Stalinist terror in Eastern Europe

Manchester University Press

Stalinist terror in Eastern Europe

Elite purges and mass repression

Edited by
Kevin McDermott and Matthew Stibbe

Manchester University Press

Manchester and New York

*distributed in the United States exclusively
by Palgrave Macmillan*

Copyright © Manchester University Press 2010

While copyright in the volume as a whole is vested in Manchester University Press, copyright in individual chapters belongs to their respective authors, and no chapter may be reproduced wholly or in part without the express permission in writing of both author and publisher.

Published by Manchester University Press
Oxford Road, Manchester M13 9NR, UK
and Room 400, 175 Fifth Avenue, New York, NY 10010, USA
www.manchesteruniversitypress.co.uk

Distributed in the United States exclusively by
Palgrave Macmillan, 175 Fifth Avenue,
New York, NY 10010, USA

Distributed in Canada exclusively by
UBC Press, University of British Columbia, 2029 West Mall,
Vancouver, BC, Canada V6T 1Z2

British Library Cataloguing-in-Publication Data is available

Library of Congress Cataloging-in-Publication Data is available

ISBN 978 0 7190 8902 2 paperback

First published by Manchester University Press in hardback 2010

This paperback edition first published 2012

The publisher has no responsibility for the persistence or accuracy of URLs for any external or third-party internet websites referred to in this book, and does not guarantee that any content on such websites is, or will remain, accurate or appropriate.

Printed by Lightning Source

Dedicated to the victims,
known and unknown

Contents

List of abbreviations and glossary of terms

ACP	Albanian Communist Party
AK	Home Army (Poland)
APL	Albanian Party of Labour
ÁVH	State Defence Authority (Hungarian secret police)
BK	National Front (Albania)
CC	Central Committee (of Communist Party)
CDU	Christian Democratic Union (Germany)
CIA	Central Intelligence Agency (USA)
Cominform	Communist Information Bureau
Comintern	Communist International
CP	Communist Party
CPSU	Communist Party of the Soviet Union
CPY	Communist Party of Yugoslavia
DBD	German Democratic Peasants' Party (GDR)
GDR	German Democratic Republic (East Germany)
GRU	Military Intelligence (USSR)
Gulag	Main Administration of Camps (USSR)
GUPVI	Main Administration of POWs and Internees (USSR)
HCP	Hungarian Communist Party
HWP	Hungarian Workers' Party
Junge Gemeinde	Young Christians (Protestant Youth Group) (GDR)
KNOJ	Corps of People's Defence (Yugoslavia)
kolkhoz	collective farm
KPD	German Communist Party
KPO	Communist Party Opposition (Germany, pre-1945)
KPP	Communist Party of Poland (pre-1938)
KSČ	Communist Party of Czechoslovakia
kulak	better-off peasant
LDPD	German Liberal Democratic Party (GDR)
MASSR	Moldavian Autonomous Soviet Socialist Republic
MBP	Ministry of Public Security (Poland)
MGB	Ministry of State Security (USSR)
MHBK	Comradely Community of Hungarian Fighters

MSSR	Moldavian Soviet Socialist Republic
MVD	Ministry of Internal Affairs (USSR)
NDPD	German National Democratic Party (GDR)
NKGB	People's Commissariat of State Security (USSR)
NKVD	People's Commissariat of Internal Affairs (USSR)
NLM	National Liberation Movement (Albania)
nomenklatura	list of key administrative appointments approved by the party
NSDAP	National Socialist German Workers' Party (the Nazi Party)
OSS	Office of Strategic Services (forerunner to the CIA) (USA)
OZNA	Department for the Protection of the People (Yugoslavia)
PPR	Polish Workers' Party
PPS	Polish Socialist Party
PSL	Polish Peasants' Party
PZPR	Polish United Workers' Party
RCP	Romanian Communist Party
RWP	Romanian Workers' Party
SAP	Socialist Workers' Party (Germany, pre-1945)
Securitate	Romanian secret police
SED	German Socialist Unity Party (GDR)
Sigurimi	Albanian secret police
SKOJ	Union of Communist Youth (Yugoslavia)
SMERSH	Military Counter-Intelligence (USSR – acronym of 'Death to Spies')
SOE	Special Operations Executive
SPD	German Social Democratic Party
SSR	Soviet Socialist Republic
Stasi	East German secret police
StB	State Security (Czechoslovakia)
TRJN	Provisional Government of National Unity (Poland)
UDBA	Administration for State Security (Yugoslavia)
USSR	Union of Soviet Socialist Republics
WiN	'Freedom and Sovereignty' resistance movement (Poland)
ZPKK	Central Party Control Commission (GDR)

List of archives and archival abbreviations

ÁBTL	State Security Historical Archive (Hungary)
a.e.	*arhivna edinitsa* (archival folder)
a.j.	*archivní jednotka* (archival unit)
AMV	Archive of the Ministry of Interior (Czech Republic)
AMVR	Archive of the Ministry of Internal Affairs (Bulgaria)
AOSPRM	Archive of Social and Political Organisations of the Republic of Moldova
ASRI	Archive of the Romanian Security Service
AÚV KSČ	Archive of the Central Committee of the Communist Party of Czechoslovakia
Bl.	*Blatt* (folio)
cs.	*csoport* (group)
d.	*dosar* (file)
dob.	*doboz* (box)
dos.	*dosszié* (file)
f.	*fond* (depository)
fas.	*fascicula* (portfolio(s))
FO	Foreign Office (UK)
inv.	*inventar* (inventory)
k.	microfilm frame
kn.	*karton* (box)
l. (ll.)	*list(y)* (portfolio(s))
MAÉ	Ministry of Foreign Affairs (France)
MOL	Hungarian National Archive
NA	National Archive of the Czech Republic
NARA	National Archive and Record Administration (USA)
ő.e.	*őrzési egység* (storage unit)
op.	*opis* (inventory)
OSA	Open Society Archive (Hungary)
SAPMO-BArch	Foundation of the Archive of Parties and Mass Organisations of the former GDR in the Federal Archive (Germany)
sv.	*svazek* (volume)
t.	*tom* (volume)

TNA	The National Archives (UK)
TsDA	Central State Archive (Bulgaria)

Notes on contributors

Robert C. Austin is a specialist in the history of the Balkans. The author of numerous scholarly articles published in *ORBIS, East European Politics and Societies, East European Quarterly* and *RFE/RL Research Reports* and newspapers, Dr Austin is Senior Lecturer and Graduate Coordinator at the Centre for European, Russian, and Eurasian Studies, Munk Centre for International Studies at the University of Toronto.

Jordan Baev is Associate Professor in Contemporary History and Senior Research Fellow in Security Studies at Rakovsky Defense College, Sofia. He serves as the Vice-President of the Bulgarian Association of Military History and is Coordinator of the Bulgarian Cold War Research Group. Dr Baev has written more than 220 works in twelve languages, among them several books and documentary volumes on Cold War political, diplomatic, military and intelligence history.

László Borhi is Senior Research Fellow at the Hungarian Academy of Sciences, and formerly guest professor at ELTE University, Budapest and the University of Pécs. He holds the Ránki György Hungarian Chair at Indiana University, Bloomington and is Fulbright Guest Professor at Dartmouth College. He is the author of *Hungary in the Cold War 1945–1956: Between the United States and the Soviet Union* (Budapest, 2004). His main research interests are the history of international relations in the twentieth century and the history of post-war Hungary.

Igor Caşu is Research Fellow at the Institute of History, Chişinău, Moldova. As a Fulbright Scholar-in-Residence, he taught Balkan history at Lenoir-Rhyne College, North Carolina and currently teaches at Moldova State University and Moldova Pedagogical University. He has published widely, including 'Political Repressions in Soviet Moldavia, 1940–1941, 1944–1989', in V. Tismăneanu et al. (eds), *The Report of the Presidential Commission for the Analysis of Communist Dictatorship in Romania* (Bucharest, 2007).

Dennis Deletant is Professor of Romanian Studies at the School of Slavonic and East European Studies, University College London, and at the University of Amsterdam. He is the author of *Ceaușescu and the Securitate: Coercion and Dissent in Romania, 1965–89* (London, 1996); *Romania under Communist Rule* (Bucharest, 1998); and *Communist Terror in Romania: Gheorghiu-Dej and the Police State, 1948–1965* (London, 1999). His most recent monograph is *Ion Antonescu: Hitler's Forgotten Ally* (London, 2006). He has also co-edited, with Ottmar Trașca, *German Documents on the Holocaust in Romania* (Bucharest, 2007).

Łukasz Kamiński is a lecturer at the University of Wrocław and the director of the Public Education Office of the Institute of National Remembrance (Warsaw). His main research interests are the history of communism in east central Europe, particularly anti-communist resistance. He is the author, editor and co-editor of several monographs, including *Poles and the New Reality* (Toruń, 2000); *About the Prague Spring* (Warsaw, 2004); and *A Handbook of the Communist Security Apparatus in East-Central Europe, 1944–1989* (Warsaw, 2005).

Kevin McDermott is Senior Lecturer in Political History at Sheffield Hallam University. He has published widely on Czech and Soviet history, including *Stalin: Revolutionary in an Era of War* (Basingstoke, 2006); *The Comintern: A History of International Communism from Lenin to Stalin* (London, 1996) (co-authored with Jeremy Agnew); *Revolution and Resistance in Eastern Europe: Challenges to Communist Rule* (Oxford, 2006) (co-edited with Matthew Stibbe); and *Stalin's Terror: High Politics and Mass Repression in the Soviet Union* (Basingstoke, 2003) (co-edited with Barry McLoughlin). He is currently researching a study of communist Czechoslovakia.

Aldis Purs has published numerous articles on Baltic history and is co-author of *Latvia: Challenges of Change* (London, 2001). He has taught in Canada, the USA and Latvia and was a research scholar at the Woodrow Wilson Center for International Studies, Washington DC. He has worked closely with Peter Gatrell and Nick Baron on population displacement, and organised the first joint conference of the Society for the Advancement of Scandinavian Study and the Association for the Advancement of Baltic Studies held in Seattle in April 2010.

Matthew Stibbe is Reader in History at Sheffield Hallam University. His previous publications include *Women in the Third Reich* (London, 2003) and *British Civilian Internees in Germany. The Ruhleben Camp, 1914–18* (Manchester, 2008). He is also editor of *Captivity, Forced Labour and Forced Migration during the First World War* (London, 2009) and joint editor, with Kevin McDermott, of *Revolution and Resistance in Eastern Europe: Challenges to Communist Rule* (Oxford, 2006). A further book, *Germany, 1914–1933: Politics, Society and Culture,* is due to be published by Pearson in 2010.

Jerca Vodušek Starič is Professor of Contemporary History at the Faculty of Arts of the University of Maribor, Slovenia. She has served as President of the Slovene Historical Society, Director of the Institute for Contemporary History in Ljubljana and as a member of the Slovene Research Council, as well as sitting on several editorial boards. In 2003 she was awarded the national award for scholars. She has published widely on the political history of the Second World War and the post-war period, especially on the Communist Party and secret services of Yugoslavia and Slovenia.

1

Stalinist terror in Eastern Europe: problems, perspectives and interpretations

Kevin McDermott and Matthew Stibbe

Communism in Eastern Europe was consigned to the dustbin of history in the late 1980s. Stalinist purges and mass repression 'died' with their creator in the mid-twentieth century. So why publish a book on one specific aspect of an extinct political system? Why do such unsavoury historical events matter in a world that is rapidly forgetting the communist past and healing old wounds? These questions can be addressed at several inter-related levels. First, many scholars argue that state-sponsored terror represented the very essence of communist governance, not just in Stalin's Russia, but in modified form throughout the world wherever and whenever communist parties established themselves in power. In this interpretation, most notoriously expounded by the lead editor of the *Black Book of Communism*, around one million east Europeans, and approximately 100 million people worldwide, were killed in the name of Marxism–Leninism during the 'short twentieth century'.[1] Leaving aside for the time being the problematic issue of determining exact numbers in the different countries and regions, it is extraordinary that such a significant theme in contemporary European history has been largely unexplored in western, and particularly English language, historiography.[2]

Second, the sheer scale of wartime and post-war Stalinist terror in the eastern half of the continent left few completely untouched. Societies for decades after were composed of victims, perpetrators and bystanders, the last burdened by tacit conformity and silence in face of flagrant illegalities and immoralities. Individuals and whole communities were profoundly affected, physically, materially and psychologically, often in ways that lie beyond historical investigation and reconstruction. Even the fortunate survivor had cause for anxiety. Many people, communists and non-communists, had to live with the uncomfortable knowledge that they had once been denounced by friends or political colleagues, with all the future uncertainty and sense of guilt that this realisation entailed.[3]

Third, a holistic analysis of post-war Stalinist terror sheds new light on the baleful consequences of the Second World War and the vicious retributions that followed in its wake. Rather than viewing Stalinist repression as, alternately, a cause or result of the Cold War, it is perhaps more enlightening to interpret it as a continuation (by other means) of the cataclysmic ideological, social and ethnic conflicts and tensions that wracked the region between 1939–45, even, arguably, well before. The barbarism of the war, the anarchical post-war anti-German expulsions of 1945–46 and the ever-present potential for political violence in societies which were still coming to terms with the experience of Axis occupation or internal civil war, or both, should never be neglected.[4] This *longue durée* is central to any understanding of Stalinist terror in the region.

Fourth, the overthrow of communism in 1989–91 was itself in part a reflection of a growing societal revulsion against state coercion and the failure of the authorities to honestly and fully reassess their past depredations. In short, the inability to come to terms with, let alone overcome, the 'demons in the closet' ate away at the legitimacy of communist regimes.

Finally, at a personal level grappling with Stalinist terror is edifying because it forces us to ponder pretty hard about moral choices. Transported back to this other world in which it was difficult, if not impossible, to hide behind private façades how would *we* have acted? As 'conformists', noisily clamouring for the death penalty against the 'enemies'? Or as 'sceptics', casting doubt on the stage management of the show trials and even bravely criticising the actions of leading communists (as quite a few east Europeans did, by the way)? And if we had been 'conformists', would this be because we were genuinely convinced of the 'traitor's' guilt, because we merely followed the baying crowd, because we expected some personal benefit from our compliance, or simply because we were afraid? Complicity in the terror process can be taken a step further. All communist party members were required to constantly update their biographies, in the process of which it was not uncommon to unwittingly (sometimes wittingly?) implicate friends and comrades.[5] By bringing these existential dilemmas to the fore, the study of communist repression compels us to evaluate the human condition and the varying motivations for individual behaviour. It suggests that people do not always operate on 'liberal', rational and enlightened principles. Above all, it teaches us to be extremely mindful of leaping to moral judgements and induces humility before the objects of our study – 'ordinary' men and women, communist and non-communist, often living under intolerable physical and psychological strain, of which we can have little, if any, real comprehension.[6]

Two other major issues arise at the start: where, for our purposes, is 'Eastern Europe'?; and what is our definition of 'Stalinist terror'? We have adopted an unusually broad geographical scope, including not only the nominally independent 'sovietised' lands lying between the Union of Soviet Socialist

Republics (USSR) and Germany (Poland, Czechoslovakia and Hungary), but also four regions that were incorporated into the Soviet Union in the 1940s: Estonia, Latvia, Lithuania and Moldavia. The Balkans are fully represented (Yugoslavia, Romania, Bulgaria and Albania), as is the German Democratic Republic (GDR). This extensive sweep permits analytical and empirical breadth and facilitates the arduous task of contrasts and comparisons across states and societies. It is essential to note, however, that use of the composite term 'Eastern Europe' does not make us insensitive to national specificities, distinct paths of development and the impact of contingency. Events in Czechoslovakia were not replicated exactly in Romania or Albania.

The term 'Stalinist terror' commonly refers to the murderous elite purges and mass repressions that engulfed Soviet officialdom and society in the late 1930s and beyond. It is intimately associated with the aims and actions of the Soviet dictator, Josef Stalin.[7] No historian today can doubt Stalin's signal organising role in these events, but this personalised view does not imply that the goals, mentalities, perceptions and fantasies of a single human being, no matter how powerful, adequately explain the complex nature of what was a multifaceted process comprising political, socio-ideological and ethnic dimensions. The millions of arrests, the hundreds of thousands of executions and non-judicial murders and the mass denunciations of 'enemies' involved and implicated very large numbers of people, not least 'ordinary' citizens. Many of the methods and mechanisms perfected in Stalinist Russia in the 1930s – sham show trials, pervasive secret police services, forced labour camps, deportations of peoples, state propaganda campaigns – were transposed to the infant communist regimes in Eastern Europe during and after the Second World War, culminating in the mass persecutions of the late 1940s and early 1950s. It is these events that lay at the heart of the chapters in this volume.

'Stalinist terror' for us, then, denotes the conscious attempt by communist leaderships to crush civil society and its autonomous institutions primarily by means of mass arrests, forced labour, relocation of suspect peoples, police brutality and judicial and non-judicial executions, the overall aim – not always achieved, it must be said – being to entrench the parties' monopoly of power by eliminating alternative sources of authority and allegiance. But in addition to the purely violent aspects of state repression, we have extended our understanding to cover such practices as police surveillance, enforced conscription, confiscation of property, loss of employment and status and evictions from dwellings. No physical harm may have been inflicted by these practices, but countless lives were ruined in the process.[8] Finally, as Igor Caşu argues in Chapter 3 on Soviet Moldavia, a strong case can be made to include state-sponsored famine under the heading 'Stalinist terror', although this remains a highly contentious issue not least in the debates on the Ukrainian *holodomor* of 1932–33.[9]

A key question is: how can we begin to understand the collective psychology of communist leaders who implemented, rationalised and justified what we term 'terror' and 'mass repression', but which they called 'class justice' and the elimination of 'enemies'. First, the process of the 'Bolshevisation', and later 'Stalinisation', of communist parties, initiated by the Communist International (Comintern) in the mid-to-late 1920s, signalled an unswerving commitment to, and ultimate dependence on, Moscow in terms of party strategy, selection of leadership cadres and financial backing.[10] It also signified a drastic curtailment of inner-party democracy and debate, a concomitant ideological ossification and organisational bureaucratisation and, at least until the mid-1930s, a profound rupture from mainstream national political cultures. Second, emergent Stalinism exacerbated the communists' almost hermetic way of life and their self-identification as 'outsiders'. The Stalinist project demanded that comrades 'work on themselves' to internalise the values of total party loyalty, collectivity and Bolshevik self-sacrifice, and to expunge deviant 'bourgeois individualistic' thoughts and actions.[11] Crucial for our purposes, this 'hermeneutics of the soul' inculcated a mental landscape of criticism, self-criticism and conspiracy in which 'enemies', both within and without, were deemed ubiquitous. Stalin's terror of the late 1930s immeasurably strengthened such attitudes. To the extent that this mindset was appropriated by east European communists, particularly those who studied or worked in the Soviet Union, its persistence helps to explain the events of the late 1940s and early 1950s. Finally, it may well be obvious, but it is worth stressing nonetheless that communists were not liberals – they were Marxist revolutionaries who were intent on *reforging the world* and this necessarily entailed recourse to coercion.

There were multiple motivations behind the terror. To some extent, they varied from country to country, were subject to change over time, depended on the nature of the target/victim, and were heavily influenced by the specific historical conjuncture of the emergent Cold War, divergent national circumstances, and personal and factional rivalries, jealousies, intrigues and score-settling. Retribution played a prominent role, especially in countries that had fought against the USSR in the Second World War. Thus, in Hungary, Romania, Slovakia and the Soviet-occupied parts of Germany the old political and military elites were extensively purged in the early post-war period and hundreds of thousands of ordinary people were selected for deportation and imprisonment in the gulag system.[12] In Poland, as Łukasz Kamiński demonstrates in Chapter 5, Stalin cast the underground Home Army, which had fought for many years against the Germans, as 'anti-Soviet' because of its loyalty to the London-based government-in-exile as opposed to the communist-controlled Lublin committee; many of its leaders and rank-and-file members were executed or put in camps. Jordan Baev's chapter on Bulgaria likewise describes the mass purges and killings of alleged 'fascist elements' in September and October 1944 following that country's defeat and occupation by the Red Army. Another important motive, apart from 'anti-fascist' retribution, was 'class justice': farmers, businessmen and artisans opposed to communist economic policies were perennial regime targets in all the countries under consideration. For instance, *kulaks* (better-off peasants) were systematically harried, just like they were in the Soviet Union, as a means of redistributing their wealth and property for the benefit of state-directed industrialisation programmes. And there were other perceived economic benefits to be derived from the use of terror, notably in the form of forced labour extracted in the numerous camps established throughout the region.

Our contributors, unsurprisingly, do not arrive at a general consensus or theory on the burning issue of motivations behind the terror.[13] Some strongly emphasise exogenous determinants, insisting that communist mass repression was above all the result of Soviet occupation and Stalin's international and ideological goals, executed on the ground by Soviet secret police 'advisers' despatched from Moscow to oversee events in Eastern Europe. Others posit what amounts to an inherent 'totalitarian' urge among communist leaders to remove all real and perceived opponents in a manic drive for monopolistic power. Others discern a complex interaction of external and internal factors, or, as Aldis Purs puts it, the terror was 'Soviet in form, local in content'. The relative weight attached to these variants is crucial.

From our perspective, the bottom line is Stalin's *Realpolitik* and never-ending quest for Soviet state security. Domestic developments in the countries of Eastern Europe in these years can thus never be divorced from wider international relations. As the Cold War grew hotter from 1947 and the Stalin–Tito split in 1948 opened up fractures in the Soviet 'bloc', the imperative for near monolithic homogeneity became ever more urgent in the Kremlin – unity meant strength. This, in turn, demanded an assault on omnipresent class 'enemies', 'spies', 'saboteurs' and 'traitors' within and outside the communist parties. These 'enemies' were identified primarily on 'traditional' Soviet lines: '*kulaks*', priests, private entrepreneurs, anti-communist activists, 'Mensheviks' (social democrats), *ancien régime* military, police, judicial and state officials. In some cases, it signified an attack on suspect ethnic 'minorities': Balts, Moldavians and, by the early 1950s in line with Stalin's perverse anti-Semitic tendencies, Jews. But these actions were not simply vindictive and arbitrary campaigns aimed at bolstering the cohesion of state and society in dangerous times. For the Stalinists were motivated by an *idée fixe*: prophylactic strikes against multifarious 'anti-social elements' would 'purify' society and lay the class foundations for the over-riding task of 'constructing socialism', as they understood it. In this sense, a deformed Marxist ideological utopianism undoubtedly underlay mass repression and it is clear that many communists, particularly at a leadership level, regarded political violence as the sharp end of class war and as an indispensable weapon in the struggle for the 'radiant future' purged of 'alien dross'.

But where precisely is the 'local' input? How valid is the polemical claim that the terror was not simply enacted by the guilty 'them' (Stalin, the People's Commissariat of Internal Affairs (NKVD), megalomaniac domestic communist leaders) on an innocent 'us' (undifferentiated and resistant east European societies)? The creation and consolidation of communist regimes after the war can never be understood solely in terms of an imposition by 'Big Brother' to the east. There were at all times indigenous factors at work. One crass manifestation of this was the zeal of some east European communist leaders to 'outdo' Stalin in their assault on 'enemies'. As László Borhi shows in Chapter 7, the Hungarian party boss, Mátyás Rákosi, was a particularly avid advocate of state terror, even to the extent that Stalin apparently vetoed one of his attempts to eliminate perceived rivals. In Romania, it was party leader Gheorghe Gheorghiu-Dej, not the Kremlin, who ordered the trial and execution of Dej's adversary Lucreţiu Pătrăşcanu in April 1954, while in the GDR Walter Ulbricht's obsession with combating 'left sectarianism' and 'right deviationism' set the tone for purges in the Socialist Unity Party (SED). It is true that Klement Gottwald, the Czechoslovak party chief, briefly vacillated before agreeing to the arrest of his friend and right-hand man Rudolf Slánský and the party as a whole was wary of self-purging, but generally when it came to repression few east European communist luminaries had to be compelled by Moscow into action. It was axiomatic that enemies existed and they had to be removed from the body politic. What is more, victims as a rule were targeted, detained and interrogated by local state security officers, tried by local judges, overseen by local prison wardens, and, in some cases, put to death by local executioners. The guiding hand of Soviet secret police 'advisers' was often evident, but was largely restricted to top level arrests and major show trials.

Furthermore, the purging of 'class exploiters', marginal 'anti-social elements' and 'alien' minorities fed into pre-existing social and ethnic tensions and prejudices and, to a certain degree, made sense to local populations radicalised and brutalised by years of economic depression, war, the Holocaust and post-war retributions. Many citizens – as many as 83,000 in Hungary in 1953 – found themselves, willingly or unwillingly, entrapped into 'offering' their services to the secret police, informing on or even denouncing relatives, friends and acquaintances, sometimes in a genuine attempt to assist suspect colleagues.[14] Finally, unpalatable as it may be, we have to acknowledge that there were local beneficiaries of mass repression: the ill-educated peasant now promoted and honoured to be a secret security agent; the upwardly mobile industrial worker now stepping into a dead man's shoes in the burgeoning state bureaucracies; the hard-up pensioner who denounces a neighbour to get their hands on a bigger apartment. Stalinist terror meant more than just an evil dictator concocting plans in his Kremlin office.

Intriguing and perplexing questions remain: why were highly publicised show trials of prominent communists staged in some countries (Bulgaria, Hungary and Czechoslovakia), but not in others (GDR, Poland and Romania)? What were the goals behind these carefully staged theatrical productions? Conversely, why were some trials, such as those of Pătrășcanu in Romania and Paul Merker in the GDR, repeatedly delayed and then held *in camera*? Can an overarching pattern to the elite purges be discerned, linking the diverse practices and motivations outlined above? Similarly, were the mass repressions operated on generic lines, or were there significant national variations? There are no simple 'answers' here, even if we adopt a strict comparative methodology.

Turning first to elite purges and show trials against leading communists, it is notable that these came in two separate waves. The first wave, in 1948–49, was directly related to the Yugoslav–Soviet split, with the main victims (Koçi Xoxe in Albania, László Rajk in Hungary and Traicho Kostov in Bulgaria) being accused of 'nationalist deviationism' or 'Titoism'. Significantly, the countries targeted represented the 'southern tier of Communist states', all of them having borders with the outcast Yugoslavia.[15] Less well-known is the fact that Yugoslavia underwent its own, no less bloody internal party purges during the same period, although in a reverse image of what was happening elsewhere in Eastern Europe, the targets were not 'national deviationists' but 'Stalinists' and 'Cominformists'; that is, those suspected of continued and 'treasonous' loyalty to Moscow. Indeed, as Jerca Vodušek Starič explains in Chapter 9, the 'anti-Stalinist' Tito regime in Belgrade paradoxically became even more Stalinist in terms of its methods of state terror after its split with the Soviet Union in 1948.

The second wave of show trials and elite purges came in the years 1950–53, when anti-Semitism (dressed up as 'anti-cosmopolitanism' or 'anti-Zionism') became an increasingly important motive, mirroring events in the USSR itself. Now the principal countries involved were Romania, the GDR and Czechoslovakia; in all three states, various factions within the ruling parties proceeded to target Jews, or non-Jewish comrades accused of being too friendly towards Jews or towards the new state of Israel. Even so, as noted by Kevin McDermott, it was only the Czechoslovak regime which actually staged a major anti-Semitic show trial, the Slánský trial, in November 1952, during which several senior members of the party and government were jointly accused of participating in a 'Trotskyite-Zionist' conspiracy to restore capitalism. Of the fourteen men convicted, eleven were identified as Jews.[16]

Given the marked increase in international tensions during the years 1948 to 1953, especially after the outbreak of the Arab–Israeli war in 1948–49 and the Korean war in 1950, and given that events like the Slánský trial were overwhelmingly Soviet inspired, even if they did garner local support, it is tempting to cast these elite purges as part of a more general build-up to possible armed conflict with the west. Indeed, there is no doubt that the Central Intelligence Agency (CIA) did attempt to penetrate agents into Eastern Europe during this period, placing the USSR and its satellites in turn on a 'permanent war footing'.[17] What is more, one high-ranking British intelligence officer privately feared that the USA was planning a 'preventive war' against the Soviet Union to start in 'mid or late 1952', a view partially shared by Winston Churchill no less.[18] Stalin's apprehensions, then, while in no way justifying the new waves of terror in the late 1940s and early 1950s, not to mention previous waves, were at least in part solidly grounded. In spite of this, and contrary to the claims of some historians, there does not appear to be any tangible proof that Stalin was seeking to steal a march on the west by launching a pre-emptive strike. A more plausible scenario, as Richard Overy puts it, is that the 'war psychosis was exploited, as it was in the 1920s and 1930s, as a factor in domestic politics'.[19] And anybody who had western – or Jewish – contacts was now automatically under suspicion, even if they had several years or even decades of loyal service to the communist cause behind them.

So, what were the motives aside from anti-Semitism and anti-Americanism? In some ways, the elite trials and purges were modelled on the Soviet terror of the 1930s. Here, too, communists were among the principal targets and the court proceedings were carefully scripted and rehearsed in advance, the sentences determined by political, not judicial, authorities. But in the Moscow trials the chief defendants were old Bolsheviks, men like Zinoviev, Kamenev and Bukharin who had once been close comrades of Lenin, whereas in post-war Eastern Europe they were mostly hard-line Stalinists (apart from Xoxe in Albania who was a fully-fledged Titoist).[20] The post-1945 show trials were also much cruder in tone, 'shameless copies' as Tony Judt calls them, and far less imaginative.[21] The Kostov trial in Bulgaria in particular turned into a fiasco when the chief defendant unexpectedly withdrew his confession – which he had only signed under extreme torture – and had to be removed from the court. When he was brought back a few days later, on 14 December 1949, for the summing up of the case, he continued to deny any wrong doing, declaring that he had 'always acted as a communist, always respected and esteemed the Soviet Union'.[22] Within the next forty-eight hours he was convicted, sentenced to death and executed, but despite this 'unseemly' haste and despite the fact that the full court proceedings had been broadcast uncensored on Bulgarian radio and exposed to detailed and hostile coverage in the western media, the trial was still considered by some to have been a success.[23]

One possible motive for the elite purges was to end the threat of 'independent roads to socialism' by removing popular communist leaders with nationalist or 'Titoist' tendencies. Yet ironically the more popular (and more independent-thinking) purge victim in Poland, Władysław Gomułka, was spared a show trial, possibly – as Kamiński shows in Chapter 5 – because Stalin feared alienating a country of such great strategic importance to the USSR and one with intense anti-Russian sentiment. By contrast, Xoxe in Albania and Rajk in Hungary were decidedly unpopular figures in their own countries and had shown little or no tendency to stand up for national interests in the face of Soviet demands. As the Hungarian author and former political prisoner Ferenc Aladár Györgyey writes:

> When László Rajk, the bloodthirsty Minister of Internal Affairs, was arrested, convicted, and executed as an agent of the Yugoslav government [in 1949], the whole [of Hungary] was laughing. Finally the murderers were turning on one another. He was the only high-ranking Communist butcher who had even been brought to justice. His own kind of justice.[24]

Another motive was undoubtedly to produce scapegoats for economic and political failures, or to mobilise supporters of communist regimes against 'spies', 'class enemies' and 'treasonous scum', labels given to show-trial victims even before they were found guilty. Thus hundreds of thousands of young people and ordinary workers were recruited into the party during these years, and party discussion groups at local or factory level in all of the countries involved zealously passed resolutions condemning the 'Trotskyite', 'Titoist', 'Zionist', 'bourgeois' or 'nationalist' traitors whose crimes had now been exposed in the press and in the courts. In this sense, Stalinism in post-war Eastern Europe could be seen, provocatively, as a form of 'plebiscitary democracy', defined by Tim Kirk as 'a political system which employs techniques of mass mobilisation to elicit acclaim and consent without enabling genuine political participation'.[25]

Stalin's suspicion of communists who had spent the 1930s and early 1940s in exile in the west, who had fought in the Spanish civil war, or who had been in Nazi concentration camps was also a factor. Among the many examples here would be several prominent East German communists, including Franz Dahlem, Gerhart Eisler and Merker, and several of the defendants in the Slánský trial (though not Slánský himself). Rajk was also a veteran of the war in Spain, and an internee in France, before escaping and returning to underground political activities in what was then still neutral Hungary in 1941.[26]

Finally, with or without Soviet involvement, there were also inevitably some local power struggles and personal score-settling going on, as Robert Austin and Dennis Deletant indicate in the cases of Albania and Romania respectively. A confidential British Foreign Office assessment of the motives behind Slánský's arrest in Prague in November 1951 came to similar conclusions, noting that the 'more probable' explanation was not that Slánský was guilty of any of the crimes he was accused of, or that he had 'erred from [Stalinist] orthodoxy' but that 'his position [as party general secretary] had become dangerously powerful in the eyes of President Gottwald or his advisers'.[27] Nevertheless, and perhaps most importantly of all, it was the apparent randomness of the victim selection process which struck many observers, causing them to draw parallels with similar events in the Soviet Union itself. As the German historian Tobias Kaiser has written in a slightly different context:

> The purges of individuals did not operate in a predictable way. Psychologically this meant a further heightening of feelings of uncertainty and terror. What was taking place was a series of connected events which nonetheless had no recognisable or identifiable pattern.[28]

Other aspects of the show trials, besides the motives of those who planned and instigated them, are also revealing. Many questions remain unanswered. For instance, how did the minor security officials who turned into interrogators and torturers understand their role? Some, as the former Slánský trial defendant Artur London tells us, were simply 'fanatical and violent', but others were able to think politically; that is, to understand that the point of the elite purges was to get 'rid of certain categories of men in power' so that the party could 'make a leap forward'. As one interrogator told him:

> If you had stayed in France . . . you would have remained a militant Party member of great value in a capitalist country. But men like you, with your past, your ideas, your concepts, your international contacts are not made for countries in the process of constructing socialism. We must get rid of you. When the difficult moment is over the Party may revise your case and give you a living, although you will not, of course, be able to play a part in politics.[29]

In fact, this was to be the experience of many prominent communist purge victims in Czechoslovakia, Poland, Hungary and the GDR in the early 1950s, some of whom were later partly or fully rehabilitated (London himself, Gomułka, Kádár, Merker, Dahlem, Eisler and others). Only the unlucky few were put on public trial and executed. Admittedly, in cases where the death penalty had been applied, it was much harder for the party to admit – even within its own inner sanctums – that mistakes had been made, as the example of Czechoslovakia in the late 1950s and early 1960s clearly shows.

Another more obscure dimension of the elite purges was their personal impact on those who narrowly avoided losing party, academic or government posts (albeit possibly with damaged career prospects), but nonetheless faced hours of questioning about their contacts with the west or with newly exposed 'spies' or 'traitors' in their own or neighbouring communist countries. Did this experience in any way shake their faith in the communist system or in the integrity of its political–judicial processes? Matthew Stibbe, for instance, in his chapter highlights the case of Jürgen Kuczynski, the East German labour historian and communist intellectual, who came under increasing pressure in early 1953, so much so that even MI5 in London speculated, wrongly as it turned out, that he might be on the verge of defecting to the west to evade possible arrest.[30] As a leading figure in the German Communist Party in London from 1936 to 1944, Kuczynski had many western friends and associates and must have found his lengthy interrogation by the SED Central Party Control Commission extremely worrying, especially in the context of the Slánský trial and the Doctors' Plot in Moscow.[31] He was also known to have worked during the war for the United States' Strategic Bombing Survey, helping to analyse intelligence on Nazi Germany for the American Joint Chiefs of Staff. On top of this he had made a number of personal enemies in the party, including fellow London exiles Wilhelm Koenen, Kurt Hager and Heinz Schmidt, making his position even more precarious. Yet in spite of numerous run-ins with the SED party machine, then and later in his career, he remained steadfast in his communist convictions. Even the numerous memoirs and autobiographical writings he published before and after 1989 fail adequately to acknowledge the extreme dangers he had faced, as a middle-class Jewish intellectual and former 'western' exile, in the GDR of the early 1950s.[32]

The final question relates to the relative importance of (false) denunciations compared with self-incrimination in the preparation of show trials. Clearly, denunciations, including those given willingly and those forced out of other prisoners by torture, were important. Yet the Czechoslovak victim Evžen Löbl also placed great weight on the background biographical statement that he wrote 'voluntarily' for his interrogators: 'what they wanted to do was turn that into an indictment'. Over and above this his chief 'sins' were 'that I was not of a working-class family, that I had been in the West, and that I had dealings with Western journalists, politicians and economists'.[33] Even so, not all communist purge victims were of 'bourgeois' origins and some had never been in the west, at least before 1945. In fact, those who were selected as victims but who did not quite fit in terms of background or contribution often had their personal biographies rewritten simply for the purposes of their trial. Heda Margolius Kovály, for example, whose husband Rudolf Margolius was one of the eleven Slánský trial defendants to be sentenced to death and executed on 3 December 1952, later wrote:

> At one point, I heard Rudolf's voice [during the trial proceedings] say that he had been trained in espionage in London during the war when, of course, he had spent the entire war as a prisoner in German concentration camps. This item was dutifully reported in the Party newspaper the following day, but later edited out of a book in which the transcript of the trial was published.

In their last meeting together, Rudolf had exhorted her: 'Don't question the trial. Believe it! . . . Please. Think of Ivan [our son], not of me'.[34]

The terrible tragedy of these individual cases should not obscure the fact that high-ranking communist victims were a small minority, in the view of some scholars accounting for less than 1 per cent of the total number. Outside the ranks of the party, hundreds of thousands of supposed 'enemies of the people' were arrested, deported to labour camps, sacked from their jobs or expelled from schools and universities, simply because they were real or imagined opponents of the communist regime. Several thousands of those arrested and tried were executed or suffered extrajudicial murder. Many politically active non-communists, notably social democrats and other moderate leftists, were targeted, religious orders, particularly the Catholic church, were decimated and a wide array of 'class enemies' were persecuted. The scale, intensity and timing of arrests differed from country to country. As Krystyna Kersten has argued in the Polish case: 'Measured simply by the number of victims, the terror was much greater in the period 1944–48 than in subsequent years'.[35] The chapters in this volume by Vodušek Starič, Caşu, Purs and Kamiński make a similar point, the former beginning her account in 1941–42 when the Yugoslav communists made their first determined bid to dominate the armed struggle against the Axis invaders, and the last three going back even further in time to the Soviet occupations of 1939–40. In those areas 'liberated' by the Red Army in the early stages of the Second World War – eastern Poland, Moldavia and the Baltic republics – mass deportations of indigenous populations and individual acts of terror, such as the Katyń massacre, were intended to eliminate national elites and other perceived 'anti-Soviet' strata of society. Hence, conventional wisdom on the periodisation of Stalinist terror in Eastern Europe (normally 1948–53) may need to be revised since in many parts of the region we can detect a continuum of repression stretching from 1939–40 to the early or mid-1950s with only relatively brief interludes of respite.

In other countries, such as the GDR, Czechoslovakia, Hungary and Bulgaria, mass repression did indeed peak in the years 1948–53 after the communists' seizure of power. Regardless of the problematics of chronology, it can safely be said that political persecution was endemic in communist Eastern Europe. No social category was exempt: blue-collar workers, farmers, artisans, traders, office employees, priests, intellectuals, teachers, professors, students, pensioners, military officers, soldiers, ethnic minorities, young and old, men and women. The broad aim of the authorities was threefold: first, to remove all sources of real or perceived opposition to communist rule by targeting 'hostile' sections of the population; second, to subordinate potentially alternative centres of political and spiritual authority, like the Catholic and Orthodox churches, opposition parties, intellectual and cultural elites or the army, to the communist power monopoly; and third, as we have already intimated, to identify scapegoats held responsible for the political and economic failings of the government. In short, it appears that repression was closely related to the intense drive of the new rulers to 'construct socialism', as they understood it.

One major conundrum is why so many industrial workers, the ostensible social pillar of the communist regimes, fell prey to the meat-grinder of Stalinist repression? This was particularly the case in Czechoslovakia, the most industrially advanced communist state. Here, it has been argued that initially 'workers accounted for the largest social group in the forced labour camps', comprising approximately 30–40 per cent. What is more, 'politically unreliable' workers 'who had protested most vehemently and publicly against wage cuts or had incited strike action would be dismissed from their factories, transferred to lower-paid jobs, given fines, their social benefits would be unlawfully curtailed while many of them would end up in prison.'[36] One explanation is that party and trade union leaders sought to break working-class solidarity in the factories by targeting 'social democratic remnants', 'class alien' migrants and other 'vacillating' strata who had infiltrated and led astray the class-conscious proletariat. Often, though, persecution against workers originated in the extremely harsh living and working conditions of rapid Stalinist industrialisation, conditions that engendered demonstrations, strikes and, by 1953, even localised workers' revolts and uprisings.[37]

The overall numbers involved in Stalinist mass repression are breathtaking, though subject to heated debate and imprecision, not least because official archives do not always indicate whether victims were arrested for directly political reasons. This caveat notwithstanding, our contributors have suggested the following totals: in Hungary, a staggering 750,000 people were convicted between 1948 and 1953; in Romania, a highly conservative estimate is that 60,000 were arrested in the same period; in Bulgaria, about 40,000 were imprisoned and 300,000 more placed under police surveillance; in Czechoslovakia, around 90,000 were prosecuted for political crimes and many tens of thousands of others suffered socioeconomic hardships of varying kinds; in Albania, 80,000 people were arrested between 1945 and 1956 from an overall population of less than two million; in Moldavia, the terror process was even worse: 300,000–350,000 were direct victims of Stalinist repression (if famines are included); in the Baltic republics, around 500,000 were forcibly deported.

In Poland, exact figures seem to be even more difficult to obtain than elsewhere, but the latest research suggests at least 350,000–400,000 arrests in the years 1944 to 1956, plus roughly 8,000 death sentences, 3,100 of which were actually implemented, although not all of these were for political offences.[38] As for the GDR, a comprehensive study published in the 1990s, which admittedly covers the entire Ulbricht era (1949–71), concluded that 'estimates of around 200,000 to 250,000 victims of the political justice system are certainly not exaggerated'.[39] On top of this 154,000 Germans and 35,000 non-Germans were interned in special NKVD/MVD-run camps between 1945 and 1950; and a further 30,000 soldiers and 40,000 civilians were convicted of various offences by Soviet military tribunals in a period stretching from 1945 to the early 1950s, including several hundred who were sentenced to death and up to 25,000 who were deported to Soviet labour camps.[40] Finally, Yugoslavia went through at least three waves of mass repression: in 1941–42, at the beginning of the armed resistance against the Axis powers; in 1945–46, the years of 'liberation' from foreign invasion and murderous retribution against fascist 'collaborators'; and in 1948–50, at the height of the Stalin–Tito split. In the latter period as many as 50,000 'Cominformists' were identified by the regime as enemies of the state, although it is still unclear how many were interned in camps and how many died.[41] The bare statistics, then, taken together are by any stretch of the imagination a depressing litany and the human suffering involved is incalculable. And this is, ultimately, the raw meaning of those two dreaded words – 'Stalinist terror': the ruination of countless lives, the ripping apart of families, the trampling on human dignity, the moral and spiritual degradation of entire societies.

The Stalinist mentality that rationalised, and indeed condoned, this physical assault on very large numbers of people is amply demonstrated in an important speech by Antonín Zápotocký, the president of the Czechoslovak republic, as late as September 1953. Having decried 'alien views' such as 'social democratic opportunism' and 'bourgeois humanist "Masarykism"',[42] Zápotocký conjured up the demon of active collaboration between 'foreign reaction', the 'traitorous emigration' and 'illegal networks' in Czechoslovakia itself: 'former capitalists, agrarian nobility, bankers, big business nabobs (*nabobů*) and . . . the petit-bourgeoisie'. Zápotocký concluded that this 'class enemy' had still not been defeated, despite the deluded 'bragging' of 'many of our comrades', and that socialism could only be achieved by confronting these 'dangers' and overcoming 'all incorrect ideological opinions in our own ranks'.[43] It was left to Václav Kopecký, the leading Czechoslovak ideologue, to spell out precisely what this meant in practice: the party had to be 'mercilessly purged' of all 'renegades'.[44] The Stalinist mindset – several months after the 'Great Leader's' death – was palpable: we are surrounded by foreign imperialist enemies organically linked to wide-ranging reactionary domestic cliques and 'anti-social elements'. Hence strict party unity, class vigilance and ideological purity are essential. These irreconcilable enemies, both within and without the party, must be eliminated if socialism is to be constructed. It was this mentality, steeped in an ideologised phantasm of omnipresent external and internal capitalist encirclement, that underlay elite purging and mass repression in Eastern Europe in the years of late Stalinism.

Notes

1 S. Courtois, 'Introduction: The Crimes of Communism', in S. Courtois et al. (eds), *The Black Book of Communism: Crimes, Terror, Repression* (Cambridge: MA, 1999), p. 4.

2 As far as we know, only one specialist book exists in English on the subject of Stalinist terror in Eastern Europe, and even this focuses on elite, not mass,

repression: G. H. Hodos, *Show Trials: Stalinist Purges in Eastern Europe, 1948–1954* (New York, 1987). The German edition of this book has been revised and up-dated: *Schauprozesse: Stalinistische Säuberungen in Osteuropa 1948–1954* (Berlin, 2001). Another important source is K. Bartošek, 'Central and Southeastern Europe', in Courtois et al., *The Black Book of Communism*, pp. 394–456. Many general histories of post-war Eastern Europe also discuss aspects of state repression, but necessarily the coverage is relatively brief and tends to concentrate on elite purges. See, for instance, J. Rupnik, *The Other Europe* (London, 1989); I. T. Berend, *Central and Eastern Europe, 1944–1993: Detour from the Periphery to the Periphery* (Cambridge, 1996); and G. Swain and N. Swain, *Eastern Europe since 1945*, 3rd edn (Basingstoke, 2003). The picture is much healthier, however, in other parts of Europe, particularly in central and Eastern Europe itself where scholars have been active in this field for many years, as witnessed by the long list of publications cited by our contributors.

3 For example, János Kádár, the Hungarian communist leader imprisoned between 1950 and 1954 on false charges of having spied for the inter-war Magyar dictator Admiral Miklós Horthy and subsequently rehabilitated in 1956, revealed something of this in a conversation with François Mitterand in 1976: 'The worst thing is to doubt one's own people. Horthy took my physical freedom. Rákosi [Hungarian party first secretary between 1948 and 1956] also took my moral freedom'. Cited in R. Vinen, *A History in Fragments. Europe in the Twentieth Century* (London, 2000), pp. 411–12.

4 Our ideas here are derived from C. Gerlach and N. Werth, 'State Violence – Violent Societies', in M. Geyer and S. Fitzpatrick (eds), *Beyond Totalitarianism: Stalinism and Nazism Compared* (New York, 2009), pp. 133–79; and I. Deák, J. T. Gross and T. Judt (eds), *The Politics of Retribution in Europe: World War II and Its Aftermath* (Princeton, 2000). Indeed, one might go back even further to the pre-communist era. The Russian army's forcible displacement of hundreds of thousands of people in the borderlands of the Tsarist Empire between 1914 and 1917 also suggests that governments and societies were deeply fragmented along political, national and ethnic lines, although, to be sure, these forced migrations occurred under wartime conditions. For details, see P. Gatrell, *A Whole Empire Walking: Refugees in Russia during World War I* (Bloomington, 1999); and Gatrell, 'Refugees and Forced Migrants during the First World War', in M. Stibbe (ed.), *Captivity, Forced Labour and Forced Migration in Europe during the First World War* (London, 2009), pp. 82–110.

5 On this important aspect of Stalinist terror, see C. Epstein, *The Last Revolutionaries: German Communists and their Century* (Cambridge: MA, 2004), esp. pp. 130–57.

6 For a graphic description of the physical and mental torment involved, see the memoirs of two prominent victims: E. Loebl, *Stalinism in Prague: The Loebl Story* (New York, 1969) and A. London, *On Trial* (London, 1970).

7 Texts on mass repression and terror in the USSR include D. R. Shearer, *Policing Stalin's Socialism: Repression and Social Order in the Soviet Union, 1924–1953* (New Haven, 2009); P. Hagenloh, *Stalin's Police: Public Order and Mass Repression in the USSR, 1926–1941* (Baltimore, 2009); P. R. Gregory, *Terror by Quota: State Security from Lenin to Stalin (An Archival Study)* (New Haven, 2009); W. Z. Goldman, *Terror and Democracy in the Age of Stalin: The Social Dynamics of Repression* (Cambridge,

2007); H. Kuromiya, *The Voices of the Dead: Stalin's Great Terror in the 1930s* (New Haven, 2007); O. Figes, *The Whisperers: Private Life in Stalin's Russia* (London, 2007); M. Ilič (ed.), *Stalin's Terror Revisited* (Basingstoke, 2006); and B. McLoughlin and K. McDermott (eds), *Stalin's Terror: High Politics and Mass Repression in the Soviet Union* (Basingstoke, 2003).

8   It must be emphasised that our focus on terror is not meant to deny the sources of conformity and support that existed for communist regimes, particularly among sections of the industrial working class and intelligentsia, or to obscure the more conventional, less coercive strategies employed by the authorities to ensure political legitimacy: progressive welfare, educational and labour legislation; land reform; the promotion of upward social mobility; the 'democratisation' of national culture; rising levels of consumption; and the search for a 'socialist modernity'. For details, see B. Apor, P. Apor and E. A. Rees (eds), *The Sovietization of Eastern Europe: New Perspectives on the Postwar Period* (Washington DC, 2008).

9   There is a huge literature on the Ukrainian famine. Contrasting views can be found in R. Conquest, *The Harvest of Sorrow: Soviet Collectivisation and the Terror-Famine* (London, 2002); and R. W. Davies and S. G. Wheatcroft, *The Years of Hunger: Soviet Agriculture, 1931–1933* (Basingstoke, 2004).

10   The Comintern, formally the Communist (or Third) International, was founded by the Bolsheviks in March 1919 to foment worldwide revolution. It was dissolved by Stalin in May 1943, not having fulfilled its prime task.

11   See J. Hellbeck, *Revolution on my Mind: Writing a Diary under Stalin* (Cambridge: MA, 2006); I. Halfin, *Terror in my Soul: Communist Autobiographies on Trial* (Cambridge: MA, 2003); and B. Studer and H. Haumann (eds), *Stalinistische Subjekte/Stalinist Subjects/Sujets staliniens: Individuum und System in der Sowjetunion und der Komintern, 1929–1953* (Zürich, 2006).

12   For details, see Bartošek, 'Central and Southeastern Europe', pp. 394–5; and N. M. Naimark, *The Russians in Germany: A History of the Soviet Zone of Occupation, 1945–1949* (Cambridge: MA, 1995), pp. 385–6.

13   Indeed, when we distributed earlier drafts of this introduction to our authors for their comments and critiques, some took umbrage at the perceived 'relativism' of our position, which was seen as placing undue emphasis on pre-existing indigenous sources of political conflict. A healthy debate ensued as reflected in this final version, which has taken on board many of the interesting comments and concerns raised in that discussion, especially regarding Soviet and communist culpability, while continuing to give substantial weight to 'local' factors, and in particular the impact of the Second World War, the Holocaust and post-war retributions on the region.

14   For a fictionalised, but real life, account of the longer-term noxious effects of such 'innocent' actions from the 1950s, see J. Škvorecký, *Two Murders in My Double Life* (New York, 2001).

15   T. Judt, *Postwar. A History of Europe since 1945* (London, 2005), pp. 178–9.

16   But again interesting anomalies arise. All three of the survivors in the Slánský trial were Jews: Vavro Hajdů, Evžen Löbl and Artur London.

17   Judt, *Postwar*, pp. 188–9; S.-J. Corke, *US Covert Operations and Cold War Strategy: Truman, Secret Warfare and the CIA, 1945–1953* (London, 2008), pp. 2 and ff. Stalin's fears of 'capitalist encirclement' and infiltration went back a very long way.

See J. Harris, 'Encircled by Enemies: Stalin's Perception of the Capitalist World, 1918–1941', *Journal of Strategic Studies*, vol. 30, no. 3 (2007), pp. 513–45.

18 For details, see P. Hennessy, *The Secret State: Whitehall and the Cold War* (London, 2003), pp. 28–30.

19 R. Overy, *Russia's War* (London, 1997), pp. 317–18. For the opposing view, which suggests that Stalin might well have been preparing the material and psychological groundwork for an early strike against the west, see Bartošek, 'Central and Southeastern Europe', p. 433.

20 Hodos, *Show Trials*, p. 10.

21 Judt, *Postwar*, p. 178. For a contemporary comparative approach, see N. Leites and E. Bernaut, *Ritual of Liquidation* (Glencoe: Illinois, 1954).

22 Hodos, *Show Trials*, pp. 21–2. A similar debacle occurred at the Bukharin-Rykov trial in Moscow in March 1938, when Nikolai Krestinskii, the former deputy commissar of foreign affairs, refused to acknowledge his guilt in open court. For details, see R. Medvedev, *Let History Judge: The Origins and Consequences of Stalinism*, revised edn (Oxford, 1989), pp. 369–73.

23 Judt, *Postwar*, p. 179.

24 F. A. Györgyey, *True Tales of a Fictitious Spy. A Hungarian Gulag Grotesquerie* (King: North Carolina, 2005), p. 15.

25 T. Kirk, *Nazi Germany* (London, 2007), p. 7.

26 Judt, *Postwar*, p. 189. On the difficulties facing Spanish civil war veterans in the GDR in particular, see J. McLellan, *Antifascism in East Germany: Remembering the International Brigades, 1945–1989* (Oxford, 2004), esp. pp. 57–63.

27 Confidential communiqué from the Foreign Office, 12 December 1951, in The National Archives, Kew, London (TNA), KV 2 /2041. The same communiqué went on to suggest that Slánský's arrest may also have been caused by his 'identification with a discredited system of Party control' and by a more general desire 'to distract attention from, and to provide a scapegoat for, the shortcomings which have been revealed in Czech economic achievements'.

28 T. Kaiser, *Karl Griewank (1900–1953) – ein deutscher Historiker im 'Zeitalter der Extreme'* (Stuttgart, 2007), p. 275. Kaiser makes this point in the context of persecution of members of the Protestant *Junge Gemeinde* (Young Christians) and related groups in the GDR in 1952–53, but it would be equally applicable to communist purge victims expelled from the party or worse during the same period.

29 London, *On Trial*, pp. 158–9.

30 See the relevant correspondence in TNA, KV 2 /1880.

31 The transcript of Kuczynski's interrogation can be found in the Foundation of the Archive of Parties and Mass Organisations of the former GDR (SAPMO-BArch), DY30/IV-2/4/123.

32 Admittedly, in his highly controversial book *Dialogue with My Great Grandson*, written in 1977 but not approved for publication in the GDR until 1983, Kuczynski wrote, somewhat candidly, that 'in the Soviet Union under Stalin anti-Semitic views came to the surface now and again'. Nonetheless, he vigorously denied that there was 'even the slightest hint of such attitudes within our own [East German] party leadership'. See J. Kuczynski, *Dialog mit meinem Urenkel: Neunzehn Briefe und ein Tagebuch*, 2nd edn (East Berlin and Weimar, 1984), pp. 51–2, and the very similar

assertions he made after 1989 in J. Kuczynski, *Ein linientreuer Dissident: Memoiren 1945–1989* (Berlin, 1992), p. 47, and J. Kuczynski, *Ein treuer Rebell: Memoiren 1994–1997* (Berlin, 1998), pp. 137–9.

33   Loebl, *Stalinism in Prague*, pp. 18 and 20.

34   H. Margolius Kovaly, *Prague Farewell* (London, 1988), pp. 166 and 172.

35   K. Kersten, 'The Terror, 1949–1954', in A. Kemp-Welch (ed.), *Stalinism in Poland: Selected Papers from the Fifth World Congress of Central and Eastern European Studies, Warsaw, 1995* (Basingstoke, 1999), pp. 78–94 (here p. 79).

36   K. Kaplan, *Political Persecution in Czechoslovakia 1948–1972* (Cologne, 1983), pp. 15–16.

37   There were brief worker revolts in Brno in late 1951 and, more notably, Plzeň (Pilsen) in June 1953.

38   A. Dudek and A. Paczkowski, 'Poland', in K. Persak and Ł. Kamiński (eds), *A Handbook of the Communist Security Apparatus in East-Central Europe, 1944–1989* (Warsaw, 2005), pp. 221–83 (here p. 273).

39   F. Werkentin, *Politische Strafjustiz in der Ära Ulbricht: Vom bekennenden Terror zur verdeckten Repression*, 2nd edn (Berlin, 1997), p. 13. Given that this study also suggests that the numbers fell back considerably in the 1960s, when 'open terror' gave way to 'hidden repression', it can safely be assumed that most victims of the East German political-judicial terror system served their sentences in the late 1940s and 1950s (see Werkentin, p. 276).

40   See J. Gieseke, 'German Democratic Republic', in Persak and Kamiński (eds), *A Handbook of the Communist Security Apparatus*, pp. 163–219 (here pp. 203–4); E. Neubert, 'Politische Verbrechen in der DDR', in S. Courtois et al. (eds), *Das Schwarzbuch des Kommunismus: Unterdrückung, Verbrechen und Terror* (Munich and Zurich, 1998), pp. 829–84 (here p. 864); and R. J. Evans, *Rituals of Retribution: Capital Punishment in Germany, 1600–1987* (London, 1996), pp. 805–6, 814 and 845–6.

41   Compare here M. Glenny, *The Balkans, 1804–1999: Nationalism, War and the Great Powers* (London, 1999), p. 536 with Bartošek, 'Central and Southeastern Europe', pp. 424–5. As Jerca Vodušek Starič pointed out in an email to the editors on 3 July 2009, some of the Yugoslav party members who were expelled and/or interned after 1948 may have fallen foul of the authorities for reasons other than alleged pro-Cominform views. In particular, local rivalries and jealousies, as well as outright corruption, played a role in some cases.

42   Tomáš G. Masaryk was the inter-war president of Czechoslovakia, who is revered by a majority of Czechs for his democratic and humanitarian principles.

43   National Archive of the Czech Republic (NA), Archive of the Central Committee of the Communist Party of Czechoslovakia (AÚV KSČ), f. 01, sv. 21, a.j. 34, ll. 39–42.

44   NA, f. 018, sv. 15, a.j. 110, ll. 4 and 6.

Soviet in form, local in content: elite repression and mass terror in the Baltic states, 1940–1953

Aldis Purs

To many Estonians, Latvians and Lithuanians, the experience of the Second World War is a sorrowful mantra: Soviet occupation and annexation → Nazi invasion → the Holocaust → the return of Soviet occupation → more deportations → occupation until 1991. The idea that the war continued until the restoration of independence in 1991 has widespread currency in the Baltic states. To general Baltic sensibilities, some of the final deciding battles in this long war centred on exposing the 'historical truths' about Soviet occupation. These truths include: the veracity of the secret protocols to the Nazi–Soviet Non-Aggression Pact of 23 August 1939, the imposition of Soviet bases on Baltic soil in the autumn of 1939, the forced nature of Soviet occupation in June 1940, and the bogus and illegal method of the Baltic states' incorporation into the USSR in August 1940. There is today near universal academic and international consensus about these events. The few politicians that continue to deny these truths dissent more for their constituents than for international or academic audiences.

Estonians, Latvians and Lithuanians assumed that continued archival research would complement ongoing study elsewhere to cement the agreement on the nature of Soviet rule. Instead, academic consensus has diverged into two paths: one focused on understanding repression in the USSR as a whole, the other on repression in the Baltic states specifically. Historians of the Soviet Union, such as Terry Martin, Yuri Slezkine, Ronald Grigor Suny and Amir Weiner, have produced thoughtful nuanced descriptions of an 'affirmative action empire', a 'communal apartment', a 'state of nations', and a 'socio-ethnic body' respectively.[1] Baltic historians, however, use a genocidal paradigm for their understanding of Soviet hegemony. The political scientist Dovilé Budryté succinctly paraphrased this emerging difference of opinion by viewing the Soviet Union as either a 'nation builder' or 'nation killer'.[2] Budryté attempts to bridge these differences in the contemporary ethnic politics of the post-Soviet Baltic states. Baltic historians, however, remain convinced that Soviet occupation intended genocide and have neither adopted Budryté's conciliatory approach nor embraced the conceptual ideas of Martin, Slezkine, Suny or Weiner.

The understanding of Stalinist terror and repression remains one of the few surviving pillars of Baltic identity. Estonians, Latvians and Lithuanians have critically re-examined their collective identity, as have their politicians and political scientists such as Daunis Auers, who has contended that 'historically the Baltic States usually have been more separated than united.'[3] Toomas Hendrik Ilves, while Estonia's minister of foreign affairs, famously and derisively argued that:

> Unfortunately most if not all people outside Estonia talk about something called 'The Baltics'. This is an interesting concept, since what the three Baltic states have in common almost completely derives from shared unhappy experiences imposed upon us from outside: occupations, deportations, annexation, sovietization, collectivization, Russification. What these countries do not share is a common identity.[4]

Baltic identity perseveres, however, in the work of Baltic historians on Soviet rule. They share a conceptual understanding of Soviet repression as something approaching genocide. Still, even in the most coercive years of Soviet dominance, when the Baltic label seems most apt, the construct shows its limitations as Estonians, Latvians and Lithuanians (communist and nationalist) acted in ways unique to their own experiences. The ever-expanding, almost encyclopaedic, scope of Baltic research is establishing the groundwork of how Soviet occupation repressed independent Baltic elites and then became mass terror. In both instances, the form was based on prior practices in the USSR, while the actual content of how repressions were executed depended also on indigenous factors.

Background

The Baltic republics broke from the nascent Bolshevik state in the aftermath of the First World War and the October Revolution.[5] Independent statehood was not the result of a long political struggle, but a fortuitous circumstance of defeated empires, successful local alliances and military prowess. Although the states cooperated in their wars of independence, petty territorial claims derailed any substantive partnership. The occupation of Vilnius by Polish forces torpedoed relations between Poland and Lithuania and scuttled any potential regional military or political bloc. Many contemporaries assumed the small states were 'seasonal phenomena' doomed to eventually fall. Lacking any meaningful multilateral guarantees of their independence, Baltic foreign policy alternated between a delicate balancing act vis-à-vis Germany and the

USSR or a desperate attempt at self-preservation through neutrality. Baltic unity did not extend beyond a few formal diplomatic exchanges and declarations of intent.

The Baltic states' domestic position was more stable, although with troublesome unresolved issues. Land reform coupled with elections to constituent assemblies and parliaments solidified political legitimacy. Minority communities had many grievances, but could address these through parliamentary politics. National elites emerged from many backgrounds: some were active in Tsarist service, others in the Russian revolutionary underground, while others still developed from the new political milieu of independence. Illegal communist parties in Estonia, Latvia and less so Lithuania challenged the political status quo, but were largely contained by the police. The most dramatic communist assault on these states during the inter-war years was the short-lived and spectacularly unsuccessful communist coup attempt in Estonia in 1924. Global depression compromised Baltic economies and the European tilt towards fascism and authoritarianism claimed all three states: Lithuania in 1926, Estonia and Latvia in 1934. Conservative authoritarian regimes led by powerful presidents were the norm by the late 1930s. State-controlled media, particularly in Estonia and Latvia, reassured inhabitants that European war would not come to the Baltic states. In Lithuania, however, territorial realignments presaged war, either catastrophically in losing Klaipeda/Memel to Hitler in March 1939 or potentially advantageously in the open case of Vilnius and a suddenly weakened Poland. In the summer of 1939, Baltic foreign ministries watched the dalliances among the western powers, Nazi Germany and the Soviet Union with great and justified trepidation.

Hitler secretly offered his ideological enemy an opportunity to divide Eastern Europe into spheres of German and Soviet influence. The resultant non-aggression pact of 23 August 1939 unleashed the invasion of Poland by the *Wehrmacht* and the Red Army and the onset of the Second World War in Europe. The pact also contained a secret protocol in which Germany ceded Estonia and Latvia to the USSR. A subsequent revision included Lithuania in the Soviet sphere of influence. Rumours of the secret protocols raced through the Baltic ministries of foreign affairs, which unofficially, yet desperately, turned to Germany and the western powers to canvas support in case of Soviet aggression. With no offers of aid forthcoming, the regimes of Estonia, Latvia and Lithuania could do nothing when the USSR demanded pacts of mutual assistance in September 1939. These pacts included the establishment of sizeable Soviet military bases in all three republics thereby effectively ending any military capability to resist full occupation when more ultimatums came in June 1940. By 17 June 1940 all three Baltic republics were occupied by Soviet military might. As Ilves stated, the republics began to share 'unhappy experiences'.

1940–41

Soviet terror began days before the occupation when Red Army forces attacked a Latvian border post near Masļenki killing five and kidnapping thirty-seven. This was a provocation, as was the charge that Lithuania had kidnapped two Soviet soldiers in May 1940. The Masļenki incident, as an unprovoked military operation on a sovereign state, is particularly important in terms of international law.[6] These provocations also open the question of advance Soviet planning for occupation and eventual terror against the citizens of Estonia, Latvia and Lithuania. Initially, émigré historians embraced NKVD Order Number 001223, supposedly from October 1939, which detailed the methods of mass deportations, as a smoking gun of Soviet plans pre-dating June 1940. More recent research, however, strongly suggests that the order was misdated and is likely from January 1941. Still, the Soviet Union, like Nazi Germany and most democratic western powers, accepted that the Baltic republics would eventually lose their independence. The Stalinist leaders assumed their power would extend to Russian imperial borders and beyond, perhaps as a result of war and occupation as with the independent states of the Caucasus in the early 1920s or through diplomatic ultimatums as in 1939 and 1940. The Soviet state understood that these republics, once 'reincorporated', would be quickly 'sovietised' with all the terror and heavy-handed measures that were used in the USSR itself from its inception.

Soviet terror and mass repression were defining components of the occupations of Estonia, Latvia and Lithuania. NKVD and communist party elites had believed for many years that untold thousands of 'enemies of the state' (foreign agents, saboteurs, traitors, class enemies and criminals) existed in the Soviet Union. In the summer of 1940, this same NKVD and communist party began to absorb independent states into the USSR. This was an unqualified strategic and territorial victory for Moscow, but these states had been caricatured as 'bourgeois', 'fascist' and 'counter-revolutionary' for decades. Clearly, to Stalinist sensibilities and notions of justice, annexation would bring thousands of new enemies into the Soviet body politic. Just as terror and mass repression were the measures used on enemies of the state in the Soviet Union, so they would become the standard *modus operandi* for dissenting (or potentially dissenting) citizens of the Baltic republics. Essentially, the terror and repression can be categorised as 'pro-active' or 'reactive'. Pro-active terror targeted victims beforehand. Targets were the politicians that Moscow labelled as enemies from the beginning or were suspect classes that the Stalinists distrusted or wanted to destroy. Reactive terror targeted those Estonians, Latvians and Lithuanians who exposed themselves as 'enemies of the people' by opposing the sovietisation of their state, economies and cultures. The first months from occupation to official incorporation into the USSR, roughly June to August 1940, clearly demonstrate aspects of both pro-active and reactive terror.

After Soviet troops marched into the capitals of the Baltic republics, Stalin's emissaries appointed left-leaning journalists, writers, poets and academics, not active communists, as the new cabinets of still nominally independent states. True power lay in the Soviet embassies and with the Red Army. Former cabinet members and leading governmental, military and business figures of the old regimes became early targets for Soviet repression. Some, such as Latvia's Border Guard General Jānis Bolšteins, avoided this fate by committing suicide as occupation began, while others, including Estonia's prime minister Jüri Uluots, went into hiding. Still others, most famously Lithuania's president, Antanas Smetona, fled abroad. For those arrested, lines of interrogation often revealed strangely hyperopic priorities. The Latvian politician Marģers Skujenieks is a case in point. His political career began before 1905 as a revolutionary and continued to evolve towards a Menshevik position in 1917, a centrist position in the 1920s, a nationalist one in the early 1930s, and finally a deputy minister president in the authoritarian regime. He was transferred to the infamous Lubianka prison in Moscow where his interrogations and charges centred on the 1937 show-trial testimony of the Latvian communists Vilis Knoriņš, Roberts Eiche and Jānis Rudzutaks.[7] Skujenieks was shot on 12 July 1941.[8] Arveds Bergs provides another example.[9] Bergs was a fantastically wealthy Latvian real estate and press mogul, who had financed and inspired many radical nationalist organisations. He was arrested in the autumn of 1940, interrogated repeatedly and ultimately charged for his role as Latvia's minister of the interior in the military field execution of communists in 1920. He was convicted primarily from the confessions of other arrested government officials. After several months crisscrossing the Gulag system, Bergs was executed on 19 December 1941.

The long memory of the NKVD extended to those who initially cooperated with Soviet occupation. In Estonia, Maksim Unt was chosen to be the minister of internal affairs and directed initial repressions against the Estonian national elite. Unt was later arrested and executed on 30 July 1941 for crimes supposedly committed during the Russian civil war in 1919. The Latvian SSR minister of welfare and subsequently commissar of education, Jūlijs Lācis, shared a similar trajectory: promotion followed by arrest and execution. These officials represented the first wave of pro-active Soviet terror. They were the Estonian, Latvian and Lithuanian elite already identified as enemies of the Soviet state from activities during the Russian revolution or from coerced testimony during the Stalinist terror of the 1930s. These elites joined the police, prison wardens, political police and intelligence agents as the first victims of Soviet terror. Russian émigré activists, Jewish bundists, Polish nationalists and homegrown fascists, such as the Perkoņkrusts in Latvia, were also arrested. The Latvian historian Irēne Šneidere has summarised this period as 'a primitive form of revenge sanctioned by the state.'[10]

The absence of the highest-ranking officials from the lists of these earliest victims of Soviet terror seems a glaring and surprising omission. In Estonia, Konstantin Päts remained in office as state president for the first month of occupation, as did Kārlis Ulmanis in Latvia. However, they were completely powerless, rubberstamped the dismantling of their regimes and were removed from office after bogus elections created people's parliaments. Päts and Ulmanis disappeared in Soviet custody and were initially believed to have become some of Estonia's and Latvia's first martyrs. Similar fates were believed to have befallen Estonia's and Latvia's most recognisable military leaders, General Johan Laidoner and General Jānis Balodis respectively. Juozas Urbšys, Lithuania's minister of foreign affairs, and Antanas Merkys, who claimed the presidency of Lithuania after Smetona fled, were treated likewise. Taken into Soviet custody and transported far from the Baltic republics, they were initially placed only under loose house arrest. By the end of July 1940, for example, Ulmanis was in a villa in Voroshilovsk where he remained until May 1941. He was free to roam the city (although most people he made contact with were concomitantly interviewed by the NKVD) and spent most of his time reading newspapers. He seemed to have little sense of the unfolding sovietisation of his native land, writing to friends and family requesting they send some of his valuables and general supplies. During this time, he was encouraged to write recollections on ten issues that interested the NKVD. These themes included the above-mentioned hyperopic ones, such as how Latvia 'found itself in the Anglo-French anti-Soviet political camp in the period 1918 to 1922.'[11]

The survival of some of these figures and their eventual return from exile fuelled occasional Baltic émigré charges of treason or collaboration with Soviet occupation (particularly regarding Balodis and Laidoner). Archival research has, to date, disproved these attacks. Apparently, Soviet authorities kept a handful of the most senior officials and their families in a more privileged state of captivity in case of need. When invading German forces rapidly approached some of these places of internment, conditions hardened. In Ulmanis's case, house arrest became incarceration followed by a series of prison moves that contributed to dysentery, kidney failure and death on 20 September 1942 in present day Turkmenistan. Päts similarly broke down from the strain of imprisonment and was placed in a psychiatric hospital, where he died in 1956. Still, as late as 1952, the remaining leading statesmen of the independent Baltic republics (and their families) were all legally interned, not imprisoned, in a prison in Ivanovo. Likely, they were kept together and in slightly more privileged conditions (better rations, access to newspapers, magazines, radio and each other) as a potential trump card to be used in the Soviet Baltic republics if need be.[12]

If Soviet occupation began by targeting the most senior Baltic elites in a pro-active assault on prior enemies of the Soviet state, the election of people's parliaments in July 1940 showcased reactive, but anticipated, terror. Soon after occupation, the new Soviet-picked cabinets called for elections for new people's parliaments. The bogus nature of these polls is well documented, but the facade also served to identify enemies of the new order. Ultimately, the communist party's sponsored electoral list was the only option in all three states, but in each republic politicians and activists raced to offer alternatives. In Lithuania an initial wave of arrests (between 500 and 2,000) began on the night of 11 July 1940, just three days before the scheduled elections.[13] Similarly, in Latvia even before the polls three organisers of 'Latvia's Democratic Voters' list were detained. In Estonia, nationalist organisations attempted to offer alternative candidates, but these were denied space on the ballot. Jüri Rajur-Liivak, a farmer, succeeded in being the only listed opposition candidate. Not surprisingly, he lost and was later arrested.[14] Most potential candidates that dared contest the elections in all three republics thereby exposed themselves as 'counter-revolutionaries' and were arrested in the autumn of 1940.[15]

This kind of reactive, but anticipated, repression became a pattern throughout 1940 and 1941. After the republics were incorporated as Soviet Socialist Republics, the laws and norms of the Soviet state were slowly introduced into the Baltic. This was done at a moderate pace to limit widespread opposition and build some degree of popular support among certain ranks of Baltic society. Raising workers' salaries and distributing small plots of land to the landless, for example, engendered a measure of legitimacy for Soviet power. Redressing some minority grievances also established support, and increased ethnic divisions as well. Most Soviet policies, however, immediately lowered the standards of living for Baltic inhabitants. For instance, the Soviet state introduced the ruble at appallingly disadvantageous exchange rates, confiscated personal savings and expropriated real estate. Societal norms of expression, through religion or the arts, were severely restricted while communist agitation, propaganda and the Russian language became ever present. As Estonians, Latvians and Lithuanians voiced their opposition to these changes, either individually or collectively, Soviet repressive organs swooped to arrest and charge these exposed 'enemies of the state'. Young people initiated this resistance activity and as a result began to be arrested in the autumn of 1940. In Lithuania, for example, Soviet authorities uncovered more than thirty youth organisations, although their total membership was very small.[16] From August 1940, all three Baltic republics saw a steady rate of monthly political arrests. In Latvia, every month between August 1940 and June 1941 had more than 200 arrests, with October recording 507 detentions. All told, more than 7,000 people were arrested for political crimes with roughly 1,500 executed.[17] Most were tried under the infamous section 58 of the criminal code of the Russian Soviet Federated Socialist Republic, even, on occasion, before it was officially introduced into the Baltic. In Estonia and Lithuania, the pattern was similar.

Repression also characterised the sovietisation of the armed forces of the Baltic republics, but perhaps to a lesser degree than anticipated. Pre-occupation planning included provisions for thousands of prisoners-of-war from Baltic armies in case of active resistance. With no such reaction, the Red Army hoped to absorb rank-and-file Baltic soldiers in a piecemeal manner by first converting armies into territorial units. However, the officer corps was, to Soviet sensibilities, almost entirely unreliable. Most senior officers had served in the Tsarist army and many had fought against the Bolsheviks during the civil war. The youngest were equally suspect because they were the products of the independent states' military academies and were vehemently nationalist. Yet, there was no Baltic parallel to the Soviet massacre of Polish officers in the Katyń forest. Instead, officers were arrested and deported. Altogether more than 850 from Latvia's army were deported, 514 of whom still actively served in the 24th Territorial Corps. Many of these arrested active-duty officers were joined by similarly arrested active-duty officers from the 29th Lithuanian Territorial Corps and the 22nd Estonian Territorial Corps (the remnants of the Lithuanian and Estonian armies respectively) en route to the Gulag in Norilsk in the Soviet far north.[18] However, others were not arrested, suggesting that prior service alone did not dictate repression in this first year of Soviet occupation. Even in the instructions for the mass deportations of June 1941, only those officers for whom compromising information was available were deported.

The first year of Soviet occupation ended with a massive wave of pro-active repression, the largest so far, and the first deportations to target class and station on a more general level. The entire year had seen a steady torrent of political arrests coupled with the rapid sovietisation of society, but there had yet to be mass deportations. The deportation of tens of thousands of 'dangerous elements' from the Baltic republics became the watershed event that defined the Soviet experience for many Estonians, Latvians and Lithuanians. In the historiography of these events, the deportations also mark the point of divergence between Baltic views of Soviet terror and those of western specialists. To Baltic sensibilities, the deportations unmask the 'genocidal' intentions of the Soviet state against the Baltic peoples, an idea initially suggested by post-war Baltic émigrés, but now commonly accepted in the independent states. To western experts, on the other hand, the Baltic deportations of June 1941 are but one of dozens of waves of deportations that stretch across Soviet history.

There is an emerging consensus about the 'nuts and bolts' of the June 1941 deportations due to the substantial amount of research and publication on the topic over the past fifteen years. The rough outline for a mass deportation of 'dangerous elements' had been established well beforehand, but ultimate approval came in May 1941 when the Central Committee of the Soviet Communist Party contemplated a project 'for the cleansing of anti-Soviet, criminal and socially dangerous elements from the Lithuanian, Latvian and

Estonian SSRs.' The specific targets were members of counter-revolutionary political parties and/or anti-Soviet nationalist white guard organisations, former police and gendarmes, including Home Guards and prison personnel, large landlords, factory owners, high-ranking civil servants and ex-army officers of the former independent states, and recidivist criminal elements.[19] The planning of the deportations included provisions for sending families into administrative exile. From this decision, historians have pieced together the preparation and execution of the expulsions in great detail. We know the fiscal resources earmarked for the operations, the number of train wagons, even the number and identity of individuals executing the actual deportations. We have early drafts of lists of those deported and local reports of how individuals were ultimately detained, transported and which of their possessions were confiscated. We have an ethnic and socioeconomic breakdown of the deportees and we even have general consensus about the number of people deported and understand why previous counts were inaccurate.

Official or quasi-official commissions of historians in all three Baltic republics have vigorously pursued a final complete accounting of all victims and martyrs of Soviet rule, particularly concentrating on the mass deportations of 1941 and 1949. All told, thousands of citizens of Estonia, Latvia and Lithuania were arrested in June 1941, and tens of thousands of their family members were concurrently deported and placed in administrative exile. In Latvia, over 5,000 were arrested and roughly 10,000 more, family members of the arrested, were deported. In Estonia, more than 9,200 people from a list of almost 14,500 were deported;[20] and in Lithuania, over 17,000 from a list of more than 21,000 people.[21] Baltic historians' devotion to finding a final tally is as much an attempt to bear witness and to memorialise, as it is a search for 'historical truth'. The massive *Name Register Books* of the Estonian Repressed Persons Records Bureau and the multiple publications of the Latvian State Historical Archives are grand efforts of intent inherently incapable of final completion; there may always be one more (or less) name. The assumption behind the massive collected databases and the prolific scholarly output of the various historical commissions and museums, perhaps most notably of the Commission of the Historians of Latvia and the Yearbooks of the Museum of the Occupation of Latvia, is that the deportations of 1941 were the first clear proof of the Soviet Union's intent to destroy Estonia, Latvia and Lithuania. Although scholars occasionally refer to the geographic nation, the implicit assumption is that these were crimes against ethnic nations. In Lithuania, the very name of the Museum of Genocide blatantly infers that Soviet terror was just one weapon from the arsenal of Soviet rule meant to destroy the Baltic peoples. Often, Baltic historians invoke Article 2 of the United Nations' 'Convention on the Prevention and the Punishment of the Crime of Genocide' to 'prove' Soviet genocidal intentions.

This assumption of genocide (in intent or consequence) separates Baltic historiography of Soviet terror from much of the current discourse on Stalinism elsewhere. Research has suggested that although certain groups were targeted precisely because of their ethnicity, on the whole 'the Soviets persistently rejected the primacy of the biological over the sociological.'[22] Furthermore, in-depth research into decision making at the All-Union level has found no evidence supporting the frequent Baltic implication (or the very real perceived belief during and after deportations) that Soviet terror was designed to destroy the Baltic nations. Instead, as Amir Weiner has argued, there were:

> twin pillars of Soviet population policies: the application of state violence anchored in political rationale and the simultaneous cultivation of ethno-national particularism. Without them, one could hardly understand the simultaneous eradication of entire national elites and intelligentsias along with the persistent delineation of particularistic identities.[23]

Ultimately, the difference between Baltic historians and Soviet specialists is one of perspective. The former see Stalinist terror as a phenomenon visited upon the Baltic republics, whereas the latter place the terror and deportations of 1940–41 (and those after the Second World War) into a larger context and as such resist the implied or explicit genocidal framework offered by Baltic historians. Pavel Polian, a leading expert on population displacement in the USSR, raised exactly these concerns at an international conference on the June 1941 deportations held in Riga in June 2001. Polian asserted that the Latvian deportation 'was one of many such operations, carried out by Soviet power in the controlled areas and it can be most correctly comprehended only in this actual historic context.' He further added that it 'was a relatively small operation ... undoubtedly tragic, but at the same time a typical page in Soviet and, unfortunately, Latvian history.'[24]

Other historians, such as Nataliia Lebedeva and Dmitrii Smirnov, have followed Polian's suggestion and placed terror in the Baltic in a broader Soviet context. Lebedeva, for example, details how the June 1941 deportations in some respects mirrored the Polish deportations of 1939.[25] Both followed the same rationale and operational organisation and shared a familial resemblance to the mass deportations of the 1930s in the USSR. Smirnov has tried to link terror and repression with Soviet norms and contemporary Russian views.[26] Others have looked beyond the genocidal framework to explain the motivation for deporting tens of thousands of Estonians, Latvians and Lithuanians precisely in 1941. Such motivation came from below, within the 'sovietising' Baltic republics themselves, and from the most commanding heights – Stalin and his inner entourage. From 'below', there were calls among some circles for more radical action against class enemies and the old regimes' elites. In certain places, such as Daugavpils or Vilnius, almost all such appeals for punishment carried ethnic connotations. Geoffrey Swain and Tomas Balkelis respectively have written about simmering ethnic conflict in the inter-war years that became more agitated in times of crisis.[27] As in the Soviet Union itself, Stalinist terror in the Baltic states included local spontaneous forms of the banality of evil – jealousies, petty feuds, revenge, retribution, careerism and naked greed.

From 'above', Stalin, fearing a German invasion of the USSR was likely within the year, viewed the deportations as necessary security precautions. This decision proved to be a massive miscalculation, as was his prediction for when an invasion would come. The deportations did not speed sovietisation, nor root out enemies that could potentially side with Germany. Instead, the Nazi attack on the USSR, less than a fortnight after the mass deportations, found stunned and bewildered nations convinced that Soviet rule intended to destroy their very existence. In these circumstances, German armies were initially viewed as liberators and Nazi plans for terror against national elites were shelved in favour of an aggressive propaganda campaign heralding a crusade against Bolshevism. Nazi ideologues and Baltic collaborators linked Soviet terror with native Jewish communities and by December 1941 German troops and local volunteers had murdered the great majority of Jews in the shameful Baltic chapter of the Holocaust. Similar to Soviet occupation, German rule was Nazi in form, but local in content. Ultimate decision making rested solely in Nazi hands, but local peculiarities influenced policy. Examining Nazi terror is beyond the scope of this work, except in how returning Soviet forces viewed Estonian, Latvian and Lithuanian (collective or individual) behaviour during Nazi occupation.

1944–53

Sustained and orchestrated Soviet terror returned with the victorious Red Army towards the end of the war. The first waves of repression included the mass deportation of Germans living in Estonia, Latvia and Lithuania, the only mass deportations determined solely by nationality.[28] Soviet repression also targeted Balts who worked with the German occupying forces, but differentiating between degrees of guilt proved difficult. The most senior and public faces of German rule were arraigned in show trials for crimes committed on the territory of the Estonian, Latvian and Lithuanian Soviet Socialist Republics (SSRs). Several were publicly executed soon after the war.[29] Less well-known, but equally guilty, criminals such as five Latvian policemen who murdered several local Jewish teenagers at Jēkabpils were prosecuted in Soviet courts over decades.[30] Accounting for the prosecution of such war criminals within the larger picture of Soviet repression of innocents continues to confuse contemporary Baltic historians. For lesser officials, conscripted soldiers and others, association with German rule became a serious stigma, but did not guarantee repression. Prisoners of war from German ranks were detained in screening camps for months, often under horrible conditions and great want, but some were then released. These screenings remain one of the least studied and most incompletely understood dimensions of post-war Soviet policy in the Baltic. If these individuals were arrested or detained in some other operation, their wartime past could resurface and figure prominently in criminal charges. The historians' dilemma, however, is that often the Soviet state added charges of collaboration haphazardly and inconsistently.

The return of Soviet rule in 1944 mirrored the imposition of Soviet rule in 1940 and 1941. Although the proverbial carrot was used to engender some popular support, the stick and the threat of the stick rebuilt Moscow's hegemony. As before, the strategy combined pro-active repression against clear enemies of Soviet power and reactive terror against individuals and groups that moved into opposition because of the nature of Soviet rule. This mechanism is most evident in the war against Estonian, Latvian and particularly Lithuanian partisans.

The Soviet state labelled partisans as 'bandits' and leftovers of Nazi and nationalist forces. There was a kernel of truth to these claims. Nazi policy included deploying diversionary groups behind Soviet lines. Moreover, some Baltic soldiers in German uniforms refused to give up the fight after the armistice and became partisans. Most partisans, however, were Estonians, Latvians and Lithuanians who took to the woods to fight for Baltic independence, escape from expected Soviet repression, and/or take revenge for friends and family already persecuted. Lithuanian partisan activity was the fiercest, longest lasting and most accomplished, but partisan resistance stretched across all three republics. Their vague strategic belief was that war would commence between the USSR and the west. Until that battle, partisans hoped to act as a deterrent and irritant to the ongoing sovietisation of the Baltic. They succeeded in killing hundreds of Soviet troops and local communist activists, and even symbolically raised national flags for short periods of time. Militarily, they were doomed.[31]

Still, the initial Soviet armed response to partisan activity was equally unsuccessful. Throughout 1945 and 1946, Soviet tactics favoured brute force and sheer numbers. Local supporters were organised in ad hoc 'destroyer battalions', or 'exterminator battalions', that joined more regular military forces in search and destroy actions. Massive shows of strength were used in attempts to comb haphazardly through woods suspected of harbouring partisans, but with little or no success. The use of locals in destroyer battalions further contributed to a chaotic and vindictive countryside. Members of the battalions looted and pillaged, while partisans took revenge against these local representatives of Soviet power. Red Army soldiers and partisans alike were guilty of forced requisitions and atrocities against perceived opponents.[32] By the end of 1946 and into 1947, Soviet tactics changed. The use of destroyer battalions slowed and partisans were attacked through subterfuge. Soviet special forces (*spetsgruppy*) infiltrated partisan ranks and proceeded to disorganise their activities and expose them to regular Soviet troops. These tactics, first perfected in western Ukraine, were used across the Soviet western borderlands.[33] Ultimately the use of agents and tactics such as corpse desecration proved decisive in paralysing partisan effectiveness and provoking an intensely bitter and distrustful atmosphere among surviving partisan units. Soviet intelligence agents were particularly successful in disrupting and manipulating attempts by western intelligence agencies to forge contacts with Baltic partisans.

Not content with neutralising the partisans, the Soviets struggled to force a decisive defeat or surrender of their adversaries. Early amnesties proved deceptive and deterred partisans from believing subsequent offers. Furthermore, the continued use of Soviet repression created steady streams of new partisans. In Lithuania, where partisan activity was most pronounced and disruptive, Stalin himself took part in planning a 1948 deportation aimed against partisan families. Ultimately, the 18 May 1948 operation deported almost 40,000 of a target list of 48,000 Lithuanian 'illegal residents, the families of those killed in armed skirmishes, the families of convicted bandits, nationalistic families, and those *kulaks* [better-off peasants] and their families who aided them.'[34] Little more than suspicion was needed to 'prove' any of these charges. Still, deportations alone did not defeat the partisans. In the Latvian case, Heinrihs Strods has charted a correlation between deportations and new waves of volunteers.[35] In short, after each wave of repression more young men (and occasionally women) moved to the forest and joined the partisan cause. This pattern held true for the 1949 deportation of Estonian, Latvian and Lithuanian '*kulaks*'.

The 25–28 March 1949 deportations were the largest deportations in Estonia and Latvia (the 1948 deportations were Lithuania's largest). They were the culmination of Soviet efforts to collectivise agriculture and vanquish '*kulaks*' and represented the last major step in homogenising Baltic practices with Soviet norms. The pattern used in Stalinist Russia was replicated. First, model collective farms and machine tractor stations were showcased to encourage voluntary collectivisation. When these failed to produce results, increasingly more draconian restrictions were placed on private farms, notably in tax policy and the employment of labour. Finally, the '*kulaks*' as a class were deported to 'break' their hold on the countryside. In the Soviet paradigm, '*kulaks*' were believed to be the material backbone of the partisan movement. Therefore, in the preparatory work building up to the deportations, family members of 'bandits' were often targeted. This action may have incapacitated the partisan movement, but in the short run it produced a new crop of recruits (those who escaped deportation or the family and friends of deported '*kulaks*'). As a result, the mass deportations of 1949 hurried the collectivisation of agriculture, not the demise of the partisan movement. Organised partisan resistance continued until Stalin's death.

Recent studies of the 1949 deportations mirror the work on the 14 June 1941 deportations in content and assumptions. In Estonia and Latvia, massive tomes painstakingly record the victims with formidable accompanying databases (age, sex, place of residence, deportation destination and fate). Similarly, researchers have identified individuals involved in the planning and execution of the deportations and some of them have been held criminally accountable in the newly independent Baltic republics. Again, we know quite a lot about the deportations: how pre-war government data were used to identify '*kulaks*', how people were detained, transported to rail hubs and what their life was like after deportation. We are reasonably sure of the numbers involved, although precise figures are impossible to establish. In Estonia, more than 20,000 people were deported.[36] In Latvia, over 42,000 people, and in Lithuania, more than 33,000 people were deported in March, April and May 1949.[37]

But the 1949 mass deportations were not the last. In 1950, 'bourgeois nationalists' were targeted at Estonia's university. In 1951, Jehovah's Witnesses were deported from all three Baltic republics.[38] In Lithuania, Jews were deported as part of the 'Doctors' Plot'.[39] All told, deportations came with tidal frequency. In Lithuania, Soviet authorities ordered thirty-five separate actions, deporting more than 125,000 people between 1940 and 1953. In total, 'more than 280,000 Lithuanians experienced forced migration to labour camps and prisons.'[40] In Latvia, similar waves led to the repression of over 190,000 people during the entire Soviet period. In Estonia, at least 34,000 were deported and roughly 122,000 suffered forms of repression.[41] Since entire families were deported, many victims were elderly, women and children. Deportations subsided only after the death of Stalin and the conditions for those already deported began to improve only after Khrushchev's 'secret speech' in February 1956. Deportees did not begin to return to their native lands *en masse* until 1956. Their past, however, stayed with them throughout their lives leading to diminished career and educational opportunities, and sub-par housing arrangements.

As with the 1941 deportations, there is a considerable gap between Baltic perceptions of the operations and Soviet specialists' evaluations. To Baltic commentators, particularly in the public sphere, there is little differentiation between deportations and political arrests. All are lumped together as Soviet terror directed against Estonians, Latvians and Lithuanians and prove that genocide was perpetrated against the Baltic nations.[42] For Soviet specialists, however, these claims are simplistic at best and frequently wilful distortions. The mass deportations were not akin to Gulag sentences. '*Kulaks*' were 'administratively exiled' and not arrested on political charges. In other words, they were forcibly displaced, usually to desolate but not penal regions of Siberia, and denied permission to return. Conditions were often horrific, deprivation and want were extreme, and police surveillance present, but this did not constitute a prison term. For example, survival rates from deportation compared to political arrest attest to the great difference between the two. In some cases, deportees even recalled their years in exile with some nostalgia citing that the sense of ethnic community and identity was strong.[43] As with the deportations of 1941, directives did not single out ethnicity as the determinant for repression. There is simply no proof that deportations were designed to destroy nations. The historiographical impasse centres on contested definitions of genocide. For generalists, intent is needed, or overwhelming consequences must demonstrate genocidal effects. For Baltic specialists, national survival is seen as dependent on autonomous statehood and vibrant political nationalism. Attacks against states are therefore attacks against nations.

Many Baltic historians fall into a deleterious cycle of beginning with an assumption and building histories that reinforce these claims. They believe Soviet rule was a genocidal threat to the Baltic nations and therefore Soviet terror had genocidal intent. To strengthen this argument, statistical proofs are often forwarded that suggest Estonia, Latvia and Lithuania suffered equally or greater than other countries or peoples through the dark twentieth century. This relativist debate, the 'our suffering matters because it was nearly total' argument, distorts all academic and public discourse on Soviet terror and repression. Instead, the absolute argument about the illegality of the occupation should be the starting point. Soviet rule was not illegitimate because it aspired to genocidal dimensions, but because it trampled on existing independent nation-states. This approach was already apparent to a trained Latvian lawyer in 1941. Hermanis Apsītis, a minister of justice in the Republic of Latvia, was arrested by Soviet police on 19 October 1940. He was sentenced to death, appealed his conviction, but was nonetheless executed on 19 January 1942. His appeal, worth quoting at length, was an attack on the legitimacy of Soviet rule in Latvia (and by extension in Estonia and Lithuania):

> My work in different positions in the Republic of Latvia cannot be qualified as an offense, since I worked in these positions in an independent state, whose sovereignty was recognized and more than once asserted by the Soviet Union . . . Thus, as of 18 November 1918, Latvia as an independent state had laws of its own, and the laws of another country, the laws of the RSFSR [Russian Soviet Federated Socialist Republic] included, were not binding for any official of this state, nor were they obliged to be familiar with or to obey these laws . . . Since I, as an officer of the court, as a soldier and later as a governmental official, was not bound by any laws of a foreign state, it is completely incorrect to judge my thoroughly lawful activities retroactively on the basis of Paragraphs 4 and 13 of Article 58 of the Criminal Code of the RSFSR. Each criminal offense implies an intention to commit the respective offense, while I had and could not have had such an intention, as it was in Latvia and not in the USSR that I was fulfilling my lawful functions. In theory, I could have violated the laws of the USSR only as of 5 August 1940, i.e. as of the moment of Latvia's accession to the Soviet Union, something I obviously did not do.

The application of Paragraphs 4 and 13 of Article 58 is incorrect also because some necessary elements of these articles are missing. Thus, for instance, Latvia's government could never be counterrevolutionary as there has never been any revolution in Latvia ... All the time I was and still am regarded as a citizen of Latvia, rather than a Soviet citizen (see the indictment). Thus, even if it was concluded (which would be contrary to the truth!) that I have committed a political crime in Latvia before the arrival of the Soviet troops, only a competent Latvian court in the territory of Latvia, rather than a court of another state beyond Latvia's borders and on the basis of laws of another state, would have been entitled to try me.[44]

Apsītis's legally grounded defiance to the repression directed against him personally is the most defensible and productive approach to Soviet terror in Latvia and the Baltic states more generally. Instead of arguing that the root evil of Soviet occupation was genocidal intent against Estonians, Latvians and Lithuanians, a case unsupported by archival evidence and one that distorts all other inquiry into the Soviet occupation, the root crime is the violation of independence and the fundamental illegitimacy of Soviet rule. This approach does not minimise or seek to justify the crimes committed by the Stalinist state. Instead the thousands of executed, the tens of thousands of political arrests, and the hundreds of thousands deported underline the extremity of Soviet conduct. If the crimes were not genocide, they were crimes against humanity and crimes against citizens of independent states.

This shift in approach could ameliorate a charged contemporary political discourse that uses genocide for callous electoral advantage and keeps alive the concept of 'communities of sufferers'. Changing the perceived focus to an attack against a state, rather than an attack against a nation, could mollify some ongoing ethnic tensions. For the discipline of history, a changed framework could bridge the chasm between Baltic historiography and Soviet studies, allowing more detailed nuanced studies of hundreds of aspects of Soviet governance and the Baltic place within Soviet rule. Some historians have already pushed at this door to examine Baltic participation in, and direction of, policy during the Stalinist era. As with the 1941 deportations, increased scholarly attention can find fruitful avenues of pursuit from 'above' and 'below'. In the former vein, historians are beginning a revision of the role of prominent Baltic communists, particularly the first secretaries of each Soviet Socialist Republic's party. Initially they were viewed as puppets, sociopaths or slavish devotees to Moscow's line. More recent research suggests, however, that Nikolai Karotamm and Estonia's Communist Party 'played a leading role in the 1949 deportation.'[45] Similarly, Geoffrey Swain has outlined political struggles and radical differences in policy between Latvia's Central Committee, Political Bureau (Latburo), and local activists. Latvia's first secretary, Jānis Kalnberziņš, often played a mediating role.[46] In Lithuania, the power of the republic's first secretary, Antanas Sniečkus, is most apparent. He was able to shield Lithuanian communists from persecution, yet directed repression and terror against anti-Soviet Lithuanians, including his own brother, with zeal. He was even able to negotiate All-Union politics so well that he remained at his post until his death in 1974. Recent scrutiny also reveals Baltic involvement in creating and executing Soviet policy at a micro level. Anu-Mai Köll has shown, for instance, how victims of the dekulakisation campaign were chosen on a local level in Estonia.[47] Heinrihs Strods and Matthew Kott, writing in defence of the genocide paradigm, documented that while close to 90,000 people were deported in the 1949 actions, more than 76,000 people participated, and over 60 per cent were locals.[48] More surprisingly, Baltic initiative could reverse certain acts of repression as in 1946 when the Latvian SSR ministry of education successfully returned 1,500 children to Latvia who had been deported in 1941. This power, however, was limited as many of the children were subsequently re-deported. Ultimately, Baltic history even in its darkest moments cannot become solely an examination of trauma. Flexibility for the discipline will become even more necessary as the Baltic historical commissions and various museums move away from the excessively repressive Stalinist years and analyse the greater complexity, ambiguity and controlled use of terror in the 1960s, 1970s and 1980s.[49]

Apsītis's appeal acts as more than just a call for revising Baltic views of Stalinist terror as genocidal. His reasoned arguments in the most dire and hopeless of circumstances are also a sharp rebuke to Soviet specialists who see Baltic deportations as relatively minor deportations in the long durée of Soviet history. *Kulak* deportations in Stalinist Russia in the early 1930s may have dwarfed those of 1948 and 1949 in the Baltic, and Crimean Tatars or Volga Germans may have suffered proportionally larger assaults on their historical ethnic communities, but these were a state's attacks on its own citizens. Soviet repression of national elites and mass terror directed against Estonians, Latvians and Lithuanians were violent unprovoked hostile acts against citizens of independent states. The signature of terror and repression may have grown from past Soviet experiences, but the place was different, and in this case the locale matters.

Notes

1   T. Martin, *The Affirmative Action Empire: Nations and Nationalism in the Soviet Union, 1923–1939* (Ithaca, 2001); Y. Slezkine, 'The USSR as a Communal Apartment, or How a Socialist State Promoted Ethnic Particularism', *Slavic Review*, vol. 53, no. 2 (1994), pp. 415–52; R. G. Suny and T. Martin (eds), *A State of Nations: Empire and Nation-Making in the Age of Lenin and Stalin* (New York, 2001); and A. Weiner, 'Nature and Nurture in a Socialist Utopia: Delineating the Soviet Socio-Ethnic Body in the Age of Socialism', in D. L. Hoffmann (ed.), *Stalinism* (Oxford, 2003), pp. 243–74.

2   D. Budryté, *Taming Nationalism?: Political Community Building in the Post-Soviet Baltic States* (Aldershot, 2005), p. 39.

3   D. Auers, 'Igaunija, Latvija un Lietuva Eiropas Savienībā: Vai Baltijas valstu sadarbība?', in Z. Ozoliņa (ed.), *Latvia's Foreign Policy and "Border Spanning"* (Riga, 2006), p. 49.

4   T. H. Ilves, 'Estonia as a Nordic Nation'. Speech to the Swedish Institute for International Affairs, 14 December 1999.

5   A standard history of each republic is D. Smith, A. Pabriks, A. Purs and T. Lane, *The Baltic States: Estonia, Latvia and Lithuania* (New York, 2002).

6   A. E. Feldmanis, *Masḷenku traģēdija – Latvijas traģēdija* (Riga, 2000).

7   Eiche and Rudzutaks recanted their forced confessions, but were shot in 1940 and 1938 respectively. Both cases featured prominently in Khrushchev's 'secret speech' denouncing Stalin, and both were posthumously rehabilitated. Skujenieks was not.

8   I. Ronis (ed.), *Kārlis Ulmanis Trimdā un Cietumā: Dokumenti un materiāli* (Riga, 1994), pp. 11–13.

9   U. Lasmanis, *Arveds Bergs: Politiskās apceres, ceturtā grāmata 1934–1941: Neizsūtītā trimdinieka piezīmes Pēdējais vārds* (Riga, 2000), pp. 476 and 489.

10 I. Šneidere, 'The Occupation of Latvia in June 1940: A Few Aspects of the Technology of Soviet Aggression', in Latvijas vēsturnieku komisijas raksti 14. sējums, *The Hidden and Forbidden History of Latvia under Soviet and Nazi Occupations 1940–1991: Selected Research of the Commission of the Historians of Latvia* (Riga, 2005), p. 42.

11 Ronis (ed.), *Kārlis Ulmanis*, pp. 160–3 and 222.

12 Ronis (ed.), *Kārlis Ulmanis*, p. 222.

13 Z. Kiaupa, *The History of Lithuania* (Vilnius, 2004), p. 282.

14 Estonian State Commission on the Examination of the Policies of Repression, *The White Book: Losses Inflicted on the Estonian Nation by Occupation Regimes, 1940–1991* (Tallinn, 2005), p. 12.

15 Ronis (ed.), *Kārlis Ulmanis*, pp. 151–6.

16 J. R. Bagusauskas, 'Formation and Activity of Youth Resistance Organizations in Soviet-Occupied Lithuania', *Lithuanian Historical Studies*, vol. 3 (1998), p. 87.

17 R. Vīksne and K. Kangers (eds), *No NKVD līdz KGB: Politiskās Prāvas Latvijā 1940–1986: Noziegumos pret Padomju valsti apsudzēto Latvijas iedzīvotāju rādītājs* (Riga, 1999), p. 971.

18 Ē. Jēkabsons and A. Bambals, 'Latvijas armijas iznīcināšana un represijas pret tās karavīriem', in Latvijas vēsturnieku komisijas raksti 3. sējums, *Totalitārie režīmi un to represijas Latvijā 1940–1956. gadā* (Riga, 2001), pp. 152 and 160.

19 J. Riekstiņš, 'The 14 June 1941 Deportation in Latvia', in *The Hidden and Forbidden History*, p. 65.

20 *The White Book*, p. 12.

21 V. Kasauskiene, 'Deportations from Lithuania under Stalin, 1940–1953', *Lithuanian Historical Studies*, vol. 3 (1998), p. 75.

22 Weiner, 'Nature and Nurture', p. 269.

23 Weiner, 'Nature and Nurture', p. 272.

24 P. Polian, 'Deportation of 14 June 1941 in the Context of the Soviet Deportation Policy', in Latvijas vēsturnieku komisijas raksti 6. sējums, *1941 gada 14. jūnija*

deportācija – noziegums pret cilvēci: Starptautiskās conferences materiāli 2001. gadā 12.-13. jūnijs, Riga (Riga, 2002), p. 710.

25 N. Lebedeva, 'Deportations from Poland and the Baltic States to the USSR in 1939–1941: Common Features and Specific Traits', *Lithuanian Historical Studies*, vol. 7 (2002), p. 110.

26 D. Smirnov, 'Sovietization, Terror and Repression in the Baltic States in the 1940s and 1950s: The Perspective of Contemporary Russian Society', in O. Mertelsmann (ed.), *The Sovietization of the Baltic States, 1940–1956* (Tartu, 2003), pp. 58 and 60.

27 G. Swain, *Between Stalin and Hitler: Class War and Race War on the Dvina, 1940–1946* (New York, 2004), pp. 17–46; and T. Balkelis, 'War, Ethnic Conflict and the Refugee Crisis in Lithuania, 1939–1940', *Contemporary European History*, vol. 16, no. 4 (2007), p. 475.

28 H. Strods and M. Kott, 'The File on Operation "Priboi": A Reassessment of the Mass Deportations of 1949', *Journal of Baltic Studies*, vol. 33, no. 1 (2002), pp. 1–31; Kasauskiene, 'Deportations', p. 77.

29 Ronis (ed.), *Kārlis Ulmanis*, p. 30.

30 D. Ērglis, 'A Few Episodes of the Holocaust in Krustpils: A Microcosm of the Holocaust in Occupied Latvia', in *The Hidden and Forbidden History*, pp. 175–87.

31 For a very sympathetic telling of Estonian partisans, see M. Laar, *War in the Woods: Estonia's Struggle for Survival, 1944–1956* (Washington, DC, 1992).

32 G. Swain, 'Divided We Fall: Division within the National Partisans of Vidzeme and Latgale, Fall 1945', *Journal of Baltic Studies*, vol. 38, no. 2 (2007), p. 196.

33 G. Reklaitis, *Cold War Lithuania: National Armed Resistance and Soviet Counterinsurgency*, The Carl Beck Papers in Russian and East European Studies, no. 1806 (Pittsburgh, 2007), pp. 6–7 and 34.

34 Reklaitis, *Cold War Lithuania*, pp. 16–17.

35 Strods is the authoritative historian of partisans in Latvia. See his three volume *Latvijas nacionālo partizānu karš* (Riga, 1996–2003).

36 *The White Book*, p. 31.

37 Kasauskiene, 'Deportations', p. 80.

38 Kasauskiene, 'Deportations', pp. 79–80; A. Rahi, 'On the Current State of Research Into Soviet and Nazi Repressions in Estonia', in *Latvijas okupācijas muzējs gadagrāmata 2002: Varas patvaļā* (Riga, 2003), p. 22.

39 V. Tininis (ed.), *Komunistinio režimo nusikaltimai Lietuvoje 1944–1953 m.: Istoriné studija ir faksimilinis documents rinkiny II Tomas* (Vilnius, 2003), pp. 63–7.

40 Tininis (ed.), *Komunistinio*, pp. 63–7.

41 Budryté, *Taming Nationalism?*, p. 180.

42 See, for example, A. Bergmanis, 'LPSR valsts drošības dienesta attīstība un loma genocīda īstenošana Latvijā (1944–1953)', and D. Bleiere, 'Represijas pret zemniecību Latvijā 1944–1953. gadā', both in *Totalitārie režimi*, pp. 255 and 282–3. Also A. Anusauskas, 'Crimes of Communism in Lithuania (1944–1953): A Historical Study', in *Totalitārie režimi*, pp. 146–7.

43 T. Balkelis, 'Ethnicity, Identity and Imaginings of Home in the Memoirs of Lithuanian Child Deportees, 1941–1952', in P. Gatrell and N. Baron (eds), *Warlands: Population Resettlement and State Reconstruction in the Soviet-East*

European Borderlands, 1945–1950 (Basingstoke, 2009). See also I. Saleniece (ed.), *1949. Gada 25. Martā izvesto balsis* (Daugavpils, 2008).

44 Quoted and translated in R. Vīksne, 'Soviet Repressions against Residents of Latvia in 1940–1941', in *The Hidden and Forbidden History*, p. 61.

45 Rahi, 'On the Current State of Research', p. 31.

46 G. Swain, '"Cleaning up Soviet Latvia": the Bureau for Latvia (Latburo), 1944–1947', in Mertelsmann (ed.), *The Sovietization of the Baltic States*, pp. 69, 76 and 80–3.

47 A. M. Köll, 'Tender Wolves. Identification and Persecution of Kulaks in Viljandimaa 1940–1949', in Mertelsmann (ed.), *The Sovietization of the Baltic States*, pp. 127–49.

48 Strods and Kott, 'The File on Operation "Priboi"', pp. 18 and 24.

49 E. C. Onken, 'The Politics of Finding Historical Truth: Reviewing Baltic History Commissions and their Work', *Journal of Baltic Studies*, vol. 38, no. 1 (2007), pp. 114–15.

Stalinist terror in Soviet Moldavia, 1940–1953

Igor Caşu

The scale of Stalinist terror in Soviet Moldavia remains virtually unknown in the west. This chapter seeks to redress the balance by focusing on these key issues: first, the aim and timing of three mass deportations, the first organised in mid-June 1941 just ten days before the German invasion, the second in July 1949 and the third in May 1951; second, the causes and consequences of the mass famine of 1946–47; and third, other individual or small-scale arrests, deportations and executions. In addition, I will try to make estimates about the overall number of political victims of the Stalinist regime in Soviet Moldavia, including their ethnic and social background. Other facets, such as anti-Soviet resistance and the rehabilitation of victims, are covered only in passing, if at all.

Soviet Moldavia did not exist as a separate political entity prior to 1940. With a Romanian speaking majority, it comprised the great bulk of historical Bessarabia, plus a tiny territory on the left bank of the Dniester River. Before 1812, Bessarabia was part of the Moldavian Principality, created in 1359, a state stretching from the Carpathian Mountains in the west to the Dniester in the east. In the early sixteenth century it fell under Ottoman suzerainty and following the Russo-Turkish war of 1806–12, the eastern part of the Principality was occupied by the Tsarist Empire and named Bessarabia. In March 1918, after more than a century of Russian rule, the local Bessarabian parliament voted for union with Romania, an act backed not only by Germany, but also by France and Great Britain.[1] In the inter-war period, the Soviet Union did not recognise Romanian authority in Bessarabia and tried to destabilise it. This included organising several uprisings, such as the one in Tatarbunar in September 1924. Failing to reach a diplomatic solution to the 'Bessarabian question' during the Vienna conference the same year, Moscow set up a Moldavian Autonomous Soviet Socialist Republic (MASSR) on the left bank of the Dniester on 12 October 1924. Its permanent capital was envisaged to be Chişinău (Kishinev in Russian) and its western frontier the Prut river. Initially, the provisional capital was established at Balta and after 1929 at Tiraspol. The MASSR was comprised of only 30 per cent Moldavians/Romanians and was intended to serve long-term Soviet interests, based on the so-called Piedmont principle.[2] During the collectivisation campaign of 1932–33, there were about 3,600 families deported from the MASSR to the regions of Archangelsk, Tomsk and the Solovki islands, around 15,000 persons in total. A further 18,000 persons died during the famine in the early 1930s. During the Great Terror of 1937–38, another 4,913 individuals, mainly from the state and party *nomenklatura*, were executed. Hence, out of a population of 600,000 in 1939, approximately 38,000 fell victim to the regime in the 1930s.[3]

In June 1940, Moscow sent an ultimatum to Bucharest demanding that it give up Bessarabia peacefully, threatening to employ military force if it refused. Romania, isolated after the fall of France and wishing to avoid the fate of Poland, finally surrendered to Soviet claims. As in the case of the Baltic states, Western Ukraine and Western Belorussia, the occupation of Bessarabia was a consequence of the Nazi–Soviet Pact of 23 August 1939. Another territory annexed by the USSR from Romania – Northern Bukovina, a former Habsburg province before 1918 – was claimed as compensation for the twenty-two years 'exploitation' of Bessarabia. In 1940, more than 60 per cent of the local population of these territories was Romanian. Northern Bukovina, as well as the territories of Southern Bessarabia on the Black Sea coast, was ceded to Ukraine (then part of the Soviet Union). In the summer of 1940, there were a mere 285 communists of Bessarabian background, of whom 186 were Jews, twenty-eight were Ukrainians, twenty-one were Russians and twenty-one were Romanians and others.[4] Even though minorities, especially Jews, dominated the Bessarabian communist organisation, this number is not representative if one compares it to the total share of minorities in Bessarabian society. In others words, it was not only the majority of Romanians, but also the minorities who did not view the Soviet model as a better alternative to the Romanian pre-war regime.[5] At the same time, one should add that the local Bessarabian members of the inter-war Communist Party of Romania were not trusted by the regime, and thus they were marginalised (but not persecuted) in favour of the Transnistrians, that is, communists from the former MASSR.[6]

Repressive policy in Soviet Moldavia, 1940–41

After the Soviet occupation of Bessarabia in 1940, a rapid process of Sovietisation was launched, the main aim of which was to marginalise or eliminate those social strata capable of organising resistance against the new authorities. The first group perceived as potentially inimical or hostile to the Soviet regime comprised former administrators, gendarmes or other persons suspected of working as agents of the Romanian government. Between 28 June and 4 July 1940, 1,122 persons were arrested from this category.[7] The second category included seventeen former members of the Bessarabian parliament (*Sfatul Ţării*), who voted for union with Romania in March 1918 as well as ex-members of Tsarist State Dumas.[8] In the next few months the NKVD arrested around 2,000 other people, the majority being railway workers.[9] Another category perceived as anti-Soviet was the priesthood. On 28 June 1940 about half of all Bessarabian priests succeeded in fleeing to Romania (487 out of 1,013). Of those who remained, 48 were killed or deported.[10]

Mass repressions of potentially dangerous anti-Soviet elements were organised on the eve of the Nazi invasion. On 31 May, Moscow's special envoy, S. A. Goglidze, sent a report directly to Stalin saying that among the most dangerous elements to be annihilated were the former Iron Guardists, the inter-war Romanian fascist body, characterised as 'the most clandestine organisation, having years of experience in illegal activities' and 'terrorist cadres organised in special paramilitary groups.' Other persons susceptible to deportation were ex-members of the National Christian Party, National Peasant Party and National Liberal Party (the former two being the main democratic parties in inter-war Romania), who were accused of preparing illegal activities. The list also included other social categories such as landowners, tradesmen, dealers, former members of the Romanian gendarmerie and ex-Tsarist White Guard officers.[11] The operation itself was planned for the night of 12–13 June 1941, and it was envisaged that a total of 32,423 persons from Bessarabia, Northern Bukovina and Hertza county would be involved. Of this number, 26,173 persons were to be deported and the remaining – 6,250 persons – were to be arrested. As for inhabitants of the Bessarabian territories incorporated into the new Moldavian Soviet Socialist Republic (MSSR), 5,033 were to be arrested and 14,542 were to be deported, a total of 19,575 people.[12]

However, according to a report sent to Stalin, Beria and Molotov by the deputy commissar for state security of the USSR, Bogdan Kobulov, the number of those deported or arrested from all occupied Romanian territories was actually 31,419 individuals, not 32,423. How can this difference be explained and what is the meaning of this reduction? There are data only for Bessarabian territory. Here 516 individuals were excluded from the initial list of those to be arrested for various reasons such as: three escaped, thirty were exempted because of illness, 263 for lack of sufficient compromising documents, and 220 changed their place of residence. At the same time, a further 667 individuals were not deported, as 103 were ill, 98 changed their residence and 466 persons (children and wives) were excluded as the decision to deport the head of their families had been meanwhile annulled. Geographically, the operation covered the entire territory of the MSSR, except the districts situated on the left bank of the Dniester, the former MASSR where terror had been organised prior to 1940. From this total, 13,682 persons were deported and 4,342 arrested according to the directives of the People's Commissariat of State Security (NKGB – political police) and only 165 persons were arrested and 203 deported as a result of decisions made by the NKVD (internal affairs).[13]

While the documents make clear that those included in the lists of deportees were resettled mainly in Siberia and Kazakhstan, there are no data relating to those arrested; that is, one quarter of the total touched by the operation of 12–13 June. A letter sent by Sazykin, commissar of state security of MSSR, to Merkulov, commissar of USSR state security, on 19 June 1941, reveals that 113 individuals were deported as their head of families were condemned to the 'highest measure of punishment', meaning immediate execution.[14] What happened to the other persons arrested is not clear: they were either executed or sent to concentration camps. Nicolas Werth has maintained that the heads of the families arrested in the Baltic states during the night of 13–14 May 1941 in all probability were executed, and that could well be the case in the MSSR.[15]

As a rule, the deportations during the night of 12–13 June 1941 took place as follows. The exact lists of victims were drawn up in advance, and hence the local authorities helped the secret police and military identify precisely where the households were located. The families were awakened in the deep of night, around 2.30 am, and the documents of those in the house were verified to match those from the list. Any luggage had to be ready in forty minutes, the limit being forty kilograms for each family.[16] Then, the victims were transported by trucks to nearby railway stations and despatched to their place of destination. A total of 1,315 wagons, distributed all over the territory of Bessarabia and Northern Bukovina, were allocated for the deportations. Official documents disclose that each wagon transported twenty individuals and each person was entitled to 600 grams of bread daily.[17] In contrast, the memoirs of survivors give an altogether grimmer picture: up to 70–100 persons shared a wagon for two to three weeks before arriving at the final destination and the daily norm of water was 200 millilitres, while some deportees received salted fish as their only food.[18] Others received boiled water and 300 grams of bread in the morning and nothing else for lunch or dinner.[19] According to other testimonies, many deportees were old and sick. Among them was a pregnant woman, deported together with her twelve children only because her husband had fled to Romania in the summer of 1940. She gave birth to her thirteenth child in the train on the way to Siberia.[20]

The heads of families were separated from their loved ones and sent to concentration camps – 5,000 to the Kozel'shchansk camp and another 3,000 to Putivl'sk – and the members of their families were despatched to special settlements for exiles (*ssylnoposelentsy*) in the regions of Karaganda, Aktiubinsk, Kustanai, Kzyl-Orda (Kazakhstan), and Omsk and Novosibirsk (Central Siberia).[21] According to a document signed by M. V. Konradov, the chief of special settlements of the Gulag, dated 15 September 1941, the number of special settlers from the Moldavian SSR was 22,648 persons, distributed geographically in Kazakhstan, Komi Autonomous SSR, and the Krasnoiarsk, Omsk and Novosibirsk regions.[22] Thus, in the autumn of 1941 there were almost twice as many individuals in special settlements compared with the total of deportees of

12–13 June 1941. This means that before the mass deportation operations and thereafter, a series of other arrests and deportations were carried out. A possible explanation is that those deported previously in the 1930s from the MASSR were sent to other regions than the ones listed above.

Besides the number of arrested, deported or executed during the first year of Soviet occupation of Bessarabia, there were another 53,356 persons mobilised for forced labour in different parts of the USSR.[23] Given the conditions in which they were mobilised and lived, these people could also be added to the victims of Stalinist repression.[24] In sum, there were about 86,000 persons who suffered on account of the Soviet regime between June 1940 and June 1941 in all the Romanian territories annexed by the USSR – Bessarabia, Northern Bukovina and Hertza county.[25]

The reoccupation of Bessarabia and the mass famine of 1946–47

Stalinist terror against the local Moldavian population recommenced immediately after the Red Army reached the River Dniester in March 1944. One of the main tasks of the Soviet security forces was to identify 'collaborators' with the Romanian administration during the period 1941–44. The local population feared that repressions would recommence on a mass scale and these attitudes were expressed by peasants to communist agitators and propagandists sent by Moscow into Bessarabian territory on the back of the advancing Red Army.[26]

In the next few years, Soviet repressive organs in Moldavia focused on identifying, arresting and deporting 'collaborators' with the enemy. In the first instance, these measures were aimed at communists who, for various reasons, had remained on Moldavian territory during the war. In 1944 and 1945, hundreds of individuals from this category were identified. The majority were rank-and-file communists expelled from the party on the grounds that they displayed passivity towards the Romanian and German authorities or were not willing to help the partisans or Soviet agents sent in during the war. Only those who had actively collaborated with the 'enemy', meaning those who helped disclose party activists or used violence against Soviet citizens, were condemned to imprisonment for up to fifteen years.[27] That said, no purges were organised against the Moldavian party *nomenklatura* under Stalin, in contrast with Estonia in 1949–52.[28] The other category of 'hunted' was the non-communist collaborators, basically former members of Romanian political parties and various cultural associations. Among them were 'Moldavian-Romanian nationalists', described as the 'most dangerous enemies of the Moldavian people.'[29]

The little-known famine of 1946 and 1947 struck various regions of the Soviet Union, and its consequences in Moldavia were catastrophic. In less than a year, the human costs were comparable to the total losses during the three years of war from 1941 to 1944. The overall number of victims is estimated at approximately two million dead, including half a million in Russia.[30] In Moldavia, the death-toll was around 150,000–200,000.[31] What were the peculiarities of the famine in Moldavia compared with other regions of the USSR and what were its main causes? In Soviet historiography, the dominant interpretation of the cause of the famine was the hardships brought by the war, exacerbated by the drought of 1946. The archival documents on the famine in Moldavia published in 1993 give another picture: the mass death could have been avoided if the regime had acted in due time. Initially, the grain procurement plan for Moldavia in 1946 was set at 265,000 tonnes. It is true that because of the drought, on 26 June 1946 the council of ministers and the party Central Committee (CC) adopted a resolution stipulating a reduction in the amount of grain to 161,000 tonnes. Later, even this plan was considered unrealistic. Thus, on 19 August 1946 it was further dropped to 72,000 tonnes.[32] But in light of the harsh conditions of 1946 even this figure was beyond the possibilities of peasant homesteads. The Moldavian historian, Mihai Gribincea, has calculated that with a population of 2,183,000 inhabitants and for a minimum of 300 grams of bread per diem per person, Moldavia needed for its own internal consumption about 240,000 tonnes of cereals. Besides, the peasantry needed tens of thousands of tonnes for feeding cattle and poultry,[33] as well as further tens of thousands for sowing the land the following year. As the harvest in 1946 was about 365,000 tonnes of cereals, for the people to survive it was imperative that the Soviet authorities completely abolish the collection of bread. By way of comparison, in 1945, when bread was already in short supply in Moldavia, about 710,000 tonnes of cereals remained after fulfilling the plan.[34]

In August–September 1946 the famine had spread to become a mass phenomenon and in November the number of 'dystrophic' (a euphemism for those affected by famine) exceeded 30,000. At this stage, the majority of those touched by the famine were poor and middle peasants. In spite of the officially expressed willingness of the Soviet government to help Moldavia, the distribution of grain in August 1946 mainly to these two categories of peasants was far from sufficient to eradicate the hunger. Furthermore, fearing repressive measures from the centre, the local authorities wanted to meet the grain procurement plan by 1 November 1946. The plan was not fulfilled by this date and subsequently it was decided that the deficit had to be extracted from rich peasants, who were being persecuted for hiding bread in their struggle for survival. In the district of Cahul, for instance, of the 250 *kulak* homesteads made responsible for 'sabotage', fifty-three heads of families were condemned on the basis of the civil code, with another thirteen on the basis of the criminal code. By 1 January 1947 the amount of grain collected was slightly over the necessary quota, reaching 101 per cent. However, these results were catastrophic for the so-called *kulaks*, who thereafter joined the army of 'dystrophic' and thus could not be of any help to their poorer neighbours. For the first time in the history of the province numerous cases of cannibalism were registered.[35] In the meantime, the Soviet government allocated a loan of 24,000 tonnes of grain and in January 1947 the first canteens were established all over the republic. By March their number had increased to 1,023, but they were not very effective in combating the famine because of a combination of bad management and theft.

Despite the mass hunger, the Central Committee of the Moldavian party did not ask the centre for assistance, probably fearing that Stalin would order the repression of the local party elite on the grounds that they were 'saboteurs'. According to some testimonies, when Nikita Khrushchev dared to inform Stalin personally about the famine in Ukraine, he immediately lost his post as first secretary of the Ukrainian SSR, but the republic received help.[36] If this was the case, then it seems that the leaders of Soviet Moldavia did not have the right to address themselves directly to Stalin or if so, they could not hope for the same mild reaction Stalin had towards Khrushchev, one of his most loyal lieutenants at the time. In late February 1947, Molotov and Stalin were eventually informed about the situation in Moldavia. However, this was done not by the local party, as one would expect, but by the procuratorial organs and via citizens' private letters. As a result, Alexei Kosygin, vice president of the council of ministers, was sent to check the situation on the ground. Meeting with the local Central Committee on 24–27 February 1947, Kosygin criticised party officials for failing both to report the scale of the famine and to organise rescue operations for the population.[37] Nevertheless, the outcome of Moscow's direct intervention was meagre. Indeed, 'mass dystrophy' peaked in the period February to March 1947: of the 389,000 cases of dystrophy in 1946–47, 240,000 were registered in these two months alone. In addition, the death rate continued to grow in the subsequent months, reaching its height in March and June-July 1947. Only in the autumn of 1947 with the new harvest did it decrease to levels characteristic of the period before the mass famine.

These facts strongly support the opinion of the editors of the documentary volume *Golod v Moldove* (*The Famine in Moldova*), who, while admitting that the visit of Kosygin was highly important, maintain that it was not crucial for putting a stop to the famine, as Soviet era historians had argued. In other words, the mass famine was ended not because the Soviet government demonstrated its ability to handle a catastrophe, but rather because the harvest – that is, natural causes – contributed to overcoming the tragedy.[38] Thus, the Stalinist regime is responsible for the death of a huge number of people and it is no exaggeration to include these in the list of political victims of the regime. At the same time, one cannot simply assume that the local authorities were less responsible for the death toll than Moscow. More exactly, before February 1947, when Stalin and Molotov were informed of the scale of the famine in Moldavia, the local party apparatus should be considered more responsible than the centre; after that date, however, the latter should be blamed as the famine continued until August 1947.

There are numerous memoirs related to the mass famine of 1946–47, many of which indicate that although conditions were hard because of the drought, the regime's inhuman requisitioning policy was largely responsible for the horrendous death toll. For instance, Alexei Guzun from the village of Chiţcani, remembers:

> For the peasants, the land is sacred; the peasant fought and will fight for the land as long as he lives . . . In 1946 I was 14 years old. Then the greatest tragedy of the Moldavian people and, of course, our family started. There were five children in our family, but two of them were serving in the army. So, at that moment there were just five of us – mother, father, my sister and two brothers, Pavel and me. The reason so many people died was that they cleaned out all our reserves . . . The soldiers swept the last barley we had in the garret. In our house, twelve soldiers were lodged in one room and twelve in the other. And these soldiers, as well as others who were in our houses, fed the horses with barley, but did not care about the people of the village. Probably, if they had left us a few pounds of barley in the garret, we would have had a chance to survive, but without it and when the drought came, the people remained with nothing.[39]

Another survivor, Victor Volcinschi, recalls even more vividly the tragedy of those years:

> We had . . . very serious cases . . . in Bădrăganii-Vechi . . . There were brothers eating each other, and after a few years, those remaining alive lost their minds . . . It was about March–April [1946] when the crisis started. My father tried to hide in the stable and elsewhere, but the authorities were searching everywhere, they pierced every outhouse with forks and iron sticks . . . What is most regrettable is that we had been 'sold' by the people from the village . . . those you had grown up with . . . As for those from the district . . . they were at least 'foreigners' . . . In 1946 they climbed without any remorse in the garret and swept the small savings we had – yes, it's true there was a poor harvest in the summer and autumn, but nevertheless we could have survived with what we had . . . But in this way they amassed everything, and not the foreigners, but our lot, from the village, just to meet the expectations of those from the district![40]

Collectivisation of agriculture and the mass deportations of 1949

The total collectivisation of agriculture, based on the Stalinist model of the early 1930s, was a permanent aim of the Soviet regime in the newly occupied western territories, including Moldavia. Initially, however, the government postponed the comprehensive 'socialist transformation of agriculture' for a variety of reasons: the consequences of the war, scarce state resources, especially machinery, the lack of specialised personnel, as well as peasant resistance.[41]

From another point of view, individual non-collectivised homesteads were tolerated for a while as they were more heavily taxed than the collectives (*kolkhozy*). Hence, there was a certain economic rationality in this policy. The most difficult issue related to those rich or middle peasants, who did not want to renounce their properties and become entirely dependent on the discretion of the state. Until 1948, the official policy of the Stalinist regime tried to limit and then marginalise the influence of these 'inimical elements'. At first, all peasants were susceptible to inclusion in the list of *kulaks*, but later this category was separated according to more or less precise criteria. The amount of land was not decisive for inclusion in the category *kulak*, although it was certainly most important for the calculation of taxes (the more land one had, the more taxes one had to pay). Already in September 1940, the limit of land plots was established at no more than ten hectares in the central and northern districts and twenty hectares in the south, where the quality of land was inferior and precipitation lower.[42] In the years 1944–46, a significant amount of land under pasture, as well as vineyards and orchards owned by the *kulaks*, was nationalised.[43] In this way, by January 1946 land distribution among individual farmers in Soviet Moldavia did not reveal great social discrepancies, as shown in the following table:[44]

Table 1: Land distribution among farmers in Soviet Moldavia

Hectares in property	Total of homesteads (%)
More than 30	0.1
From 20 to 30	0.2
From 15 to 20	0.6
From 10 to 15	2.7
From 5 to 10	23.3
From 1 to 5	65.3
Less than one or nothing	7.9

Of the total of 463,274 homesteads, only 4,144 (8.8 per cent) had two cows and only sixty-one peasants owned more than three; a mere 3.4 per cent of homesteads possessed more than two horses, while only 263 farmers owned more than three.[45] In the context of the famine, on the eve of the new harvest in the summer of 1947 it was decided that only poor homesteads would be absolved of paying back their taxes or loans for the previous years. Instead, the 'kulak and rich' (*kulatsko-zazhitochnye*) were instructed to liquidate all their debts to the state without delay. On 30 August 1947, the CC of the Moldavian party adopted a decision 'On the identification of *kulak* homesteads', according to which *kulaks* were those who had hired seasonal workers during or after the war, bought products from other peasants in order to sell them for a profit on the market, and hired their machinery to other peasants in exchange for products or money, or had revenues from rented land and mills.[46] In other words, all those peasants who adopted some rudimentary elements of a capitalist market economy and thus were independent of the state were perceived as potential enemies of the Soviet regime. A list was drawn up in ten days and included 10,154 homesteads, or 2.1 per cent of peasant farms. After the list was checked by a special commission, only 7,338 were confirmed as *kulaks*.[47] The identification of *kulaks* and their separation into a special taxation category anticipated the next stage of the collectivisation of Moldavian agriculture. From 1947, the Soviet regime tried to use its fiscal policy in a more discriminatory and discretionary manner in order to encourage rich or middle peasants to enter the *kolkhoz*. At the same time, in 1948 it was decided that, as in the early 1930s, this social category was the main obstacle to the final and complete 'socialist transformation of agriculture' and should thus be eliminated.

Several decisions anticipating the mass deportations of the summer of 1949 were adopted in the second half of 1948. The period of voluntary collectivisation and marginalisation of *kulaks* was over; it was time, according to Stalinist logic, to deport them from Moldavia. From the autumn of 1948, and especially from the spring of 1949, rumours, partly inspired by foreign radio stations like the 'Voice of America', began to spread about a future mass deportation.[48] Local *kulaks*, as in the Baltic states, tried to escape being categorised as such by the regime. One of the main strategies was to split the land formally among relatives and thus enter the category of poor or middle peasant. Others joined the *kolkhoz* as it was perceived as a shelter against repressive measures. This phenomenon took on an alarming scale for the authorities as a few months before the mass deportation of July 1949, one of the main tasks of the local party and state organisations was to identify and expel in due time the 'real' *kulaks* from the *kolkhoz*. Ad hoc meetings on the collectives were held for this purpose just days before the deportations took place.[49] If a *kulak* successfully remained in the *kolkhoz*, his personal security as well as that of his family was assured.

On 12 October 1948, after the lists of *kulaks* had been verified, the Soviet minister of internal affairs, N. S. Kruglov, sent a secret letter to his Moldavian counterpart, announcing that:

> collectivisation of agriculture in the Moldavian SSR is taking place in an atmosphere of intensifying class struggle . . . In order to fulfil the state economic plan for the . . . collectivisation of agriculture in the Moldavian SSR, as well as for restraining the anti-Soviet activities of *kulaks*, I beg you to ask the Soviet government for permission to deport the *kulaks* from the MSSR to remote regions of the Soviet Union. In total, there are about 15,000 *kulaks* in Moldavia. In any case, it is necessary to deport at least the most inimical and most economically powerful, about 5,000 individuals.[50]

According to numerous local reports, there was a definite intensification of anti-Soviet activities. Peasants entering the *kolkhoz* were threatened with reprisals by *kulaks* should the Soviet Union lose a future war with the United States and Great Britain. Thus, one can see that the context of the first years of the Cold War and the emergence of east-west confrontation nurtured illusions about the provisional character of the Soviet regime in the newly occupied territories and inspired certain social categories to resist the authorities. At the same time, there can be no doubt that the deportations played an instrumental role in the establishment of the Soviet regime in Moldavia.

On 28 June 1949, the Moldavian government adopted the decision 'On the deportation of *kulak* families, landowners and big merchants from the MSSR'. This decree, based, as in the case of the Baltic states, on a previous decision taken by the USSR council of ministers, identified 11,342 families to be deported, but the final lists had once again to be thoroughly verified. In this sense, local soviets and district and city executive authorities were obliged urgently to present the lists to the Moldavian ministry of state security. The tragic event, dubbed Operation 'South', started as scheduled at 2.00 am on 6 July and ended at 8.00 pm on 7 July 1949.[51] It ended in the forced displacement to Siberia and Kazakhstan of 11,239 families, or 35,050 individuals. Of these families, 7,628 were regarded as *kulaks*, landowners and tradesmen (23,056 persons), and the remainder were labelled as collaborators with the 'German-fascist occupiers'. One must point out that, just as during the mass deportations of 12–13 June 1941, not all those included in the basic lists were deported. In July 1949, of the total of 12,860 families originally listed, 1,567 were not deported for various reasons: 274 families had entered collective farms; 240 produced evidence attesting that certain members of the family were serving in the Red Army; 35 families were exempted on the grounds that their members had received Soviet decorations or medals;[52] 508 changed residence; and 105 families, informed about the operation, were able to hide at the homes of relatives or in the surrounding forests.[53] Some 1,000 escapees were caught by state security officers in the following days.[54] It should be mentioned that 305 families, or approximately 1,000 people, deported during Operation 'South' were from the former MASSR, the majority of them peasants who had settled beyond the Dniester under Romanian administration during the Second World War.[55] Another difference with the deportation of mid-June 1941 is that in July 1949 all the repressed were deported to special settlements and the heads of families were not sent to Gulag labour camps.

What happened to those individuals who in one way or another escaped? The Chişinău authorities took several initiatives, one by Leonid Brezhnev, who served as first secretary of the Communist Party of Moldavia from July 1950 to October 1952. On 16 March 1951, he asked the Central Committee in Moscow for permission to deport escapees from Operation 'South', but the central authorities did not sanction the request. Later, on 28 May 1952, the USSR ministry of interior re-examined the idea of deporting those 3,120 individuals who had escaped. On 10 June 1952, this recommendation reappeared once again in a report of a deputy chief in the ninth directorate of the ministry of interior, but it too never materialised.[56] As a compromise between those insisting on another deportation and those rejecting this solution, it was decided that escapee families were to be doubly taxed.[57] Others had problems entering the *kolkhoz*, this being the only way of social integration in the rural areas under the Soviet regime. As they were not able to join the *kolkhoz*, they could not receive salaries and pensions and their children were susceptible to stigmatisation by the community as 'enemies of the people'.

What were the shorter and longer term consequences of the displacement of tens of thousands of Moldavians to Siberia? The immediate impact was on the pace of collectivisation, as expected by the Soviet authorities. In the five months following the operation, from July to November 1949, the proportion of collectivised homesteads rose from 32 per cent to 80 per cent. By January 1951, 97 per cent of individual farmers had entered the *kolkhoz*.[58] In other words, the peasantry had dramatically altered their attitude toward the Soviet regime in a matter of a few months. Fearing similar operations, they reluctantly accepted the rules of the potentates of the day and renounced their properties in favour of collective farms. This fear was deeply ingrained as the deportees of 1949 had been displaced 'in perpetuity', in line with a decision taken by the Moscow authorities.[59] This time, some categories of deportees fell under the decree of 8 March 1941 'On obtaining Soviet citizenship by the inhabitants of Bukovina and the re-acquisition of Soviet citizenship by the inhabitants of Bessarabia'. Thus, the logic of the Soviet authorities was that on receiving Soviet citizenship – actually against their will – Bessarabians were susceptible to accusations of treason against the Soviet state by 'collaborating' with the Romanian government during the war.[60] The above-mentioned law had been used before the deportations of 1949 in order to prosecute all those 'guilty' of remaining under 'enemy territory', acting as a juridical basis for the forced repatriation of Bessarabians fleeing to Romania after 1944. In 1946, local authorities had registered 40,000 'repatriated', many of them hunted by the Romanian police and sent to the USSR. All of them were treated with great suspicion and some were sent to Siberia as 'dangerous social elements'.[61]

The tragic fate of the deportees was vividly described by Nicolae Negru, nowadays a journalist at one of the best Romanian-language weeklies in the Republic of Moldova, *Jurnal de Chişinău*:

> We were educated, all of us, as janissaries . . . I myself, being in the eighth grade, reproached my father for the bad things he used to say about the Soviet regime and socialism. It was not, however, a reproach made in public; I was not yet a fully-fledged Pavlik Morozov, but the case demonstrates that the children of the

deportees were intoxicated to such a degree that they started to accept that they deserved to be deported in perpetuity . . . I have suffered a lot because my father was unlike others and I have lived many shocking moments. One of them I will never forget. I was in the first grade and I was returning home in a very good mood as I had received my first book from the school library . . . It was a book with the image of Volodea Ulianov [Lenin] on the cover. 'I don't want to see the image of that bandit in my house!', yelled my father and threw the book out. I know of other cases, when the offspring of deportees renounced their parents . . . I had to re-learn a lot of things before agreeing with my father, but it was not as easy as one would think.[62]

The final mass deportation of the Moldavian population took place on 1 April 1951 and was aimed at religious elements, who were seen as a potential danger to the regime. The majority of those resettled during this phase were members of religious sects, in particular 'Jehovah's Witnesses', who were accused of anti-Soviet activities.[63] As a result of this operation, which started at 4.00 am and ended at 8.00 pm on 1 April, 723 families, or 2,617 individuals, were deported. Over 2,000 ministry of interior officers and soldiers were involved in the organisation of the deportation, as well as 750 members of the party and state *nomenklatura*. Some 415 trucks were allocated to transport the deportees to nearby railway stations, and from there 135 wagons carried them to their final destinations.[64] Members of religious sects were deported simultaneously from the other newly occupied territories – the Baltic states, Western Ukraine and Belorussia.[65]

The ethnic and social composition of victims

What was the ethnic and social composition of the political victims of the Stalinist regime in Moldavia? The most complete list of victims is provided by the *Book of Memory*, published in four volumes between 1999 and 2005, but this does not include ethnic identities. According to official Soviet statistics, in January 1953 there were approximately 40,000–45,000 ethnic Moldavians/Romanians in the deportee settlements (*spetsposeleniia*).[66] Another report from 1950 claims that there were 94,792 deportees from Soviet Moldavia.[67] Thus, one can conclude that the share of Moldavians/Romanians in the total of displaced persons was about 50 per cent. Others, as one can deduce from their names in the *Book of Memory*, were Jews, Russians, Ukrainians, Gagauzes, Bulgarians and Gypsies.[68] Hence, Stalinist terror should be categorised as genocide or crimes against humanity, rather than ethnocide as it was not directed exclusively or even mainly against one ethnic or national group.

That said, it is possible to estimate the social composition of the victims of the deportations of mid-June 1941 and early July 1949. During the mass deportations organised in 1941, there were five main categories: 'anti-Soviet elements'; former gendarmes, police and prison personnel; ex-landowners, traders and state clerks; former officers in the Romanian, Polish and Tsarist armies; and refugees from the USSR arriving before 1940. One can see that *kulaks* were not yet in a special category and that rich peasants constituted a minority among the deportees.[69] In the second mass deportation of July 1949, however, the *kulaks* were the majority, representing 70 per cent of the total.[70] The goal of the first deportation was clearly to cleanse the western borderlands of 'hostile elements' in the wake of a Soviet–German confrontation; the latter was launched in order to fulfil an internal agenda. In this, the Moldavian deportations of June 1941 are similar to those organised almost simultaneously in the Baltic states, Western Ukraine and Belorussia.[71] However, there are differences. In the Baltic states and Western Ukraine, for instance, the deportees included family members of the armed resistance movement, such as Latvia's 'forest bandits'.[72] While there was sporadic violent resistance in Soviet Moldavia up to 1952, no such mass armed movement existed. This may reflect a weaker national consciousness, in part because many Bessarabian intellectuals and representatives of the liberal professions – the main carriers of modern national identity – emigrated to Romania.[73] Another factor accounting for more active peasant resistance in Western Ukraine and the Baltic states could be the predominance of the *khutor* sector in those societies.[74] In other words, the Moldavian deportations of July 1949 were more of a prophylactic strike than those in the other territories, where they were aimed at both ending an insurgency and speeding up collectivisation.

Conclusions

This chapter has attempted to calculate the number of victims resulting from Stalinist rule in Soviet Moldavia, and has relied primarily on archival research, secondary sources and memoirs. While it is always difficult to arrive at precise figures due to the deliberate fusing of the 'political' and 'criminal' under a totalitarian regime, I have nonetheless been able to establish fairly accurate figures for victims of the three major deportations, the post-war famine and a variety of additional persecutions.[75] First, Soviet repression in the immediate aftermath of Bessarabia's annexation in 1940 until June 1941 claimed approximately 86,000 political victims. In an attempt to liquidate elements of society deemed 'anti-Soviet', a total of 26,173 people were deported, primarily to Siberia and Kazakhstan, and 6,250 were arrested in June 1941; this figure includes Bessarabia, Northern Bukovina and Hertza county, all Romanian territories occupied by Moscow in June 1940. Additionally, 53,356 people were subjected to forced labour in different regions of the USSR and, given their status and work conditions, these should also be included as political victims of Stalinist terror.

The second era of mass suffering occurred during the famine of 1946–47. While hundreds of accused 'collaborators' were arrested and deported in the immediate aftermath of the Second World War, these numbers are dwarfed by the 150,000–200,000 residents of Soviet Moldavia who died as a result of the famine. Although the drought was not caused by Stalin, there is sufficient evidence to conclude that Soviet agricultural and fiscal policies caused the deaths in Moldavia. It is quite probable that, with different policies, deaths would have been nominal, if not avoided altogether.

The third period of mass victimisation occurred during collectivisation and culminated with mass deportations in 1949. Adopting policies used in Soviet territories during the 1930s, central administrators prepared lists of *kulak* 'class enemies' as early as 1948 and began deportations in early July 1949. A total of 35,050 people were deported to Kazakhstan: 23,000 were supposed *kulaks*, and the remainder were accused of collaborating with the Romanian and German authorities. I also discussed some of the long-term consequences of this mass displacement, both for the deportees and for the peasants who remained behind in Soviet Moldavia.

All in all, if we include the repressions in the inter-war Moldavian Autonomous Republic, the total number of direct victims of the Stalinist period in the territories of the present day Republic of Moldova amounts to approximately 300,000–350,000 individuals. The number of those who suffered indirectly from the terror of this regime is incalculable. Finally, a brief analysis of the social and ethnic composition of the victims suggests that Stalinist terror in Soviet Moldavia should not be categorised as ethnocide, but rather as genocide or a crime against humanity. I concluded with some comparisons of victimisation in the Baltic states from the same period, but this comparison is under-explored and remains a promising avenue for future research.

Notes

1 For details, see G. Torrey, *Romania and World War I* (Iaşi-Oxford-Portland, 1999), p. 326.
2 According to Terry Martin, the 'Piedmont principle' was the 'belief that cross-border ethnic ties could be exploited to project Soviet influence into neighbouring states'. See T. Martin, *The Affirmative Action Empire: Nations and Nationalism in the Soviet Union, 1923–1939* (Ithaca, 2001), pp. 274–5. Also M. L. Schrad, 'Rag Doll Nations and the Politics of Differentiation on Arbitrary Borders: Karelia and Moldova', *Nationalities Papers*, vol. 32, no. 2 (2004), pp. 457–96.
3 E. Negru, 'Republica Autonomă Sovietică Socialistă, 1924–1940', in D. Dragnev (ed.), *O istorie a regiunii transnistrene din cele mai vechi timpuri până în zilele noastre* (Chişinău, 2007), pp. 268–72.
4 V. Stăvilă, *De la Basarabia românească la Basarabia sovietică, 1939–1945* (Chişinău, 2000), p. 14.

5   Arhiva Organizaţiilor Social Politice a Republicii Moldova [Archives of Social and
    Political Organisations of the Republic of Moldova, archives of the former Central
    Committee of the Communist Party of Moldavia – hereafter AOSPRM], f. 51,
    inv. 15, d. 99, fas. 3–8.
6   AOSPRM, f. 51, inv. 15, d. 99, fas. 3–8.
7   I. Scurtu (ed.), *Istoria Basarabiei, de la începuturi până la 1998* (Bucharest, 1998),
    p. 224.
8   E. Postică, *Deputaţii Sfatului Ţării represaţi în anul 1940*, in *Cugetul*, no. 1 (1998),
    pp. 92–8.
9   A. Moraru, *Istoria românilor. Basarabia şi Transnistria* (Chişinău, 1995), p. 337.
10 M. Gribincea, *Basarabia în primii ani de ocupaţie sovietică, 1944–1950* (Cluj, 1995),
    p. 35.
11 V. Pasat, *Trudnye stranitsy istorii Moldavii, 1940–1950* (Moscow, 1994), p. 147.
12 Pasat, *Trudnye stranitsy*, p. 164.
13 Pasat, *Trudnye stranitsy*, pp. 166–7.
14 V. Pasat, *Surovaia pravda istorii. Deportatsii s territorii Moldavskoi SSR, 40–50 gody*
    (Chişinău, 1998), pp. 98–100.
15 N. Werth, 'A State Against Its People: Violence, Repression, and Terror in the Soviet
    Union', in S. Courtois, et al. (eds), *The Black Book of Communism: Crimes, Terror,
    Repression* (Cambridge: MA, 1999), pp. 212–13.
16 Memoirs of Vadim Pirogan, in S. Saka (ed.), *Basarabia în GULAG* (Chişinău, 1995),
    p. 84.
17 Pasat, *Trudnye stranitsy*, p. 153.
18 V. Olaru-Cemârtan, 'Deportarea masivă de populaţie din RSSM din 12–13 iunie
    1941', *Destin românesc*, no. 3 (2006), p. 65.
19 Memoirs of Vadim Pirogan, in Saka (ed.), *Basarabia în GULAG*, p. 99.
20 E. Kersnovskaia, *Skol'ko stoit chelovek*, edited by V. Pasat (Moscow, 2006),
    pp. 132–3.
21 Pasat, *Trudnye stranitsy*, pp. 159–60.
22 S. V. Mironenko et al. (eds), *Istoriia stalinskogo Gulaga*. vol. 1: *Massovye represii v
    SSSR* (Moscow, 2004), p. 407.
23 Moraru, *Istoria românilor*, p. 337.
24 Pasat, *Surovaia pravda istorii*, pp. 107–23.
25 I. Caşu, '*Politica naţională' în Moldova Sovietică, 1944–1989* (Chişinău, 2000), pp. 32–3.
    See also M. I. Semiriaga, *Tainy stalinskoi diplomatii* (Moscow, 1992), p. 270.
26 AOSPRM, f. 51, inv. 2, d. 127, fas. 34.
27 AOSPRM, f. 51, inv. 2, d. 16, fas. 267–77; inv. 3, d. 14, fas. 351–72; inv. 3, d. 21,
    fas. 99, 107, 115.
28 E. Zubkova, 'Fenomen "mestnogo natsionalizma": "Estonskoe delo" 1949–1952
    gg. v kontekste sovetizatsii Baltii', *Otechestvennaia istoriia*, no. 3 (2001), pp. 89–102.
29 AOSPRM, f. 51, inv. 3, d. 7, fas. 1–10, 17–19.
30 E. Zubkova, *Russia after the War: Hopes, Illusions and Disappointments, 1945–1957*
    (New York, 1998), p. 47.
31 A. Ţăranu et al. (eds), *Golod v Moldove (1946–1947). Sbornik dokumentov* (Chişinău,
    1993), p. 10.
32 Ţăranu et al. (eds), *Golod v Moldove*, pp. 7, 205–7.

33 Gribincea, *Basarabia în primii*, p. 75.

34 Ţăranu et al. (eds), *Golod v Moldove*, p. 7.

35 Ţăranu et al. (eds), *Golod v Moldove*, pp. 321, 387, 408, 465, 480, 487, 546, 604, 606–8, 612, 636, 669, 687.

36 Ţăranu et al. (eds), *Golod v Moldove*, p. 10.

37 Ţăranu et al. (eds), *Golod v Moldove*, pp. 498–512.

38 Ţăranu et al. (eds), *Golod v Moldove*, pp. 12–13. See also Gribincea, *Basarabia în primii*, pp. 99–100.

39 L. Turea and V. Turea, *Cartea foametei* (Chişinău, 1991), p. 32.

40 Turea and Turea, *Cartea foametei*, p. 38.

41 E. Postică, *Rezistenţa antisovietică în Basarabia, 1944–1950* (Chişinău, 1997), pp. 96–107.

42 V. Ţaranov et al. (eds), *Kolektivizatsiia krest'ianskikh khoziaistv v pravoberezhnykh raionnakh Moldavskoi SSR. Dokumenty i materialy* (Chişinău, 1969), pp. 27–8.

43 Pasat, *Surovaia pravda istorii*, p. 200.

44 Ţăranu et al. (eds), *Golod v Moldove*, p. 198.

45 Ţăranu et al. (eds), *Golod v Moldove*, p. 198.

46 Ţaranov et al. (eds), *Kolektivizatsiia krest'ianskikh*, pp. 173–4.

47 Pasat, *Surovaia pravda istorii*, pp. 201–2.

48 R. Şevcenco, *Viaţa politică în RSS Moldovenească, 1944–1961* (Chişinău, 2007), p. 99.

49 Pasat, *Trudnye stranitsy*, pp. 348–9, 421–2.

50 Pasat, *Surovaia pravda istorii*, pp. 220–1.

51 Gribincea, *Basarabia în primii*, pp. 129–30.

52 This probably concerned not only medals received during the war, but also special merits in the reconstruction of roads and railways, for which many peasants were mobilised. AOSPRM, f. 51, inv. 2, d. 5, ff. 345–59.

53 Pasat, *Trudnye stranitsy*, p. 485.

54 Pasat, *Trudnye stranitsy*, pp. 43, 491.

55 S. Digol, 'Operatsiia "Iug" v levoberezhnoi Moldavii: zabytyi fragment "reabilitirovannoi pamiati"', *AB IMPERIO*, no. 2 (2004), pp. 269–96.

56 T. V. Tsarevskaia-Diakina (ed.), *Istoriia stalinskogo Gulaga*. vol. 5: *Spetspereselentsy v SSSR* (Moscow, 2004), pp. 677–8, 686.

57 V. Ţaranov, 'O likvidatsii kulachestva v Moldavii letom 1949 goda', *Otechestvennaia istoriia*, no. 2 (1996), p. 78.

58 Pasat, *Trudnye stranitsy*, pp. 46–7.

59 *Istoriia stalinskogo Gulaga*, vol. 1, p. 530.

60 E. Şişcanu, *Basarabia sub regimul bolşevic, 1940–1952* (Bucharest, 1998), p. 107.

61 Pasat, *Trudnye stranitsy*, p. 31.

62 *Contrafort*, no. 9 (September, 2003), p. 6.

63 Pasat, *Trudnye stranitsy*, p. 635.

64 Pasat, *Trudnye stranitsy*, pp. 632–5.

65 *Istoriia stalinskogo Gulaga*, vol. 5, p. 665.

66 N. F. Bugai, '40–50-e gody: posledstviia deportatsii narodov', *Otechestvennaia istoriia*, no. 2 (1992), p. 142; Pasat, *Surovaia pravda istorii*, p. 370. See also *Argumenty i fakty*, no. 39 (1989), p. 8.

67   Werth, 'A State against Its People', in Courtois et al. (eds), *The Black Book*, p. 237.

68   E. Postică (ed.), *Cartea Memoriei*, vols 1–4 (Chișinău, 1999–2005).

69   Pasat, *Trudnye stranitsy*, p. 167.

70   Pasat, *Trudnye stranitsy*, p. 392.

71   See A. Statiev, 'Motivations and Goals of Soviet Deportations in the Western Borderlands', in *Journal of Strategic Studies*, vol. 28, no. 6 (2005), pp. 977–1003; and G. Swain, 'Deciding to Collectivise Latvian Agriculture', *Europe-Asia Studies*, vol. 55, no. 1 (2003), pp. 38, 48–9.

72   A. Anušauskas (ed.), *Anti-Soviet Resistance in the Baltic States* (Vilnius, 2006), pp. 63–70.

73   Șevcenco, *Viața politică*, p. 77–8.

74   The *khutor* system refers to the existence of large individual households, isolated from each other, unlike the traditional village communities, characteristic of Bessarabia and most of Russia.

75   The official Soviet statistical division between 'politicals' and 'criminals' was highly arbitrary. See M. Ellman, 'Soviet Repression Statistics: Some Comments', *Europe-Asia Studies*, vol. 54, no. 7 (2002), p. 1156. For example, there is broad unanimity among prominent Russian historians that those condemned according to the law of 7 August 1932 (re-established on 4 June 1947), on the theft of public property, should be counted as political victims of the regime. See O. V. Khlevniuk, *The History of the Gulag. From Collectivization to the Great Terror* (New Haven and London, 2004), p. 306; and N. Werth, '"Déplacés spéciaux" et "colons de travail" dans la société stalinienne', *Vingtième Siècle. Revue d'histoire*, no. 54 (1997), pp. 34–50.

East Germany, 1945–1953: Stalinist repression and internal party purges*

Matthew Stibbe

The years 1945 to 1953 were a crucial period in the formation of the East German dictatorship, marking it out as similar to, and yet in many ways distinct from, the other communist states of Eastern Europe.[1] A key event here was the merger of the old Communist Party (KPD) and Social Democratic Party (SPD) to create the German Socialist Unity Party (SED), which held its founding conference in Berlin in April 1946. In theory the new party was based on an equal partnership between the two socialist traditions: 680,000 former social democrats and 600,000 former communists were now joined under the same roof, and the fourteen-member Central Secretariat was made up of seven representatives from each side.[2] In theory, too, the new party ruled out slavish adherence to Soviet forms of political organisation, and instead committed itself to the development of a 'special German path to socialism', a phrase developed by one of its leading ideologues, the veteran communist Anton Ackermann.[3] Beginning with the completion of the 'unfinished' bourgeois democratic revolution of 1848, the SED would follow a gradual approach to socialism through forging a broad alliance with anti-fascist and progressive forces in all four occupation zones. This also fitted in with Stalin's early post-war aims in Germany, which were more complex and more ambitious than the mere sovietisation of the eastern half of the country. Ultimately his main interest was in the coal and steel resources of the Ruhr in the British zone, and for this reason he kept his options open regarding future relations between the USSR and the German Left.[4]

By 1953, however, as Peter Grieder puts it, the SED had been 'transformed into a highly centralized, hierarchical organization, based on the model of the Communist Party of the Soviet Union (CPSU)' and claiming absolute control over all aspects of East German society.[5] The fourteen-member Central Secretariat had been replaced by an eleven-member Politburo dominated by communists loyal to Moscow, and all pretence at parity with former social democrats had been dropped. The new party had also narrowed its definition of anti-fascism to the point where it was virtually synonymous with Stalinism. Meanwhile, tens of thousands of middle-ranking officials and 'ordinary' party members had been purged or had fled to the west, and some had been imprisoned or deported to the Soviet Union. The same applied to members of the West German KPD and the various non-Marxist parties and mass organisations in the Soviet zone now gathered together in the new, single-bloc National Front for Democratic Germany.[6]

The aim of this chapter is to explore how East Germany was transformed into a communist dictatorship between 1945 and 1953 with particular reference to the use of purges as a means of destroying any sources of internal party opposition – or potential opposition – to the process of Stalinisation. Purges thus took place of social democrats, 'left sectarians', 'right deviationists', advocates of a 'special German path to socialism', so-called 'Titoists' and 'Trotskyists', and – moving beyond the SED itself – opponents of communism within the wider sphere of politics and society. At the same time, the chapter will consider two broad explanations for the purges, firstly that they were enacted on Moscow's orders, and reflected the primacy of Soviet security concerns and interests, and secondly that they were also inspired, to some extent at least, by personal rivalries and 'Stalinist' tendencies within the top levels of the KPD/SED leadership in Berlin.[7] A final section will then go on to consider why, in the end, there were no elite show trials in East Germany in the late 1940s and early 1950s to match those taking place in neighbouring socialist countries like Hungary, Bulgaria and Czechoslovakia.

Purges of former social democrats

One of the principal aims behind the formation of the SED was the removal of the social democrat threat to communist hegemony, especially in areas where the SPD had been strong before 1933, such as Thuringia and Saxony. The fear of KPD leaders like Wilhelm Pieck and Walter Ulbricht was that the SPD would triumph politically in the eastern zone by developing an anti-Soviet (as well as anti-fascist) programme. There was also a long history of ideological enmity between the two parties which had only partly been buried, if at all, by the new spirit of unity which followed the defeat of Nazism. Not surprisingly, therefore, the communists were soon making moves to shift former social democrats out of important party and government offices at local, regional and zonal level, a process which began as early as 1945 and continued with greater openness after the 2nd SED party congress of September 1947.[8] Between 1946 and 1950, hundreds of anti-unity/anti-communist social democrats were also jailed or imprisoned at a number of special detention centres (*Speziallager*) run by agents of the Soviet interior ministry (the NKVD and the Ministry of Internal Affairs (MVD)), including at former Nazi concentration camps like Sachsenhausen and Buchenwald.[9] One SPD source from September 1947 suggested that 400 social democrats were being held at Zwickau prison, 900 at

Dresden prison and 800 at Buchenwald. Others had been arrested and deported to the Soviet Union itself.[10]

Having said this, it is important to acknowledge that Soviet occupation policy was at least partly determined by broader developments in the Cold War, such as the removal of communists from coalition governments in Italy and France in May 1947 in the run-up to the announcement of the Marshall Plan, and the fierce anti-communism prevalent among the mainstream political parties in the western zones of Germany, who worked together to isolate the KPD from positions of power.[11] As east-west tensions grew, Soviet officials also became increasingly concerned about the agitation of so-called 'Schumacher agents' in their zone, i.e. members of the *Ostbüro* (eastern office) of the West German SPD, led by Kurt Schumacher. The latter had pursued a policy of non-recognition towards the SED and implacable opposition to the Soviet presence in the east, with the hope that the SPD might still become the largest left-wing party throughout Germany.[12] The 'Schumacherites' clearly had some popularity within the lower ranks of the SED itself, as the Holocaust survivor Victor Klemperer noted in his diary on 2 September 1947 after a conversation with a couple of old 'SPD'ers' in Görlitz. Even so, he was not willing to endorse their anti-Soviet sentiments, which he saw as opening the way for a dangerous revival of fascism and militarism in the eastern zone: 'I believe I *must* stick with the radical and Russophile line, it is not nice, but probably necessary nonetheless'.[13]

Matters came to a head in the summer and autumn of 1948, with the beginning of the Soviet blockade of West Berlin, and, perhaps more importantly, the first open indications of a split between Stalin and Tito's Yugoslavia. At the end of June, at a meeting of the SED party executive, Otto Grotewohl, the most senior former social democrat in the Central Secretariat, declared that the party had committed a 'grave error' in believing that the problem of 'Schumacher agents' and other anti-communist elements in the eastern zone could be left to the Soviets to contend with:

> We must confront this issue ourselves . . . on the political level. We must deal with this threat clearly and openly in our party organisations. The more clearly we address it, the easier it will be to isolate the seat of the disease and render it impossible . . . we must have the strength to throw these people out.[14]

This was followed, on 29 July 1948, by a resolution passed by the party executive calling for a major purge of 'hostile and degenerate elements', and in September 1948 by an official renunciation of the idea of 'special German path to socialism', including a statement by Anton Ackermann exercising a dialectical U-turn in relation to his previous views: 'The theory [of a special path] provides a perfect cover for secret Schumacher operatives, for enemy agents of all kinds, for wavering, semi-opportunistic elements, for elements who have been corrupted by the spirit of nationalism'.[15]

The subsequent campaign against 'hostile' forces within the party at first affected former social democrats more than any other group, and led to the exclusion of up to 80,880 party members by the end of March 1949.[16] In the same period around 5,000 ex-social democrats were arrested by the Soviet occupation authorities, over 400 of whom died in NKVD/MVD-run prisons in Germany or in forced labour camps in Siberia.[17] Usually their alleged offence was to have made illegal contacts with the West German SPD or its *Ostbüro*, although the charges often included fabricated stories about secret dealings with western intelligence agencies and/or the Gestapo. One example, among many, is that of Joseph Scholmer, a social democrat doctor from Berlin who worked for the Central Health Administration (*Zentralverwaltung für Gesundheitswesen*) in the Soviet zone from 1945 and joined the SED in 1946. Initial enthusiasm soon turned to disgust at the behaviour of the Soviet occupation authorities, as he later reported:

> In the period leading up to 1 May 1947 many bad things happened. The Soviets refused for a whole year to allow extra rations for half a million tuberculosis patients. They dismantled all the industrial plants which produced children's food in the eastern zone, so that infants died in tens of thousands from dystrophy. At the same time they banned us from accepting thousands of tons of food offered by the Quakers, the International [Committee of] the Red Cross and the Swedish Red Cross from their depots in West Germany.[18]

After the President of the *Zentralverwaltung für Gesundheitswesen* was arrested in February 1947 for his outspoken criticism of Soviet policy, Scholmer decided not to take part in the May Day festivities, and in 1948 he resigned from the party. His own arrest came in April 1949, and after months of questioning by the MVD at their special interrogation centre at Hohenschönhausen, followed by a further period of waiting at Lichtenberg jail, he was sentenced to twenty-five years penal servitude and deported to Siberia. Like many others who experienced the same fate, he was only released from Soviet captivity after 1954, and went immediately to West Berlin.[19]

Other social democrats fled the Soviet zone before the knock on the door came. This applied most famously to Erich Gniffke, formerly second chairman of the SPD in the east and the only member of the SED Central Secretariat to vote against a resolution condemning Tito and supporting Yugoslavia's expulsion from the Cominform on 3 July 1948. In his resignation letter, published after his flight to the west in October 1948, he condemned 'the separatist path, in which the "class struggle" is carried into every corner of the zone' and continued:

> I openly admit that the decision is easier to make now than it was half a year ago. Then I would have had to resign from the SED, now I am resigning from the 'party of the new type', or rather the Ulbricht KPD of 1932. For this is the transformation which we have seen taking place at the last three meetings of the party executive.[20]

Otto Grotewohl, the erstwhile chairman of the SPD in the Soviet zone, had for a while been able to put a brake on this move away from internal party democracy, especially as he enjoyed close contacts with several senior Soviet officials, including Colonel Sergei Tiul'panov, head of the Propaganda Department of the Soviet Military Administration (SMA). However, he fatally underestimated his own power within the SED, which was not inconsiderable in the first two years of the party's existence, and, perhaps more importantly, felt abandoned by the west. In any case, his address to the party executive at the end of June 1948 in effect transformed him into the role of 'chief mouthpiece' for the purges, as one historian puts it.[21] In July 1948 and again in January 1949 he voted in favour of the transformation of the SED into a Leninist 'party of the new type', although he was not entirely uncritical of subsequent developments.[22] His primary concern, however, was to prevent his arch-rival Walter Ulbricht from becoming the dominant voice within the party and the Soviet zone, and to claim for himself the leading position of party general secretary. In this case, too, he failed completely, as events in the years 1950 to 1953 clearly showed.

Purges of 'left sectarians', 'right deviationists', 'Trotskyists', 'Titoists' and other party veterans

While the purges within the SED at first mainly affected former social democrats, the target was soon widened to include dissident communist groups who opposed – or who might oppose – the official party line. Here the relevance of quarrels going back to the 1920s and 1930s is much more evident, particularly given that many figures who had belonged to left-wing splinter groups like the Communist Party Opposition (KPO) or the Socialist Workers' Party (SAP) in the Weimar and Nazi eras eventually found their way back into the KPD/SED after 1945.[23] Other German communists, while remaining inside the party through thick and thin, had developed a more critical stance as a result of their experiences in Spain, in Nazi concentration camps or in areas that had come under Red Army occupation in 1945. Wolfgang Leonhard, himself a party loyalist who had spent the Nazi period in the Soviet Union and had never questioned the Moscow line, later explained his shock at discovering KPD members who were prepared to challenge aspects of the Stalinist system:

> It was inevitable that former [Moscow] émigrés would come into contact with those who had fought against the Nazis at home, leading to critical reflection on both sides. Was the Hitler-Stalin pact really a necessary compromise made because of the international situation? ... Wasn't it ... more an imperialist carve up of Poland? ... Wasn't the leadership cult, the constant emphasis on Stalin's wisdom and infallibility, at total variance with the founding principles of the socialist movement? ... And what about Stalin's policy on the nationalities' question? Wasn't the privileging of everything Russian and the systematic promotion of the Russian people as the leading nation a complete retreat from socialist ideals?[24]

Interestingly, Ulbricht and his Soviet mentors seemed to fear such 'old communists' even more than the 'Schumacherites'. The danger was that they could develop a Marxist–Leninist critique of 'Soviet imperialism' and also appeal to nationalist sentiment by challenging the imposition of the Oder-Neisse line and the subsequent loss of Germany's eastern territories to Poland.[25] On top of this, some former KPD members openly rejected the SED's anti-fascist bloc policy, i.e. its cooperation with the bourgeois parties on 'national' and economic questions, as 'opportunistic'.[26] This was particularly apparent among dissident communist groupings in West Berlin, who were not so easily brought into line as their counterparts in East Berlin or in the eastern zone.[27] A new set of ideological enemies was also created across the Soviet bloc following the expulsion of the Yugoslav Communist Party from the Cominform on 28 June 1948. Henceforth even those who had been prisoners of war in Yugoslavia during and after the war or who had links with Belgrade were seen as suspicious.[28]

In this sense the creation of the Central Party Control Commission (*Zentrale Parteikontrollkommission*, ZPKK) under Hermann Matern in September 1948 was a crucial tool in the Stalinisation of the party and the tightening of ideological control over individual party members. Its chief task was to review the party records and individual biographies of thousands of SED officials at zonal, regional and local level, many of them veteran communists with periods of service to the party going back to the 1920s and 1930s, in order to root out possible spies and counter-revolutionaries.[29] Membership was also made harder to acquire, with new applicants expected to fill out a detailed questionnaire about their history and previous political affiliations, and from January 1949 to spend at least a year as probationers (*Kandidaten*) before becoming full party members.[30] This 'Foucauldian strategy of discipline'[31] was supported by Ulbricht, Pieck and Grotewohl, but clearly took place at the instigation of Soviet advisers who had the power to issue orders and had free access to the ZPKK's files. For them, the defection of Wolfgang Leonhard to communist Yugoslavia in March 1949 added to the sense of threat and urgency. The ZPKK was now ordered to collect evidence of a broader conspiracy, particularly in relation to party members in East Berlin. How was it possible, the Soviet advisers asked, that Leonhard, one of the first German communists to be returned from Moscow as part of the 'Ulbricht group' in May 1945, could turn out to be a traitor? And why had none of his colleagues or students in the 'Karl Marx' party high school noticed his pro-Tito (and therefore pro-fascist) views?[32]

On top of this came the so-called Field affair, caused by the trial in Hungary in 1949 of an American citizen, Noel Field, on fabricated charges of spying for the American Office of Strategic Services (OSS) while working with communist resistance groups in Switzerland and France during the Second World War. In September 1949 Ivan Serov, the overall chief of the Soviet security apparatus in Berlin, ordered Matern to investigate all German communists who had come into contact with Field, and as a result dozens of party veterans were purged or demoted from senior positions.[33] Other former western émigrés came under suspicion if they had worked in any capacity for the Americans during the war, or – following developments in Moscow and across the Soviet bloc in 1948/9 – simply if they were Jewish or had links to the new state of Israel. Joachim Schwarz, for instance, who came back to East Berlin from Palestinian exile in 1950, later recalled the following incident concerning one of his fellow returnees:

> Because of a feud over a woman, one Tel Aviver denounced the other as an English spy. The proof was that he had served in the intelligence corps of the British 8th army [in North Africa] and was therefore a friend of the British Intelligence Service, the chief instigator of all counter-revolutionary undertakings in the modern world … His father had also been a Social Democrat councillor in a small German town during the Weimar era. It was obvious that the son was an agent, an enemy spy. He was immediately arrested.[34]

By the late 1940s, indeed, it was in many ways safer to be an ex-Nazi living in the Soviet zone than it was to be a western émigré, Jew, social democrat, admirer of Tito or former member of a communist splinter group.[35] Left party veterans, 'international socialists', 'Trotskyists' and ex-KPO members or 'Brandlerites'/ 'right deviationists' were especially vulnerable to investigation by the ZPKK, with suspicions about their activities being raised as early as 1947.[36] By July 1951 only around 5,000 of them remained in the party, including 515 erstwhile adherents of the KPO line, compared to 108,675 former members of the NSDAP and affiliated organisations.[37] Even so, the vast majority of ex-Nazis were also kept out of the SED – for one thing, their commitment to Marxism–Leninism was at best doubtful, and for another, their presence would interfere with Stalin's ongoing attempts to seize the initiative from the west on the German question. Instead, at Tiul'panov's instigation, two new parties had been formed in the Soviet zone in 1948, the Democratic Peasants' Party (DBD), which sought to win over farmers who were reluctant to join the SED, and the National Democratic Party (NDPD), which aimed to recruit 'nominal' Nazis and patriotic army veterans for a policy of anti-fascist reconstruction.[38] Both parties were ostensibly led by non-Marxists, but with communist sympathisers in key positions. Indeed, unlike the other bloc parties, the Christian Democrats (CDU) and Liberal Democrats (LDPD), the SED rightly considered that it had little to fear in terms of opposition to its policies from the DBD and the NDPD.[39]

Purges of members of bloc parties

In spite of their very cautious approach, and their absolute refusal to engage in overt anti-Soviet propaganda, as their western counterparts demanded, the CDU and LDPD parties represented a threat to the SED in terms of their electoral popularity as well as their non-Marxist ideology. In August 1947, for instance, the diarist Victor Klemperer noted 'I am convinced that in a truly free election today the SED would become a tiny minority party'.[40] As it was, the bloc system, which discouraged or prevented genuine competition during elections, allowed Soviet and later East German officials to manipulate, outflank and bully members of the 'bourgeois' parties in order to improve the chances of SED candidates. Where these tactics failed (as they did in the *Kreis, Land* and Greater Berlin elections in October 1946), or where members of the CDU or LDPD distanced themselves too much from the SED, purges within these parties became necessary, including, in some cases, arrests on trumped up charges of 'maladministration' or 'anti-Soviet activity'.[41]

During the first two and a half years of military occupation, however, the preferred method used by the Soviet authorities was to impose restrictions on individuals that stopped short of actual arrest. This was the case, for instance, with the first zonal leaders of the CDU, Andreas Hermes and Walther Schreiber, who were dismissed from office in December 1945, and with their successor Jakob Kaiser, who met the same fate in December 1947.[42] The latter had recommended a policy of non-cooperation with the first SED-dominated *Volkskongress*, a pseudo-representative body which claimed to be the voice of the German people and whose appearance was designed to coincide with the meeting of the foreign ministers' conference in London in December 1947. Soon afterwards Kaiser and nine of his colleagues from the fourteen-member CDU executive fled to West Berlin from where they continued to act as a spearhead for opposition to SED rule.[43] The SPD *Ostbüro*, while based in Hanover and later Bonn, also had offices and agents in West Berlin, and access to all four sectors of the city.[44]

By 1948 the Berlin question itself was becoming more acute on the international stage as well as on the domestic front. In March of that year, during a meeting in Moscow, Wilhelm Pieck told Stalin that it would be better if the western Allies could be persuaded to leave Berlin as soon as possible. Otherwise he feared that the municipal elections, due for December 1948, would not produce better results for the SED than the 19.8 per cent gained in October 1946.[45] Worse still, many CDU officials in the Soviet zone continued to recognise Jakob Kaiser as their real leader, rather than the new Soviet appointee Otto Nuschke,[46] and even SED members of the Berlin Magistrat could be found voting with the ruling SPD against the official party line.[47] For all of these reasons the SED leadership turned to Stalin for a quick resolution of the Berlin question, but, following the Soviet blockade of June 1948 to May 1949 and the successful Allied response, it was clear that Stalin could not force the western powers out, at least in the short term. As an alternative, the SED formed a new city government for East Berlin in November 1948, which existed separately from the West Berlin Magistrat under SPD mayor Ernst Reuter.[48]

Apart from the particular problems associated with the western military presence in Berlin, it was also feared that the CDU at local and provincial level might become a haven for former social democrats opposed to the transformation of the SED into a Marxist–Leninist organisation. Indeed, Gary Bruce notes an escalation of arrests of middle- and lower-ranking CDU officials by the MVD in 1948/9, particularly in relation to opposition to the *Volkskongress* movement and its slogans in favour of national unity under SED leadership:

> During one of these waves in the spring of 1948, Soviet security organs shot outright the CDU chair of *Kreis* Delitzsch, Hans Georg Löser, in his apartment. The CDU mayor of Falkensee, Hermann Neumann, was arrested and died in prison. On December 31 [1948], the entire executive of the CDU in Woltersdorf (*Kreis* Niederbarnim) was arrested. After a trip to Saxony-Anhalt, one CDU correspondent reported that the 'NKVD' was playing a decisive role in forcing the CDU into line. Because of the repression of its members, the CDU refused to participate in the [Anti-Fascist] Block until August [1949].[49]

Arrests also took place of LDPD representatives, including Hermann Becker, leader of the party in the Thuringian Landtag and editor of its local newspaper, who was seized by the MVD in July 1948,[50] and Wolfgang Natonek, the chair of the Leipzig University student council, who was held for questioning on charges of 'conspiracy with the capitalist west' in November 1948; later he and twenty-five of his fellow 'conspirators' received twenty-five years in a Soviet labour camp.[51] Another leading figure from the same circle of 'Young Liberals', Arno Esch, was arrested by the MVD in October 1949 because of his vocal resistance to the meeting of the third *Volkskongress*, and along with seven others was sentenced to death by a Soviet military tribunal for 'preparing an armed revolt'. The sentence was carried out in the Soviet Union on 24 July 1951.[52]

Overall by 1948/9 so-called 'bourgeois reactionaries' in the CDU and LDPD were taking up as much of the MVD's time as illegal SPD and dissident communist groups. Yet the SED and the Soviets still needed these parties in order to continue the anti-western/pro-unity line developed at Stalin's behest.[53] This was all the more important given the poor showing of the West German KPD in elections to the first Bundestag in August 1949, where it achieved only 5.7 per cent of the vote and was therefore powerless to shape future events.[54] It was this setback which finally persuaded the Kremlin to endorse arrangements for the creation of a separate East German state, the German Democratic Republic, during a visit of SED leaders to Moscow in September 1949, although some of the details had already been worked out at a previous meeting in December 1948.[55] At the same time, plans were laid for the final dissolution of the NKVD/MVD-run special camps set up in the Soviet zone in 1945, with the last inmates being released or transferred to the East German courts and political justice system in early 1950.[56] A subsequent set of trials, mostly held in secret at Waldheim prison in Saxony, led to the conviction of over 3,000 alleged fascist war criminals, thirty-two of whom were sentenced to death and twenty-four of whom were actually executed. This was in spite of ongoing concerns expressed by Otto Nuschke and other leading CDU members of the new government as to the legality of the proceedings and the reliability of the verdicts. Helmut Brandt, a senior Christian Democrat official inside the Justice Ministry who had also criticised the high level of political interference in the trials, was less fortunate; he was arrested in late 1950 and sentenced to ten years in prison in 1954 in a trial which also saw the GDR's former CDU Foreign Minister Georg Dertinger receiving fifteen years for a separate (but in the eyes of the court, related) political offence.[57]

New developments, 1950–53: why were there no elite show trials in the GDR?

While the failure of the West German KPD was something of a blow to Stalin, the foundation of the GDR in October 1949 was an enormous boost for the SED, and for Ulbricht personally, who won unanimous backing as general secretary of the new Central Committeee at the third party congress in July 1950.[58] Lingering CDU opposition in the Soviet zone was also broken in 1949–50 when the party seemed to accept SED hegemony in the new National Front, the holding of delayed 'single list' elections to the new parliament, the *Volkskammer,* and the reorganisation of the political justice system so that it became de facto an executive branch of the party-state.[59] However, individual bourgeois politicians continued to face harassment, including Hugo Hickmann, who was removed as chair of the Saxon CDU in early 1950, and Karl Hamann, second chairman of the zonal LDPD who was arrested by agents of the new ministry of state security (Stasi) in 1952.[60] In 1950–51 the struggle against 'sectarians', 'deviationists', 'cosmopolitans', 'Trotskyists', 'Brandlerites' and 'Schumacher agents' also continued and was indeed accelerated.[61] Thus, according to one Soviet source, some 80,593 members and candidate members were recommended for expulsion by the ZPKK between January and October 1951, 26,225 as 'unequivocal enemies of the party', 32,375 as 'party or class aliens' [*partei- und klassenfremde Elemente*], 3,295 because of 'moral corruption', 14,043 'because they were no longer in agreement with the policies of the party', and 4,655 'for other reasons'.[62] Some of those interrogated were threatened with loss of employment, prosecution or imprisonment if they refused to collaborate or to implicate others, so that an atmosphere of terror now reigned at all levels of the party.[63] SED and non-SED teachers, academics and students were also subject to intensified surveillance, culminating in a systematic campaign of harassment and exclusion directed against members of the Protestant *Junge Gemeinde* and associated Christian groups in 1952–53.[64] At the same time pressure was on from the Soviets to produce a show trial against leading German communists who had supposedly spied for the west to match those taking place elsewhere in the eastern bloc. This was also to Ulbricht's liking as it helped him in his power struggles against potential rivals.[65]

Indeed, while new evidence since 1989 suggests that the GDR President Wilhelm Pieck tried to put a brake on East German preparations for a show trial of selected western émigrés, Ulbricht emerges even more clearly as the key instigator, alongside Soviet advisers.[66] After an abortive attempt to create a German 'Rajk trial' in 1950–51, which was abandoned on Stalin's orders,[67] things finally came to a head on 30 November 1952 with the arrest of Paul Merker, an ex-member of the Politburo who had spent the war years in Mexico and had been expelled from the party in August 1950 in connection with the Field affair. Already accused of working for the Americans, Merker was now charged with the additional crime of 'war mongering and incitement to racial hatred' because of his support for Israel during the wars in Palestine in 1948–49. As in the parallel case of the Slánský trial in Czechoslovakia, there was more than a hint of anti-Semitism here too. Merker was not Jewish, but he and his Free Germany movement had strongly identified themselves with the Jewish victims of Nazi persecution, and three of his co-accused were also German-Jewish communists who had been part of the wartime Mexico group: Alexander Abusch, Erich Jungmann and Leo Zuckermann.[68] Merker's arrest became all but inevitable when he was cited as a co-conspirator by several of the defendants at the Slánský trial, a fact widely reported in the East German press. To add fuel to the fire, in December 1952 the Politburo drew up a resolution on 'the lessons of the Slánský trial' which accused Merker and Zuckermann of being 'agents of the USA-financial oligarchy' and supporters of 'Zionist policies' who had encouraged the illegal transfer of Jewish capital from Germany to Israel in order to support US imperialist interests in the Middle East.[69] By now Merker was under 'investigative detention' and Zuckermann had fled with his family to West Berlin.

In a separate but related development, Franz Dahlem, leader of the KPD Central Secretariat in Paris in the late 1930s and survivor of Mauthausen concentration camp, was criticised for allowing the 'voluntary internment' of German communists by the French authorities in 1939, and was finally expelled from the Central Committee and the Politburo in May 1953. Like Merker, he had been critical of aspects of Stalin's pre-1945 foreign policy, especially the Nazi-Soviet Pact, and had also fallen out with Ulbricht over key issues concerning post-war cadre policy and relations with West Germany. Like Merker, he had also been marked out by the Soviets as a possible defendant in an East German show trial from at least 1950 onwards.[70]

Finally, in March 1953 the ZPKK ordered a re-examination of the records of all party comrades who had been in western exile during the war, on the grounds that the earlier investigations of 1949–50 had been 'insufficient'.[71] One person who was targeted for extensive questioning was the economic historian and former London exile Jürgen Kuczynski. Already removed from his position as President of the German-Soviet Friendship Society in 1950, possibly as a result of his middle-class Jewish background,[72] he was now denounced by a fellow British émigré, Wilhelm Koenen, as an imperialist agent who had worked in London for the Americans and the 'Jewish-Trotskyist' newspaper *Left News*, owned by the 'anti-Soviet propagandist' Victor Gollancz.[73] Koenen in turn was denounced by Politburo member Elli Schmidt because in the late 1940s he and his wife Emmi Damerius-Koenen 'were often in Prague' and usually returned with 'handsome gifts' and tales of meetings with former friends from the Czech exile group in Britain. Two other German communists, Gerhart Eisler and Alexander Abusch, were also denounced by Schmidt because of their 'very close relations' with André Simone (Otto Katz), one of Slánský's Czech co-defendants, who they had met in Paris in 1939–40 and again after the war. Both were Jewish and had ties to known anti-Soviet groups in the 'imperialist' west.[74]

By now, even the British security services suspected that a major purge of Jewish communists in East Berlin was imminent, and were considering the possibility of trying to persuade one or two of them to defect. In particular they were interested in Jürgen Kuczynski, his sister Ursula, a.k.a. Ruth Werner or 'Sonya', her husband Leon Beurton, and another former member of the KPD in Britain, Johanna Klopstech. All four had been involved in Soviet military espionage during the Second World War, and especially in the atomic spy case which had come to light with the arrest of Klaus Fuchs in London in February 1950. As a senior MI5 officer wrote to one of his counterparts in MI6 on 23 January 1953:

> The essential point is that all these persons are likely to possess valuable information about Russian espionage, and that it is worth going to considerable lengths to get them, and with them their information . . . If any of them is in any way accessible to a personal approach, direct or indirect, we feel that this might well justify a special operation, with the ultimate object, of course, of getting them into British hands.[75]

It is not known whether the Kuczynskis or any of the other targets were contacted, but a few months later MI5 were forced to recognise that the reports it had received of Jürgen's arrest were inaccurate, and that both he and his sister had somehow managed to survive the purges unscathed.[76]

So why in the end were there no show trials in East Germany to match those taking place elsewhere in the Soviet bloc? One explanation, and until recently the most popular one, is that the SED leaders did not really have the appetite for such a stage-managed event and pursued a series of delaying tactics for as long as they could. In particular they disliked the official anti-Semitism which had been increasingly evident in the Soviet Union since late 1948 and which allegedly had been introduced into the GDR by Vladimir Semyonov, political adviser to the head of the Soviet military administration.[77] However, the Slánský trial in November 1952 and the revelations concerning the 'Doctors' Plot' in Moscow in January 1953 meant that they now 'had no option but to follow Stalin's and Beria's orders'.[78] Stalin's death in March 1953 and Beria's arrest in June 1953 removed the external pressure, and thus the need for the show trials, while Khrushchev's denunciation of Stalin in 1956 allowed for the eventual – albeit partial – rehabilitation of both Dahlem and Merker.[79]

Even so, the uncomfortable fact remains that senior SED officials fully backed the Hungarian, Bulgarian and Czechoslovak trials, and seemed to have no problem in accepting the defendants' guilt as self-evident. Kurt Hager, for instance, who headed the Central Committee's propaganda department, argued in a foreword to the official East German edition of the Rajk trial proceedings that the Hungarian defendants were part of a broader 'network of spies with lines of communication to the traitor Tito . . . and through him to the intelligence services of the American and British imperialists'.[80] He also clearly regarded Paul Merker as a traitor and refused to accept any other version of events – including the possibility that Merker had fallen victim to an anti-Semitic conspiracy – until after 1990.[81]

In the parallel case of Franz Dahlem, Anton Ackermann led the denunciations in a secret speech to the thirteenth plenum of the Central Committee on 13–14 May 1953, accusing his former colleague of 'capitulating [before the French authorities] at the beginning of the war' while 'under the influence of the secret Soviet enemy Paul Merker', and of arrogantly dismissing the party's criticisms of him 'even after the revelations concerning Merker have been made known'.[82] The Politburo's recommendation that the matter be referred back to the ZPKK for further investigation, with the possibility of criminal charges to follow, was also supported by two other Central Committee members, Paul Wandel and Dahlem's son-in-law Karl Mewis, the latter insisting that when duty called 'I have only one family, namely the party'.[83]

Finally, as Peter Grieder has persuasively argued, Ulbricht added his own personal stamp to the preparations for the show trials and, furthermore, pursued a vendetta against Dahlem and Merker even after the show trials themselves had been abandoned and Field and his wife released without charge in Budapest in 1954. Thus Dahlem's repeated requests for rehabilitation were rejected between 1953 and 1956, and Merker was actually placed before the GDR supreme court in 1955 in a secret trial in which he was found guilty on the original charge of 'war mongering and incitement to racial hatred' and sentenced to eight years in prison.[84] Another veteran communist, Hans Schrecker, also received eight years in a separate trial in 1954, having first been arrested by the Stasi in November 1952, while Gerhart Eisler, who at one time was picked out by Wilhelm Pieck for potential membership of the

Politburo, was sacked as head of the SED Office of Information in January 1953 and subjected to over two and a half years of investigations by the ZPKK between 1953 and 1955.[85]

The explanation for the absence of a show trial in East Germany must therefore be sought elsewhere, and not in any collective squeamishness or *Bauchschmerzen* on the part of the GDR's rulers. One factor may have been the continuance of Moscow's 'zig-zag' course on the German question in 1952–53, leading to ongoing doubts about the applicability of Soviet methods to the GDR, and another the East German regime's greater vulnerability to the pressures of international (i.e. western) public opinion owing to the open border in Berlin.[86] The fact that Merker – in contrast to the fourteen defendants in the Slánský trial – did not make any false confessions, and indeed continued to assert his innocence while under interrogation, is also significant.[87] Finally, it does seem that the GDR President Wilhelm Pieck played an important role personally in protecting Merker and Dahlem from the threat of a public show trial, and in ensuring their belated and partial rehabilitation after 1956. This again suggests that the peculiar manner in which the show trials were prepared and then abandoned had as much to do with power struggles in East Berlin as with pressures coming from Moscow.[88]

Conclusion

The evidence presented above partly confirms the older Cold War view that there was an important link between the East German purges and the more murderous campaigns against 'Zionists', 'Trotskyists' and 'Titoists' taking place elsewhere in Eastern Europe.[89] In particular it is clear that elements within the SED leadership – most notably Ulbricht, Matern and the rising star in the Stasi, Erich Mielke – were determined to stage a German 'Rajk trial' in 1950/1 and later a German 'Slánský trial' in 1952/3. The fact that Paul Merker was cited as a co-conspirator in the Slánský trial also suggests strong levels of collaboration between the Czechoslovak, Soviet and East German security services, and the possibility of anti-Semitic motives, although senior SED officials were careful to avoid using the word 'Jew' and instead spoke of the 'sins of Zionism' or of 'Jewish-nationalist agents'.[90]

However, it is also important to look at the differences as well as the similarities. One of these differences lies in the complex relationship between the two Germanys and the fact that there was not just one communist party but two, the SED in the east and the KPD in the west. Here Christoph Kleßmann's notion of post-war German history as the record of an asymmetric process of 'intertwining and differentiation' (*Verflechtung und Abgrenzung*) proves very useful.[91] Thus the fear in Moscow was that an East German show trial involving accusations against senior German communists could more easily be challenged by information available in the west, thereby 'unmask[ing] . . . [the] obvious lies and distortions' behind all of the charges.[92] It might also encourage dissension within the West German KPD and the formation of new anti-Stalinist groups there, particularly in the aftermath of the Yugoslav–Soviet split.[93] The strict secrecy surrounding the arrest and interrogation of Kurt Müller, the most senior member of the West German KPD to be accused of 'Trotskyist' crimes after being invited by Ulbricht to East Berlin in March 1950, is itself highly revealing. Müller was eventually sentenced to 25 years in a Soviet labour camp for espionage, but released and repatriated to West Germany in late 1955.[94]

A further factor influencing events was the existence of a strong democratic socialist tradition in eastern Germany, particularly in areas like Saxony and Thuringia. This was also apparent, for instance, in June 1953, when the main centres of unrest during the uprising of that month corresponded to the strongholds of Imperial and Weimar German Social Democracy.[95] Much of the new evidence presented in the 1990s indeed suggests that social democrats were still seen as the main ideological enemy, as they had been by German communists since 1919, in spite of the lip-service paid to the idea of socialist unity after 1946. A similar refusal to move on from the past is evident in Ulbricht's obsession with left-wing *Abweichler*, which can be traced back at least in part to internal divisions within the KPD in the late 1920s and early 1930s. Yet ironically, as Norman Naimark has noted, Ulbricht also had a great deal in common with those he accused of 'sectarianism', including 'intolerance of diversity, dogmatic attachment to Soviet Leninism, and inability to compromise'.[96]

All of the above factors help to explain the very limited rehabilitation of purge victims in the GDR in 1956, especially when contrasted with the situation in Poland, Hungary and the Soviet Union itself. Indeed, unlike some of its socialist neighbours, the East German state never came to terms with its violent, repressive origins, as Erich Honecker's hostile response to Gorbachev's reforms in the 1980s also suggests. While in the 1960s and 1970s the regime developed a broader accommodation with the people, and was not set in advance on a 'downfall in stages',[97] it nonetheless remains the case that the events of the late 1940s and early 1950s continued to haunt SED leaders. Kurt Hager, for instance, wrote somewhat belatedly in his post-1990 memoirs:

> The proceedings against Merker, Dahlem and others . . . represent a dark chapter in the history of the GDR. The trials and other acts of repression, the fear of spies and constant demands for vigilance created a virus inside the SED which could not be removed and which over time weakened the entire organism. From this point on mistrust and vigilance played an ever greater role, which had a negative impact on the inner life of the party and on the social climate.[98]

Even so, some open questions remain – why did Ulbricht and Matern survive the years 1945 to 1953 unharmed, even though attempts were made by some of their rivals to implicate them in imaginary 'anti-party' conspiracies?[99] Why did Hager, a western émigré married to a Jew, emerge unscathed, and Honecker for that matter, who had spent much of the Nazi era in Brandenburg jail and was said to have cracked under Gestapo interrogation?[100] And how could the ZPKK launch an extensive investigation into the defection of Wolfgang Leonhard to Yugoslavia in March 1949, causing a veritable witch hunt inside the 'Karl Marx' party high school, yet fail to discover that a colleague had accompanied him on one of his clandestine trips to meet Yugoslav representatives in East Berlin in 1948?[101] The fact that we do not have complete answers to these questions, in spite of the opening of the relevant archives, underlines Catherine Epstein's point that there was something 'arbitrary and irrational' about the purges – as indeed there was about the purges throughout the Soviet bloc during this period.[102]

Notes

*   I would like to thank Peter Grieder for his helpful comments and suggestions on an earlier draft of this essay.

1   The best study in English is G. Pritchard, *The Making of the GDR, 1945–53: From Anti-Fascism to Stalinism* (Manchester, 2000). Also useful is M. Fulbrook, *History of Germany, 1918–2000: The Divided Nation*, 2nd edn (Oxford, 2002). Many of the differences stem from the fact that East Germany represented not a single, indivisible people like the Poles, or a multi-national empire like the USSR, but the smaller half of a defeated and bitterly divided nation.

2   H. Weber, *Geschichte der DDR*, revised edn (Munich, 2000), p. 82.

3   A. Ackermann, 'Gibt es einen besonderen deutschen Weg zum Sozialismus?', *Einheit*, 1 (February 1946), pp. 22–32.

4   On Stalin's *Deutschlandpolitik*, see in particular D. Staritz, 'The SED, Stalin and the German Question: Interests and Decision-Making in the Light of New Sources', *German History*, vol. 10, no. 3 (1992), pp. 274–89; and W. K. Wolkow, 'Die deutsche Frage aus Stalins Sicht (1947–1952)', *Zeitschrift für Geschichtswissenschaft*, vol. 48, no. 1 (2000), pp. 20–49. More controversial, but still a good read, is W. Loth, *Stalins ungeliebtes Kind: Warum Moskau die DDR nicht wollte* (Berlin, 1994). Loth's central argument, that Stalin did not want the GDR, even after 1949, has been challenged by a number of other studies, including, most recently, D. Spilker, *The East German Leadership and the Division of Germany: Patriotism and Propaganda, 1945–1953* (Oxford, 2006).

5   P. Grieder, *The East German Leadership, 1946–73: Conflict and Crisis* (Manchester, 1999), p. 8.

6   Weber, *Geschichte der DDR*, p. 128.

7   The best works take both of these factors into account, albeit with differing shades of emphasis. Compare, for instance, G. H. Hodos, *Show Trials: Stalinist Purges in Eastern Europe, 1948–1954* (New York, 1987), pp. 113–28, and H. Weber, 'Schauprozeß-Vorbereitungen in der DDR', in H. Weber and U. Mählert (eds),

Terror: Stalinistische Parteisäuberungen 1936–1953 (Paderborn, 1998), pp. 459–85, with Grieder, *The East German Leadership*, pp. 8–36, and C. Epstein, *The Last Revolutionaries: German Communists and their Century* (Cambridge: MA and London, 2003), pp. 130–57.

8 H. Hurwitz, *Die Stalinisierung der SED: Zum Verlust von Freiräumen und sozialdemokratischer Identität in den Vorständen 1946–1949* (Opladen, 1997); F. T. Stößel, *Positionen und Strömungen in der KPD/SED 1945–1954* (Cologne, 1984). On the 2nd party congress see also Spilker, *The East German Leadership*, pp. 132–3.

9 In 1946 the NKVD, or People's Commissariat of Internal Affairs, was officially renamed MVD or Ministry of Interior, although the old acronym continued to be used in popular and academic parlance for many years afterwards. For further details see N. M. Naimark, *The Russians in Germany: A History of the Soviet Zone of Occupation, 1945–1949* (Cambridge: MA and London, 1995); and M. Klonovsky and J. von Flocken, *Stalins Lager in Deutschland 1945–1950: Dokumentation, Zeugenberichte* (Munich, 1993).

10 Naimark, *The Russians in Germany*, pp. 385–8.

11 On the West German KPD see P. Major, *The Death of the KPD: Communism and Anti-Communism in West Germany, 1945–1956* (Oxford, 1997). Also Spilker, *The East German Leadership*, passim.

12 See e.g. the concerns raised by the Soviet official I. F. Filippow in his report 'Die Sozialistische Einheitspartei Deutschlands', 9 October 1946, reproduced in G. Bordjugow, 'Das ZK der KPdSU(b), die Sowjetische Militäradministration in Deutschland und die SED (1945–1951)', in Weber and Mählert (eds), *Terror*, pp. 283–349 (here pp. 316–24 and esp. 319–20).

13 V. Klemperer, *The Lesser Evil: The Diaries of Victor Klemperer, 1945–1959*, translated by M. Chalmers (London, 2003), p. 217 (entry for 2 September 1947).

14 Protokoll der 11. (25.) Tagung des SED-Parteivorstandes am 29./30. Juni 1948, in Stiftung Archiv der Parteien und Massenorganisationen der DDR im Bundesarchiv Berlin (henceforth SAPMO-BArch), DY30/IV-2/1/48, p. 199.

15 Protokolle der 12. (26.) und 13. (27.) Tagungen des SED-Parteivorstandes am 28./29. Juli 1948 und 15./16. September 1948, in SAPMO-BArch, DY30/IV-2/1/51 and 2/1/52. See also Hurwitz, *Die Stalinisierung der SED*, pp. 427 and 446; and Spilker, *The East German Leadership*, p. 168.

16 Hurwitz, *Die Stalinisierung der SED*, p. 459.

17 W. Buschfort, *Das Ostbüro der SPD: Von der Gründung bis zur Berlin-Krise* (Munich, 1991), p. 46.

18 J. Scholmer, *Die Toten kehren zurück: Bericht eines Arztes aus Workuta* (Cologne, 1954), p. 8.

19 Scholmer, *Die Toten kehren zurück*, pp. 267–81.

20 E. Gniffke, *Jahre mit Ulbricht* (Cologne, 1966), p. 369.

21 A. Malycha, *Die SED: Geschichte ihrer Stalinisierung, 1946–1953* (Paderborn, 2000), p. 377.

22 Grieder, *The East German Leadership*, pp. 21–2.

23 Stößel, *Positionen und Strömungen*, p. 59; Pritchard, *The Making of the GDR*, pp. 176–7.

24 W. Leonhard, *Die Revolution entläßt ihre Kinder* (Cologne, 1955), pp. 434–6.

25 Hurwitz, *Die Stalinisierung der SED*, pp. 490–1. See also N. M. Naimark, 'The Soviets, the German Left and the Problem of "Sectarianism" in the Eastern Zone, 1945 to 1949', in D. E. Barclay and E. D. Weitz (eds), *Between Reform and Revolution: German Socialism and Communism from 1840 to 1990* (Oxford, 1998), pp. 421–41 (here p. 433).

26 Stößel, *Positionen und Strömungen*, pp. 73–84; Pritchard, *The Making of the GDR*, pp. 178–80.

27 Naimark, *The Russians in Germany*, p. 283; Malycha, *Die SED*, pp. 423–4.

28 See the evidence in SAPMO-BArch, DY30/IV-2/4/156.

29 Gniffke, *Jahre mit Ulbricht*, pp. 329–30; Pritchard, *The Making of the GDR*, pp. 166–9.

30 Hurwitz, *Die Stalinisierung der SED*, p. 436.

31 Epstein, *The Last Revolutionaries*, p. 157.

32 See Naimark, 'The Soviets, the German Left and the Problem of "Sectarianism"', p. 437. Also W. Leonhard, 'Im Fadenkreuz der SED: Meine Flucht von der Parteihochschule "Karl Marx" im März 1949 und die Aktivitäten der Zentralen Parteikontrollkommission', *Vierteljahrshefte für Zeitgeschichte*, vol. 46, no. 2 (1998), pp. 283–310.

33 Hodos, *Show Trials*, pp. 113–15; Epstein, *The Last Revolutionaries*, pp. 138–9.

34 C.-J. Danziger (i.e. Joachim Schwarz), *Die Partei hat immer Recht: Auto-biographischer Roman* (Stuttgart, 1976), p. 22.

35 Grieder, *The East German Leadership*, p. 19.

36 See e.g. the report 'Organisierte feindliche Oppositionsgruppen', 9 January 1947, giving details of the activities of 'organised communist opposition groups' in various parts of East and West Berlin, in SAPMO-BArch, DY30/IV-2/4/385, Bl. 603–9.

37 'Bericht über den Stand der Überprüfung am 31. Juli 1951', in SAPMO-BArch, DY30/IV-2/4/47, Bl. 9. On the purge of former KPO members see also Malycha, *Die SED*, esp. pp. 424–8.

38 Stößel, *Positionen und Strömungen*, pp. 299–300; Naimark, *The Russians in Germany*, pp. 347 and 394.

39 Spilker, *The East German Leadership*, pp. 157–8.

40 Klemperer, *The Lesser Evil*, p. 211 (diary entry for 3 August 1947).

41 M. Allinson, *Politics and Popular Opinion in East Germany, 1945–68* (Manchester, 2000), pp. 27–9.

42 Loth, *Stalins ungeliebtes Kind*, pp. 55–6 and 103; Spilker, *The East German Leadership*, p. 43.

43 G. Bruce, *Resistance with the People: Repression and Resistance in Eastern Germany, 1945–1955* (Lanham, Maryland, 2003), p. 80.

44 Cf. Buschfort, *Das Ostbüro der SPD*, passim.

45 Wolkow, 'Die deutsche Frage aus Stalins Sicht', p. 32.

46 Bruce, *Resistance with the People*, p. 86.

47 Hurwitz, *Die Stalinisierung der SED*, p. 440.

48 Cf. Loth, *Stalins ungeliebtes Kind*, pp. 115–28.

49 Bruce, *Resistance with the People*, p. 87.

50 Allinson, *Politics and Popular Opinion*, p. 29.

51 Klonovsky and von Flocken, *Stalins Lager in Deutschland*, p. 25.

52 Bruce, *Resistance with the People*, pp. 90–1.

53 Wolkow, 'Die deutsche Frage aus Stalins Sicht', p. 36.

54 Loth, *Stalins ungeliebtes Kind*, pp. 158–9.

55 Staritz, 'The SED, Stalin and the German Question', p. 283; Wolkow, 'Die deutsche Frage aus Stalins Sicht', p. 38.

56 Klonovsky and von Flocken, *Stalins Lager in Deutschland*, pp. 187–92. Cf. J. Gieseke, 'German Democratic Republic', in K. Persak and Ł. Kamiński (eds), *A Handbook of the Communist Security Apparatus in East-Central Europe, 1944–1989* (Warsaw, 2005), pp. 163–219 (here p. 204); and F. Werkentin, *Politische Strafjustiz in der Ära Ulbricht: Vom bekennenden Terror zur verdeckten Repression*, 2nd edn (Berlin, 1997), pp. 161–83.

57 Werkentin, *Politische Strafjustiz*, pp. 179–80 and 300–1; Klonovsky and von Flocken, *Stalins Lager in Deutschland*, pp. 205–18; R. J. Evans, *Rituals of Retribution. Capital Punishment in Germany, 1600–1987* (London, 1996), pp. 814–15.

58 Hurwitz, *Die Stalinisierung der SED*, p. 456.

59 Bruce, *Resistance with the People*. p. 103; Werkentin, *Politische Strafjustiz*, pp. 25–31.

60 Weber, *Geschichte der DDR*, p. 141.

61 See e.g. 'Bericht über die Tätigkeit von Genossen ehemaliger parteifeindlicher Gruppierungen', 6 November 1950, and 'Bericht der LPKK Sachsen über parteifeindliche Gruppierungen', 5 January 1950, both in SAPMO-BArch, DY30/IV-2/4/385.

62 Report by Soviet official M. Kijaktin, 13 December 1951, reproduced in Bordjugow, 'Das ZK der KPdSU(b)', pp. 340–9 (here p. 341).

63 Leonhard, 'Im Fadenkreuz der SED', p. 299.

64 See E. Ueberschär, *Junge Gemeinde im Konflikt: Evangelische Jugendarbeit in SBZ und DDR 1945–1961* (Stuttgart, 2003), esp. pp. 170–202.

65 Hodos, *Show Trials*, p. 126; Grieder, *The East German Leadership*. p. 31.

66 Weber, 'Schauprozeß-Vorbereitungen', p. 473; W. Otto, 'Erinnerung an einen gescheiterten Schauprozess in der DDR', *Jahrbuch für Historische Kommunismusforschung*, vol. 14 (2008), pp. 114–30.

67 Hodos, *Show Trials*, pp. 122–3; Weber, 'Schauprozeß-Vorbereitungen', p. 474. According to fresh evidence which has come to light since the end of the Cold War, the trial was intended to include as principal defendants the West German KPD politician and Bundestag deputy Kurt Müller, who had been arrested in East Berlin in March 1950, and the East German Politburo member Franz Dahlem, one of Ulbricht's chief rivals. See here K. Müller, 'Der geplante Schauprozeß', in H. Knabe (ed.), *Gefangen in Hohenschönhausen. Stasi-Häftlinge berichten* (Berlin, 2007), pp. 101–29.

68 For a detailed discussion see J. Herf, *Divided Memory: The Nazi Past in the Two Germanys* (Cambridge: MA, 1997), pp. 106–61.

69 'Lehren aus dem Slansky-Prozeß – endgültige Fassung', 19 December 1952, in SAPMO-BArch, DY30/IV-2/4/124. A version of the document was published in the party newspaper *Neues Deutschland* on 4 January 1953 and confirmed at a plenary session of the Central Committee in May of that year. Cf. Otto, 'Erinnerung an einen gescheiterten Schauprozess', p. 126.

70 Grieder, *The East German Leadership*, pp. 33–5; Epstein, *The Last Revolutionaries*, pp. 143–7; Hodos, *Show Trials*, p. 126.

71 'Plan zur Durchführung der Überprüfung von Genossen, die in kapitalistischen Ländern in Emigration waren', 1 March 1953, in SAPMO-BArch, DY30/IV-2/4/445.

72 J. Kuczynski, *Ein linientreuer Dissident. Memoiren 1945–1989* (Berlin, 1992), p. 47.

73 Wilhelm Koenen to Hermann Matern, 13 January 1953, in SAPMO-BArch, DY 30/IV-2/4/123.

74 Elli Schmidt to Hermann Matern, 4 December 1952, in SAPMO-BArch, DY30/IV-2/4/124.

75 MI5 to MI6, 23 January 1953, in The National Archives (TNA), Kew, London, KV 2 /1880.

76 See the undated note in TNA, KV 2 /1880. Just how close Jürgen Kuczynski came to arrest in 1953 is difficult to say with certainty, but judging by the extensive interrogations of him and several of his London associates by the ZPKK – available to read in transcript form in SAPMO-BArch, DY30/IV-2/4/123 – he may well have been singled out by Matern and his Soviet advisers as another possible defendant in an anti-Semitic show trial. Certainly his extensive wartime contacts with exiled German communists in London and Paris, and his work for the London branch of the United States' Strategic Bombing Survey in 1944–45, made him an ideal target. For the background to MI5's interest in the Kuczynskis see also R. C. Williams, *Klaus Fuchs, Atom Spy* (Cambridge: MA, 1987).

77 Kuczynski, *Ein linientreuer Dissident*, p. 47.

78 P. O'Doherty, 'The GDR in the Context of Stalinist Show Trials and Anti-Semitism in Eastern Europe, 1948–54', *German History*, vol. 10, no. 3 (1992), pp. 302–17 (here p. 317).

79 Cf. Weber, 'Schauprozeß-Vorbereitungen', p. 481.

80 K. Hager, *László Rajk und Komplicen vor dem Volksgericht* (Berlin, 1949), p. 3.

81 K. Hager, *Erinnerungen* (Berlin, 1994), pp. 181–2.

82 Protokoll der 13. Tagung des Zentralkomitees der SED am 13. und 14. Mai 1953, in SAPMO-BArch, DY30/IV-2/1/115, p. 263.

83 Protokoll der 13. Tagung des Zentralkomitees (as note 82), p. 273.

84 Grieder, *The East German Leadership*, pp. 29 and 35–6. Merker was released in early 1956 and later that year all the charges against him were formally dropped; he in turn agreed to remain silent about his mistreatment at the hands of the party.

85 Epstein, *The Last Revolutionaries*, pp. 140–3.

86 Hodos, *Show Trials*, p. 127.

87 Grieder, *The East German Leadership*. p. 29; Herf, *Divided Memory*, p. 141.

88 Grieder, *The East German Leadership*. p. 31; Otto, 'Erinnerung an einen gescheiterten Schauprozess', passim. Significantly, Jürgen Kuczynski also believed that Pieck had protected him and many other party intellectuals from 'the most terrible persecution' in the early 1950s: 'Nicht wenige, darunter auch ich, haben ihm viel zu verdanken' – see Kuczynski, *Fortgesetzter Dialog mit meinem Urenkel: Fünfzig Fragen an einen unverbesserlichen Urgroßvater* (Berlin, 1996), p. 120.

89 See e.g. M. McCauley, *Marxism-Leninism in the German Democratic Republic. The Socialist Unity Party* (SED) (London, 1979), p. 65.

90 Cf. the report in the London *Times*, 2 December 1952 ('Self-Examination in E. Germany: Consequence of the Czech Trial').

91 C. Kleßmann, 'Verflechtung und Abgrenzung: Aspekte der geteilten und zusammengehörigen deutschen Nachkriegsgeschichte', *Aus Politik und Zeitgeschichte*, B29–30, 16 July 1993, pp. 30–41.

92 Hodos, *Show Trials*, p. 123.

93 Leonhard, 'Im Fadenkreuz der SED', p. 309. On oppositional groups in the West German KPD see also Major, *The Death of the KPD*, pp. 210–12.

94 On Müller see Major, *The Death of the KPD*, pp. 204–5; Grieder, *The East German Leadership*, p. 29; and Hodos, *Show Trials*, p. 119. Also note 67 above.

95 Cf. my essay, 'The SED, German Communism and 17 June 1953: New Trends and New Research', in K. McDermott and M. Stibbe (eds), *Revolution and Resistance in Eastern Europe: Challenges to Communist Rule* (Oxford, 2006), pp. 37–55.

96 Naimark, 'The Soviets, the German Left and the Problem of "Sectarianism"', p. 438.

97 See in particular the evidence presented by M. Fulbrook, *The People's State: East German Society from Hitler to Honecker* (New Haven and London, 2005). The phrase 'downfall in stages' refers to the controversial book by A. Mitter and S. Wolle, *Untergang auf Raten: Unbekannte Kapitel der DDR-Geschichte* (Munich, 1993).

98 Hager, *Erinnerungen*, pp. 183–4.

99 Grieder, *The East German Leadership*. p. 36.

100 Epstein, *The Last Revolutionaries*, p. 256.

101 Leonhard, 'Im Fadenkreuz der SED', p. 309.

102 Epstein, *The Last Revolutionaries*, p. 153.

Stalinism in Poland, 1944–1956

Łukasz Kamiński

The first experience that Polish society had with the Stalinist system was in 1939–41. Under a secret clause of the Nazi-Soviet non-aggression pact of August 1939, the USSR remained neutral when Germany attacked western Poland on 1 September, and actually launched its own invasion of eastern Poland on 17 September. On 28 September, the two powers concluded another agreement under which they divided the territory of Poland between themselves. Slightly more than half was over-run by the Soviets and this part of Poland was now subjected to wide-ranging sovietisation. As early as 22 October 1939 'elections' to the people's assembly of Western Byelorussia and Western Ukraine took place. A few days later the elected representatives addressed the Soviet authorities with a 'request' to annex the occupied Polish lands to the Byelorussian and Ukrainian Soviet Republics.[1]

The institutions of the Polish state were liquidated and replaced with Soviet ones. The collectivisation of agriculture and nationalisation of private ownership in industry, commerce and craft were pushed through. The inhabitants of the occupied territories were inundated by an enormous wave of propaganda. However, from the very beginning they resisted in spontaneous and organised ways. Thus they tried to celebrate Polish national holidays and to preserve the spirit of resistance via underground leaflets and publications. Large and small partisan units also operated, all of them ultimately answerable to the Polish government-in-exile in London. The Soviet authorities responded with mass reprisals. Tens of thousands of Polish citizens were arrested and deported to Soviet labour camps and hundreds were sentenced to death. In the spring of 1940, on the direct orders of the Politburo of the Communist Party of the Soviet Union (CPSU),[2] over 25,000 persons, mainly army officers and representatives of the Polish state elites were murdered at Katyń and elsewhere.[3] At the same time 320,000 Polish citizens were compulsorily sent into the interior of the USSR in the wake of four big deportation actions. Immediately after the outbreak of the Soviet–German war in June 1941 many Polish political detainees in NKVD prisons located in the occupied Polish territories were murdered.[4]

The outbreak of the Soviet–German war nonetheless enabled a temporary normalisation of Polish–Soviet relations. As a result of the Sikorski–Maiskii agreement, signed on 30 July 1941 between Władysław Sikorski, prime minister of the government-in-exile, and Ivan Maiskii, the Soviet ambassador in London, new ties of mutual recognition were established, an amnesty was declared for Polish citizens deported to the USSR and the formation of a Polish army in the Soviet Union was announced. However, this did not mean that Stalin had changed his general approach towards Poland. For instance, he refused to discuss the restoration of the pre-1939 Polish–Soviet border in any future peace settlement. He also continued to make plans for a future Soviet-dominated Poland. Thus in December 1941, in the vicinity of German-occupied Warsaw, Soviet planes dropped a dozen or so agents of the Comintern (Communist International), all former members of the Communist Party of Poland (KPP) until the latter's liquidation by Stalin in 1938. On 5 January 1942 they set up the Polish Workers' Party (PPR), which in accordance with long-term Soviet intentions was to become the vanguard for a new communist-ruled Polish state. Significantly, this organisation did not operate in the areas annexed by the USSR in 1939, instead confining itself to the territories invaded by Nazi Germany in the same year. Even then, the PPR played only a marginal role among the Polish resistance groups, devoting most of its energies to producing propaganda aimed at discrediting the legal Polish authorities in London and the policies of the Polish underground at home, in particular the Home Army (AK). It also passed information on the AK and other non-communist resistance groups to Soviet intelligence agencies.

An important turning point in Polish–Soviet relations came in 1943 when the Germans discovered the mass graves of murdered Polish officers at Katyń. The decision of the government-in-exile in London to refer the matter to the International Committee of the Red Cross provided Moscow with an excuse to break off diplomatic relations with its erstwhile ally. Meanwhile, although the western powers were still committed to the government-in-exile and although up to 150,000 Poles had fought in various western theatres of war against the Germans, President Franklin D. Roosevelt still gave his tacit consent to the redrawing of the pre-1939 borders in a private conversation with Stalin which took place during the Tehran Conference of December 1943. In effect this meant an acceptance of Stalin's claims to the eastern Polish territories annexed by the USSR in September 1939.[5]

The Lublin Committee

In July 1944 Soviet troops started approaching the territories which, according to the Nazi–Soviet non-aggression pact of 1939, were under German rule. This resulted in the intensification of efforts to create Polish authorities controlled by Moscow. Thus on 20 July a new Committee of National Liberation in Poland (known as the Lublin Committee) was set up at the request of Stalin. Edward Osóbka-Morawski, a socialist politician, became its first head. In order to mislead the public, it was announced that the Lublin Committee had been established spontaneously on 'liberated' Polish territory at Chełm on 22 July, although in fact it had been formed two days earlier in Moscow. This fabrication later became an important part of communist mythology. Meanwhile, the representatives of the Lublin Committee, even before their departure from Moscow, signed a secret agreement with the Soviet Union renouncing Polish claims to the pre-war eastern territories, including the cities of Wilno and Lwów (now renamed Vilnius and Lviv). The only concession Stalin was willing to make was the return of the Białystok district in northeastern Poland; all other Soviet conquests of 1939 were retained.[6]

The Lublin Committee at first held sway over a small area of Poland occupied by the Red Army in July and August 1944. The establishment of the new authorities required the liquidation (with the help of NKVD troops) of the Polish national underground and in particular members of the Home Army, who were seen as suspect because of their loyalties to the government-in-exile. Indeed, members of the Home Army faced the same fate as the underground political activists and soldiers from those eastern territories which remained in Soviet hands. Around 27,000 who refused to join the new Polish army led by General Zygmunt Berling (in which over half of the officers were citizens of the USSR) were sent to Soviet camps. Many others were put on trial and sentenced to death or to long terms of imprisonment by Soviet military tribunals or by the newly created Polish security service, which operated with the help of Soviet advisers and was composed of several hundred people trained at the NKVD officers' school in Kuibyshev. Over 1,000 judicial executions were carried out in the first year after 'liberation'.[7]

The communists and their allies in the Lublin Committee tried in vain to gain wider social support, appealing to national pride, the need for further resistance against the Germans and the importance of land redistribution. However, conscription into the new communist-controlled Polish army met with a mass boycott, with over 30 per cent of the soldiers deserting, including the entire 31st infantry regiment. The agricultural reform launched in Lublin Poland in September 1944, despite the fact that it was fulfilling the old demands of village inhabitants, did not gain the approval of the peasants. After one month the communist authorities were forced to issue a special decree accelerating the implementation of land reform.[8] Stalin too criticised the Polish communists for dragging their feet, noting revealingly that: 'The abolition of a whole class (rich landowners) is not a reform but a revolution and cannot be carried out with the full majesty of law'.[9]

For most Poles the real Polish government was the one in exile in London, which had worked together with the representatives of the anti-German resistance on the home front throughout the war. After July 1944 the civilian and military structures of the Polish underground state continued to function not only in the territories occupied by the Germans but also in Lublin Poland. On 25 July 1944 the government-in-exile, now led by prime minister Stanisław Mikołajczyk, indeed denounced the Lublin Committee as 'an attempt by a handful of usurpers to impose on the Polish nation a political leadership which is at variance with the overwhelming majority'.[10] However, due to the presence of the Red Army in Lublin Poland, any military resistance there was initially out of the question.

Instead, on 1 August 1944 the Home Army launched the Warsaw uprising against the Germans with the intention of liberating the Polish capital before the Red Army reached the city from the east. The defeat of the uprising by the Nazis after two months of desperate fighting, during which Stalin deliberately withheld logistical support from the insurgents, destroyed the last hopes for Polish freedom while further undermining relations between the government-in-exile and the Soviet Union. Not surprisingly, Mikołajczyk's two visits to Moscow in August and October 1944 ended in failure. Stalin's demands that the USSR be allowed to retain the eastern territories seized from Poland in 1939, coupled with his insistence on a new coalition government for the remainder of Poland in which communists would take over a number of significant posts, was unacceptable to most non-communist Polish politicians. Mikołajczyk resigned and was replaced by a socialist, Tomasz Arciszewski, who went on to play only a secondary role in diplomacy between the western Allies and the Soviet Union.[11]

The fate of Poland was finally determined in the first months of 1945. On 31 December 1944 the Lublin Committee was transformed into the Provisional Government, which was formally recognised by the Soviet Union, and after a few weeks by France and Czechoslovakia. In this way two Polish governments operated in the international arena – the legal one and the one which exercised real power over the country. In January 1945 the Soviet offensive started as a result of which, within a few weeks, all Polish territories were liberated, including Warsaw, which had been razed to the ground by the Germans after the defeat of the uprising. In the meantime, in order to avoid further repressions General Leopold Okulicki formally dissolved the Home Army on 19 January 1945. During the Yalta Conference (4–11 February 1945) Stalin, Churchill and Roosevelt agreed in principle that the pre-war eastern border of Poland would be changed in accordance with the demands of the Soviet Union (no decision was made concerning the new western border),[12] and that a new Provisional Government of National Unity (TRJN) would be established, including communist and non-communist politicians, whose task would be to organise democratic multi-party parliamentary elections 'as quickly as possible'. These decisions were made without the approval of the government-in-exile, which subsequently rejected them. However, the leaders of the anti-Nazi underground in Poland and the former prime minister Mikołajczyk took a slightly different stand, agreeing to participate in talks on the establishment of the TRJN provided that the negotiations, to be held in Moscow, took place on the basis of mutual recognition and equality.[13]

Although the Home Army had been formally disbanded, the fact that a wide variety of independent politicians from the anti-Nazi underground, who had strong support from Polish society, now came out of hiding to demand a role in government was inconvenient for Stalin. That is why General Ivan Serov, a key figure in Red Army counter-intelligence and the chief NKVD adviser to the Polish ministry of public security, organised a trap whereby sixteen leaders of the Polish underground were arrested at the end of March 1945 for 'anti-Soviet activities' and taken to the Soviet capital. Among them were the commander of the Home Army General Okulicki, the deputy prime minister of the underground government Stanisław Jankowski and several members of the council of national unity, a body which had served as an underground parliament during the German occupation. The captives were held at the Lubianka, the notorious NKVD prison, although the Soviets feigned for several weeks that they knew nothing about their fate or whereabouts.[14]

At the same time, the movement of the front line into German territory in March–April 1945 and the subsequent departure of most of the Red Army forces from Poland resulted in the spontaneous revival of underground structures, this time directed against the threat of sovietisation rather than the Nazi occupation. Older partisan units, based on the former Home Army, were rebuilt, while new units were also set up. Many men were recruited into armed combat against the new state as a result of their own direct experience of communist reprisals. The armed underground was not only able to crush dozens of communist militia posts but also to free prisoners from state jails and seize whole towns and villages.[15]

In June 1945 the talks promised at Yalta on the establishment of the TRJN started in Moscow. Although the communists pretended that genuine representatives of different political forces took part, the only really independent voice was that of Mikołajczyk. Additional pressure on him was brought by the fact that at the same time a show trial of the leaders of the Polish underground kidnapped earlier by the NKVD took place in Moscow. It was suggested outright that their fate depended on the outcome of negotiations on the establishment of the TRJN. The secretary general of the PPR, Władysław Gomułka, clearly specified the scope of negotiations by stating that: 'we will never give back power once seized'.[16] In the end, Mikołajczyk and his allies got only three ministerial seats in the new government. Despite this they decided to accept the establishment of the TRJN as they believed in the promise of free elections. On

5 July 1945 the USA and Britain recognised the new government and thereby severed their relations with the government-in-exile (a body which nonetheless continued in existence until 1990). The trial of the leaders of the Polish underground state ended with prison sentences of up to ten years for the main defendants, sentences which were quite lenient in Soviet terms. However, three of the victims, including General Okulicki and deputy prime minister Jankowski, died while serving their time and it is suspected that they were murdered. The trial also allowed the Soviets and their Polish communist allies to present the wartime Home Army as a group of fascists and collaborators, when in reality it had led the underground resistance against German occupation.[17]

The participants in the Moscow talks soon returned to Poland. Tens of thousands of people took to the streets of Polish towns and cities to greet Mikołajczyk, who was now deputy prime minister and minister of agriculture in the new government. Partly in order to free himself from ongoing attempts at communist subjugation, he decided to establish a new party which was called the Polish Peasants' Party (PSL). This body soon became the most popular political force in the country with over one million members (not only peasants). The PSL offered Polish society hope that democratisation was feasible and that is why the vast majority of Poles supported it. The eminent emigré politician, Karol Popiel, returned to the country as leader of the Christian Democratic Labour Party, but its structures quickly became controlled by politicians subordinated to the communists. This led to the suspension of the party's licence to operate in July 1946 and to Popiel leaving the country shortly thereafter. Other parties were more indirectly subjected to communist control, including the Socialist Party (PPS) of prime minister Osóbka-Morawski. An attempt to rebuild the legal structures of the National Party ended up with its activists being arrested.[18]

Opposition and mass repression

The establishment of the new government and the return of Mikołajczyk to the country aroused fervent hope in Polish society. People believed that the free elections promised by the victorious Allies would enable them to oust the communists from power. In the summer of 1945 the activities of the armed underground declined. As a result of the amnesty declared in August, 30,000 people came out of hiding. Numerous Home Army veterans decided to put their faith in the democratic process believing that it presented their best opportunity to help shape the transformations taking place in the country.[19]

However, not all shared this conviction. On 2 September 1945 the largest illegal resistance movement was established – 'Freedom and Sovereignty' (WiN). It was an organisation based on Home Army structures, although initially it saw its main task as mobilising political resistance and educating society in preparation for genuinely free elections. However, it soon came to the conclusion that armed combat could not be avoided. Many of the older partisan units still in existence subordinated themselves to WiN and new groups were constantly being set up. The second largest conspiracy group was the National Military Union, which had strong armed units at its disposal in many regions. Apart from nationwide organisations there were also many regional ones in operation, mostly deriving from the Home Army. Other groups operated in the eastern territories annexed by the Soviet Union, most notably the Exterritorial Vilnius Area of the Home Army. It is estimated that between 120,000 and 180,000 people took part in this underground resistance to sovietisation, although only 10,000 to 15,000 were involved in armed combat at any one time. However, the force was sufficient to control a large part of the country in 1945–46 and to wage successful battles with the Polish communist militia and the NKVD, including attacks on jails and the liberation of prisoners. About 10,000 partisans lost their lives during such actions.[20]

Polish communist leaders, who later described these early post-war years as a period of 'civil war',[21] responded by undertaking a major revision and expansion of the burgeoning police state. Thus the number of members of the security apparatus, known since 1945 as the ministry of public security, increased on a regular basis and a network of agents and informers was also developed. In the spring of 1946 special regional courts martial were established to judge civilians for 'political crimes'. Those found guilty were sent to an ever increasing number of prisons and forced labour camps.[22] In November 1945 the special commission for the fight against abuse of the law and harmful economic activity was also set up. It was an administrative rather than judicial body and could send people to labour camps for periods of up to two years. Despite its name, the activities of this unit were largely political. Thus the commission was used to wage systematic campaigns of persecution against private entrepreneurs, peasants and persons spreading political rumours (so-called 'whispered propaganda'). By February 1946 around 120,000 people were imprisoned.[23] The legal basis for these reprisals was also developed. On 13 June 1946 the 'Decree on especially dangerous crimes in the period of statehood restoration', known as the so-called 'small penal code', was adopted. It was one of the main tools used to crack down on political opponents until the late 1960s.

The total number of people who were sentenced for political crimes in the whole period down to 1956 is not known. We have at our disposal only fragmentary data. As many as 8,000 death sentences were passed, at least half of them in political trials. Precise estimates are hampered by the fact that it was characteristic of communist reprisal methods that political opponents were often accused of criminal offences. This was done to make them more repugnant to society.[24]

In the autumn of 1945 and the spring of 1946 hopes for the future were mostly centred on the elections promised at Yalta. Knowing the outcome of the polls in Hungary in November 1945, which were won outright by the Polish equivalent of the PSL, the Hungarian Smallholders' Party, and realising that they had very little support in Polish society, the communists aimed at delaying the elections for as long as possible. The negotiations over the proposal for the establishment of a single electoral bloc for all political parties were a sort of 'smoke screen' for this. When the proposal was finally rejected by the PSL, which left the government in April 1946, the idea of calling a referendum to place three central political questions before the public vote appeared as an alternative to the promised free elections. The referendum would also allow the communists to measure the extent of their control over the state and their level of support in Polish society without having to risk losing power.[25]

In the run up to the referendum, which took place on 30 June 1946, various types of political opposition appeared. In the countryside there was strong resistance to the compulsory grain deliveries imposed by the communists.[26] The wave of industrial unrest which started in the spring of 1945 also intensified. In May 1946 there were over 100 strikes and in total there were at least 1,220 in the period 1945–48. Many of them were violent. In 15 per cent of the strikes political demands were directly raised, but even during economic strikes the anti-communist attitude of workers was revealed.[27] Strikes in the regions of Łódź, Katowice and Kraków were particularly numerous. These were also the areas where the wartime and post-war movement of people was the least intense and where traditional patterns of worker solidarity remained largely intact.[28]

Traditionally, 3 May is a Polish national holiday, marking the anniversary of Europe's first, and the world's second, modern constitution in 1791. In the immediate post-war period it was still a national holiday, but from the communists' point of view it came too soon after the new holiday of 1 May. For this reason, and also due to fear of renewed youth protests (the largest took place in December 1945 in Łódź and in April 1946 in Szczecin), a last-minute ban on celebrating the 3 May constitution day was issued. It led to mass demonstrations in dozens of towns and cities, which were brutally suppressed by the militia and the internal security corps (KBW).[29] In twelve towns and cities firearms were used against the protesters, and, according to different sources, between three and twenty people were killed, hundreds injured and thousands arrested. The events of 3 May in Kraków were especially infamous because of the use of machine guns against protesters and the arrest of 1,200 people, mainly students of the Jagiellonian University. Follow-up demonstrations as well as strikes of university and secondary school students, even primary school pupils, took place all around the country in response to these events. It seems that this was the first mass social protest against communist rule in post-war Eastern Europe. The strikes were defeated through propaganda and arrests, with scores of people being sentenced to terms of imprisonment. As a result of the disturbances, the autonomy of universities was severely limited and proposals were considered to punish rebellious students with a two-year period of imprisonment in labour camps.[30]

The referendum was held on 30 June 1946. Three questions were asked: (i) whether the senate should be liquidated, (ii) whether the agricultural reform should be introduced and whether heavy industry should be nationalised, and (iii) whether the new western border with Germany, the Oder-Neisse line, should be approved. The first question was designed to make the situation of the PSL even harder as this party had demanded the liquidation of the senate in the inter-war period. In 1946 in order to differentiate itself from the communists the PSL had to call for people to vote against its former position – 'no' to the first question, and 'yes' to the second and third questions. Communists and their supporters called for three 'yes' votes. The resistance group WiN appealed to its supporters to vote in accordance with PSL guidelines, whereas the national underground advocated voting 'no' to all three questions. The communists organised a mass propaganda campaign before the referendum in the wake of which, *inter alia*, they printed tens of thousands of brochures, leaflets, handouts and posters (several for each citizen). But the campaign did not bring the expected results. According to the most optimistic estimates only 20–25 per cent of society voted 'yes' three times. No wonder the decision was made to forge the results of the referendum. A group of professional NKVD counterfeiters arrived from Moscow and proceeded to fabricate the minutes of electoral commissions. It was publicly announced that 68.2 per cent voted 'yes' to all three questions. Genuine results were made public only in Kraków where electoral commissions were still controlled by the PSL.[31]

The communists nonetheless drew conclusions from the real results, which had shown how unpopular they were. The campaign of repression against the activists of the underground and the PSL subsequently gathered pace. Special militia groups of the PPR and the secret police murdered over 100 activists of the party led by Mikołajczyk, while thousands of others were imprisoned. Local branches of the PSL were systematically liquidated. In September 1946 the Sejm (national parliament) electoral law was adopted, paving the way for general elections to be held in January 1947. It contained many provisions enabling the communists to manipulate the results. At the same time the bloc of democratic parties and trade unions, which included the communists and allied political groups, was set up. The bloc had exclusive access to state structures and the media, an advantage which it exploited ruthlessly in the course of the election campaign.[32]

During the campaign the terror intensified enormously. It is estimated that as many as 100,000 activists of the PSL were detained or arrested.[33] A series of show trials started in the summer of 1946 directed against opposition and armed underground activists. The propaganda acted by fair means or foul, accusing the PSL of all possible crimes. The *Gazeta Ludowa* ('People's Paper') published by Mikołajczyk's party was subjected to strict censorship. The communist bloc all around the country registered lists with number 3, whereas the PSL received lists with different numbers for each constituency. Pro-communist military security and propaganda groups were sent to the villages, allegedly to protect electoral commissions but in fact to terrorise the peasants. Communist campaigners intruded upon hundreds of thousands of people in their homes and made them declare their support for the PPR. Half a million citizens were deprived of their voting rights by administrative fiat. PSL lists were also revoked in a number of constituencies. The opposition did not have any representatives in electoral commissions, whereas nearly half the commission members were recruited from the agents of the secret police. In order to make sure that counting took place in accordance with the pre-arranged results, special tables were prepared to facilitate the rewriting of votes. In this way, each party managed to obtain the 'required' number of seats in parliament.[34]

The last mass protest took place just before the election on 19 January 1947 when students and pupils demonstrated and went on strike for a few days in Lublin. The election itself was a complete farce. The majority of Poles were forced to vote in full view of communist election officials and those who opted for the secret ballot were scrupulously noted down. In contrast to the referendum, the results hardly needed fabricating after the event. Officially, 80.1 per cent of voters opted for the communist bloc and 10.3 per cent for the PSL, the remaining votes being cast for several other lists of minor pro-communist parties. The complaints over electoral irregularities filed by the PSL as well as protests submitted to the ambassadors of the USA and Great Britain met with no response.[35]

The elections were an important turning point, seriously undermining the morale of the by now exhausted and demoralised opposition parties. Thus the activities of the PSL almost ceased entirely after the elections, allowing the communist authorities to dissolve the party's structures in several provinces. Finally, the PSL fell under complete communist control after its leader Mikołajczyk fled to the west in October 1947. The activities of the illegal armed resistance movements also tailed off significantly. In February 1947 the next amnesty was declared as a result of which 53,517 conspirators came out of hiding. Between April and July 1947 virtually all Ukrainians living in southeastern Poland, roughly 140,000 people in total, were expelled from their homes and resettled in scattered communities in Silesia, Pomerania and other regions annexed from Germany in 1945, a process which destroyed the last remnants of Ukrainian resistance to communist rule in Poland. In November 1947 the 4th Main Board of WiN was dissolved, marking the end of the last nationwide Polish resistance group. Individual partisan units, with dwindling numbers, nonetheless continued to fight an increasingly hopeless battle against the communists until the early 1950s.[36]

Terror

The strengthened position of the communists after the manipulated January 1947 election result enabled them to proceed more directly to the full-scale sovietisation of Polish society. In the autumn of 1947 the so-called 'battle for the economy' started. The battle was aimed at combating small businesspeople – owners of shops, warehouses, mills and so on.[37] In 1948 all youth organisations were 'united' under communist supervision in the Stalinist Union of Polish Youth. In the first half of 1948 a great cleansing operation was conducted in the PPS, the communist-controlled Polish Socialist Party, as a result of which social democrats and others with anti-communist views were eliminated from the ranks of the party. This formed the background to the 'unification' of the PPR and the PPS, which took place in December 1948. The new party, the Polish United Workers' Party (PZPR), exercised absolute power over Poland until 1989. The sovietisation of the Polish political system ended in 1949 when the United Peasants' Party was established following the compulsory 'unification' of the pro-communist Peasant Party with the remnants of the PSL. In this way a formal system with three parties was created, although there is no doubt that the PZPR played the dominant role in state and society.[38]

The period of the most intense development of Stalinism in Poland (1948–56) also meant deep economic transformations. At the request of the newly created Communist Information Bureau (Cominform) in the summer of 1948 the collectivisation of villages was announced. However, in spite of the use of mass terror (over half a million peasants were sentenced for oppositional activities in the period to 1956), collectivisation failed. At its peak in 1955 less than 10 per cent of farms were included in the collective system. Following the Soviet model of five-year plans, the six-year plan was announced in 1950. Dubbed by state propaganda as the 'plan for the construction of the basis of socialism', it anticipated the rapid modernisation of the country's infrastructure, first and foremost through the development of heavy industry. The propaganda intent of the government was symbolised by the building of the gigantic Nowa Huta metallurgical plant. However, the implementation of the plan was mainly based on the extreme exploitation of workers, who were burdened with systematic increases in work norms as well as the introduction of the Soviet-style *Stakhanovite* 'labour race'. As a consequence, the number of fatal industrial accidents rose year after year.[39] Meanwhile, the 1950 law on socialist work increased the severity of punishments imposed on those accused of sabotage, ill-discipline or absenteeism in the workplace. 'Slack workers', as Tony Kemp-

Welch puts it, were de facto redefined as 'enemies of the state' and could be sent for 're-education' in one of several forced labour camps dotted around the country.[40]

Owing to the increase in tensions between the Soviet Union and the west, Stalin decided to take direct control over the Polish army. In November 1949 Konstantin Rokossowsky, a Soviet marshal, was appointed as the new Polish minister of defence. Several hundred senior Soviet military officers came with him to Poland and they were given the vast majority of leading positions in the army. After the outbreak of the Korean war in 1950, an unprecedented build-up of the armed forces took place, as happened in other eastern bloc countries like Czechoslovakia and Hungary. The Polish army at its height numbered half a million soldiers and maintaining and equipping it put an enormous strain on the economy. The need to supply many million of tons of coal to the USSR annually was equally burdensome as the price paid by the Soviets did not even cover the cost of transportation.[41]

In the second half of 1948 the apparatus of terror also began to seek new targets, not least among communists themselves. The starting point was the removal of Gomułka from his post as secretary general of the PPR in the autumn, mainly as a result of his apparent opposition to the Cominform's resolution condemning Tito, his doubts about the wisdom of the policy of collectivisation and his concerns about the brutal manner of the forthcoming unification of the PPR with the PPS. He was replaced by Bolesław Bierut, a loyal Stalinist, who, together with party colleagues Jakub Berman, Stanisław Radkiewicz and Hilary Minc, organised a ruthless campaign to 'uncover and eliminate foreign agents and anti-party groups' within the new United Workers' Party. They did this largely through the formation in early 1949 of a new public security commission, the rough equivalent of the Central Party Control Commission in East Germany, which had access to the files of all party members and was directed from above by Soviet 'advisers'. According to Krystyna Kersten, 'Bierut and Berman systematically and scrupulously monitored materials concerning [alleged traitors in the party], authorised the most important arrests, and approved or directed draft indictments'.[42] They also followed closely, and sought to draw lessons from, the Rajk trial in Hungary and the Kostov trial in Bulgaria and acquired lists of Polish communists who supposedly had had contact with Noel Field and other newly exposed 'imperialist agents'.[43] Above all they began making preparations for a Polish show trial, with Gomułka the most likely defendant alongside two or three other senior colleagues. In the period November 1948 to October 1949, 104 key party officials were arrested and interrogated in order to reveal their part in this imagined conspiracy. As in Hungary and Bulgaria, and later in the Slánský trial in Czechoslovakia, the initial intention was to build up a case using 'falsified documents and statements extracted by torture'.[44]

Another important staging post was the trial before the supreme military court in July–August 1951 of a number of senior officers charged with having built up a 'diversionary-espionage group in the Polish Army' and with having conspired to 'restore the rule of landowners and capitalists'. All of the defendants, including General Stanisław Tatar and Lieutenants Marian Utnik and Stanisław Nowicki, who had been under arrest since February 1949, were found guilty and sentenced to lengthy terms of imprisonment.[45] Most had served in the pre-war Polish army and/or in the non-communist underground resistance against the Germans during the Second World War. Clearly this particular trial was linked to Stalin's quest for greater control over the Polish armed forces, but it had obvious implications for the position of leading communists suspected of organising a 'provocation in the workers' movement' as well, and seemed to signal the possibility that an even bigger 'imperialist' plot was about to be revealed.

In July 1951, on the first day of the generals' appearance before the supreme military court, Gomułka himself was detained and held under close house arrest for the next three years, but surprisingly he was not charged or brought to trial. Nor was he tortured or forced to make a confession of guilt, although he was placed under considerable psychological pressure to play ball with his interrogators. The trial of another top communist who was arrested in 1950, Marian Spychalski, also failed in the end to materialise, but he was held for longer than Gomułka and was only set free following Bierut's death in March 1956.[46]

Various explanations have been offered for the absence of a show trial in post-war Poland, though the lack of solid documentary evidence means there can be no definitive answer to this question. One theory focuses on internal politics in the PZPR, suggesting that Bierut secretly took steps to protect his formal rival, albeit not for humanitarian reasons, but because he feared that too thorough an investigation of Gomułka's past activities might endanger his own freedom and reputation. Berman, the party's chief 'power behind the throne', also had much to fear, not only because he was Jewish and therefore potentially a 'Polish Slánský', but also because the emigration of his brother to Israel in 1950 made him even more vulnerable to charges of disloyalty or treason if the tables should suddenly be turned. Both Bierut and Berman therefore had good reasons to tread carefully. But, equally, another theory suggests that it was Stalin who did not wish for a show trial in Poland, particularly as he was concerned about the popularity of Gomułka and the potential for a nationalist backlash against communism in a country which not only had a long tradition of anti-Russian feeling, but which was of great strategic and military importance to the Soviet Union against the background of the Cold War and ever worsening east-west relations. It may even be that Stalin secretly admired Gomułka for his courage and willingness to speak out against the official Cominform line on issues like collectivisation. Finally, it could be that in the new context of the early 1950s Gomułka simply did not have the right profile for a plausible show-trial defendant: he was not Jewish or pro-Zionist, he had not spent the war years in western exile, he had no obvious contacts with Tito, he refused to 'confess' and above all there was no concrete evidence linking him with Rajk or Slánský, or at least no evidence that could be convincingly fabricated for a public audience.[47]

The absence of a show trial, however, should not lead us to underestimate the terror in Poland. By January 1953, according to Andrzej Paczkowski, the secret police had expanded its file system to cover some 5.2 million people, or one in every three adults. Numerous death sentences were still being passed by the courts and then signed by Bierut in person, further underlining the fact that he was not inclined to clemency in most cases. Prosecutions for political offences also continued, so that in the last six months of 1952 there were almost 50,000 political prisoners in Poland. Some were put on trial and convicted, while others were held for years without being charged and others still were sent to administrative detention in labour camps. Even young political 'delinquents' were not spared; those considered to come from 'improper' social backgrounds or who were registered in police files for 'hostile activities' were held in a special prison at Jawor which held 2,500 inmates by 1953.[48] When they reached adulthood, instead of military training they were sent to the mines where they had to work for twelve hours a day. In total, over 200,000 people were subjected to forced labour of one kind or another in the period to 1956, several hundred of whom died as a result of industrial accidents.[49]

The Catholic church

After the removal of all avenues for independent political activity, even in the ruling PZPR itself, the last barrier standing in the way of the complete sovietisation of Polish society was the Catholic church. Already in September 1948, 400 priests were arrested for a catalogue of supposed offences.[50] The terror was stepped up in 1949 following a Cominform conference in the February of that year devoted to the 'struggle against religion'. Of course, church–state conflicts took place in all eastern bloc countries during this period. However, in Poland a further dimension of this struggle was the unwillingness of the Vatican to recognise the Oder–Neisse line as the new border between Germany and Poland and its alleged support for West German (and therefore American) 'imperialism' against the national interests of the Polish people.[51]

On 5 August 1949 the 'Decree on the protection of conscience and religion' was adopted by the Polish communist authorities. Despite its name it served the purpose of victimising clerics and lay persons (not only Catholics but also Jehovah's Witnesses) rather than protecting religious liberties. On 1 September 1949, on the tenth anniversary of the outbreak of the Second World War, the 'movement of patriotic priests', which aimed at destroying the unity of the church, was set up. In March 1950 the state confiscated the Catholic charity organisation 'Caritas' and took over its property, just as previously it had sequestered agricultural land, hospitals and other immovable property belonging to the church. However, one month later, and rather unexpectedly, a new agreement between the state and the church was signed. The communists now committed themselves to upholding basic religious freedoms, including the return of Caritas and other Catholic bodies to church control. But the agreement was systematically breached. Religion classes were limited in schools, Catholic papers were closed down and hundreds of clerics were imprisoned. So too were over 2,000 Jehovah's Witnesses who were accused of being American agents and 'enemies of the people'.[52] In 1951 the authorities even made an attempt to initiate a schism in the church by imposing their own diocese managers in the 'Recovered Territories' (i.e. the former German lands annexed to Poland in 1945), thereby creating positions which the Vatican had previously and deliberately left vacant. However, this scheme failed when the new managers were recognised by Archbishop (later cardinal) Stefan Wyszyński, the primate of Poland since 1948.

Stalin's death in March 1953 led to a gradual reduction in terror in most parts of Eastern Europe, but in Poland the persecution of the church continued unabated and in many ways intensified during the period 1953–54.[53] For instance, the 'Decree on the appointment to the church seats' was made public in February under which the state was authorised to nominate all new bishops and parish priests. Moreover, all clerics were required to swear an oath of allegiance to the state. The episcopate responded with a famous letter titled 'Non possumus', in which they refused to accept the new law. In September 1953 a grand show trial of the Bishop of Kielce, Czesław Kaczmarek, was organised. He was depicted as 'a Gestapo collaborator' and 'a spy of the Vatican City' and was eventually convicted and sentenced to twelve years imprisonment on charges of 'weakening the defensive spirit of Polish society in the face of threatened Hitlerite aggression, disrupting the reconstruction of the country and planned economy, and of sabotage on Polish soil in the interests of American imperialism'.[54] When primate Wyszyński refused to condemn the bishop, he too was arrested and interned for over three years, from September 1953 to October 1956. Thereafter the episcopate of Poland, deprived of its leader, submitted to the authorities. In 1954 many convents were liquidated and the nuns were sent to special labour camps. However, despite such persecutions the authorities failed to break the church completely and, even more noticeably, failed to pull the Polish people away from their religion.[55]

More generally, terror could not destroy Polish society itself or its resistance to ongoing sovietisation. True, the various partisan units were significantly weakened in the period after 1947–48, but they did not disappear entirely and the last time an underground soldier was killed in action was in 1963. Industrial stoppages were shorter and had fewer participants after 1948, but 200 strikes were still recorded in 1950. Above all the opposition of the peasants towards collectivisation remained very strong. Examples here include the destruction of agricultural machinery, the slaughtering of cattle and pigs, migration from villages to the towns and boycotts of work on collective farms. Various attempts were also made to try and break the government's monopoly in the sphere of information and communications, for instance by listening to foreign radio stations, spreading gossip and rumours ('whispered propaganda') and telling anti-communist political jokes. All the above activities were defined as criminal and were violently punished with sentences of up to twelve years' imprisonment.[56]

The continuing resistance of Polish society, the increasing economic crisis and the power struggles taking place inside the Soviet Union after 1953 were the main causes of de-Stalinisation, a process which began later in Poland than in other socialist states and did not really get started until well into 1955. Needless to say, several events in the first half of 1956, including Khrushchev's secret speech to the twentieth congress of the CPSU in February, the death of party general secretary Bierut in March and large-scale rioting in the city of Poznań in June, accelerated the move towards reform. In October 1956 Gomułka returned to power with Khrushchev's approval and a temporary liberalisation of the system took place.[57] A similar pattern of events occurred after further workers' protests in 1970 and 1980. However, although the system was gradually opened up, its main features (the absolute power of the communist party, dependence on the Soviet Union, the all-pervasive control over society exercised by the security apparatus and the readiness to turn to mass reprisals) remained unchanged until its fall in 1989.

Conclusion

A Soviet-style communist regime was successfully installed in Poland after the Second World War because Polish territory was occupied by the Red Army, not because of any indigenous support for the communist cause. The terror system which emerged in the years 1948 to 1954, and which built on an earlier period of mass repression between 1944 and 1948, had its own internal peculiarities, partly reflecting the personalities of the individuals concerned, Bierut first and foremost, and partly reflecting the unique circumstances of Poland's transition from brutal wartime German occupation to large-scale public and underground resistance to sovietisation. But it is also difficult not to conclude that in the Polish case in particular, Stalin's influence was crucial. This can be seen on two different levels.

Firstly, the underground armed conflict of 1945–46, waged by remnants of the wartime Home Army and other anti-communist groups, confirmed Stalin's suspicion that Polish society would never voluntarily submit to Soviet influence. Above all he was deeply suspicious of three defining Polish institutions: the Catholic church, the landowning class and the military, all of which had been bastions of nationalist resistance against Tsarist rule in the nineteenth century and all of which, in their own way, refused to accept the 'reality' that Poland owed its liberation from fascism to the heroic struggles of the Red Army in the war against Hitler's Germany.[58]

But secondly the Soviet dictator feared and perhaps even respected Poland because of its potential to offer large-scale resistance to Moscow's hegemony in Eastern Europe. Such precautionary fears were compounded by the strategic importance of Poland as a supply route for hundreds of thousands of Red Army soldiers now stationed in East Germany in readiness for the possible outbreak of World War Three.[59] It is this consideration which probably explains Stalin's reluctance to give the green light for a show trial against Gomułka in the early 1950s and equally Khrushchev's decision to bring Gomułka back as party first secretary during the political crisis of October 1956. In both cases, the Soviet leadership appears to have followed the logic of Gomułka's own advice to the PPR Central Committee in 1945: 'The masses should see us as a Polish party. Let them attack us as Polish communists, not [as Soviet or Russian] agents'.[60]

Notes

1   J. T. Gross, *Revolution from Abroad: The Soviet Conquest of Poland's Western Ukraine and Western Belorussia* (Princeton: NJ, 2002), pp. 17–113.
2   At this time, the Soviet party was formally known as the All-Union Communist Party (Bolsheviks), but for ease of reference we shall use the acronym CPSU.
3   This tragic event has gone down in history as the Katyń massacre, although the victims were murdered not only in Katyń but also in other places, for instance Kharkiv and Tver. For documents on the executions, see A. M. Cienciala, N. S. Lebedeva and W. Materski (eds), *Katyn: A Crime Without Punishment* (New Haven, 2008).
4   S. Ciesielski, W. Materski and A. Paczkowski, *Represje sowieckie wobec obywateli polskich* (Warsaw, 2002).
5   A. Kemp-Welch, *Poland under Communism: A Cold War History* (Cambridge, 2008), pp. 1–6.
6   K. Kersten, *Narodziny systemu władzy Polska 1943–1948* (Poznań, 1990), pp. 42–63.
7   L. Pietrzak, S. Poleszak, R. Wnuk and M. Zajączkowski (eds), *Rok pierwszy. Powstanie i działalność Aparatu Bezpieczeństwa Publicznego na Lubelszczyźnie (lipiec 1944 – czerwiec 1945)* (Warsaw, 2004), pp. 15–34.
8   Kersten, *Narodziny systemu władzy Polska*, pp. 74–107.
9   Kemp-Welch, *Poland under Communism*, p. 20.
10 Kemp-Welch, *Poland under Communism*, p. 5.

11 A. Paczkowski, *Pół wieku dziejów Polski* (Warsaw, 1996), pp. 117–26.

12 The issue of the western border was decided on at the Potsdam Conference of July–August 1945.

13 K. Kersten, *Jałta w polskiej perspektywie* (London, 1989), pp. 101–34.

14 A. Leinwand, *Przywódcy Polski Podziemnej przed sądem moskiewskim* (Warsaw, 1992), pp. 15–113.

15 R. Wnuk, S. Poleszak, A. Jaczyńska and M. Śladecka (eds), *Atlas polskiego podziemia niepodległościowego 1944–1956* (Warsaw and Lublin, 2007), pp. xxiv–xxv.

16 Kersten, *Narodziny systemu władzy Polska*, p. 108.

17 Kersten, *Narodziny systemu władzy Polska*, pp. 136–44; Leinwand, *Przywódcy Polski Podziemnej*, pp. 115–62; Paczkowski, *Pół wieku dziejów Polski*, p. 375.

18 J. Wrona, *System partyjny w Polsce 1944–1950. Miejsce, funkcje, relacje partii politycznych w warunkach budowy i utrwalania systemu komunistycznego* (Lublin, 1997), pp. 136–248.

19 Wnuk et al. (eds), *Atlas polskiego podziemia*, p. xxx.

20 Wnuk et al. (eds), *Atlas polskiego podziemia*, p. xlii–li. Figures for the number of deaths among the opposing Red Army and NKVD forces are not available. Cf. A. Dudek and A. Paczkowski, 'Poland', in K. Persak and Ł. Kamiński (eds), *A Handbook of the Communist Security Apparatus in East Central Europe, 1944–1989* (Warsaw, 2005), pp. 221–83 (here p. 273).

21 Kemp-Welch, *Poland under Communism*, p. 40. Today's Polish historians, on the other hand, tend to reject the term 'civil war', arguing instead that this was a national war waged by Polish society against the Soviet and NKVD troops occupying their towns and villages. See A. Paczkowski, 'Poland: "The Enemy Nation"', in S. Courtois (ed.), *The Black Book of Communism: Crimes, Terror, Repression* (Cambridge: MA, 1999), pp. 363–93 (here p. 376).

22 There were over 200 of these at one point. See B. Kopka, *Obozy pracy w Polsce 1944–1950: Przewodnik encyklopedyczny* (Warsaw, 2003).

23 K. Madej, J. Żaryn and J. Żurek (eds), *Księga świadectw: Skazani na karę śmierci w czasach stalinowskich i ich losy* (Warsaw, 2003), p. xxii.

24 Madej et al. (eds), *Księga świadectw*, pp. xx–xxxviii.

25 Kersten, *Narodziny systemu władzy Polska*, pp. 206–20.

26 Ł. Kamiński, 'Ekonomiczny opór wsi polskiej 1944–1948', in Ł. Kamiński (ed.), *Studia i materiały z dziejów opozycji i oporu społecznego* (Wrocław, 1998), vol. 1, pp. 3–13.

27 Ł. Kamiński, *Strajki robotnicze w Polsce w latach 1945–1948* (Wrocław, 1999), pp. 107–20.

28 It is worth noting that as a result of the war Poland not only suffered huge demographic losses but also forced migration on a large scale, a phenomenon which directly affected 25 per cent of the population. Thus both the Germans and the Soviet occupiers deported large numbers of people, while others were forced to leave their homes because of racial or political persecution, or as a consequence of changes in state boundaries.

29 As regular units of the Polish army often refused to participate in battles against underground partisans, the task was largely taken over by the KBW from the spring of 1946.

30 Ł. Kamiński, *Polacy wobec nowej rzeczywistości 1944–1948: Formy pozainstytuc-jonalnego ż ywiołowego oporu społecznego 1944–1948* (Toruń, 2000), pp. 160–92.

31 A. Paczkowski, *Referendum z 30 czerwca 1946 r. Przebieg i wyniki* (Warsaw, 1993), pp. 5–16.

32 Kersten, *Narodziny systemu władzy Polska*, pp. 252–92.

33 Cz. Osękowski, *Wybory do Sejmu z 19 stycznia 1947 roku w Polsce* (Poznań, 2000), p. 74.

34 J. Wrona (ed.), *Kampania wyborcza i wybory do Sejmu Ustawodawczego 19 stycznia 1947* (Warsaw, 1999), pp. 5–45; Osękowski, *Wybory do Sejmu*, pp. 15–162.

35 See Osękowski, *Wybory do Sejmu*, pp. 130–59, and Kamiński, *Polacy wobec nowej rzeczywistości*, pp. 193–8.

36 Paczkowski, 'Poland: "The Enemy Nation"', pp. 376–7; Kamiński, *Polacy wobec nowej rzeczywistości*, pp. 249–50; Wnuk et al. (eds.), *Atlas polskiego podziemia*, p. xxxii.

37 The 'battle for the economy' was the continuation of the policy of nationalisation of industry which began in early 1946.

38 Paczkowski, *Pół wieku dziejów Polski*, pp. 229–54.

39 D. Jarosz, *Polityka władz komunistycznych w Polsce w latach 1944–1956 a chłopi* (Warsaw, 1998); and D. Jarosz, *Polacy a stalinizm 1948–1956* (Warsaw, 2000).

40 Kemp-Welch, *Poland under Communism*, p. 35.

41 E. Nalepa, *Oficerowie Armii Radzieckiej w Polsce 1943–1968* (Warsaw, 1995).

42 K. Kersten, 'The Terror, 1949–1954', in A. Kemp-Welch (ed.), *Stalinism in Poland: Selected Papers from the Fifth World Congress of Central and Eastern European Studies, Warsaw, 1995* (Basingstoke, 1999), pp. 78–94 (here p. 90).

43 Kemp-Welch, *Poland under Communism*, pp. 42–3.

44 Kersten, 'The Terror', pp. 90 and 93.

45 Kersten, 'The Terror', p. 92.

46 Kersten, 'The Terror', p. 93.

47 For a more detailed discussion, see Ł. Kamiński, 'Why did Gomułka not become a Polish Slánský?', paper presented at the international conference 'Political Trials of the 1950s and the Slánský case', Prague, 14–16 June 2003, available on-line at: www.sipa.columbia.edu/ece/research/intermarium/vol7no1/kaminski.pdf (accessed 23 November 2009).

48 All figures in this paragraph from Paczkowski, 'Poland: "The Enemy Nation"', p. 382.

49 Ł. Kamiński, 'Schauprozesse in Polen 1945–1956', in U. Bräuel and S. Samerski (eds), *Ein Bischof vor Gericht: Der Prozeß gegen den Danziger Bischof Carl Maria Splett 1946* (Osnabrück, 2005), pp. 263–80.

50 Kemp-Welch, *Poland under Communism*, p. 46.

51 Cf. M. Phayer, *Pius XII, the Holocaust and the Cold War* (Bloomington and Indianapolis, 2008), pp. 167–8.

52 Paczkowski, 'Poland: "The Enemy Nation"', p. 382.

53 Kemp-Welch, *Poland under Communism*, pp. 47–8.

54 Kemp-Welch, *Poland under Communism*, p. 48.

55 J. Żaryn, *Dzieje Kościoła katolickiego w Polsce (1944–1989)* (Warsaw, 2003), pp. 88–156.

56 Ł. Kamiński, A. Małkiewicz and K. Ruchniewicz, *Opór społeczny w Europie Środkowej w latach 1948–1953 na przykładzie Polski, NRD i Czechosłowacji* (Wrocław, 2004), pp. 177–92, 254–308.

57 On the Polish October, see J. Granville, 'Poland and Hungary, 1956: A Comparative Essay Based on New Archival Findings', in K. McDermott and M. Stibbe (eds), *Revolution and Resistance in Eastern Europe: Challenges to Communist Rule* (Oxford, 2006), pp. 57–77.

58 Paczkowski, 'Poland: "The Enemy Nation"', pp. 363–4.

59 Kemp-Welch, *Poland under Communism*, pp. 9–10 and 98–9.

60 Kemp-Welch, *Poland under Communism*, p. 20.

Stalinist terror in Czechoslovakia: origins, processes, responses

Kevin McDermott

Between 1948 and 1954, Czechoslovak society was subjected to multiple forms of repression by the newly installed communist regime. Political trials, internment in forced labour camps and prisons, even executions were commonplace in those dreadful years, and a wide range of less coercive measures was fiercely imposed. No stratum of society escaped the depredations. Ever since, experts have attempted to explain the origins and processes of these troubling events.[1] A recurrent question haunts historical scholarship and indeed the Czech, though less so Slovak, collective consciousness: why did political violence on this scale take place in a country with the humanist and pluralist credentials of Czechoslovakia, the only state in inter-war Eastern Europe in which democratic structures survived and in many ways prospered? Does the comforting answer lie in external pressures exerted most obviously by Stalin and the Soviet political and secret police hierarchies? Or was there a disconcerting internal determinant at play, sometimes referred to as 'indigenous Stalinism'? Or were the broader geo-political conflicts and constraints of the emerging Cold War more relevant? Other no less intractable issues abound. Who were the prime targets? By what mechanisms were the repressions actually carried out, and who organised them? What was the political impact and longer-term significance of the Stalinist terror? Most intriguingly perhaps, what was the popular reaction to the purges, particularly of leading communists such as ex-party general secretary Rudolf Slánský, who was condemned to death in November 1952 on trumped up charges? This chapter addresses these difficult themes drawing on recent historiography and, where appropriate, archival sources declassified in the Czech Republic since 1989.

Stalinist repression in Czechoslovakia: an overview

In February 1948, the Communist Party of Czechoslovakia (*Komunistická strana Československa* – KSČ) came to power in a bloodless *coup*. This is not the place to reconstruct the communist seizure of power in any detail. Suffice it to say that the KSČ was the largest party in the country, polling 40 per cent of the vote in the Czech lands of Bohemia and Moravia (but only 30 per cent in Slovakia) in the free elections of May 1946, had accumulated key power positions in the coalition governments that ran Czechoslovakia from May 1945 to February 1948, enjoyed relatively buoyant popularity among industrial workers, intellectuals and other social groups, and was tactically and ideologically more astute than its non-communist rivals.[2] 'Pro-Sovietism', shared even by influential politicians of the centre-left, and a profound anti-western sentiment following the Munich 'betrayal' of September 1938 undoubtedly contributed to the appeal of the KSČ. The communists were also not averse to using strong-arm methods and populist forms of anti-German nationalism to discredit opponents and garner mass backing. In short, there were powerful endogenous reasons for the communists' triumph. Nevertheless, there can be little doubt that Stalin played an important, if murky, strategic role in the Prague events, seeking to confirm Soviet hegemony over central and Eastern Europe in light of the worsening international atmosphere and the first signs of confrontation with Yugoslavia.

The immediate political goal for the KSČ after the 'victorious February' was to consolidate and extend its monopoly of power. To this end, within a few months approximately 28,000 employees were removed from state and public administration, including in the army, secret services and judiciary. Leading non-communist officials, especially National Socialists,[3] were summarily dismissed, their parties infiltrated, and effectively decimated, by communist-dominated 'action committees' which were given the power to purge mass organisations regardless of normal legal procedure. The social democrats were politically emasculated by a merger with the KSČ in June 1948, by which time Czechoslovakia had become in essence, if not formally, a one-party state.[4] In the following months and years, persecution affected all sections of society: communists, non-communists and anti-communists, Czechs and Slovaks,[5] young and old, men and women.[6]

Numerically, it is still impossible to arrive at precise overall figures as the term 'repression' covers a wide variety of meanings and measures: non-judicial murder, judicial execution, detention in labour camps or prison, enforced military service, expulsion from the party, loss of employment and status, and a host of other social and material restrictions including evictions from dwellings, exclusions from schools and universities, arbitrary reduction or cessation of pension payments and confiscation of personal property. Neither is it always evident whether a victim was targeted specifically for 'political' or 'anti-state crimes'. Moreover, it has been argued that 'the number of murders carried out by the State Security can never be determined.'[7] That said, the 'orthodox' statistics calculated by the renowned expert Karel Kaplan have now been largely superseded by more recent research. Writing in the early 1980s, Kaplan maintained that victims of political and military trials resulting in internment in prisons and labour camps amounted to roughly 250,000; approximately 750,000 others suffered economic and social sanctions of various kinds; and a further 500,000 to 750,000 were driven to the fringes of society because of their political or religious beliefs.[8] But these extremely high figures have been updated by the latest archival findings (not least by Kaplan himself), which indicate that just under 90,000 citizens were prosecuted for 'political crimes' in the years 1948–54; over 22,000 were incarcerated in 107 labour camps; almost 10,000 suspect soldiers and conscripts were condemned to back-breaking work in special construction battalions; and as many as 1,157 people perished in detention.[9]

Regardless of these perennial numerical uncertainties, it is widely agreed that in the period October 1948 to December 1952, 233 death penalties were pronounced, of which 178 were carried out. This figure notoriously included Milada Horáková, a National Socialist parliamentary deputy and the first, and only, woman to be executed in Czechoslovakia on political grounds. More death penalties were approved in 1953 and 1954, a total of 181 being passed between 1953 and 1967. However, even these numbers may be misleading. A former Czech judge has insisted that 'there were more people tried in secret . . . and subsequently executed than the government has ever been willing to admit.' Tens of others were shot while trying to escape from prison or attempting to flee the borders. Among the communist elite, 278 high-ranking party functionaries were convicted, although it must be said that communist victims represented a tiny fraction of the total sentenced (some have estimated a mere 0.1 per cent). In addition, party purges and expulsions reduced the size of the KSČ by several hundred thousand in the years 1949–54.[10] By any standards these are shocking statistics, but according to one recent controversial text Czechoslovakia, particularly its elites, did not suffer disproportionately from Stalinist political violence compared with other central and east European socialist states, as several authors have claimed.[11]

Origins: indigenous and exogenous factors

To seek the longer-term roots of the post-war repressions we need to examine briefly the historical development of the Communist Party of Czechoslovakia in the inter-war period, notably the process of 'Stalinisation' from the late 1920s.[12] Formed in 1921, the KSČ remained for most of the decade essentially a product of its origins in the left wing of the social democratic movement. Although it was affiliated to the Moscow-based Communist International (Comintern) and thus subject to gradual 'Bolshevisation' and 'russification', the party operated legally, competed, rather successfully, in parliamentary and municipal elections, sought and achieved a mass membership and was led by figures, such as Bohumír Šmeral, who could not easily be described as militant

Bolsheviks. It endeavoured to maintain organic links with the Czech and Slovak labour movements and with the various national minorities in the multi-ethnic state. Hence, to a certain extent the KSČ shared a pluralist conception of politics and was influenced by the dominant democratic political culture which characterised the first republic.

This situation was to change markedly from 1928–29 with the advent of a new party leadership under Klement Gottwald. Most of the older 'right-wing' luminaries were acrimoniously expelled and replaced by younger 'proletarian' elements, steadfastly loyal to the USSR and its Stalinist bosses. The process of 'Stalinisation', duplicated throughout the international communist movement, was reaching fruition.[13] Gottwald himself gave a clear inkling of what this meant in his inaugural address to the Czechoslovak national assembly in December 1929. Responding to accusations from non-communist deputies that the KSČ was under the command of a foreign state, Gottwald boasted: 'We are the party of the Czechoslovak proletariat and our highest revolutionary headquarters are in Moscow . . . We go to Moscow to learn from the Russian Bolsheviks how to wring your necks. (*Outcry*) And you know that the Russian Bolsheviks are masters at that! (*Uproar*).'[14]

It would be wrong, however, to imply that the KSČ (or any other communist party) became a monolithic Stalinist body completely divorced from national political currents by its utter devotion to the USSR and an 'alien' ideology, or that its entire membership fully imbued Stalinist values. For the rest of its existence, the Czechoslovak party was to experience a constant tension between on the one hand 'its insertion in the national community and [on the other] in the international communist movement'.[15] The boundary lines between these so-called 'national communist' and 'muscovite' tendencies may have often been blurred, running even through individual leaders and functionaries, but the two mentalities were nonetheless palpable. At the risk of over-simplification, the 'national communist' inclination came to the fore during the anti-fascist 'popular front' strategy in the years 1934–38, the 'democratic interlude' of 1945–47 with its defining slogan of a 'Czechoslovak road to socialism', and most conspicuously during the reformist Prague Spring of 1968, while the 'muscovite' tendency predominated in the Stalinist phase of construction in 1948–54 and in the 'normalisation' process after 1969. This dichotomy helps to explain the longer-term indigenous factors behind both the prosecution of the mass repression and its eventual refutation.[16]

The medium-term origins of Stalinist terror in Czechoslovakia must be contextualised in the traumatic experiences of the preceding decade: the humiliation of Munich, Nazi tutelage during World War Two, the Holocaust, the forcible expulsion of the Sudeten German minority in 1945–46, and, strikingly, the fearsome retribution process of the first post-war years. In the words of one expert, the period 1938–48 was 'the most fateful in the history of Czechoslovakia, encompassing truncation, dissolution, occupation, war, liberation, radical social reform, and absorption into the communist bloc.'[17] Following the Munich agreement of September 1938 and the subsequent *Wehrmacht* invasion of Czechoslovakia in March 1939, a Nazi-controlled Protectorate of Bohemia and Moravia was created in Prague and a nominally independent Slovak state was established in Bratislava. Six years of war and oppressive Nazi hegemony brutalised society, promoted a 'statisation' of the economy and labour relations and encouraged a moral devastation in social and ethnic relations, most evident in a marked radicalisation of Czech animosity towards the 'traitorous' Sudeten Germans, who numbered approximately 3.1 million.[18] With the agreement of the Allied powers, the vast majority of these citizens were deemed 'collectively guilty' and forcibly removed from Czechoslovak territory in two waves of expulsions in 1945 and 1946, the first (the 'wild transfer') being accompanied by chaotic violence and terror.[19]

Intimately linked to these demographic upheavals was the regulated retribution implemented by president Edvard Beneš's government in the aftermath of the war. This campaign was directed primarily against Sudeten Germans and their Czechoslovak collaborators and was enforced with ferocious zeal. Indeed, in the Czech provinces 723 death sentences were pronounced, of which 686 were actually carried out, by some way the highest ratio (95 per cent) in the whole of Europe and, it should be noted, far exceeding the number of judicial executions during the Stalinist period.[20] According to a leading authority, the significance of this is that 'the Czech postwar court system developed into something of an efficient killing machine – banning appeals, limiting the mitigating circumstances to a bare minimum and ruling that the death sentences must be carried out within two hours of the pronouncement of the capital verdict.'[21] What is more, this far-reaching retribution was inflicted by a 'democratic' government, was not produced under pressure from the Kremlin and preceded the communist regime by two to three years, thus helping to forge the mechanisms and mentalities for future Stalinist illegalities.

The barbarities of the Second World War also fostered deeply ambivalent attitudes towards Czechoslovak Jewry and exacerbated pre-existing anti-Semitic moods and sentiments.[22] The Holocaust decimated Czechoslovakia's Jewish population, only around 40,000–45,000 surviving from a total of circa 255,000 in 1938–39.[23] On their return from the camps, the repatriates were often met with a mixture of low-level anti-Semitism, stemming largely from property disputes, and occasionally outright physical violence, bordering on pogroms, as in several parts of Slovakia in the years 1945–48. Many Jewish cemeteries and synagogues were desecrated throughout Bohemia and Moravia.[24] What is more, a survey of religious life among Czechs and Moravians conducted by the Institute of Public Opinion in July 1946 revealed that almost 16 per cent of the 1,000 interviewees felt 'an antipathy' towards Jews, compared to 1.3 per cent towards Protestants, 7.4 per cent towards Catholics, and 8.2 per cent towards atheists.[25] Given that some of the respondents may have been disinclined to indicate their real beliefs in a semi-public forum, it seems reasonable to surmise that, soon after the Holocaust, as many as one in five Czechs held marked anti-Jewish sentiments. Leading party ideologue, Václav Kopecký, contributed to this inflamed atmosphere when in a speech in spring 1947 he referred to Jews as 'bearded Solomons' and 'scum' (*svoloč*), who falsely claimed to have participated in the anti-Nazi resistance.[26]

The overall relevance of these experiences and mentalities for our purposes is that the Munich 'betrayal', Nazi occupation, wartime horrors and widespread post-war retributions and population transfers made plausible the notion of the 'enemy within', undermining, to a certain extent at least, Czechs' and Slovaks' commitment to humanist beliefs, democratic procedures and legal norms. In this sense, important continuities existed between Nazi (1939–45), 'democratic transition' (1945–48) and communist rule (1948–54), and these socio-cultural interconnections are, arguably, just as salient as politico-ideological ruptures. It would thus appear that Stalinist repression is best contextualised by a complex combination of, on the one hand, deep-seated indigenous social and ethnic conflict exacerbated by war, foreign occupation and post-war fears and retributions, and, on the other, more immediate largely externally generated pressures.

What were these immediate pressures? When assessing short-term catalysts, it is tempting to see a monolithic hand at play: Stalin and the Soviet political and secret police bosses carefully orchestrating the purges in order to 'sovietise' the country, remove all 'Titoist', 'bourgeois nationalist' and 'Zionist' conspiracies and challenges to the emerging 'socialist camp', and thus secure the international and ideological position of the USSR in the dangerous uncharted waters of the Cold War. Tito's defiant attitude towards Soviet strictures was particularly alarming, threatening as it did the Kremlin's dominance of the embryonic communist systems throughout the region. These goals were given added urgency in Czechoslovakia's case by its exposed geopolitical location at the frontline of east–west frictions and intrigues. To be sure, such analyses are well-founded and, at one level, highly persuasive. Stalin's actions were undoubtedly informed by the darkening international conjuncture and the belief that war between socialism and capitalism was inevitable. It should also be recognised that western and émigré spies really did exist and attempted to recruit agents in Czechoslovakia, compounding communist fears and insecurities. Therefore, society needed to be 'protected', mobilised and prepared for the decisive battles ahead and the political trials of 'renegade' communists and 'anti-state' oppositionists were an indispensable method of inculcating uniformity and passivity among potentially unruly Soviet bloc allies. Moreover, Stalin's long-standing theory that the class struggle would heighten and 'bourgeois' resistance intensify as socialism approached provided the ideological underpinnings of terror by exposing the machinations of the 'class enemy' as the root of all problems.

Finally, it is often affirmed that Stalin's increasingly anti-Semitic tendencies in the last years of his life, associated with crass 'anti-cosmopolitanism' and the notorious 'Doctors' Plot', impacted on Czechoslovak and wider bloc developments. Indeed, such sentiments were given full reign in the late 1940s and early 1950s when the KSČ unleashed a vicious 'anti-Zionist' campaign dutifully following Stalin's shift to a pro-Arab and anti-Israeli foreign policy. This drive effectively degenerated into an anti-Semitic onslaught most grossly manifested in the Slánský trial in which eleven of the fourteen defendants were officially designated 'of Jewish origin'. There is little doubt, then, that the Soviet dictator bears ultimate responsibility for the repressive campaigns in Czechoslovakia and elsewhere, though his exact role is almost impossible to verify, subject as he was to vacillation, obfuscation and tactical change.[27]

Beyond Stalin's nefarious personal role, there was another international dimension to the Czechoslovak terror. Once started, the political trials in Eastern Europe possessed a certain logic and momentum of their own. Thus, the László Rajk affair in Hungary in autumn 1949 had a profound impact on Czechoslovakia. In the course of the investigations into Rajk's alleged traitorous activities, it had been 'discovered' that an extensive network of spies existed among Czechoslovak communists. As a result, the Hungarian party boss, Mátyás Rákosi, curtly informed his KSČ counterparts and demanded action. Prague's response was portentous. Gottwald invited Moscow to send Soviet secret police 'advisers' to assist the Czechoslovak authorities in their hunt for 'enemies', a request duly granted by Stalin but not fulfilled until the summer of 1950. It was the height of irony that within two years Slánský would be turned into the 'Czechoslovak Rajk' on the direct intervention of these advisers.

However, regardless of the explanatory potency of this exogenous interpretation, it is, in my opinion, uni-dimensional and overly restrictive. Even if we accept that the purges were initiated and coordinated in Moscow, they often fell on fertile soils, were adapted for domestic purposes and were not always amenable to strict party control 'from above', as we shall see in the Slánský case. They could be, and were, used to 'solve' power struggles, organisational rivalries and personal jealousies among the Czechoslovak political elite,[28] target class and in some instances ethnic 'enemies', identify scapegoats for the gross economic and material hardships,[29] serve as a reservoir of forced labour for developmental and military goals,[30] and act as propaganda and educative tools for the masses.[31] They emerged initially as a response to the sense of crisis and social tension that afflicted the regime as early as the summer and autumn of 1948, the origin of which was the failure to satisfy unrealistic economic targets and aspirations. Ultimately, however, mass repression had a direct political goal based on an ideological imperative steeped in Stalinist brutality: to bolster the legitimacy of the infant communist state by declaring a 'class war' on the 'bourgeois', 'impure' and 'socially harmful elements' who stood in the way of the communist project.

In short, repression was closely related to the intense drive of the new rulers to 'construct socialism', as they understood it. The unpalatable truth is that many Czech and Slovak communists, from all ranks of the party, condoned this violent campaign; some actively participated in it. Prime responsibility for the carnage most assuredly resides with the leading cohort, but it is hard to avoid the conclusion that many lower-level functionaries and ordinary members, and not a few non-communist citizens, were complicit by their 'silence', illiberal attitudes and tacit consent. In the controversial words of one Czech writer: 'We are all collectively responsible for the political trials – the nation as a whole, as a continuum.'[32]

Processes

The aim of this section is to analyse the mechanisms by which the terror was perpetrated – which institutions and individuals organised the mass repressions and trials, what specific forms did they take, and who were the prime targets? During the Prague Spring of 1968, the reformist party leadership under Alexander Dubček ordered an official enquiry into the Stalinist repression of the late 1940s and early 1950s as previous party-led investigations were widely regarded as inadequate and self-limiting. The archival based findings, known as the Piller Report after the chair of the commission, were not published at the time, being one of the many victims of the Soviet-led invasion in August 1968.[33] However, the damning account appeared in English translation in 1971 and concluded that the mechanism for the purges consisted of three main elements: the political institutions, the state security service (Státní bezpečnost – StB) and the judiciary.

In the first category, determining roles were played by named individuals: most consistently party chairman and president of the republic Gottwald and prime minister Antonín Zápotocký, but also 'at times' Viliam Široký, Ladislav Kopřiva, Karol Bacílek, Alexej Čepička, Jaromír Dolanský, Antonín Novotný, Kopecký and other ministers and members of the KSČ political secretariat, the security commission and the party control commission. Gottwald 'usually' took the decision to arrest leading officials, he was informed of the course of interrogations and he 'intervened in the preparation of the big trials.' The indictment and length of sentence in all the main political trials were also approved by him and his closest colleagues. To this extent, 'he bears full and major responsibility for the trials.' The general significance of these political actors and institutions lay in their ability to issue specific directives and articulate ideological justifications for the repression, while at the same time extending their domination over the judiciary and, more ambivalently, the secret police.[34]

Underlying these personal responsibilities, according to the report, was the 'deformed political system', notably the monopoly of power of the communist party and the way its 'leading role' in political and social affairs was exercised. Hypertrophied centralisation and bureaucratisation meant that power became concentrated in ever fewer hands and any independent control over that power by parliament and the judiciary was eliminated. Moreover, 'in assuming governmental functions, the Communist Party usurped the sovereign status of the organs of State', permitting the party leaders to operate 'in defiance of the Constitution and to pave the way for illegality.' In turn, fiercely applied party discipline ensured 'unquestioning obedience' among subordinates, many of whom genuinely believed in the guilt of the accused and acted in good faith.[35]

The state security service – or to be more precise, those departments of the service devoted to preparing and staging the trials – played a pivotal role in the whole terror process, becoming in typically Stalinist fashion a virtual law unto itself. The falsification of written evidence, verbal and physical abuse of prisoners and the extortion of 'confessions', all of which were sanctioned by the political leadership, including successive ministers of the interior and national security, were routinely employed by notorious StB agents, such as Bohumil Doubek and Karel Košt'ál. From a broader perspective, it has been claimed that the secret police heavily influenced the political conception of the main trials and that leading communist functionaries themselves were at times fearful of the StB. Indeed, Kaplan has gone so far as to argue that the security service:

> acted as the driving force of the entire mechanism for the manufacture of political trials . . . [it] had become such a powerful political force that it was able to act even behind the back or even against the party leadership . . . most importantly, its actions determined the decisions of political institutions, [and] it pursued its own objectives or those of its Soviet colleagues in selecting future victims and preparing trials.[36]

The reference to 'Soviet colleagues' is noteworthy. Having been invited by Gottwald in September 1949, many Soviet agents worked in the Czechoslovak central and regional security administrations right through to the mid-1950s. As representatives of Moscow, they wielded enormous power and prestige; indeed, 'their advice and instructions had the weight of orders' and most Czech and Slovak officials, up to and including the minister of national security, accepted their prescriptions as correct.[37] What is more, the Soviet advisers, led by Alexei Beschasnov, introduced harsher forms of interrogation, recommended the composition of groups to be tried, intervened in the formulation of the indictments and, it appears, injected distinct anti-Semitic overtones in the preparation of the Slánský trial.[38] In a real sense, they were Stalin's eyes and ears in Prague.

The third component of the mechanism of state coercion was the judiciary. Although the Piller Report absolved the judicial profession as a whole from implication in the terror and suggested that it played a relatively minor part, the principal function of the relevant judicial organs was not inconsiderable: to legalise the trials and publicise the proceedings in line with party directives. As such, many judges, prosecutors and defence lawyers were unable or unwilling to maintain the independence of the courts and oversaw 'a system of administering justice behind closed doors', in effect condoning gross violations of the law bordering on arbitrary misrule. In the words of the report:

> The guilt of the judiciary in this respect lies primarily in allowing itself to be used as an executive arm of the political system and of Security, thereby lending its decisions a semblance of legality and professionalism . . . By its conduct during the trials, the judiciary delivered a crushing blow to the authority of the law and to public confidence in the administration of justice.[39]

Top officials in the ministry of justice, the supreme court and the prosecutor-general's office enthusiastically endorsed this politicisation of the judiciary and initiated key repressive legislation, including the infamous Act on the Protection of the People's Democratic Republic No. 231/48.[40]

In sum, the Piller Report concluded that 'an instrument of power had come into being, accountable to no one, beyond all control and outside the law; it had placed itself above society and usurped a power to which it had no right. Its very existence was unconstitutional.'[41] And it was this supreme 'instrument of power', founded on a firm alliance of monopolistic communist political hegemony and untrammelled secret police authority, which unleashed the mass repressions.

These campaigns took two main inter-related forms: socioeconomic and political. A crucial component of the former were the special 'actions' organised by the leading party authorities, supported by the ministries of the interior, defence and national security. 'Action B', lasting from May 1952 to July 1953, targeted 'anti-state elements' who were to be evicted from the major cities. Several thousand families were affected.[42] 'Action K' was aimed at resettling so-called *kulaks* (richer farmers), a total of 8,246 people being hit between November 1951 and summer 1953.[43] 'Action P' was directed at the Roman and Greek Catholic churches under the terms of which virtually all bishops and thousands of priests, monks and nuns, especially in Slovakia, were demoted, interned in assembly camps or placed under house arrest. People deemed of 'bourgeois' and 'petit-bourgeois origin', both urban and rural, were systematically harassed. For instance, plans were enacted in April 1950 to liquidate private craft businesses and by 1958 such firms had been cut from 247,404 to just 6,552. In the countryside, Soviet-style collectivisation of agriculture and accompanying 'elimination of the *kulaks*' were initiated in April 1949 and reportedly hit over one million farmers, drastically reducing the amount of farm-holdings above twenty hectares.[44]

Even industrial labourers, the social backbone of the system, were far from immune from persecution. Kaplan has argued that initially workers comprised approximately 30–40 per cent of prisoners in the labour camps.[45] At the same time, it must be emphasised that very large numbers of blue-collar employees experienced upward social mobility, being plucked off the shop-floor to become newly appointed managers and administrative officials. For communist leaders, the repression of 'class enemies' and promotion of working-class cadres represented a double-edged sword in the struggle for the socialist transformation of the country, and permitted the creation of a supportive stratum of 'beneficiaries of terror'.

Political persecution was endemic between 1948 and 1954. The first mini-wave of trials occurred in September and October 1948 and involved primarily young people accused of writing and distributing anti-state propaganda and leaflets. It is estimated that up to 1,800 were sentenced. Thereafter, other categories of society were earmarked for attack, affecting in some cases KSČ members: army officers and former participants in the anti-fascist resistance; officials of non-communist parties, notably national socialists and social democrats; so-called 'Trotskyites'; 'external enemies' connected in some way with western agencies and organisations; and economic officials, managers, and white-collar workers. Some of these mockeries of justice – the great 'show trials' of communist luminaries, non-communist politicians and Catholic bishops – had national, even international, significance, and were carefully staged performances designed to expose 'the enemy', intimidate the population and act as educative and propaganda tools. The prime example here was the trial of the 'anti-state conspiratorial centre', which will be discussed below. Other trials were secret in nature, generally having local and regional connotations. The victims were invariably non-communist citizens often charged under the notorious Act on the Protection of the People's Democratic Republic. It is estimated that between 40,000 to 45,000 people were sentenced in accordance with this law and the Penal Act of 1950.[46] It should be noted that at a regional and district level, local communist party officials composed 'security groups' which appear to have had a degree of autonomy from the 'centre' in deciding repressive policy.

Responses

The most infamous case of Stalinist terror in Czechoslovakia concerned the second-in-command of the communist system – Rudolf Slánský. A brief study, based largely on archival sources, of his show trial illustrates not only the stifling degree of centralised control exerted by the communist authorities, but also the multifarious responses and level of criticality exhibited by 'ordinary' citizens to the purges that rocked Czechoslovak political life.[47] From the end of the Second World War to September 1951, Slánský was general secretary of the KSČ and without doubt one of the most powerful figures in the country.[48] Reasons for his arrest, on Stalin's orders, in November 1951 are still obscure. According to the Soviet dictator, he had 'committed a number of errors in promoting and posting leading personnel' which had allowed 'conspirators and enemies' to go on the rampage in the party.[49] Beyond this, Stalin's broader geo-political concerns, Slánský's Jewish background and relative unpopularity in the KSČ, and inner-party elite rivalries all served to make the ex-general secretary a perfect scapegoat for the socioeconomic travails afflicting the communist regime.

Physically and mentally tortured for many months by Czech and Soviet secret police agents, Slánský eventually confessed to having acted as the head of a fictitious 'anti-state conspiratorial centre' composed of fourteen prominent party and state leaders, eleven of whom were 'of Jewish origin'.[50] The men were charged *inter alia* with high treason, espionage, sabotage, and economic and military subversion with the ultimate aim of tearing Czechoslovakia from the Soviet camp, undermining socialism and restoring capitalism. Amid tumultuous public fanfare, the falsely condemned were brought to trial on 20 November 1952 having diligently memorised predetermined scripts. After a week's ordeal, Slánský and ten others were sentenced to death and three received life imprisonments. All eleven were hung in the early hours of 3 December, their ashes unceremoniously scattered on an icy road near Prague.[51]

At one level, the Slánský trial and its reception exemplify all too clearly the centralised organisational grip and ideological manipulation of the top party leadership. After Slánský's arrest, Gottwald and a handful of his closest aides were informed in minute detail about the progress of the interrogations,[52] and in the weeks before the trial they decided the date of the proceedings, the composition of the court[53] and the sentences to be administered. The mass media covered the proceedings on a daily basis, newspapers were reportedly sold out immediately, and the public followed the trial on state radio (and, subversively, on foreign stations such as Radio Free Europe) with intense interest. Contrary to all legal norms, the guilt of the accused was pre-assumed. Between 20 November and 2 December 1952, 8,520 resolutions and telegrams flooded the Central Committee and the state court.[54] The wording and structure of these communications are formulaic, and stock phrases, though not always entirely identical, recur, suggesting orchestration from above.[55] In them, many thousands of factory workers, collective farmers, clerical and institute employees, teachers and even schoolchildren from all over the republic expressed their outrage and righteous indignation at the 'crimes' of the 'Slánský gang'. Some were accompanied by long lists of hand-written signatures. While a minority of the resolutions explicitly demanded the death penalty, the vast majority called for 'the strictest punishment' of the 'traitors', 'villains' and 'imperialist agents'. The 'masses', then, seemingly endorsed the party's version of the affair and positively welcomed the harsh sentences. Many other documents in the party and ministry of interior files attest to these strident popular moods.

However, a closer reading of the archival sources reveals a more variegated picture. Local party functionaries and secret police agents despatched daily reports to their superiors indicating that many citizens, including party members, adopted non-conformist and sceptical attitudes to the trial. For example, some, generally older, workers refused to accept that Slánský, a long-serving 'co-fighter' with Gottwald, was capable of betrayal, intimating that he was 'a lightning rod who is blamed for all mistakes and scarcities while the guilty lot stay clean'. A few brave souls doubted the charges brought against him and even one party official expressed surprise at Slánský's demise, regarding him as a 'model Bolshevik worker'. The conduct of the trial itself came in for scathing criticism among the more independent minded. For them, it was 'a show (*divadlo*) rehearsed in advance', 'a well-staged comedy', 'a filmed circus' and 'farce'. One citizen complained: 'you can't listen to such crap (*kraviny*).' It was commonly suggested that 'drugs', 'pills', 'injections', 'narcotics' and 'chemicals', even beatings, were responsible for the abject performances of the accused.[56] There were also rare expressions of outright opposition. Leaflets and posters appeared in some parts of the country bearing inscriptions such as 'Long Live the USA, Death to Communism', 'The Death of Stalin Means Death to Communists' and 'Shit on Gottwald'.[57]

Anti-Semitic outbursts were depressingly legion, ranging from unreflective knee-jerk stereotyping to quasi-Hitlerian vituperation. Several representative comments will suffice: 'we worked' while these 'Jewish pigs fleeced us of our money'; 'Jews always shirk honest labour and do well for themselves'; 'what else can you expect from Slánský, a Jew who's never known manual work and has always been affluent' – he should be sent to the Jáchymov uranium mines so at least once in his life he gets used to hard labour. Among the more violent diatribes are the following: 'All Jews should be shot'; 'Hitler shot lots of them [Jews], but still not enough'; 'I'd like to get my hands on this Slánský and tear him limb from limb' (*řezal řemínky od nohou až k hlavě*); these 'scoundrels' (*lumpy*) should be 'cut to pieces' (*z nich řezat kousky*); 'they should hang him [Slánský] immediately'; this 'stinking Jew' (*smradlavý žid*) should be 'cut into strips' (*řezat řemeny*).[58] These vicious sentiments confused and worried some party officials and even Gottwald felt constrained to offer publicly a distinction between ideologically sound 'anti-Zionism' and crass racist 'anti-Semitism'.[59]

Less common, but one suspects more disturbing to the party elite, were those voices which implicitly and explicitly criticised leading figures in the KSČ for their gullibility and lack of vigilance in the Slánský case. Even party members were not afraid to express their distrust of specific ministers and Central Committee dignitaries, up to and including Gottwald and Zápotocký, who were on occasion openly blamed for ignoring warning signals from below. How come these people are so divorced from rank-and-file complaints? Why are party 'comrades' isolated from the workers and never move among them – surely, 'this is not a communist attitude'? Why aren't leaders subject to rigorous 'cadre review' like everyone else? Shouldn't Gottwald carry out 'self-criticism'? Shouldn't there be a 'screening' (*prověrka*) of all responsible figures in party, state and economic life in order to guarantee that they have the appropriate 'class origins' to defend workers' interests?[60] Proletarians understood that the 'higher-ups' must have decent houses and other amenities if they are to represent the republic, but 'luxury and gross differences' should not be permitted.[61] Secret police agents reported that factory workers were apparently 'signing resolutions demanding the resignation of the entire government and the establishment of a new government composed of people whose past life is unambiguous and well known to the public'.[62] Likewise, regional party officials in Brno noted ominously that workers were calling on 'members of the CC [Central Committee] KSČ to give up their functions.'[63] A perspicacious Prague security agent stated the obvious: 'among some workers, even party members, faith in the government and the CC KSČ is shaken.'[64] It appears, then, that the Slánský trial was used by discontented and frustrated citizens to vent their anger against the communist regime per se, not just against the few designated 'enemies'.

What do these diverse popular responses tell us about the impact of terror in Czechoslovakia? As far as the KSČ is concerned, it seems that internal party discipline generally held firm, but, that said, the leadership could never blithely rely on strict Leninist dictate among the rank and file. Ordinary members, and not a few lower-level functionaries, aired views that were disquieting to the centre and were critical by name of top party and state bosses. The accountability and trustworthiness of the executive were cast into doubt, the reality of 'inner-party democracy' was impugned and the gap between 'us' and 'them' clearly identified. In the process, it is possible that the administrative competence and loyalty of some party-state cadres were undermined. In sum, these unintended consequences of the leadership's policy of repression hint at the muted limits of 'Stalinisation' at the base of the Czechoslovak party, even if we accept that the KSČ elites were growing increasingly accustomed to obeying Moscow's orders.

At a societal level, given the scale and range of the repression, there can be little doubt that many citizens lived in fear and were scarcely able to voice their opinions openly and publicly. Nevertheless, attitudes towards the Slánský trial, as we have seen, ranged from strident, sober and selective support to passive compliance and resigned accommodation, to apathy, doubt, guarded dissent and overt opposition. In the absence of hard statistics and regardless of the ostensible loud consensus behind the party line, it is impossible to assess the relative weights of these positions. However, the numerous signs of non-conformism, evident even among industrial workers, suggest that public backing for the trial and the government's version of it was exaggerated and that the communist authorities were never able to completely manipulate popular opinion and eliminate negative comment. We are palpably not dealing with a fully-fledged 'totalitarian' system capable of moulding public discourse at will. A minority was not afraid to speak critically, even if many others, enthusiastically or passively, played by the rules of the game. Not everyone, it appears, was intimidated by the terror.

Conclusion and aftermath

Elite purges and mass repressions in Stalinist Czechoslovakia were multifaceted processes with distinct, but closely inter-related, exogenous and indigenous origins and multiple politico-ideological and socioeconomic aims. Precisely because of this complex web of causes and effects, they cannot be interpreted as merely a product of 'evil' megalomaniac men bent on creating a 'totalitarian' order. Neither were they simply imposed by Moscow on a resistant party and society. Neither is there a single over-arching explanation for their emergence after the communist *coup* of February 1948. I have argued in this chapter that Stalinist terror in Czechoslovakia is best located in a framework which emphasises both longer- and shorter-term factors: the pre-war 'Stalinisation' of the KSČ and the creation of a mentality of ubiquitous 'enemies'; the traumatic experiences of the Munich 'betrayal', Nazi occupation, the Holocaust and, notably, post-war ethnic and class retributions, all of which went some way in tearing the fabric and cohesiveness of Czechoslovak society; and the sense of internal crisis and external pressure generated by the failings of the infant communist regime in an intense international atmosphere of breakdown between two hostile camps. The emerging Cold War imparted a clear, albeit grossly distorted, ideological imperative to the terror: the need to construct 'socialism' as rapidly as possible, a mission which was broadly supported and justified not only by Czech and Slovak communists, but also by many non-communist citizens. This required *inter alia* the removal of all class 'aliens' and 'enemies' who by definition were suspected of allying with the 'imperialist capitalist' west.

In addition to these 'objective' circumstances, the goals, ambitions, perceptions and misperceptions of concrete actors should never be ignored – individual agency is crucial. Stalin, Gottwald and other Czech and Soviet political and security bosses operated in an almost Byzantine network of personal rivalries and clandestine conflicts, and the elite purges are explained, in part at least, by these ultimately impenetrable intrigues and cabals. In the

'Slánský Affair', it appears that scapegoating for economic failures and personal enmities played a not inconsiderable role in identifying the ex-general secretary as the 'Czechoslovak Rajk'. In short, structural and contingent factors combined to produce a toxic form of lawlessness.

The legacy of Stalinist terror in Czechoslovakia was far-reaching and long-lasting. State-sponsored repression did not cease with the deaths of Stalin and Gottwald in March 1953. The final show trial was held as late as April 1954, when leading Slovak communists, including Gustáv Husák, were sentenced to lengthy terms of imprisonment for 'bourgeois nationalism'. Even Khrushchev's groundbreaking 'secret speech' in February 1956, in which he famously denounced aspects of Stalin's despotic rule and 'cult of personality', did not put a definitive end to the depredations. Certainly, under Gottwald's rather colourless successor, Novotný, a measure of liberalisation did occur: labour camps were closed down, grandiose show trials were eschewed, punishments were less severe, conditions in prisons improved and limited attempts at rehabilitation were undertaken. But persecution, harassment and arrests continued well into the 1960s, albeit at a reduced level, and peaked again during Husák's 'normalisation' after the crushing of the Prague Spring.[65]

However, the sheer longevity of repression was only a part of its historic significance. At a far deeper level, the political trials 'were a manifestation of inhumanity that shook socialism to its foundations both in Czechoslovakia and abroad. The effects were felt in all areas: economic, political and cultural, in the minds of the people, in relations between citizens and in the country's international standing.'[66] To take just two examples: in the economy, the ingrained notion that the hand of the largely fictitious 'enemy' lay behind all setbacks meant that the real causes of the malaise were often obscured, hence exacerbating rather than solving the problems. In political life, the numerous violations of the law and the constant search for the 'enemy within' bred mistrust and suspicion, engendered widespread feelings of fear and legal insecurity in the population, and undermined public faith in the constitution and politics in general. In many ways, then, the persecutions and purges of the period 1948–54 lay at the root of the social crises that culminated in the Prague Spring. But even the cataclysmic and painful re-evaluations of the past associated with Dubček's 'socialism with a human face' did not adequately fulfil the demands for rehabilitation and justice on the part of the unjustly condemned. Indeed, the wounds are still apparent to this day, an ugly and unwanted reminder of a dark past which implicated and tainted too many people.

Notes

1 Key works in English are J. Pelikán (ed.), *The Czechoslovak Political Trials, 1950–1954: The Suppressed Report of the Dubček Government's Commission of*

Inquiry, 1968 (London, 1971); H. G. Skilling, *Czechoslovakia's Interrupted Revolution* (Princeton, 1976), pp. 373–411; K. Kaplan, *Political Persecution in Czechoslovakia 1948–1972* (Cologne, 1983); R. K. Evanson, 'Political Repression in Czechoslovakia, 1948–1984', *Canadian Slavonic Papers*, vol. 28, no. 1 (1986), pp. 1–21; and M. Hauner, 'Crime and Punishment in Communist Czechoslovakia: The Case of General Heliodor Píka and his Prosecutor Karel Vaš', *Totalitarian Movements and Political Religions*, vol. 9, no. 2–3 (2008), pp. 335–54. Among the voluminous Czech historiography, see A. Kratochvil, *Žaluji*, vols 1–3 (Prague, 1990); F. Gebauer et al., *Soudní perzekuce politické povahy v Československu 1948–1989. Statistický přehled* (Prague, 1993); K. Kaplan, *Nekrvavá revoluce* (Prague, 1993); K. Kaplan, *K politickým procesům v Československu 1948–1954: Dokumentace komise ÚV KSČ pro rehabilitaci 1968* (Prague, 1994); K. Kaplan and P. Paleček, *Komunistický režim a politické procesy v Československu* (Prague, 2001); and J. Pernes and J. Foitzik (eds), *Politické procesy v Československu po roce 1945 a 'případ Slánský'* (Brno, 2005). There are several harrowing and poignant memoirs by surviving victims and close relatives of the purged: E. Loebl, *Sentenced and Tried: The Stalinist Purges in Czechoslovakia* (London, 1969); A. London, *On Trial* (London, 1970); T. Bouška and K. Pinerová, *Czechoslovak Political Prisoners: Life Stories of 5 Male and 5 Female Victims of Stalinism* (Prague, 2009); M. Šlingová, *Truth Will Prevail* (London, 1968); J. Slánská, *Report on My Husband* (London, 1969); and H. Margolius Kovaly, *Prague Farewell* (London, 1988). See also the insightful observations of I. Margolius, *Reflections of Prague: Journeys through the 20th Century* (Chichester, 2006).

2   The most recent text is B. F. Abrams, *The Struggle for the Soul of the Nation: Czech Culture and the Rise of Communism* (Lanham, 2004). The latest contribution by Czech and Slovak historians is Z. Kokošková et al. (eds), *Československo na rozhraní dvou epoch nesvobody* (Prague, 2005).

3   The Czech National Socialists bore no ideological relation to their German namesake, being a democratic centre-left party.

4   Kaplan, *Political Persecution*, pp. 7–11; and M. Myant, *Socialism and Democracy in Czechoslovakia, 1945–1948* (Cambridge, 1981), pp. 219–26. Emphasis on the repressive nature of the post-February regime is not meant to obscure the more 'progressive' and broadly popular reforms initiated by the communist government, such as a free health service and improved pensions.

5   For reasons of space I have concentrated on repression in the Czech lands. For details on Slovakia, see E. Steiner, *The Slovak Dilemma* (Cambridge, 1973), pp. 93–104; and S. Sikora, 'K reakcii slovenského obyvateľstva na politické procesy v 50. rokoch', in Pernes and Foitzik (eds), *Politické procesy*, pp. 171–8.

6   I have not been able to discover comprehensive figures on the number of Czech and Slovak women sentenced in the years 1948–54, but fragmentary evidence suggests that it may be as high as 10 per cent of the total. See P. Blažek, 'Politická represe v komunistickém Československu 1948–1989', in *Moc verzus občan. Úloha represie a politického násilia v komunizme* (Bratislava, 2005), p. 15. This percentage is corroborated by an unofficial and incomplete estimate from 1951 asserting that there were over 9,000 women labour camp inmates out of a total of 90,400. See M. Dowling, *Czechoslovakia* (London, 2002), pp. 90–1. If accurate, this figure is

twice as high as in the USSR during the Great Terror. See M. Ilič, 'The Forgotten Five per cent: Women, Political Repression and the Purges', in M. Ilič (ed.), *Stalin's Terror Revisited* (Basingstoke, 2006), pp. 116–39.

7 Kaplan and Paleček, *Komunistický režim*, p. 238.

8 Kaplan, *Political Persecution*, p. 24.

9 Statistics are taken from several Czech sources cited in Hauner, 'Crime and Punishment in Communist Czechoslovakia', pp. 343–4, notably Blažek, 'Politická represe v komunistickém Československu', pp. 8–22. See also Evanson, 'Political Repression', p. 4; and Gebauer et al., *Soudní perzekuce politické povahy v Československu*. According to the Rehabilitation Law No. 119 of 1990, in the entire period of communist rule in Czechoslovakia – 1948 to 1989 – 257,864 people were prosecuted for political 'crimes', although even this figure does not appear to cover all cases. See Kaplan and Paleček, *Komunistický režim*, p. 39.

10 The ex-judge is O. Ulč, *The Judge in a Communist State: A View from Within* (Columbus: Ohio, 1972), p. 131. All statistics are drawn from Pelikán (ed.), *The Czechoslovak Political Trials*, pp. 56–7; J. Foitzik, 'Souvislosti politických procesů ve střední a východní Evropě' and K. Kaplan, 'Politické procesy 50. let v Československu', both in Pernes and Foitzik (eds), *Politické procesy*, pp. 11, 13, 15–16, 109; K. Kaplan and J. Váchová (eds), *Zemřelí ve věznicích a tresty smrti, 1948–1956: Seznamy* (Prague, 1992) pp. 53–60 and non-paginated addendum; Hauner, 'Crime and Punishment in Communist Czechoslovakia', p. 344; and K. Bartošek, 'Central and Southeastern Europe', in S. Courtois et al. (eds), *The Black Book of Communism: Crimes, Terror, Repression* (Cambridge: MA, 1999), pp. 427–37. On the Horáková trial in May–June 1950, see K. Kaplan, *Největší politický proces: M. Horáková a spol.* (Brno, 1995); and P. Formánková and P. Koura, *Žádáme trest smrti! Propagandistická kampaň provázející proces s Miladou Horákovou a spol.* (Prague, 2008).

11 See M. Blaive, *Promarněná příležitost: Československo a rok 1956* (Prague, 2001), pp. 187–98. Also M. Blaive, 'The Czechs and their Communism, Past and Present', in D. Gard et al. (eds), *Inquiries into Past and Present* (Vienna, 2005), only available online and unpaginated.

12 For general histories of the Czechoslovak party, see J. Rupnik, *Histoire du Parti communiste tchécoslovaque: des origines à la prise du pouvoir* (Paris, 1981); and Z. Suda, *Zealots and Rebels: A History of the Ruling Communist Party of Czechoslovakia* (Stanford, 1980).

13 The latest work on the 'Stalinisation' process is N. LaPorte, K. Morgan and M. Worley (eds), *Bolshevism, Stalinism and the Comintern: Perspectives on Stalinization, 1917–53* (Basingstoke, 2008). See also K. McDermott and J. Agnew, *The Comintern: A History of International Communism from Lenin to Stalin* (Basingstoke, 1996), pp. 81–119.

14 K. Gottwald, *Spisy*, vol. 1 (Prague, 1951), p. 322.

15 J. Rupnik, 'The Roots of Czech Stalinism', in R. Samuel and G. Stedman Jones (eds), *Culture, Ideology and Politics: Essays for Eric Hobsbawm* (London, 1982), p. 306.

16 For a critique of this interpretation, see M. Blaive, 'Internationalism, Patriotism, Dictatorship and Democracy: The Czechoslovak Communist Party and the Exercise

of Power, 1945–1968', *Journal of European Integration History*, vol. 13, no. 2 (2007), pp. 55–68.

17   B. Abrams, 'The Politics of Retribution: The Trial of Jozef Tiso in the Czechoslovak Environment', in I. Deák, J. T. Gross and T. Judt (eds), *The Politics of Retribution in Europe: World War II and Its Aftermath* (Princeton, 2000), p. 252.

18   On the impact of the Nazi Protectorate, see C. Bryant, *Prague in Black: Nazi Rule and Czech Nationalism* (Cambridge: MA, 2007).

19   See R. Luža, *The Transfer of the Sudeten Germans: A Study of Czech-German Relations 1933–62* (New York, 1964); B. Frommer, *National Cleansing: Retribution against Nazi Collaborators in Postwar Czechoslovakia* (Cambridge, 2004); and E. Glassheim, 'The Mechanics of Ethnic Cleansing: The Expulsion of Germans from Czechoslovakia, 1945–1947', in P. Ther and A. Siljak (eds), *Redrawing Nations: Ethnic Cleansing in East-Central Europe, 1944–1948* (Lanham, 2001), pp. 197–219. It should be noted, however, that public criticism of the anti-German excesses and condemnation of so-called 'Czech Gestapoism' was expressed soon after the events. I am grateful to Dr Eva Hahn for bringing this to my attention.

20   Figures from Frommer, *National Cleansing*, p. 91.

21   Hauner, 'Crime and Punishment in Communist Czechoslovakia', p. 343.

22   On the evolution of Czech anti-Semitism, see H. J. Kieval, *Languages of Community: The Jewish Experience in the Czech Lands* (Berkeley, 2000); K. Čapková, *Češi, Němci, Židé? Národní identita Židů v Čechách 1918–1938* (Prague, 2005); and J. Rataj, 'Český antisemitismus v proměnách let 1918–1945', in J. Tomaszewski and J. Valenta (eds), *Židé v české a polské občanské společnosti* (Prague, 1999), pp. 45–64.

23   The figures are calculated from H. Krejčová, 'Český a slovenský antisemitismus 1945–1948', in K. Jech (ed.), *Stránkami soudobých dějin: Sborník statí k pětašedesátinám historika Karla Kaplana* (Prague, 1993), pp. 159 and 165.

24   Krejčová, 'Český a slovenský antisemitismus', pp. 164–71.

25   Č. Adamec, B. Pospíšil and M. Tesař, *What's Your Opinion? A Year's Survey of Public Opinion in Czechoslovakia* (Prague, 1947), p. 23.

26   Cited in K. Kaplan and P. Kosatík, *Gottwaldovi muži* (Prague, 2004), p. 236. See also J. Pávová, *Demagog ve službách strany. Portrét komunistického politika a ideologa Václava Kopeckého* (Prague, 2008).

27   For Stalin's direct interventions in the Rajk affair, see M. Mevius, *Agents of Moscow: The Hungarian Communist Party and the Origins of Socialist Patriotism 1941–1953* (Oxford, 2005), pp. 244 and 249.

28   For informed speculation on inner-party factional in-fighting, organisational clashes and power struggles, see P. Tigrid, 'Marx na Hradčanech (Pokus o pohled na československou otázku deset let po únoru)', *Svědectví*, vol. 2 (1958–59), pp. 325–33. For evidence of personal rivalries in the Slánský case, see the documents from the Soviet foreign ministry archive reproduced in G. P. Murashko, 'Delo Slanskogo', *Voprosy istorii*, no. 3 (1997), pp. 3–20 and no. 4 (1997), pp. 3–18.

29   For indications that some communist party members linked Slánský to material shortages and price rises, see the National Archive of the Czech Republic (NA), Archive of the Central Committee of the KSČ (AÚV KSČ), f. 100/24, sv. 108, a.j. 1401–1402, ll. 77–8.

30 Most notorious of the labour camps was the Jáchymov uranium mine complex in north-western Bohemia, which became a living hell for thousands of politically persecuted citizens.

31 For extracts from a report, dated 14 May 1952, for the Organisational Secretariat of the KSČ entitled 'On Making Full Use of Important Trials in Public Educational Campaigns', see K. Kaplan, *Report on the Murder of the General Secretary* (London, 1990), p. v.

32 Dušan Hamšík cited in A. Oxley, A. Pravda and A. Ritchie (eds), *Czechoslovakia: The Party and the People* (London, 1973), p. 88.

33 For a judicious assessment of the Piller Report, see Skilling, *Czechoslovakia's Interrupted Revolution*, pp. 397–404.

34 Pelikán (ed.), *The Czechoslovak Political Trials*, pp. 130–2, 249–54 and 260–77, quotations at pp. 131 and 261.

35 Pelikán (ed.), *The Czechoslovak Political Trials*, pp. 246–8, quotations at p. 246.

36 Kaplan, *Political Persecution*, pp. 16–17. For more details, see K. Kaplan, *Nebezpečná bezpečnost: Státní bezpečnost 1948–1956* (Brno, 1999), especially pp. 167–98.

37 Pelikán (ed.), *The Czechoslovak Political Trials*, p. 136.

38 Kaplan, *Political Persecution*, p. 17; and Kaplan, *Nebezpečná bezpečnost*, pp. 25–33.

39 Pelikán (ed.), *The Czechoslovak Political Trials*, pp. 137–40 and 256.

40 Kaplan, *Political Persecution*, pp. 17–18.

41 Pelikán (ed.), *The Czechoslovak Political Trials*, p. 131.

42 For details, see K. Kaplan and J. Váchová (eds), *Akce B – vystěhování 'státně nespolehlivých osob' z Prahy, Bratislavy a dalších měst, 1952–1953* (Prague, 1992), pp. 5–7, 121 and 176.

43 For details, see K. Jech (ed.), *Vystěhování selských rodin v Akci K ('kulaci') 1951–1953: Seznamy a vybranné dokumenty* (Prague, 1992), pp. 6–7 and 105.

44 Kaplan, *Political Persecution*, pp. 11–15. On the persecution of the Catholic church and other religious orders, see K. Kaplan, *Stát a církev v Československu v letech 1948–1953* (Brno, 1993); and Sikora, 'K reakcii slovenského obyvateľstva', pp. 171–8.

45 Kaplan, *Political Persecution*, pp. 15–16.

46 This paragraph is based on Kaplan, *Political Persecution*, pp. 16 and 19–23.

47 For a more detailed analysis of public responses, see K. McDermott, 'A "Polyphony of Voices"? Czech Popular Opinion and the Slánský Affair', *Slavic Review*, vol. 67, no. 4 (2008), pp. 840–65; and V. Brabec, 'Vztah KSČ a veřejnosti k politickým procesům na počátku padesátých let', *Revue dějin socialismu*, no. 3 (1969), pp. 363–87.

48 It is estimated that before his demise Slánský shared culpability for the imposition of 139 death penalties. See I. Lukes, 'The Rudolf Slánský Affair: New Evidence', *Slavic Review*, vol. 58, no. 1 (1999), p. 164, n. 32; and I. Lukes, 'The Birth of a Police State: The Czechoslovak Ministry of the Interior, 1945–48', *Intelligence and National Security*, vol. 11, no. 1 (1996), pp. 78–88.

49 Cited from Stalin's letter to Gottwald, 24 July 1951 in NA, f. komise 1, sv. 2, a.j. 13, ll. 6–7.

50 Aside from Slánský, the other members of the 'Centre' were Vladimír Clementis, Otto Fischl, Josef Frank, Ludvík Frejka, Bedřich Geminder, Vavro Hajdů, Evžen

Löbl, Artur London, Rudolf Margolius, Bedřich Reicin, André Simone (Otto Katz), Otto Šling and Karel Šváb. Hajdů, Löbl and London were given life sentences, but were later released and eventually rehabilitated.

51   On the complex and unsavoury origins and outcomes of the case, see Tigrid, 'Marx na Hradčanech', pp. 330–9; Pelikán (ed.), *The Czechoslovak Political Trials*; Kaplan, *Report on the Murder of the General Secretary*; Lukes, 'The Rudolf Slánský Affair', pp. 160–87; and I. Lukes, *Rudolf Slansky: His Trials and Trial*, Cold War International History Project, Working Paper No. 50 (Washington D. C., 2006).

52   See, for example, NA, f. 100/24, sv. 108, a.j. 1404 (unpaginated).

53   See NA, f. 02/5, sv. 44, a.j. 128, ll. 3–4; and f. 02/5, sv. 87, a.j. 289, l. 1.

54   This figure is given in NA, f. 014/2, sv. 9, a.j. 71, l. 2.

55   See NA, f. nezpracovaný fond and f. rezoluce Slánský, nezpracovaná část fondu.

56   These comments are located in NA, f. 05/1, sv. 416, a.j. 2460, l. 2; f. 014/12, sv. 8, a.j. 64, l. 7; f. 014/12, sv. 8, a.j. 61, ll. 8–9; f. 01, sv. 18, a.j. 29(3), ll. 272–3; and the Archive of the Ministry of Interior (AMV), f. 310–114–6; f. 310–114–7; f. 310–114–9; f. 310–114–11; f. 310–114–13 and f. 310–114–16 (unpaginated).

57   NA, f. 014/12, sv. 10, a.j. 103, l. 2; f. 014/12, sv. 10, a.j. 104, l. 2; AMV, f. 310–114–16.

58   AMV, f. 310–114–6; f. 310–114–7; f. 310–114–9; f. 310–114–11; f. 310–114–12; f. 310–114–13; f. 310–114–16; NA, f. 014/12, sv. 8, a.j. 61, l. 21. See also NA, f. 19/13, a.j. 122 (2), l. 127.

59   For confusion among party functionaries, see NA, f. 014/12, sv. 8, a.j. 64, l. 3; f. 19/13, a.j. 122 (2), l. 118; and AMV, f. 310–111–3, l. 9. For Gottwald's distinction, see NA, f. 12, jedn. 59, l. 57.

60   NA, f. 014/12, sv. 8, a.j. 61, ll. 8, 19, 24; f. 014/12, sv. 8, a.j. 64, ll. 3, 6; f. 014/2, sv. 9, a.j. 71, ll. 4, 12–13; AMV, f. 310–114–6.

61   NA, f. 014/2, sv. 9, a.j. 71, l. 4.

62   AMV, f. 310–114–6.

63   NA, f. 19/13, a.j. 122 (2), l. 127.

64   AMV, f. 310–114–6.

65   See J. Cuhra, 'In the Shadow of Liberalization: Repressions in Czechoslovakia in the 1960s', *Cahiers du Monde russe*, vol. 47, nos 1–2 (2006), pp. 409–26; Evanson, 'Political Repression', pp. 11–21; and Kaplan, *Political Persecution*, pp. 25–40.

66   Pelikán (ed.), *The Czechoslovak Political Trials*, p. 140.

Stalinist terror in Hungary, 1945–1956

László Borhi

In Hungary, as elsewhere in the emergent Soviet bloc, state repression served two main purposes. [It was designed, firstly, to liquidate political enemies and the remnants of the old elite; and secondly, to intimidate society as a whole.] In addition, the USSR directly carried out reprisals in Hungary. This paper is structured accordingly and seeks to analyse the roots and processes of state-sponsored terror. My aim is to reconstruct the unfolding terror as it gradually engulfed not only the population, but also the Hungarian Communist Party (HCP – from 1948 known as the Hungarian Workers' Party) and even the 'arm of terror' itself – the secret police (*Államvédelmi Hatóság* – ÁVH, the State Defence Authority). Although Hungary's post-war history should not be seen solely through the lens of political violence, repression was a fundamental element, no less than in Stalin's Soviet Union. It (de)formed the country's politics, society and economy. Reprisals took several forms: mass deportations, show trials and wide-scale persecution, including the loss of freedom and human rights. Terror reflected the country's domestic and international position and was a powerful political tool in the creation of a proletarian dictatorship in Hungary. Mass repression was the cement of the Stalinist political system, which exercised power in a hostile social environment. As communist ideologist József Révai explained succinctly in March 1949: 'the main function of the dictatorship of the proletariat will be the use of terror against external and domestic enemies'.[1] Coercion and violence, together with the drastic policy of circular social mobility[2] and Soviet occupation, were the pillars of communist power. Although terror was justified as a tool in the construction of a classless society, ideology – the Stalinist dogma of constantly intensifying class struggle – often went hand in glove with mundane political aims.

The repressive nature of the regime appeared in two fundamental features: the denial of liberty – which I understand in Friedrich Hayek's definition of freedom from coercion – and terror applied against society. Even in the so-called coalition era between 1945 and 1947, legislation was introduced allowing the communist party to eliminate political opponents by both legal means and police methods. This was made possible by the communist sway over the judicial system, including the courts of law. After the communist seizure of power the legal system functioned as the protector of the regime. Although officially the former ruling classes were the designated enemy of the proletarian dictatorship and were targeted by vicious propaganda campaigns, all social classes and groups were affected by the policy of reprisals irrespective of age, gender, religious or political persuasion. Even survivors of Nazi camps were not exempt. Neither did high position in the power structure guarantee immunity from persecution. For example, deputy head of the political police, Ernő Szűcs, was beaten to death by his own henchmen, and László Rajk, a former minister of interior and chief architect of state terror, was minister of foreign affairs and a member of the Politburo at the time of his arrest. Close relatives of show-trial victims were often repressed.

The definition of crime had already been lowered to an absurd threshold in the coalition era. In August 1947, a man was interned for telling a joke about party leader Mátyás Rákosi.[3] Decree 8800/1946 penalised activities violating the compulsory delivery of agricultural produce. 'Hoarding' a few croissants was enough for prison. The aim was to eliminate the better off *kulak* peasantry and to curb consumption under conditions of food shortage generated by forced industrialisation. Charges usually included several or all of the following: conspiracy, sabotage, high treason, spying on behalf of imperialist intelligence agencies, Trotskyism and economic crimes, such as embezzlement or currency violations. Self-incriminating confessions of the defendants, extracted by intimidation and torture, were sufficient proof of guilt. After 1948, one could be convicted of a crime one was *expected* to commit. For example, a military tribunal tried a certain István Szabó because his adopted son was charged with espionage. The judge acknowledged that Szabó had no knowledge of his son's alleged crime, but nevertheless stated that he was 'dangerous to society because his close relative was in the service of the treasonous Titoist gangs and therefore Szabó himself can be used for subversion against our people's democracy.'[4] Compulsory vigilance required people to report crimes about to be committed, even if the 'expected' malefactor was a family member. Non-compliance could lead to imprisonment. Perpetrators of political crimes disappeared and their fate was not disclosed even to next of kin. In certain categories of crime, such as illegal crossing of the border during military service, relatives were automatically punished and if the authorities determined a 'class alien' to be a menace to society their relatives could even be arrested.

The institutional and legal framework of terror

The political police

Party leader Rákosi defined proletarian dictatorship as 'rule based on coercion unconstrained by law'.[5] The revolutionary arm of terror – the political division of the police – was established in February 1945 with the mission of hunting down war criminals, but it mainly served to eliminate whoever the communist party designated as its political enemy. By 1947, out of 1,348 members, 1,338 were communists. Initially there were two branches led by rival communists, but soon Gábor Péter gained the upper hand and in 1946 amalgamated his rival's organisation into his own. Péter's body (ÁVO) was taken out of police jurisdiction and in 1948 subordinated directly to the Interior Ministry (ÁVH). In 1949 Péter's ambitions paid off and the ÁVH became an independent entity directly under the council of ministers and overseen by the interior minister.[6] In practice, only Rákosi held any sway over Péter, whose organisation of terror was effectively out of control. Its mission was the protection of the regime and the unmasking of enemies, and its administrative structure was built accordingly.[7] Soon Péter's fiefdom engulfed the counter-intelligence department of the defence ministry and in its heyday in 1951 the ÁVH had 8,145 employees. Two years later it was merged with the interior ministry, which now had thirteen out of twenty-five departments dealing with state security, and it employed 7,501 people in addition to 40,201 working for the police. After 1953, the ministry of interior functioned as the ministry of state security until 1988.[8] The ÁVH itself was disbanded on 28 October 1956 during the abortive revolution.

The political police kept a close watch on society and deployed an armada of spies. In 1953 over 83,000 people reported to it in a variety of arrangements: as informers and their handlers or as 'social contacts' with no formal tie to the authorities. In the same year, 1,149,659 people were kept under observation (in a population of 9.5 million). During the domestic thaw of 1953, 666,728 records were 'erased' because they were compiled 'unlawfully'. On the other hand, the ÁVH's 'observation potential' increased by 44 per cent in 1954. This was put to good use, such as counting and identifying people visiting western diplomatic missions. State censors opened almost 30,000 letters, and in 1955 close to 43,000 reports were filed on recorded phone conversations.[9] In 1955, some 70,000 people worked for the interior ministry, including the border guard.[10]

The 'enemy' was also numerous and variously defined. It included 'Zionists and Hungarian bourgeois nationalists' and the 'remnants of capitalists, *kulaks* and cosmopolitans'. In addition, 'lingering bourgeois ideas also nourished hostile elements.' According to Révai, 'reaction' was more powerful in Hungary than in the Soviet Union because the majority of the intelligentsia was bourgeois.[11] The enemy seemed to be everywhere: in the upper and lower echelons of the party, ministries, factories, mines, even Hungarian–Soviet companies. Révai argued that 'political consolidation and the intensification of class struggle' were 'not contradictory conditions.' On a higher level of development, class struggle would 'inevitably' become more intense.[12] Terror was applied 'democratically': it cut through all social classes and groups from the capital to the tiniest village, not even sparing strata that were supposed to provide the regime's social base of support.

In numerical terms, the figures are startling. Between 1946 and 1956, 43,000 people were sentenced for political crimes and, according to official findings, 500 were executed.[13] Between 1950 and 1953, courts dealt with 650,000 people and passed 387,000 sentences.[14] The tide of persecution between 1951 and 1953 was probably closely linked to Stalin's prediction that world war would break out in 1953,[15] coupled with internally generated ideological zeal.[16] According to contemporary Soviet data, 362,000 people stood trial in 1951 alone and some 500,000 'administrative' (police) procedures took place.[17] An amnesty in 1953 involved a staggering 748,000 people; 40,000 were released from prison, internment camps and forced relocation,[18] although many victims of show trials, particularly those involving alleged conspiracies, espionage and sabotage, remained behind bars until some were released in the summer of 1956. Despite massive persecutions in 1953, a leading functionary claimed that there were still half a million hostile elements.[19] After the Soviets installed the reformist communist, Imre Nagy, in 1953, measures to restore 'socialist legality' were introduced. The term still revealed the intent to use police coercion to protect the system, but the number of arrests diminished much to the chagrin of the state security apparatus. In 1955, minister of interior László Piros bemoaned the fact that 'the spirit of class struggle' had 'slackened', particularly in the war against the *kulaks*. Thus, after Nagy's removal in late 1956 arrests went up by 40–42 per cent.[20]

Repressive laws

Even these high figures for political offences may not represent the true scope of repression because in order to persecute 'class aliens' the communist system penalised a vast number of activities that would not be illegal in a democracy. From 1946, legislation appropriate for the persecution of political and social enemies was passed. Act 1946/VII on the protection of the republic threatened capital punishment for those initiating or leading a movement or conspiracy against the state. But death sentences were passed merely for 'standing ready' to overthrow the regime and the act outlawed even discussion of changing the regime. Another law – also dating from 1946 – on criminal offences threatening public supply penalised violations of compulsory deliveries from the peasantry. Yet another decree allowed capital punishment for the violation of currency regulations. In the 1950s 'hoarding' a few dollars or loaves of bread carried prison sentences. A decree passed in 1949 threatened verbal criticism of the collective farm system with punishment of up to ten years imprisonment. Decree 26 of 1950 targeted individuals who planned or attempted to flee abroad during military service, and their relatives would also be punished with five to ten years imprisonment.[21] Other decrees promulgated in 1950 made violations of the economic order and the 'social ownership' of property punishable by death.[22] Until 1953 court martial was used for the rapid implementation of death sentences in certain categories of crime. After 1948 military tribunals deliberated in excess of 6,000 cases annually, over four times as many as in the coalition years.[23]

In 1945, legal provisions were made to introduce forced labour as a form of punishment. The aim was to reduce the 'danger' prisoners posed to society by getting them 'accustomed to productive work' in the approximately 100 labour and internment camps and sub-camps. After 1951, their numbers were increased drastically to satisfy the needs of Hungary's militarised economy. Prisoners performing forced labour peaked at 28,000 in 1953, but then decreased under the 'New Course' initiated by Nagy. From 1952, forced labour was coordinated by an inter-agency organ called the Public Works' Directorate.[24] In 1945, a system of internment had been introduced for people 'suspicious or dangerous' to public order and safety, or to 'the democratic reconstruction' of Hungary in cases where courts of law were not competent. Internment was made without due legal procedure. The ÁVH exercised judicial functions: it was entitled to make arrests without authorisation, was in charge of detaining and guarding the inmates and was responsible for making them work. There were four main internment camps in 1950 where inmates from a variety of social strata performed hard physical labour under inhuman conditions. They were sent there without trial for a maximum of 24 months (but the sentences were extended indefinitely). For György Gábori, conditions in the infamous labour camp of Recsk, where some 1,600 prisoners of all backgrounds were held, compared unfavourably to German concentration camps.[25] György Steiner remembered: 'There was no hope of liberation. In Buchenwald we were kept alive by the desire for the war to end. Here . . . there was no hope.'[26] After 1948, internment was a means of eliminating undesirable elements.[27] Internment camps were disbanded in 1953, but only about half of their inmates were released. The others were tried and re-sentenced. 'Enemy elements' could still be relocated and placed under police supervision.

Literally, nobody was safe from persecution, but ultimately terror targeted well-defined social groups. Between 1951 and 1954, 13,670 members of the former 'exploiting classes' (including children and old people) were evicted from their Budapest homes to the countryside to perform forced labour. Some of them were sent to the internment camp in Hortobágy; others were put up in barns and even pigsties. Their immoveable property was confiscated and given to party, police or army cadres. An estimated 10,000 villagers, including children, were also evicted to the camp system of Hortobágy where approximately 300 people died.[28] Hence, political enemies were segregated from the rest of society and many disappeared without trace. Families of the victims (even of high level functionaries) were not told about their execution or incarceration for years. The father of a defendant in the air force trials inquired about his son two years later, because the family did not know what he had done or what had happened to him.[29]

Mass repression of non-communists

Deportations and sabotage trials

The Soviet occupation of Hungary led to massive reprisals – the wide-scale rape of women and the looting of private and national wealth, but most of all the deportation of very large numbers of people. Moscow considered Hungarians collectively responsible for the war against the USSR. This and the policy that envisioned the Soviet Union's reconstruction via the use of slave labour motivated mass deportations. Deportations particularly targeted ethnic Germans. Close to 33,000 were taken from Hungary in an operation lasting from 25 December 1944 to 31 January 1945. Only 29,101 returned.[30] From Hungary's wartime territory, an estimated 600,000 to 700,000 people were deported to the camps of the Soviet Main Administration of POWS and Internees (GUPVI), of whom 150,000 to 200,000 may not have returned. In addition, in 1947 Soviet military tribunals sent an estimated 20,000 Hungarians to the Gulag. These trials were formalities and the detainees had no opportunity to defend themselves or appeal against their verdict. Most did not commit any crime and were removed because they were deemed to pose a risk to the communist seizure of power. Many of the captives, as many as 200,000, were civilians, including women and children. They were rounded up randomly to fill pre-determined quotas. Between 15–20 per cent died either in one of the transit camps or on the way to their destinations. Brutal treatment, malnourish-ment, inhuman work conditions and disease took a huge toll on the prisoners.[31]

In 1945 and 1946, several bilateral treaties were signed that effectively made Hungary a Soviet military and economic space. In May 1946, Rákosi declared that a 'dictatorship of the proletariat' would be constructed irrespective of internal and external circumstances. The wartime Grand Alliance was dead and the Soviets regarded Eastern Europe as a bulwark against Anglo-American 'imperialism'. Pressure on the political right was stepped up. In late 1946, Hungarian military intelligence 'revealed' a right-wing plot against the republic linked to the most popular party, the Smallholders' Party. Altogether 229 people were tried in seven trials for conspiracy. Two death penalties were passed and thirteen people received prison sentences longer than five years. On 1 January 1947, Rákosi disclosed that the conspiracy was of 'tremendous significance' for the struggle against the Smallholders' Party. Thus, the indictment had to be drafted accordingly and the Politburo resolved that the trials had to be properly prepared. The presiding judge and the prosecutor received political guidance from interior minister Rajk, political police chief Péter and indirectly from Rákosi.[32] In February 1947, the Soviet authorities arrested Béla Kovács, general secretary of the Smallholders' Party, for his alleged part in the conspiracy and on 31 May Prime Minister Ferenc Nagy was forced to resign for the same reason.

The construction of a communist police state could now proceed essentially unhindered by foreign or domestic constraint. Show trials were aimed at 'beheading' civil society and were linked to external, internal and economic policy goals. They were held before selected audiences with wide and hostile media coverage serving well-defined propaganda purposes. Their scripts were written in advance, which the protagonists – political and ecclesiastical dignitaries, experts, managers and party functionaries – rehearsed and then recited in court. Top party leaders often prepared the verdicts before the proceedings began. Some trials, like that of Cardinal József Mindszenty, the head of the Roman Catholic church in Hungary, were compiled from elements of truth to arrive at wholly fictitious charges. Others, such as the Rajk trial, were entirely fabricated by the political leadership working together with the secret police and Soviet 'experts'. These trials would have been inconceivable if the judiciary had been independent of the executive branch of power, itself first dominated, later monopolised, by the communist party. But this was not the case. The accused were not entitled to defend themselves in any meaningful sense of the word. A large number of political trials involved ordinary citizens designated as 'enemies of the state'. The major show trials were accompanied by a number of 'satellite' ones. Those held behind closed doors were meant to generate 'mythic fear', but there were so many trials that it would have been impossible to focus popular attention on all of them.[33] Moreover, too many open political trials could have had the effect of weakening the regime by causing public outrage.

Sabotage trials began in 1948. The USSR was building an economic empire in Hungary while western companies were being squeezed politically and economically. Hungarian-American Oil (MAORT), a subsidiary of Standard Oil New Jersey, had concessions for the largest petroleum field in Hungary and was delivering for Soviet reparations. MAORT complained about forced over-production, which was destroying the oil field. The communist-led Supreme Economic Council agreed and recommended a 10 per cent reduction. Still, in mid-1948 Hungary's communist leadership, which was eager to seize MAORT's oil concession, 'discovered' that production levels were lowered because of US political and economic interests and that experimental rigs were deliberately misplaced where there was no hope of finding oil. These charges were made even though the company's communist organisation had claimed that there was no sign of sabotage. Documentary evidence reveals that investigations served to create a legal basis for the company's nationalisation. The trial also served propaganda purposes: a 'white book' was published on the misdeeds of the Hungarian defendants and their American superiors, and the latter were expelled after making forced confessions. Their Hungarian colleagues admitted to the crimes and declared that they were motivated by pro-American sentiments. Chief geologist, Simon Papp, confessed to his crimes in order to avoid further torture; his death sentence was later commuted to life in prison, where he was forced to work for the government. Three others received four to ten years. The propaganda message was that experts of the old regime could not be trusted.[34]

Nationalisation and 'unmasking American imperialism' may have motivated another Soviet-type 'bourgeois sabotage trial': the proceedings against Standard Rt, a subsidiary of International Standard Electric Company (ISEC). On 8 May 1949, the Hungarian government and Standard Budapest reached an agreement whereby as a special favour the government would guarantee the company's economic viability and profits in return for which Hungary would be supplied with the necessary licenses to produce modern telecommunication and aviation equipment. When Washington refused to ratify the deal, Standard's management and the vice president negotiating on behalf of ISEC, Robert Vogeler, were arrested. Vogeler confessed to spying, gathering information on Hungarian oil, gas and uranium deposits, recruiting nuclear physicists, sabotaging exports to the USSR and smuggling Romanian officials into Austria on behalf of US military intelligence. The defendants represented diverse 'hostile' segments of society – the aristocracy, the Jewish and German bourgeoisie, the clergy, 'national communists' and representatives of British and American imperialism.[35] Their 'confessions' were drafted by their interrogators and they were promised release after the trial, which Rákosi orchestrated, including the amount of time allocated to each defendant. The judge and the prosecutor were hand-picked. The proceedings 'demonstrated' the US leadership's involvement and 'proved' all foreign companies and cultural institutions, like the British Council, were covert intelligence centres. War hysteria was whipped up by revealing that the Standard 'spy ring' helped prepare a bombing map of Hungary. Standard's managing director, Imre Geiger, was sentenced to death for treason and sabotage, just like the government negotiator, Zoltán Radó, a member of the communist party who was branded a Trotskyist. Five people, including Vogeler and the Briton Edgar Sanders, were sent to jail. A further seventeen people were sentenced in satellite trials. As a result Hungary's links with the Anglo-Americans were all but severed.

The frantic pace of heavy industrialisation and military build-up required the diversion of funds from the agricultural sector. Brutal policies of collectivisation were introduced and surplus agricultural produce was confiscated leading to extreme food shortages, even famine, in the countryside of a state that had been supplying Europe with food for centuries. It is small wonder that popular ire would turn against the embodiments of the system, 'delivery inspectors', in the liberating days of the 1956 revolution. Harsh measures were introduced to curb consumption because of the severe shortage of wheat – exported to fund industrialisation – and to persecute the class enemy. The following typical cases illustrate the ratio between 'crime' and punishment: a peasant, Ferenc Reisz, received two years in jail and a fine of 1,000 forints (a good monthly salary) for buying seven kilos of bread and sixty-five croissants; and Károly Csorba went to prison because he 'possessed 150 kilos of wheat', but in his 'greed' still bought bread besides hiding twenty kilos of lard in his garden.[36] Peasants, portrayed as avaricious hoarders responsible for the food misery, functioned as scapegoats on whom the regime shifted blame, similar to the coalition period when communist propaganda attributed the economic malaise to 'black marketers' and 'speculators' (meaning Jews).

In December 1949, interior minister János Kádár announced the beginning of the 'class struggle' against the *kulaks*: if they 'make a move', the 'proletarian fist' had to strike. Proletarian dictatorship had been realised in the city, Kádár claimed, and it was now the countryside's turn.[37] The regime identified *kulaks* as the main enemy on the basis of collective guilt and sought to destroy them as a social class in the belief that the upper echelon of the peasantry was the most ardent opponent of socialist transformation. The party leadership formed action groups of the political police that toured rural areas beating 'rich' peasants. *Kulaks* were punished, even if they were innocent, in order to break the backbone of the traditional social hierarchy of the village. The severity of punitive action often exceeded party directives and efforts to rein in 'excesses' by threats of military tribunal failed. Even the Soviet ambassador, Evgenii Kiselev, protested against the atrocities, claiming that because of police brutality *kulaks* fled to the forest.[38] In sum, the agricultural division of the ÁVH constructed a system of near total control over rural production and its employees.[39]

Reprisals against the Catholic church

In 1948 the communist authorities moved against the Catholic church. Archbishop Mindszenty refused to sign an agreement with the state on behalf of the church and had already opposed the nationalisation of ecclesiastical schools. Although clergymen had been victims of show trials in the coalition period and the church's power had been gravely impaired, the showdown between the strongest religious denomination and the dictatorship reached a climax in the legal proceedings against Mindszenty. In January 1948 Rákosi declared war on 'reactionaries hiding behind the cloak of the church.'[40] Initially, he was loath to try the Cardinal and the regime attempted to rid itself of Mindszenty by finding a political solution for his removal. But after efforts to displace Mindszenty had failed, he was taken into custody on 26 December 1948 following the political police's discovery of a 'secret archive' in the Cardinal's palace at Esztergom. Charges included conspiracy, spying and currency speculation. Mindszenty's interrogation focused on his discussions with Otto Habsburg, which allegedly broached the restoration of the Habsburg dynasty. Rákosi, who was unhappy with the results of the interrogation, set the main focus of the investigations himself. The trial had to show that the Cardinal conspired to launch a world war, his 'fascist stance' being 'revealed' by the accusation that he wanted to re-enact anti-Semitic legislation. Although the Cardinal had indeed negotiated with both Habsburg and an American ecclesiastic, the 'concept' woven from this factual basis was fiction.

In his carefully staged trial Mindszenty denied conspiracy, but confessed to guilt 'in general'. It is clear that his political ideas were not liberal, but even the restoration of the Habsburg dynasty would have been far more democratic than the political course that ensued in Hungary over the next forty years. On 8 February 1949 Mindszenty was sentenced to life in prison for treason, conspiracy and currency crimes. The prosecutor appealed for the death penalty, but on 28 July the court upheld the original sentence. Six other defendants received long prison sentences. There is strong evidence to suggest that the Cardinal was beaten during his interrogation and at the time it was suggested that his meek behaviour in court was induced by the administration of psychotic drugs, but evidence does not corroborate this. It is more likely that he was broken by months of abuse.

The Mindszenty trial ushered in a period of intense reprisals against the Catholic church until an agreement on state–church relations was signed on 30 August 1950. In that year all but a few of the monastic orders and their schools were disbanded, and several hundred priests were interned. In April 1951 the party leadership decided on a showdown with the remaining monastic orders by 'proving' that they were planning to restore the *ancien régime* with the assistance of 'clerical reaction', were spying, speculating with currency and living in moral turpitude. Bishop József Grősz, the informal head of the Hungarian Catholic hierarchy in Mindszenty's absence, was picked as the protagonist of a new show trial. Grősz was arrested on 18 May 1951 on the basis of a damning report by the political police. Five separate investigations were 'amalgamated' into one concept, according to which Grősz was planning to overthrow the government with US military intervention at the price of a new world war. The alleged conspirators were to provide armed assistance to the Americans. In all, 200 people were tried and seventeen were executed in the main and satellite trials. It should be noted that there were numerous other conspiracy trials in which the accused were charged with similar offences. One defendant in the Grősz trial was arraigned for murdering thirty Soviet soldiers, but not a single body was found. Instead, the trial rested mostly on the self-incriminating confessions of the defendants who were led to believe that they would be set free if they cooperated with the authorities. The accused were in a desperate mood, some allowing themselves to believe that their only friend and hope was the merciless and sadistic leader of the political police, Péter. As in other trials the confessions were rehearsed, but faithful recital of their lines did not help the defendants. What is more, other members of the high clergy were 'implicated' in the trial. They made written pledges to 'rectify their mistakes' and took an oath of fidelity to the constitution of the People's Republic.[41]

Repression of social democrats

Ever since 1946 Rákosi had aimed to liquidate the social democratic party by merging it with the HCP. In 1948 the plan reached the phase of realisation. On 16 February 1948, fourteen defendants were tried, the main ones *in absentia*, for conspiring to overthrow the republic with American assistance. The trial was directed against the emblematic right-wing social democrats, Károly Peyer and Ágoston Valentiny, who had opposed the merger, although the latter was arrested only in 1950. Family members who had failed to report the alleged crimes to the authorities were also sentenced. A few days after the trial, the would-be defendants in the Nitrokémia affair – one of the largest military plants in central Europe – were arrested and accused of treason, fraud and sabotage. This trial targeted social democratic state secretaries and repeated the old Stalinist charge that social democracy was allied with fascism, and was an association of 'political criminals', 'fascists' and 'Horthyite reactionaries.' Right-wing social democrats had joined forces with Horthyites and national socialists to 'undermine Hungarian democracy.'[42] In this mixture of bourgeois sabotage and political show trial, the plant's managing director was sentenced to death and six others received from eight years to life in prison.

The main onslaught against social democracy came after the Rajk trial in the autumn of 1949. It appears that Rákosi saw the trial as a prelude to finishing off those social democrats who had helped him to power.[43] In February 1950, he signalled that an offensive against social democrats and trade unionists was in the offing. In June he told the Soviet ambassador, Kiselev, that 500 social democrats needed to be arrested and 'concentration camps . . . organised for them. It doesn't matter whether they are right or left wingers, they are all police informers.'[44] Thus, terror caught up with fellow travellers who had helped construct the communist state. A few days later Rákosi informed Stalin that Árpád Szakasits and György Marosán, the two social democrats most loyal to the communists, had been arrested. There is no evidence that the new round of trials originated in Moscow. The arrests coincided with the detention of army officers and initially there were plans for merging the social democratic and military trials. Eventually one such trial was held, in which social democratic officers were accused of conspiracy. Two defendants were executed and one received life imprisonment.

In accordance with party instructions, former social democratic leaders were charged with having worked for 'Horthy's police', of being British agents, conspiring to overthrow the 'democratic order' and currency crimes. The party's former general secretary, Szakasits, and eight others were tried in November 1950. Charges included war crimes, espionage on behalf of British services – Szakasits was accused of having been recruited by the Special Operations Executive in 1939, which was true – conspiracy, violation of currency regulations, embezzlement and sabotage. Rákosi wanted the death penalty for Marosán (he planned to pardon him), but his verdict (later commuted to life) was mistakenly read out to Szakasits. Six more people were condemned and Szakasits's wife spent four years in jail without an indictment. His son-in-law spent three years on death row until his sentence was changed to life, and his daughter and five grandchildren were evicted from their homes. He and his associates were eventually released in mid-1956. Despite all this Szakasits remained 'an unwavering warrior of socialism' and Marosán vowed he would 'wage a life-long struggle against' social democracy. However, another defendant, Sándor Szalai, revealed the dictatorship's brutality: 'I was in Nazi hands and went through many things, but I can say that this coercion belongs to the maximum I experienced.'[45] Former minister of justice István Ries was taken into custody in July 1950. His brutal treatment led to his death. His interrogator hit and spat at him in fury, because he urinated in his trousers.[46] Altogether 431 social democratic functionaries and industrial workers were tried in twelve group and nine individual trials in 1950 and 1952.[47] It should be noted, however, that no social democratic leaders were actually executed.

Espionage and conspiracy cases

In the officially generated war hysteria of the early 1950s, the political police investigated 924 cases of espionage. In 1954 alone they arrested seventy-one 'spies', 209 'conspirators', fifty-one industrial and agricultural 'saboteurs' and fourteen people for 'terrorist acts'.[48] In July 1956, Rákosi claimed that each month the ÁVH 'uncovered an average of two counter-revolutionary underground conspiracies.'[49] In a characteristic case, István Dudás was asked by his brother, an agent of the US Counter Intelligence Corps, to organise a group of partisans to support the Americans in the event of war. He was told that the Americans would supply arms when the time came. As Dudás never received the instruction to launch the conspiracy he took no action. He and his brother were executed nonetheless.[50] Many others, who believed the USA would unleash a war to liberate Eastern Europe, made similar preparations to help overthrow the regime, disseminated anti-communist leaflets or even undertook sabotage action.[51] The largest conspiracy was probably that of the 'White Guard' under János Kővári with an alleged 348 members, of whom 86 were sentenced. The conspirators' sociological makeup was varied. One of the largest cases, Győző Flossmann's 'Underground Front', included working-class, petit-bourgeois and bourgeois members as defined by contemporary terminology. Gedeon Ráth's plot was comprised of 'Horthyite officers and *kulaks*' and several defendants in Kálmán Horváth's group were 'poor peasants'. Thus, all social categories were represented.[52] In light of what we know about the Truman and Eisenhower administrations' strategy to subvert communist regimes, defendants' accounts of US plots to organise armed resistance groups were not far-fetched, but even these trials were partly fabricated and interrogators were told what kind of confessions to extract from the detainees. In mid-1956 these and other cases were reviewed and it was determined that many of the charges were either unfounded or blown out of proportion because, although the defendants had made plans, they took little or no action at all. Some of them were released or their sentences were lowered.

Repression of communists

The Rajk trial

The proceedings known as the Rajk trial, which took place in Budapest from 6 to 24 September 1949, came closest to the classic Soviet archetype. Moreover, it made Budapest the regional centre of east European trials. Many classical enemies were lined up: imperialists, as well as their foreign and domestic agents, social democrats, army officers, Trotskyists and 'cosmopolitans'. The concept tying all these together was complex and required the assistance of Soviet experts. Scholars differ about the origins of the trial.[53] One historian has argued that Moscow used the Rajk affair to counter the anti-Soviet allegations of the simultaneous Alger Hiss trial in the USA.[54] The Kremlin may have signalled its desire for a large show trial in 1948, but records suggest that the Hungarian regime itself was preparing for a trial to unmask domestic enemies. As Rákosi put it on 5 March 1949: 'class aliens and conscious agents of the class enemy' remain in the party; hence, communists had to 'guard vigilantly over the purity of [their] ranks.'[55] But it seems that the 'concept' did not unfold as investigations 'revealed' new elements of a conspiracy, but the other way round. Confessions were tailored so as to underpin an already existing scenario.

It is also an open question why former interior minister Rajk, a diehard Stalinist who, personal rivalries notwithstanding, helped construct the communist police state, emerged as the main defendant. Defence minister Mihály Farkas ascribed it to a 'provocation' by Rákosi and Lavrentii Beria, Stalin's secret police boss,[56] but evidence suggests that Rajk's rivals, Péter and

Farkas himself, came up with the idea. Beside political considerations, personal rivalries and hatred also played a role in the selection of the 141 defendants of the main and satellite trials. The plot of the trial kept changing: from Trotskyism and 'cosmopolitanism' to the defendants being informers of Horthy's police until the final anti-Yugoslav focus. This definitive version was the work of the Soviet security 'advisers', who, tying all the threads together, claimed that Rajk and his associates had been spies of the American Office of Strategic Services (OSS) and had conspired with Yugoslav intelligence to remove Hungary from the Soviet bloc.

Initially, members of the so-called 'Swiss group' – communist Jewish intellectuals who spent the war in Switzerland – were arrested on the basis of the confession of an American communist, Noel Field, who had formerly spied for the Soviet Union and had been running a Unitarian relief agency in Switzerland during the war. The Hungarian political police, with Soviet approval, kidnapped Field in Prague aided by Czechoslovak colleagues. Field's confession led to the arrest of Tibor Szőnyi, head of the communist party's cadre division, who 'admitted' to having worked for a leading Republican politician, Allen Dulles. Szőnyi then implicated Rajk, but it is uncertain whether at Rákosi's, Farkas's or Soviet instigation. Another kidnap victim, a former communist police agent, made Rajk out to be a police informer, who later became Szőnyi's higher contact to Dulles. At this point, the 'investigation' got bogged down and was handed over to Soviet secret police general Fedor Belkin and his associates. It was they who gave final shape to the concept of the trial. Belkin consulted with Rákosi, who kept his finger on every detail. From this point, Péter and his colleagues merely carried out their instructions. The episode demonstrated, crucially, that Hungarian sovereignty was lost to the Soviet Union. Rákosi drafted the indictment and took it to Moscow where he and Stalin pored over every word. It was then handed to the designated judges who were told not to alter a single letter. The verdicts were predetermined: Rajk, Szőnyi and another defendant were condemned to death, two others were given life sentences, and one received nine years. Rajk was executed on 16 October 1949.

The Rajk trial was in fact a series of trials. The defendants of the related cases included archetypal communist enemies who had wormed their way into the ranks of the party to serve domestic and foreign enemies. György Pálffy-Österreicher had been in charge of the military secret service and he and his associates represented the army. High-ranking officers of the political police were also purged, probably because they were Rajk's appointees. Social democrats and Yugoslav 'agents of imperialism' were also represented. All the defendants were tortured, which included brutal beatings (some were bludgeoned to death), sleep deprivation, drinking from the toilet bowl and even eating excrement, before the Soviet interrogators switched to more subtle methods. An American observer of the trial noted that Rajk spoke as if he was reciting. Indeed, the trial was rehearsed and every word spoken by the participants was written in advance. A microphone was even wired to Rákosi's study so that he could intervene in case events took an undesirable turn. Farkas and Rákosi determined the verdicts prior to the trials. Rákosi claimed that Farkas wanted every defendant put to death, but he spared some of them for political reasons and also because he needed their testimony for the reprisals against 'Titoists' and social democrats outlined above.[57] But the victims confessed to the most absurd crimes not only because they were tortured or their families threatened. They martyred themselves because they believed that their confessions would aid the communist movement. Rajk hailed Stalin and Rákosi even with the rope literally around his neck.

Further enemies were also unmasked within the communist party in the form of an 'anti-party group' headed by minister of interior Kádár. Rákosi, and possibly Farkas, were behind the investigations launched against Kádár in November 1950, which were based on Szakasits's confession alleging that Kádár had treasonously 'liquidated' the communist party in 1943 as an agent of Horthy's police. This broadened into investigations against an alleged Kádár-led 'anti-Semitic, anti-Soviet, nationalist anti-party group' made up *inter alia* of foreign minister Gyula Kállai, state secretary of culture Géza Losonczy, Ferenc Donáth and interior minister Sándor Zöld. In April 1952, Zöld was relieved of his post for failing to purge the police of 'hostile elements.' Fearing arrest and clearly unhinged, he killed his family and then committed suicide. Kádár and his associates were arrested immediately afterwards to 'avert a similar incident.' At this stage, Rákosi was going beyond even Stalin's tolerance limits, the Soviet boss vetoing Rákosi's plan to arrest Farkas and Péter.[58] Kádár, an alleged agent recruited by Rajk, confessed to subverting the party as a hostile agent and spying for imperialist services. He was sentenced to life imprisonment in December 1952 for conspiracy to overthrow the people's democracy, espionage and treason. Eventually it was determined that Kádár had 'liquidated' the party on behalf of British intelligence.[59] Péter later claimed that he had saved Kádár's life, because he did not believe some of the absurd charges.[60] Nevertheless, one defendant, Sándor Haraszti, was sentenced to death, others received fifteen years, while defendants of a simultaneous 'anti-party' trial got eight to twelve years. The sentences were overturned in 1954 and Kádár went on to lead the HWP for over thirty years from 1956.

Military trials

Stalin purged his army before World War Two and his self-proclaimed 'best disciple', Rákosi, did the same when east and west were preparing for World War Three. What is more, he did so without being told by Moscow. Purges in the Hungarian army had begun already in the coalition period. One military official was sentenced to death in 1947 as part of the communist struggle for power.[61] But the main attacks were launched after the communist takeover. A series of trials between 1948 and 1950 targeted resistance groups in contact with an émigré military organisation, the MHBK (Comradely Community of Hungarian Fighters). In 1948, staff colonel Pál Hadváry and a civilian were executed for passing secret information to the MHBK in a case that involved an officer of military intelligence. They and several others were tried by the People's Court so that they would be sentenced to death. Further investigations led to mass arrests. In February 1949, fifteen people were handed over to a Soviet military tribunal, which sentenced them to twenty-five years forced labour while thirty-five were tried in Hungary later that year, five military officers being executed. In January 1951 two officers who had previously served in Horthy's army were executed in a medical doctors' 'plot' of food poisoning, which, according to their show trial, was a conscious act of sabotage and a conspiracy to overthrow democracy when the 'international situation was becoming acute.' Separate trials were held for officers who had returned from Soviet captivity: five defendants of a trial involving twenty-five people were executed for conspiracy in 1950.[62] These trials were part of cleansing the army of the old guard, as a result of which 81 per cent of the officer corps was made up of new recruits by 1951.

Indeed, purging the 'old guard' became an obsession: a party functionary told the Soviet ambassador that local Soviet companies employed too many of them, and hence the Hungarians wanted to remove these 'unreliable' and 'hostile' elements and warned Kiselev to pay more attention to hiring reliable people.[63] In September 1952, the Soviet consul in Győr learned that Budapest was preparing something 'similar to the Tukhachevskii trial' on the grounds that the Hungarian general staff and high command was 'contaminated' with 'hostile elements and spies.' It was implied that the trial would be linked to right-wing social democrats and 'clerical reactionaries', who formed the basis of an 'anti-government' conspiracy which had just been revealed in Budapest.[64]

Earlier, in a sequel to the Rajk-Pálffy affair, sixty-six people, thirty-five of them officers and generals, had been arrested and fourteen sentenced to death.[65] On 19 August 1950 six generals, including the chief of staff of the army, László Sólyom, and a colonel were hung and buried in an unmarked grave. He and other defendants had served in the country's meagre anti-German resistance and were arrested for this activity in 1944. Defence minister Farkas, who thought that there were still too many well-trained but politically unreliable members of the officer corps, took credit for unmasking the enemy in the military. In his fabricated confession, Sólyom 'confessed' to having promoted fascists. He was also accused of heading a conspiracy to take control of the army. Rákosi insisted on adding that Sólyom and his associates had worked for the British intelligence service. Eventually charges also included conspiracy, sabotage, treason and in some cases war crimes. The absurdity of the accusations is revealed by the fact that two generals were accused of espionage for France because they had organised riding lessons for the French military attaché in 1946. Confessions were extracted by physical and psychological torture. One victim was threatened that his pregnant spouse would be beaten until she miscarried if he failed to confess.

Political reliability also eclipsed professional competence in the air force, where thirteen people, including deputy commander Lajos Tóth and several pilots, were arrested in May 1951 for spying, sabotage and hostile activity. As Farkas put it in chastising the commander of the air force, colonel András Zalka, a Soviet citizen: 'when he stands up for them [the defendants] he doesn't realise that he is supporting enemies of the people'. It is likely that the regime did not wish to train the untrusted old guard in the use of new Soviet jet fighters. Technical-bureaucratic problems relating to the introduction of the new Soviet training aircraft were thus distorted into accusations of conscious sabotage.[66] Tóth was found guilty and executed.

Repression of the political police

As in Stalinist Russia, reprisals reached the political police itself. Péter's former deputy, Szűcs, and several high-ranking ÁVH officials in his entourage were taken into custody in October 1950. Szűcs had been deeply involved in the proceedings against Rajk, Sólyom and the social democrats. He was accused of being a Trotskyist and a British spy. At Rákosi's instructions, a professional ÁVH torturing squad beat him and his brother to death, perhaps intentionally.[67] The causes of his removal are still a matter of conjecture: his knowledge of the party leadership's involvement in the Rajk trial, evidence of which Rákosi tried to cover up; a possible conflict with Soviet security officials; perhaps the fact that he was collecting compromising material on top party leaders and sending them to Moscow. Whatever, Szűcs was involved in the ÁVH's operation of selling passports to 'bourgeois' elements where he may have collided with Péter's interests. Thirteen people went to trial in the Szűcs case, two of whom were sentenced to death and executed.[68]

A second wave of arrests in the political police was connected to the preparation of a Soviet-inspired Zionist show trial. The roots of the anti-Zionist campaign reach back to 1950 when a Soviet adviser, Kartashov, called his superiors' attention to the malevolent influence of Jews in Hungary. It is noteworthy that initially the Rajk trial had an anti-Zionist focus. Later, in the wake of anti-Semitic reprisals in Moscow, the Kremlin designated Zionism as the primary enemy in Eastern Europe.[69] Preparations for a grand trial began and Hungarian authorities worked out several scenarios based on the Slánský trial, which indicated that Zionist agents, who had worked for the Gestapo, had infiltrated the highest circles of Hungarian politics, economy and state security and spied for the Americans. Zionist engineers were sabotaging production and Zionist doctors were preparing to murder political leaders. Some eighty to ninety Jews and non-Jews were arrested, including the head of the National Office of Israelites.[70] On 3 January 1951, Péter himself was arrested as a Zionist agent and former police informer and in February Rákosi announced a campaign against Jewish 'cosmopolitanism'.

As before, Rákosi instructed the political police about the direction investigations should take, but interior minister Ernő Gerő and Farkas also helped to formulate the conceptual framework. Gerő was put in charge of the anti-Zionist proceedings. Péter (whose wife was also arrested and interrogated) was accused of having subverted his agency from the outset by attracting American-Yugoslav spies into its ranks. Curiously, the charge of moral turpitude used against 'clerical reactionaries' reappeared. A particularly strange accusation surfaced against Jewish leaders: collaboration with the Germans as members of the Jewish council thereby assisting the murder of 'little Jews'. Absurd confessions, such as a Zionist seizure of power and plans to establish a rabbinical centre of espionage in Hungary, were extracted with sadistic torture. Two lines took shape: the doctors' plot and collaboration with the Gestapo. Shortly after Stalin's death the Zionist line was dropped, several people were released and ÁVH leaders were charged – not fictitiously – with embezzling state funds. Péter and seventeen associates were sent to prison for crimes against the people, abuse of power and economic crimes.[71]

The function of terror in a Stalinist society, according to George Schöpflin, was 'to enforce compliance, to destroy all pre-existing values . . . and make it easier for new revolutionary values to take root.'[72] But Hungarian terror exceeded even what the Soviets thought reasonable. Ambassador Kiselev maintained that the regime's persecution of intellectuals was alienating even those who would otherwise cooperate.[73] In late 1952, shortly before Stalin's death, he argued that far too many cases of subversion and other crimes were based on unfounded accusations and recommended the 'restoration of socialist legality.'[74] When the top leadership was summoned to Moscow in June 1953, Beria called the Hungarian reign of terror 'inadmissible and intolerable.'[75] In 1953, state terror was relaxed for a while, although the Stalinists did their best to sabotage Nagy's rather limited efforts and its machinery remained intact.[76] Until the rule of law was restored as a result of the transition in 1989–90, the political leadership retained unconstrained power and was free to resort to terror. However, after the wave of reprisals between 1956 and 1962, which cost 229 lives, the Kádár regime chose to diminish the role of terror in its exercise of power.

Notes

1 Cited by T. Zinner, 'Az egyik gyújtózsinór a Rajk-Brankov ügyhöz (is)', in I. Okváth (ed.), *Katonai perek 1945–1958* (Budapest, 2001), p. 246.
2 G. Gyáni, 'A forradalom társadalomtörténeti paradoxonjai', in G. Gyáni and J. M. Rainer, *Ezerkilencszázötvenhat az újabb történeti irodalomban* (Budapest, 2007), pp. 87–104.
3 State Security Historical Archive (ÁBTL), III/c, V-78019. Memorandum by Ferenc Münnich.
4 'Szabó István és társai', ÁBTL, 10–51048–952, V-93057.
5 M. Rákosi, *Visszaemlékezések 1940–1956*, vol. 2, edited by I. Feitl et al., (Budapest, 1997), p. 756.
6 M. Kiss, 'Péter Gábor Államvédelmi Hatósága', in I. Ötvös (ed.), *Variációk – Ünnepi tanulmányok M. Kiss Sándor tiszteletére* (Piliscsaba, 2004), pp. 135–41; G. Kiszely, *ÁVH – egy terrorszervezet története* (Budapest, 2000), pp. 13–35.
7 For the ÁVH's structure, see B. Boreczky, 'Az Államvédelmi Hatóság szervezete, 1950–1953', in G. Gyarmati (ed.), *A Történeti Hivatal Évkönyve 1999* (Budapest, 1999), pp. 91–111.
8 E. Kajári, 'Bevezető a Belügyminisztérium Kollégiuma 1953–1956 közötti iratainak tanulmányozásához', in G. Gyarmati and K. S. Varga (eds), *A Belügyminisztérium Kollégiumának ülései 1953–1956*, vol. 1 (Budapest, 2001), pp. 24–7.
9 E. Kajári, 'Az egységesített BM államvédelmi tevékenysége, 1953–1956', in G. Gyarmati (ed.) *Államvédelem a Rákosi korszakban: tanulmányok és dokumentumok a politikai rendőrség második világháború utáni tevékenységéről* (Budapest, 2000), pp. 165–78.
10 Report to the Political Committee of the Hungarian Workers' Party, 6 December 1955, Hungarian National Archive (MOL), 276 f., 53 cs., 260 ő.e.
11 'Révai feljegyzése Rákosinak', MOL, 276 f., 65 cs., 16 ő.e.
12 'Elméleti feladataink és a pártoktatás. Révai József és Andics Erzsébet hozzászólása', 1948. MOL, 276 f., 53 cs., 10 ő.e.
13 According to an older estimate 5,000 were executed. See I. Fehérváry, *Börtönvilág Magyarországon* (Budapest, 1978), p. 44.
14 Kajári, 'Bevezető', p. 23.
15 Rákosi, *Visszaemlékezések*, pp. 914–16.
16 Rákosi was planning to 'liquidate' *kulaks* as a social class during the Second Five-Year Plan. See 'Feljegyzés Rákosival folytatott megbeszélésről', 10 May 1953, in M. Baráth (ed.), *Szovjet nagyköveti iratok Magyarországról 1953–1956 – Kiszeljov és Andropov jelentései* (Budapest, 2002), p. 53.
17 'Soprovoditelnoe pismo Kiseleva Vyshinskomu', 25 December 1952, in T. V. Volokitina et al. (eds) *Vostochnaia Evropa v dokumentakh rossiskikh arkhivov, 1944–1953 gg., tom II 1949–1953* (Moscow, 1998), pp. 853–4.
18 Figures cited in J. M. Rainer, 'Állami erőszak és ellenállás Magyarországon 1956 előtt', in Gyáni and Rainer, *Ezerkilencszázötvenhat*, pp. 106–13.
19 'Zapis besedy s Biro', 3 February 1953, in Volokitina et al. (eds), *Vostochnaia Evropa*, pp. 866–71.
20 Kajári, 'Bevezető', pp. 38–42.

21   F. Kahler, 'Gondolatok koncepciós perekről', in Ötvös (ed.), *Variációk*, pp. 248–50.

22   J. Lőrincz, 'A Sztálini büntetőpolitika és konzekvenciái a hazai büntető igazságszolgáltatásban', in *1956 szilánkjai* (Budapest, 2007), pp. 96–7.

23   S. Szakács and T. Zinner, A háború 'megváltozott természete' – Adatok, és adalékok, tények és össszefüggések, 1944–1948 (Budapest, 1997), pp. 199–203.

24   G. T. Varga, 'Adalékok a börtönügy és rabmunkáltatás történetéhez', in G. Gyarmati (ed.), *A Történeti Hivatal évkönyve 2000–2001* (Budapest, 2001), pp. 159–75.

25   G. Gabori, *When Evils Were Most Free* (Ottawa, 1981).

26   For the quote and interviews with former inmates and guards of the camp, see G. Böszörményi (ed.), *Recsk, 1950–1953 – egy titkos kényszermunkatábor története* (Budapest, 2005), p. 502.

27   For an account of an internment camp, see G. Faludy, *My Happy Days in Hell* (New York, 1962).

28   Zs. W. Balassa et al. (eds), *Hortobágyi Kényszermunkatáborok 1950–1953* (Budapest, n.d.), p. 30.

29   'Beadvány Rákosinak', MOL, 276 f., 65 cs., 82 ő.e.

30   E. M. Varga and V. I. Korotajev, 'Bevezető', in E. M. Varga (ed.), *Magyar hadifoglyok a Szovjetunióban* (Moscow and Budapest, 2006), p. 31.

31   T. Stark, *Magyar foglyok a Szovjetunióban* (Budapest, 2006), pp. 19–217. A recent study based on Soviet documents estimates the number of Hungarians in Soviet camps at 500–520,000, of whom 70,000 did not return. This does not include those who died in transit, the number of whom cannot be estimated and neither can the number of deported civilians. Varga and Korotajev, 'Bevezető', pp. 30–1. For testimonies of Gulag survivors, see S. Sára (ed.), *Nehézsorsúak – magyarok szovjet rabszolgaságban* (Veszprém, 2006).

32   Kiszely, *ÁVH*, pp. 56–9.

33   Kahler, 'Gondolatok a koncepciós perekről', pp. 243–59.

34   Kiszely, *ÁVH*, pp. 83–90; L. Borhi, *Hungary in the Cold War, 1945–1956: Between the United States and the Soviet Union* (Budapest-New York, 2004); and K. Katona, 'A MAORT története a fordulat éveiben Magyarországon', in Gyarmati (ed.), *A Történeti Hivatal Évkönyve 2000–2001*, pp. 137–58.

35   I. Pál, 'A Vogeler-ügy', in T. Frank (ed.), *Gyarmatokból impérium* (Budapest, 2007), pp. 217–35.

36   'Feljegyzés a BM beszolgáltatási csoportnak', 22 January 1953. MOL, XIX-A-1-2-ee, dob. 198, dos. 39.

37   E. Kajári, 'A Hajdúnánási "kulák-ügy" 1951-ben', in Gyarmati (ed.), *A Történeti Hivatal Évkönyve 1999*, pp. 209–28.

38   'Zapis besedy s ministrom inostrannikh del', 28 August 1951, in Volokitina et al. (eds), *Vostochnaia Evropa*, pp. 600–1.

39   Kajári, 'A Hajdúnánási "kulák-ügy" 1951-ben', pp. 209–28.

40   Details on the Mindszenty affair are taken from M. Balogh, *Mindszenty József 1892–1975* (Budapest, 2002), pp. 190–255.

41   M. Balogh and Cs. Szabó, *A Grősz-per* (Budapest, 2002), pp. 5–60.

42   Szakács and Zinner, *A háború 'megváltozott természete'*, p. 367; Zs. Kádár, 'A magyarországi szociáldemokrata perek története', *Múltunk*, no. 2 (1996), pp. 3–48.

'abolzhskogo o protsesse nad Raikom', September 1949, in
'Vostochnaia Evropa, pp. 231–4.
.nim o khode peregovorov s episkopim sovetom', 2 June 1950,
.et al. (eds), Vostochnaia Evropa, pp. 371–2.
, A magyarországi szociáldemokrata perek', pp. 3–48.
See Kiszely, ÁVH, p. 235.

47 See Kádár, 'A magyaországi szociáldemokrata perek', pp. 3–48.
48 Kajári, 'Az egységesített BM', pp. 169–70.
49 'Rákosi feljegyzése a PB-nek', 13 July 1956. MOL, 276 f., 65 cs., 26 ő.e.
50 'Dudás István és társai', ÁBTL, 1951, 10–5575–51, V-81337–2.
51 In 1951, Sándor Gyimesi's Anti-Bolshevik Guard allegedly blew up a railroad section and attacked a police post. ÁBTL, 10–50517/951, V-103/408/1.
52 Győző Flossmann and associates, ÁBTL, 10–5096, ÁBTL, 10–732301; Gedeon Ráth and associates, ÁBTL, 37–5-79/1952, V-112524; Kálmán Horváth and associates, ÁBTL, VI/1a, V-111790.
53 See G. Hódos, Tettesek és áldozatok – Koncepciós perek Magyarországon és Közép-Kelet-Európában (Budapest, 2005); T. Hajdu, 'A Rajk-per háttere és fázisai', Társadalmi Szemle, no. 11 (1992), pp. 17–36; and Kiszely, ÁVH, pp. 151–214; Zinner, 'Az egyik gyújtózsinór a Rajk-Brankov', pp. 241–350.
54 M. Schmidt, Battle of Wits: Beliefs, Ideologies and Secret Agents in the 20th Century (Budapest, 2007).
55 Rákosi, Visszaemlékezések, p. 899.
56 See Kiszely, ÁVH, pp. 172–3.
57 'Dokladnye zapiski Zabolzhskogo', pp. 231–4.
58 Rákosi, Visszaemlékezések, p. 899.
59 T. Huszár, Kádár János politikai életrajza 1912–1956, vol. 1 (Budapest, 2001), pp. 158–95; Kiszely, ÁVH, pp. 258–71.
60 See Kiszely, ÁVH, pp. 271–2.
61 Szakács and Zinner, A háború 'megváltozott természete', pp. 323–6.
62 I. Zsitnyányi, '"A hazáért mindhalálig" – a magyar tisztikar ellen irányuló perek', in Okváth (ed.), Katonai perek, pp. 173–97.
63 'Zapis besedy s Kovachem', 16 June 1951, in Volokitina et al. (eds), Vostochnaia Evropa, pp. 567–70.
64 'Soobshchenie konsula SSSR v Dere Indiushkina Vyshinskomu', 9 September 1952, in Volokitina et al. (eds), Vostochnaia Evropa, p. 809. Marshal Tukhachevskii was a high-ranking Soviet general executed in May 1937 following a secret trial in Moscow.
65 The information in this paragraph is from A. Oroszi, 'A Sólyom-per', in Okváth (ed.), Katonai perek, pp. 141–62.
66 G. Markó, 'Koncepciós perek a légierő tisztjei ellen', in Okváth (ed.), Katonai perek, pp. 163–72.
67 See V. Farkas, Nincs mentség – az ÁVH ezredese voltam (Budapest, 1990), p. 646.
68 Kiszely, ÁVH, pp. 215–35 and 277.
69 T. V. Volokitina et al. (eds), Moskva i Vostochnaia Evropa: Stanovlenie politicheskikh rezhimov sovetskogo tipa (Moscow, 2002), pp. 547 and 552.

70   M. Schmidt, '"Ez lesz a perek pere" – adalékok egy torzóban maradt tisztogatási
     akcióhoz', in M. Schmidt, *Diktatúrák ördögszekéren* (Budapest, 1998), pp. 271–84.
71   Kiszely, *ÁVH*, pp. 286–315.
72   G. Schöpflin, *Politics in Eastern Europe, 1945–1992* (Oxford, 1993), p. 101.
73   'Zapis besedy s ministrom inostrannikh del', 28 August 1951, in Volokitina et al.
     (eds), *Vostochnaia Evropa*, pp. 600–1.
74   'Soprovoditelnoe pismo Kiseleva', pp. 853–4.
75   Cited in G. T. Varga (ed.), 'Jegyzőkönyv a szovjet és magyar párt- és állami vezetők
     tárgyalásairól', *Múltunk*, no. 3 (2002), pp. 234–69.
76   See M. Baráth, 'Gerő Ernő a Belügyminisztérium élén', in Gyarmati (ed.), *Évkönyv
     1999*, pp. 147–66.

Political purges and mass repression in Romania, 1948–1955*

Dennis Deletant

This chapter will assess the extent to which the Romanian Communist Party (RCP) used mass repression as a tool to eliminate opponents in the drive to consolidate power, thereby reducing Romania to subservience to the Soviet Union.[1] It will describe the coercive measures taken by the RCP to transform Romania, following the Soviet model and employing Stalinist norms and practices. The latter offered an especial blueprint for the removal, not only of members of the democratic opposition, but also, in 1952, of alleged 'deviationists' in the party itself. Although repressive measures were taken by communists against their opponents in the post-August 1944 governments, it was only in 1948 that the first steps towards the legalisation of repression were taken; 1955 is significant because many political prisoners were amnestied in the autumn of that year as a sign that Romania was prepared to comply with the human rights provisions that membership of the United Nations required, albeit most of these same prisoners were re-arrested in 1957 as part of a new crackdown in the wake of the Hungarian uprising.

Initially, Romania shared with the communist regimes of central and Eastern Europe a reliance on terror as an instrument of political power. This terror was wielded in two stages: first, to eliminate opponents in the drive to consolidate power, and second, to ensure compliance once revolutionary change had been effected. In Romania's case the first stage, broadly speaking, encompassed the period 1945 to 1964, the year in which an amnesty of political prisoners was completed, and the second ran from 1964 to 1989. There was a perceptible change in the degree of repression exercised by the regime in 1964. Until this penultimate year of Gheorghe Gheorghiu-Dej's rule as general secretary of the Romanian Workers' Party (RWP), a sense of terror pervaded most of adult society. After 1964, Romanians were marked by fear, rather than terror, of the secret police (*Securitate*) and the Ceaușescu regime, for all its appalling abuses of human dignity and contempt for civil rights, never used the tactics of mass arrests and internal deportations that were a feature of most of the Dej era.

Repression of non-communists

On 23 August 1944 King Michael ordered the arrest of Romania's pro-German dictator, Ion Antonescu, and prepared to change sides in the war. When Soviet troops entered Bucharest on 30 August, they found an interim Romanian government ready to negotiate an armistice. Stalin used the armistice, signed in Moscow on 14 September, to subvert the effects of the 23 August coup that had threatened to wrest the initiative in Romanian affairs from him. In order to regain that initiative the Soviet leader fashioned from the armistice a legal framework for securing a dominant political and economic interest in Romania. Stalin's instrument in reducing the country to subservience to the USSR was the Romanian Communist Party.[2] It did so through the political system, the trade unions and the educational system. Internally, the aim was to break the existing structures of society and in this the party succeeded. Mass arrests took place of persons deemed to have aided the 'fascist regime of Marshal Ion Antonescu'. Purges were initiated by Lucrețiu Pătrășcanu, the minister of justice, in April 1945 and continued throughout his term of office.[3] The culmination was the enforced abdication of King Michael, under the threat of civil war, on 30 December 1947. The same day, the Romanian People's Republic was declared.

With the establishment of the republic the foundations of the totalitarian state could be put in place.[4] The first step was to cement Romania into the emerging Soviet bloc from a military point of view. This was achieved by a treaty of friendship, cooperation and mutual assistance between Romania and the USSR, which was signed on 4 February 1948. The second step was the consolidation of the single mass party composed of an elite and dedicated membership. This was achieved by dissolving the major opposition parties, the National Peasant and National Liberal parties in the summer of 1947, and by the forced merger of the Social Democratic Party with the communist party on 12 November 1947. According to figures presented at the last congress of the SDP, held on 5 October 1947, the Social Democratic Party had some 500,000 members, only half of whom appear to have joined the newly-fused party which was known as the Romanian Workers' Party and had a combined membership of 1,060,000.[5]

The RWP held its first congress on 21–23 February 1948 at which Dej was re-elected general secretary and Ana Pauker, Vasile Luca and Teohari Georgescu were the other three members of the secretariat.[6] A warning of measures against perceived opponents of the regime was given in Dej's report to the congress. Here he categorised 'Iron Guardists, spies and diversionists' as 'the enemies of Romanian democracy'.[7] On 26 March 1949, this category of 'hostile elements' was augmented by 'the saboteurs' who, in Dej's view, 'must be eradicated without mercy'. Thus the Stalinist method of abstract accusation, followed by the physical liquidation of the accused, found its way into the practice of the RWP.[8]

The first move towards the legalisation of repression was the amendment on 27 February 1948 of the penal code which had been in force since 2 March 1940. The revised code borrowed a series of concepts from Soviet legislation which were alien to Romanian law, but essential for the consolidation of communist political power. Novel notions such as 'counter-revolutionary sabotage', 'counter-revolutionary diversion', and 'counter-revolutionary agitation and propaganda' were introduced and quickly applied to justify a round-up of Iron Guardists throughout the republic on the night of 14–15 May.[9] A further step in the legalisation of repression was a decree of 18 August 1948, which supplemented the Law on the Prosecution and Punishment of Those Guilty of War Crimes or of Crimes Against Peace and Security, introduced exactly one year earlier. Using this law, the ministry of interior ordered the arrest of more than 1,000 former officers of the Romanian intelligence service, the security police, and the *jandarmerie*, all of whose places were taken by communist appointees.

As a result of a Central Committee resolution of November 1948, a verification campaign in the communist party was undertaken by a so-called 'non-party *aktiv*' of some 200,000 investigators, a euphemism which covered the participation of the security police, the army and officials of the ministry of justice. The period of investigation lasted from November 1948 until May 1950 and was directed at the various waves of members who had been recruited into the party. The first of these comprised non-politically affiliated workers and young Iron Guardists, who in 1945 had been given responsible positions in factories and trade unions as a reward for joining. This group included domestic servants who had been canvassed by the communists for membership as useful instruments for reporting on the activities of their employers. The second wave had joined during 1946 and 1947 and was drawn from army units, which had been formed from Romanian prisoners of war in the Soviet Union. It also included Romanian administrative personnel working for the Red Army. A third wave had been generated by the merger of the Social Democratic Party in 1948 and a fourth by those who had joined the new bureaucracy which staffed the institutions set up to effect the communist revolution in all sectors of activity. The latter covered the personnel of the people's councils, the peasants who had joined collective and state farms, and students and teachers in the reformed education system. Most of these recruits regarded party membership either as the key to advancement and privilege, or as insurance against being disadvantaged or even arrested, and there was a good deal of opportunism in their motivation, especially among older people.[10] The verification process removed from the party 192,000 'exploiting and hostile elements' and their elimination could only but augment the feeling of terror which permeated most of Romanian society.

This purge, aimed at creating an elite, coincided with the party's programme of revolutionising agriculture, industrialising the economy and transforming society. The party moved swiftly to revolutionise Romania, following the Soviet model and employing Stalinist norms and practices. The nationalisation in June 1948 of industrial, banking, insurance, mining and transport enterprises not only allowed the introduction of centralised quantitative planning, but destroyed the economic basis of those stigmatised as class enemies. Confiscating private share holdings and threatening their owners was relatively straight-forward; agriculture posed more complex problems. On 2 March 1949, the ownership of land was completely removed from private hands. This permitted the liquidation of the remnants of the old landowning class and of the *chiaburi*, peasants who hired labour or let out machinery, irrespective of the size of their holding. The land, livestock and equipment of landowners who possessed property up to the maximum of fifty hectares permitted under the 1945 land law were expropriated without compensation. Virtually overnight the militia moved in and evicted 17,000 families from their homes and moved them to resettlement areas. The confiscated land, totalling almost one million hectares, was either amassed to create state farms or was organised into collectives which were in theory collectively owned, but were in fact state-run because the ministry of agriculture directed what crops were to be grown and fixed the prices. Members of the collective were allowed to keep small plots of land not exceeding 0.15 of a hectare.

The majority of peasants, ranging from the landless to those who worked their holdings using only family labour, were organised into state or collective farms. This required extensive coercion, despite Dej's assurance to villagers that 'under no circumstances should the peasantry be forced into collectives'.[11] On Dej's own admission – in a report made to the party's Central Committee in December 1961 – resistance to collectivisation resulted in the arrest of some 80,000 peasants, 30,000 of whom were tried in public.[12]

The final major obstacle to the imposition of the Soviet model was the church, but here the RCP did not follow to the letter the Kremlin's solution. Both the Romanian Orthodox church and the Uniate or Greek Catholic church in Transylvania had been vital in preserving a sense of national cohesion and identity during the eighteenth and nineteenth centuries, and both retained the allegiance of millions of Romanians. If both churches could be manipulated to serve the regime's ends, then there was no point in destroying them. The Orthodox church had been declared the dominant faith under the 1923 Constitution and had been given special privileges, such as the payment of its clergy's salaries by the state, and the communist party was to use this dependence to bring the Orthodox hierarchy under its control. The Uniate church presented a different problem, however. It had been created at the beginning of the seventeenth century as a result of the conversion by Jesuits of many Orthodox Romanians in Transylvania to accept certain articles of the Catholic faith, among them the primacy of the Pope. As long as authority over the church resided in Rome, it would be difficult for the new regime to bring it to heel.

Broadly speaking, the communist party, while officially condemning religious worship, nevertheless tolerated it within certain bounds prescribed by law. In this respect it was more lenient than the Soviet regime. The exception was the Uniate Church, which was terminated on 1 December 1948; its dioceses and institutions abolished, and its buildings entrusted to the Orthodox church. On the nights of 27 and 28 October 1948, the six Uniate bishops, together with some 600 priests, were systematically rounded up. Most were jailed without trial. Of the bishops, only three survived the years of imprisonment to be released into compulsory residence on Dej's orders in 1955. None of them had been brought to trial.

The machinery of terror used against the peasantry to force through collectivisation was set in motion by the party to carry out the mass deportations of Serbs and Germans living in the western area of the Banat. These groups were considered a security risk when tension between Yugoslavia and Romania grew following the former's expulsion from the Cominform in June 1948. Stalin coined a new heresy – 'Titoism' – and the satellite states were forced to conduct a witch-hunt of senior cadres who were purged as an example to those who were alleged to have placed loyalty to their country before fidelity to Moscow. The deportations from the Banat region began on 16 June 1951 and affected 40,320 persons.[13] The deportees were only allowed to take what belongings they could carry, the rest of their property being bought by specially constituted commissions who paid them only a fraction of the value of the possessions. The special trains were guarded by troops and avoided stops in the main railway stations to prevent any communication with ordinary citizens. On arrival the fortunate deportees were allocated makeshift clay-walled huts with straw roofs in special settlements, some of which had been given Soviet names, such as 'Iosif Clisitch' where 859 people were placed. Others, even on the *Securitate*'s admission, were literally 'dumped in the middle of nowhere in the full glare of the sun without the necessary means of shelter.'[14] The same reports talk of a lack of drinking water and irregular supplies of bread, and many cases of children suffering from over-exposure to the sun.

Nothing illustrated more graphically the coercive nature of the centralising policies pursued by the communist regime than its use of forced labour. As in the Soviet Union, the ministry of interior in Romania was effectively charged with managing part of the economy. Cosmetically obscured by the euphemism 'temporary labour service', forced labour was used as an instrument of punishment for the thousands charged with economic sabotage and absenteeism. Included among their number were the tens of thousands of peasants who resisted the forced collectivisation of agriculture. Forced labour was officially introduced under the labour code of 8 June 1950 although it had been practised for more than a year in the construction of the Danube–Black Sea canal. The labour camps themselves, initially known as 'labour units' (*unități de muncă*), were similarly legalised retrospectively, on 13 January 1950 by a decree of the Grand National Assembly, since they had been established for the canal project in May 1949. The decree stipulated the setting up of units for 'the re-education through labour of elements hostile to the RPR.'[15] It placed the running of the camps under the authority of the council of ministers, an authority which was transferred to the ministry of interior by a further decree of 10 March 1950. Persons liable to be interned in the camps were defined in an order issued on 3 April 1950 by Gheorghe Pintilie, head of the *Securitate*.[16]

On 22 August 1952, the council of ministers adopted Resolution 1554 by which the camps were renamed 'work colonies' (*colonii de muncă*). It was signed by Dej as president of the council. Ten new categories of persons liable for internment were added to those in the order of April 1950. The resolution also introduced the penalty of fixed domicile, or internal exile (*domiciliu obligatoriu*), which was aimed at those who had not been 're-educated' in prison or in the labour camps and were still deemed to represent a threat to state security. Within its remit also fell former landowners, bankers and wholesale merchants, the close female relatives of those who fled the country before 1944 (Iron Guardists) and those who left after 1945 and were opponents of the regime in exile. Exempted from these provisions were artists, sculptors, composers and academicians 'who work honestly and are useful to society'.

The largest concentration of labour camps – fourteen in all – was for construction work on the Danube–Black Sea canal project. Packed prisoners from every walk of life were packed into them. Members of the professional classes rubbed shoulders with dispossessed farmers, Orthodox and Uniate priests with Zionist leaders, Yugoslavs from the Banat with Saxons from Transylvania, all were victims of the denial of human rights which accompanied the Romanian regime's programme of political and economic revolution. The construction of the canal was undertaken on the initiative of Comecon and approved by the Politburo on 25 May 1949. Its official purpose, according to decree no. 75 of the Grand National Assembly of 23 March 1950, was to provide the cheapest and most direct means of transport by river to the Black Sea by building a canal cutting the Danube's passage to the sea by 260 kilometres. Construction of the canal would also help to industrialise the south-eastern corner of the country, improve the irrigation of the Dobrogea province, thereby increasing agricultural yields, and provide training in new engineering techniques to those involved in its construction.[17] Stalin authorised Soviet financial backing for the project.

Work began on the canal at the end of the summer of 1949 on the basis of construction plans drawn up by a special Soviet–Romanian commission in May. The workforce was to be supplied from three sources: volunteer paid labour, forced labour and army conscripts. Both the planning and execution of the canal was supervised by Soviet counsellors. By the spring of 1952, the number of forced labourers had reached 19,000. In addition, 20,000 voluntary civilian workers were employed together with 18,000 conscript soldiers.[18] Once they had arrived at the canal, the political prisoners were subjected to the process of 're-education through labour'. The methods used were described in an internal report of the military prosecutor's office, drawn up for the ministry of interior on 27 February 1954:

> Many prisoners were beaten without justification with iron bars, shovels, spades and whips. Many died as a result of the blows received while others remained crippled for the rest of their lives. A number of prisoners were shot dead, others were denied medical treatment when sick and forced to work against medical advice and consequently several died. Prisoners were put naked or skimpily dressed in isolation cells in winter. Prisoners were punished by making them stand in frozen water until lunchtime. Prisoners were tied by the hands and exposed naked in the summer to be bitten by mosquitoes.[19]

Construction of the canal was abandoned after Stalin's death under a resolution of the council of ministers dated 17 July 1953.[20] The reasons behind this decision were never made public during communist rule, but the documents now available reveal that bad planning played a major part. Work began long before the plans were completed and when they finally arrived, it was discovered that the original estimates in scale and cost of the construction were 50 per cent below the true costs. The geological studies made by Soviet specialists were found to be inaccurate, and the machinery imported from the USSR was either in poor condition or did not work at all. Facing huge losses and robbed of a major propaganda victory, Dej sought scapegoats and the *Securitate* was ordered to organise show trials of workers who were accused of sabotage.[21]

On 11 March 1954, the council of ministers resolved to release the prisoners in the labour camps with the exception of those who, on the expiry of their sentence 'present an especial danger to state security'. Such prisoners were to be assigned fixed domicile for a period of between six months and five years.[22]

The communist party's blunt instrument of repression was the *Securitate*. It was set up according to a Soviet blueprint and under Soviet direction. The subservience of the Romanian security and intelligence services to the interests of the USSR was ensured by making the security police responsible in 1945 to Pantelimon Bodnarenko, a Ukrainian-born Soviet agent who had been imprisoned for spying in Romania in the late 1930s. Bodnarenko assumed a Romanian name, Gheorghe Pintilie,[23] and in August 1948 he was appointed head of the newly reorganised *Securitate*. The designation signalled a new mission for the security police. Its role, defined under its founding decree no. 221 of 30 August 1948, was 'to defend the democratic conquests and to ensure the security of the Romanian People's Republic against the plotting of internal and external enemies'.[24] Defence of the 'democratic conquests' meant the maintenance of the RWP in power and thus the new People's Republic officially certified itself a police state.

The principal task of the *Securitate* was 'to seek out and destroy any form of internal resistance to the regime'. The main targets were former factory owners and landowners, members of the outlawed democratic parties and of the Iron Guard, priests, students and teachers, and retired army officers and policemen. *Securitate* files indicate that more than 70,000 people were arrested in the decade from 1948 to 1958, 60,428 of them between 1948 and 1953. These figures must be treated with caution since, as we have seen, on Dej's own admission in 1961, 80,000 peasants alone had been arrested to enforce collectivisation of agriculture. Many of the arrests were illegal for they were carried out by *Securitate* officers acting purely on telephoned instructions from their superiors without an arrest warrant issued by the procurator's office. In September 1958, Alexandru Drăghici, the minister of interior, was still complaining of cases in which arrests had been made without foundation and prematurely.[25]

The death penalty for treason and economic sabotage was introduced on 12 January 1949, and a decree promulgated in the same year punishing acts 'considered as dangerous to society', even if these were 'not specifically provided for in the law as crimes'. A law of 12 August 1950 imposed the death penalty for crimes against national independence and sovereignty, for negligence by workers 'leading to public disaster', for theft and destruction of military equipment, and for plotting against the state, spying, and economic sabotage. The death penalty was applicable for the betrayal of 'state secrets' to a foreign power, but the nature of these state secrets was not defined. 'Plotting against the internal and external security of the Romanian People's Republic' also attracted the death penalty, but once again 'plotting' was not defined. The open-endedness of this legislation permitted its arbitrary application by the authorities. The category of 'counter-revolutionary crimes' made its appearance in decree no. 83 of 1949. This provided for punishments of up to fifteen years hard labour for those who resisted the expropriation of land under the reforms of 1945 and 1949.

It is difficult to give precise figures for the numbers of persons arrested and jailed in the Dej era for the simple reason that the *Securitate's* own statistics are contradictory. One ministry of interior report states the following: in the ten years from 1948 to 1958, 58,733 persons were convicted of a multitude of crimes, all of which were of a political nature: conspiring against social order, belonging to subversive or terrorist organisations, including the former democratic political parties and the Iron Guard, 'hostile instigation against the regime', illegally crossing the frontier, failing to report a crime against the state, crimes 'against humanity and activity against the working class', treason, espionage, distributing forbidden leaflets, sabotage, and 'hostile religious activity'. Most of those convicted received sentences ranging from one to ten years imprisonment. A total of 73,310 persons were sentenced to imprisonment in the period 1945 to 1964, of whom 335 received the death penalty (for several it was commuted). A further 24,905 were acquitted or had the cases dropped against them. In addition, 21,068 people were sent to labour camps in the same period. The numbers of those who died in detention is given as 3,847, of whom 2,851 died while serving their sentence, 203 under interrogation, 137 as a result of the execution of the death sentence, and 656 in the labour camps. Yet another set of statistics shows that in the period from 1950 to 31 March 1958, 75,808 persons were arrested, of whom 73,636 were convicted. In the same period, 22,007 persons were sent to labour camps and between 1949 and 1958 about 60,000 were placed under house arrest. Independent sources have produced quite a different set of figures; an examination of court records of the period indicates that in the period 1949 to 1960, 134,150 political trials took place involving at least 549,400 accused.[26]

The majority of those sent to labour camps were not tried or sentenced. They were sent there on the orders of the ministry of interior, which itself was acting on instructions from Dej and the Soviet counsellors. The despatch of the latter to Romania had been requested by Dej in November 1949 in a letter to Andrei Gromyko, Soviet deputy foreign minister, asking for assistance in 'analysing the position of party members who had an unclear or suspect activity.' The Soviet Politburo discussed Dej's request on 9 November and the Soviet ministry of state security was authorised to send A. M. Sakharovskii and V. S. Patrikeev to assist the *Securitate* in its work.[27]

The euphemism 'administratively sentenced' (*condamnat administrativ*) was used to disguise the illegality of the plight of the occupants of labour camps and to justify their detention. Not even this fiction, however, was employed to justify the arrest between 1948 and 1950 of the ministers of the pre-communist regime, the bishops of the Greek and Roman Catholic churches, and former policemen. There was no offence in the penal code to cover their arrest and they were imprisoned on the basis of orders issued by the ministry of interior.

Political purges of communists

As was typical in the Soviet bloc during the late Stalinist period, some of the staunchest advocates of political repression were soon to find themselves the victims of it.[28] For years the conventional wisdom of the purges in the senior ranks of the RWP was that they were a response to the 'heresy' of Zionism, and that their victims belonged to the so-called 'Moscow-wing of the RCP'. Recent research has shown this conclusion to be simplistic. The second part of this chapter will review this research and present its conclusions.

At the time of its emergence in the politics of post-war Romania, the communist party leadership fell into three groups, categorised to whether they had stayed in the country or in Moscow during the war, and, if the former, whether they were in jail or were operating in successful clandestinity. The first group, conventionally called 'the native faction', was led by Dej and was composed largely of workers and activists imprisoned during the strikes of the 1930s. This group spent the war years in the Târgu-Jiu internment camp and included Georgescu, Drăghici, Nicolae Ceauşescu, Miron Constantinescu and Alexandru Moghioroş. The second faction comprised several members of the pre-war communist leadership, some of whom had taken refuge in Moscow to escape arrest, hence their name the 'Moscow bureau'. This group was led by Pauker, a member of the executive committee of the Comintern and head of the external bureau of the communist party in Romania. Pauker forged close links with Soviet luminaries Viacheslav Molotov and Andrei Vyshinskii and her associates included Luca and Leonte Răutu. The third group was made up of veteran communists who had remained in Romania and acted clandestinely. Its leading members were Ştefan Foriş, a Hungarian who was confirmed as general secretary of the RCP by the Comintern in 1940, Remus Kofler and Lucreţiu Pătrăşcanu.

It is true that these factional divisions to a large extent mapped out the targets for the party purges, which had an honoured place in communist practice.[29] Stalin provided the models and sharpened the instruments. Indeed, relationships of senior Romanian communists with the Soviet Union for many years defined interpretations in western scholarship of the purges in Romania in the early 1950s. These were seen in terms of a conflict between so-called 'local communists' led by Dej, and the 'Muscovites' under Pauker and Luca, who spent the war years in Moscow.[30] But this dichotomy is misleading. It was precisely because of Dej's loyalty to Moscow that he was able to eclipse his 'Muscovite' rivals. Newly available evidence confirms that it was a personal conflict between Dej on the one hand, and Pauker and Luca on the other, rather than a conflict of ideology, that fuelled the struggle for power.[31]

The release since 1989 of documents relating to the arrest, interrogation and trial of Pătrăşcanu have shed particular light on the struggle for dominance in the party which spanned the years 1944 to 1954. In the space of ten years, Dej oversaw the removal of three comrades whom he regarded as potential rivals for power; two of them, Foriş and Pătrăşcanu, were executed, and the third, Pauker, reduced to the state of a political corpse. That Dej should have reached this position was, in part, testimony to his own abilities, those of a patient tactician and consummate manipulator. But his consolidation of power depended on his avoidance of giving his Soviet master any reason to question his loyalty. His vulnerability to Stalin's suspicions was all the greater because he, alone, among the leading figures in the RCP, had not been schooled in Moscow and was therefore something of an unknown quantity, as Georgi Dimitrov, the former Comintern general secretary, admitted to Pauker in September 1944.[32] To correct this disadvantage Dej did two things. First, he surrounded himself with a number of NKVD agents, who had been imprisoned during the war, and appointed them to senior positions in the security services and the ministry of interior, thereby offering Stalin a guarantee of his loyalty. Second, Dej used every opportunity to exploit the potential flaws in the actions of his rivals, thereby giving Stalin grounds for doubting their reliability, while at the same time reinforcing his own credentials as a faithful servant. If Stalin was the only person who could call Dej to account, then Dej could get away with anything subject to his master's agreement.

In May 1951, at the celebration of the thirtieth anniversary of the Romanian Communist Party, Dej recognised Pauker and Luca as the oldest serving members of the party leadership, but they acknowledged Dej as the sole leader. Barely four months later, Dej was in Moscow seeking Stalin's approval for the purge of Pauker, Luca and Georgescu. One reason for Dej's eagerness was the opposition shown by Pauker and Georgescu to the trial of Pătrăşcanu. Recent research has argued strongly that Pauker and her protégé Georgescu resisted attempts to prosecute Pătrăşcanu on trumped-up charges and that their protection of him was a significant factor in the delay in bringing him to trial. This obstruction contributed to the charge of 'right-wing deviationism' launched against them both in May 1952.[33]

The arrest of Rudolf Slánský, the general secretary of the Czechoslovak Communist Party, on 24 November 1951 as part of a Zionist 'conspiracy' sent a signal to Pauker that despite her close relations with Stalin and Molotov she was not immune, and yet another to Dej that she was not untouchable. Dej acted on the signal to remove his only serious rivals for power. At a Central Committee plenary meeting held on 29 February and 1 March 1952 attacks were launched against Luca, and by implication Pauker and Georgescu, which presaged their eventual purge.

Several interpretations of the purge have been offered and require discussion. First, it was not simply a manifestation of a struggle between a 'native' Dej faction and a 'Muscovite' Pauker faction. We have only to point to the fact that Georgescu, who was an ethnic Romanian and had spent the war years with Dej, was included among the 'right-wing deviators'. Georgescu's inclusion may have resulted from Dej's fear that Stalin might use him against Dej since the Cominform had in 1950 suggested Georgescu as general secretary of the party, an elevation that he is said to have refused.[34]

Second, the attack on Pauker should not be seen in itself as evidence of anti-Semitism. When the order came from Stalin to purge alleged Zionists throughout the Soviet bloc, Pauker's Jewishness was a fortunate accident for Dej; he used the opportunity to dismiss not just Pauker, but the gentile Luca who was a Transylvanian Hungarian. Moreover, two of Dej's associates in his move to take advantage of Stalin's paranoid delusions about a Zionist 'conspiracy' were themselves Jews, namely Iosif Chişinevski, who became a leading figure in the party secretariat, and Răutu, the head of the party propaganda body. Nevertheless, Pauker may have contributed to her own downfall by her alleged support of Romanian Jews.[35]

Third, the purge should not be interpreted as the embryo of Dej's autonomous policies of the early 1960s. Dej had shown himself to be no less Stalinist than Pauker and Luca. At the Cominform conference in Bucharest in July 1949, it was Dej who carried out Stalin's brief of denouncing Tito. While the signal for the purge came from Stalin, the identity of the victims suggested itself and Dej went ahead with advice from his Soviet counsellors. The charges against the 'deviators', as Pauker, Luca and Georgescu were dubbed, were prepared by Constantinescu, Chişinevski and Moghioroş under strict supervision from Soviet advisers, the principal one of whom was Sakharovskii, the security adviser to the ministry of interior.[36]

The Central Committee plenum held on 29 February and 1 March 1952 criticised Luca for allowing 'grave' mistakes and 'frauds' to be committed by the finance ministry and the national bank when applying the currency reform of January.[37] In a break in the proceedings Pauker came to the defence of Luca, but without success.[38] Popular dissatisfaction with the reform was reported to Dej and he called upon Luca, as minister of finance, to pay the price for it, even though the reform had been drawn up with the approval of the entire Politburo at the insistence of the relevant Soviet counsellors. In Dej's reckoning Luca had to go in order to create a breach in the Pauker group. Increasingly prey to fits of anger – he suffered from chronic asthma, chronic laryngitis and problems with his liver, which forced him to follow a special diet – Luca offered the easiest target. Furthermore, Luca had lost several of his friends because of his behaviour and was therefore less difficult to remove.

Dej had not forgiven Georgescu for his defence of Luca at the Politburo meeting that preceded the plenary meeting of 29 February. At a second plenary meeting on 26–27 May, it was announced that Luca had been dismissed from the party. Pauker was strongly criticised at the same plenary meeting for having 'helped and encouraged the rightist deviations of Luca and Georgescu' and was not re-elected to the Politburo, but since she had 'acknowledged some of her errors' she was allowed to retain her post as foreign minister.[39] On 28 May, *Scînteia* reported that Georgescu had been replaced by Drăghici as minister of interior.

Dej's pre-eminence in the Romanian party was sealed by his appointment, on 2 June 1952, as president of the council of ministers (prime minister), a post which he combined with that of general secretary of the party to which he had been elected at the national conference of October 1945. At the end of June

1952, Dej intensified the attack on Luca, Pauker and Georgescu. In a speech delivered on 29 June, he blamed Luca for 'retarding the development of heavy industry', for protecting thousands of *kulaks* by disguising them as middle peasants, and for encouraging capitalism and profiteering. Pauker was condemned for obstructing the organisation of collective farms and Georgescu for allowing the abuses committed by Luca and Pauker to take place.[40]

Luca was arrested on 16 August 1952 alongside twenty-eight others. As in the Pătrăşcanu case, the interrogation of Luca and his associates was coordinated by the Soviet advisers to the ministry of interior. Colonel Francisc Butyka, charged with leading the interrogation of Luca, later recalled this: 'At that time we had Soviet counsellors who took the initiative from the very start. And as usual, as in other cases, nothing was done without their guidance. The entire strategy of the inquiry, including the questions, was translated into Russian and monitored by the counsellors.'[41]

Pauker and Georgescu were initially spared arrest, but the political assassination of the former proceeded rapidly. A rumour campaign was launched by the *Securitate* that she had contacts with western intelligence agencies through her brother who lived in Israel, and that she had money deposited in a personal bank account in Switzerland. On 5 July 1952, she was dismissed as foreign minister, but held on to her post as vice-premier of the council of ministers until 24 November when she was stripped of that as well. Her association with Stalin and Molotov may well explain her gradual elimination from public life, which contrasted with Luca's abrupt arrest. The manner of her exit from politics, as well as the fact that she was succeeded as foreign minister by Simion Bughici, also a Jew, suggests that it would be hazardous to ascribe her demise solely to Stalin's anti-Semitic drive, which was at its height at that time in the rest of central and Eastern Europe.

Pauker was arrested on 20 February 1953. Like Luca, she denied the accusations of 'rightist deviationism'. She was interrogated about her activity in Moscow during the war and her contacts with the Comintern, but she was spared the tribulations of Luca and Georgescu. Stalin's death proved her salvation. Following several telephone calls from Molotov to Dej, she was released exactly two months after her arrest, although she was assigned an official house and could not go out unaccompanied by *Securitate* agents. She was finally allowed to reside with her daughter Tatiana and her family in February 1954, but was effectively a political corpse and lived a secluded existence in Bucharest until her death on 3 June 1960.[42]

Georgescu was arrested on 18 February 1953, as was his deputy at the interior ministry, Marin Jianu.[43] Neither were brought to trial. In contrast to thousands of others, they passed through the Caudine Forks of the *Securitate* and emerged shaken, but relatively unscathed. After his release in 1956, Georgescu was sent to work as a proof-reader at the *13 December* printing press and in a sign of magnanimity from Dej was made director of this same press in which he had secured his first job in 1923 as a typesetter.

Stalin's death on 5 March 1953, and the trial and execution of Beria in December of the same year, ushered in a power struggle in the Kremlin; it also removed the pressure on Dej for a major show trial. It became clear that separation of power was to be the order of the day when Khrushchev became first secretary of the CPSU in September 1953 and Georgii Malenkov was made prime minister. Yet this very separation of power in the Kremlin gave Dej more room to manoeuvre and until April 1954 he resisted Soviet pressure to limit his own authority as general secretary and premier by introducing collective leadership. Before doing so, he took perhaps the most cynical decision of a career littered with shameful deeds of repression. In order to eliminate a possible rival to his personal power whom he anticipated might receive the support of the 'reformist' Soviet leadership, he finally ordered the trial of Pătrăşcanu, who had been held in custody since April 1948.

It must be emphasised that Pătrăşcanu's trial, some six years after his arrest, was not staged as a Soviet initiative, but on the orders of a cynically manipulative Dej determined to hold on to power in the face of de-Stalinisation. The absence of any proof of the 'guilt' of the defendant made a mockery of the principles of a fair trial and justice and showed that Dej was merely using the cover of 'legality' to remove his most serious rival. The charges against Pătrăşcanu had originally been presented on 22 February 1948 at the first congress of the Romanian Workers' Party at which Georgescu had denounced Pătrăşcanu as 'an exponent of bourgeois ideology'.[44] He was subsequently detained on 28 April and formally arrested on 24 August. Dej's decision to place Pătrăşcanu on trial was influenced by Malenkov's wish that Dej introduce collective leadership. In his submission to the Party Commission on the Rehabilitation of Some RCP Activists on 2 November 1967, Dumitru Petrescu, a veteran communist, recalled a visit made by a Romanian government delegation to Moscow in January 1954 composed of Dej, Constantinescu, Alexandru Bîrlădeanu and himself. During the visit Constantinescu confided to Petrescu that he was taking to Malenkov a fifty-page dossier in Russian containing charges to be brought against Pătrăşcanu and a demand for the death sentence. When asked by Constantinescu for his opinion Petrescu declined to give one; when Constantinescu returned from seeing Malenkov, Petrescu stated, 'he told me he had solved the problem. In what sense he did not say, but I understood "solved" to mean that the Soviets had given their agreement to Pătrăşcanu's execution.'[45]

On 14 March 1954, it was announced that the Romanian Politburo had decided 'that the trial of the group of spies headed by Pătrăşcanu should now go ahead.'[46] It was held in camera between 6 and 13 April 1954 to avoid attracting attention and to avert the possibility of political capital being made from it. No word had been published of Pătrăşcanu's arrest or interrogation and nothing was revealed about the conduct of the trial. The only information disclosed concerned the charges, which were summarised under their legal headings as articles of the penal code but not defined; the findings of the Military Tribunal; and the execution of Pătrășcanu and Kofler on 17 April. The latter was reported in a communiqué published in *Scînteia* on the following day. It was only after the 1989 revolution that fuller details of Pătrășcanu's ordeal were made public.

Pătrășcanu was tried with ten co-defendants.[47] The list of their alleged crimes ran to thirty-six pages. Pătrășcanu was charged with: a) 'crimes against peace, in that he served as an agent of the fascist and bourgeois-landowners' police, and of the British secret service in trying to break up the communist party from within and paralyse its actions in the fight against fascism and the imperialist war, and had supported Antonescu and the war against the Soviet Union'; b) 'the crime of high treason, in that as minister of justice he led a group of conspirators who, with the help of the Anglo-American imperialists and their intelligence agencies, worked for the violent overthrow of the democratic regime installed on 6 March 1945 with a view to destroy the independence of the Romanian state'; and c) 'the crime of high treason, in that he passed to the British and American intelligence agencies after 23 August 1944 secret information regarding the security of the Romanian state'.

No proof of the allegations was provided. If Pătrășcanu listened with disgust at the fabrications of his former communist colleagues, he found the use of Gheorghe Tătărescu, King Carol's prime minister and a communist stooge, too much to stomach. Rising from his seat he protested: 'Such scum of history are brought to this trial as witnesses against me, a communist. If such an individual has to prove that I am not a communist, it is only proof of the low level of the Romanian Communist Party which needs such elements, as well as evidence of the total lack of proof in this odious trial, so that it has been necessary to resort to such a witness.'[48] Pătrășcanu condemned the trial as an outrage and when invited by the judge to make his own final statement, he was reported as saying that he had nothing to say 'except to spit on the accusations made against him.'[49]

By executing Pătrășcanu, Dej was able to pre-empt any Soviet attempt to impose a post-Stalinist restructuring of the party. While in Poland and Hungary such victims of Stalinist terror as Gomułka and Nagy were elevated to the party leadership, Romania now lacked a living 'martyr'. Moreover, Dej could argue that 'Stalinists' had already been purged from the Romanian party by pointing to the removal of Pauker and Luca. To underline his point he ordered the trial of Luca in October 1954. Unlike the Pătrășcanu trial, foreign correspondents were admitted, but this time the defendant's replies were read into the record by the president of the tribunal in order to avoid the embarrassment caused in the Pătrășcanu case by the latter's outbursts.[50] Luca's trial lasted four days. He was found guilty of charges of sabotaging the economy and conspiracy, and sentenced to death on 10 October. After entering a plea for clemency, his sentence was commuted to forced labour for life.[51] Dej remained a convinced Stalinist and Stalin's death had little impact on Romania's internal affairs: there was no major change in the party leadership, no de-centralisation of the economy, and no stop to the collectivisation of agriculture. There was, however, a short-lived amnesty of political prisoners in the autumn of 1955.[52]

Conclusion

With the imposition of communist rule Romania was forced to turn its back on the west and face eastwards. The most graphic feature of this new stance was the adoption of the Stalinist practice of mass arrests, deportations and imprisonment without trial. The application of the Soviet model in the Romanian legal system brought with it the notorious show trial which enabled the regime to dispose of its opponents under a cover of spurious legality. This was in marked contrast to the pre-war judicial system which, despite its many flaws, was not the instrument of a single political party. The pre-war Romanian governments did not seek the elimination of a political class, nor did they rely on the principle of guilt by association. The methods used by Dej against the Romanian people were also used against party members, the most prominent being Pătrăşcanu, Pauker, Luca and Georgescu. This involved the violation of party statutes. Dej's interest in following the results of the stage management of Pătrăşcanu's trial by listening to the proceedings on a tape-recorder echoes Stalin's presence on the balcony in the Moscow show trials. Both communist leaders embodied the intrusiveness of the police state.

It was Dej who created the conditions for the emergence of Ceauşescu as his sucessor in 1965. Dej's removal of his opponents impoverished the political landscape and perverted Romanian society. Imprisoned husbands were divorced by their wives – and *vice versa* – so that partners and children would not carry the stigma of a political detainee which was a bar to higher education and employment. The children of political prisoners were denied entry to university education until 1963. It was precisely these children who left Romania at the first opportunity in the late 1960s and 1970s with dire consequences for the formation of an opposition to Ceauşescu.

Notes

*   This chapter is a revised version of material contained in my *Communist Terror in Romania. Gheorghiu-Dej and the Police State, 1948 to 1965* (London, 1999), chapters 6, 7 and 8.
1   I take repression to be the oppression or persecution of an individual or group for political, economic or religious reasons, particularly for the purpose of restricting or preventing their ability to take part in the life of society. Repression may be

represented by the legalised intrusion of the state into the private life of the citizen through surveillance, eavesdropping and wire-tapping, discrimination, police brutality, politically motivated imprisonment, torture and forced domicile.

2   For a recent history of the RCP, see V. Tismăneanu, *Stalinism for All Seasons. A Political History of Romanian Communism* (Los Angeles, 2003).

3   According to prime minister Petru Groza, 80,000 persons had been arrested, a figure which later fell to 2,300. Pătrăşcanu put the figure 'in the middle of April' 1945 at 60,000. See A. Gibson, 'The Communists are the Real Rulers of Romania', *The Sunday Times*, 15 July 1945.

4   See D. Deletant, *Communist Terror in Romania. Gheorghe Gheorghiu-Dej and the Police State, 1948–1965* (London, 1999), pp. 82–92.

5   R. R. King, *A History of the Romanian Communist Party* (Stanford, 1980), p. 71.

6   Dej had been elected general secretary of the party at its national conference in October 1945.

7   Iron Guardists were members of the extreme right-wing anti-Semitic movement of that name which had been removed from power in January 1941 by General Ion Antonescu with Hitler's blessing.

8   An analysis of the editorials in *Scînteia* charts the evolution of the language used to demonise the 'enemies of the state' during the years 1945 to 1953. See L. Ţirău, 'Ziarul "Scînteia" şi războiul rece. Atitudine politică şi limbaj, 1945–1953', *Revista istorică*, vol. 4, nos 7–8 (1993), pp. 725–41.

9   The terminology was borrowed in particular from Article 58 of the Soviet penal code which had been introduced on 25 February 1927 to arrest those suspected of counter-revolutionary activities.

10 G. Ionescu, *Communism in Rumania, 1944–1962* (London, 1964), p. 204.

11 *Scînteia*, 22 January 1949.

12 G. Gheorghiu-Dej, *Articole şi cuvântări, iunie 1961-decembrie 1962* (Bucharest, 1962), p. 206.

13 A register of the numbers deported from the Banat and which villages they came from is contained in *Rusalii '51. Fragmente din deportarea în Bărăgan* (Timişoara, 1994), pp. 217–31.

14 *România liberă*, 2 July 1993, p. 11.

15 *Organizarea şi funcţionarea Organelor Ministerului de Interne de la Infiinţ are pînă în prezent* (Bucharest, 1978 [mimeographed]), p. 112.

16 For details, see C. Troncotă, 'Colonia de muncă', *Arhivele Totalitarismului*, vol. 1, no. 1 (1993), p. 170.

17 D. Jela, *Cazul Nichita Dumitru. Încercare de reconstituire a unui proces comunist* (Bucharest, 1995), p. 28.

18 Jela, *Cazul Nichita Dumitru*, pp. 21, 26 and 148.

19 Troncotă, 'Colonia', p. 174.

20 Resolution no. 2404. I am grateful to Ioan Ciupea of the Museum of National History in Cluj-Napoca for this information.

21 *Cartea Albă a Securităţii* (Bucharest, 1995), vol. II, p. 96; see also Deletant, *Communist Terror*, pp. 219–20.

22 R. Ciuceanu, *Regimul penitenciar din România, 1940–1962* (Bucharest, 2001), p. 59, n. 55.

23 C. Andrew and O. Gordievsky, *KGB: The Inside Story of Its Foreign Operations from Lenin to Gorbachev* (London, 1991), p. 362.

24 *Cartea Albă a Securității*, vol. II, p. 157.

25 *Cartea Albă a Securității*, vol. II, p. 64.

26 For the sources for these figures, see Deletant, *Communist Terror*, pp. 134–5.

27 V. Tismăneanu, D. Dobrincu and C. Vasile (eds), *Comisia Prezidențială pentru Analiza Dictaturii Comuniste din România. Raport Final* (Bucharest, 2007), p. 155. See also D. Deletant, 'Influența sovietică asupra Securității române 1944–1953' in *Memoria ca formă de justiție* (Bucharest, 1995), pp. 35–46.

28 Some of the arguments that follow are based on my study *Communist Terror*, chapters 7, 8 and 11. I have refined details by referring to R. Levy, *Ana Pauker. The Rise and Fall of a Jewish Communist* (Los Angeles, 2001) and Tismăneanu, *Stalinism for All Seasons*.

29 G. H. Hodos, *Show Trials. Stalinist Purges in Eastern Europe, 1948–1954* (New York, 1987).

30 See S. Fischer-Galați, *The New Rumania. From People's Democracy to Socialist Republic* (Cambridge: MA, 1967), p. 31. Victor Frunză makes a similar division, calling the 'Muscovites' the 'externals' (*exteriori*), and the 'local communists' the 'internals' (*interiori*). See his *Istoria Stalinismului în România* (Bucharest, 1990), p. 219.

31 Three scholars in particular pointed out that neither of the two groups, 'local communists' and 'Muscovites', was so rigidly defined because personal allegiance often cut across this artificial division. See B. Vago, 'Romania', in M. McCauley (ed.), *Communist Power in Europe 1944–1949* (London, 1977), p. 113; M. Shafir, *Romania. Politics, Economics and Society* (London, 1985), p. 35; and M. E. Fischer, *Nicolae Ceaușescu. A Study in Political Leadership* (Boulder, 1989), p. 42. Extracts from the minutes of some of the RWP Politburo meetings during the period under discussion have appeared in Romanian secondary sources and are quoted where appropriate.

32 See Deletant, *Communist Terror*, p. 147.

33 R. Levy, 'Did Ana Pauker Prevent a "Rajk Trial" in Romania?', *East European Politics and Societies*, vol. 9, no. 1 (1995), pp. 143–78.

34 V. Tismăneanu, 'The Tragicomedy of Romanian Communism', *East European Politics and Societies*, vol. 3, no. 2 (1989), p. 361.

35 This theory is advanced by I. Calafeteanu, 'Schimbări în aparatul diplomatic românesc după 6 martie 1945', *6 Martie 1945. Începuturile Comunizării României* (Bucharest, 1995), p. 168.

36 Tismăneanu, 'The Tragicomedy', p. 382.

37 Archive of the Romanian Security Service (henceforth ASRI), Fond 'P', file 40009, vol. 32, pp. 308–9. At the time of writing this archive is being transferred to the custody of the National Council for Study of the *Securitate* Archives (CNSAS) where files will be given, according to practice, new reference numbers.

38 Levy, *Ana Pauker*, p. 201.

39 Ionescu, *Communism in Rumania*, p. 211.

40 Ionescu, *Communism in Rumania*, p. 213.

41 Archive of the Executive Committee of the Central Committee of the Romanian Communist Party, 264, vol. 19, pp. 90–5. At the time of writing this archive was being re-catalogued at the Central National Historical Archive (ANIC) – formerly the State Archive. I am grateful to Marius Oprea for locating this document and showing me a copy.

42 Author's interview with Eduard Mezincescu, 16 June 1994. For Pauker's final years, see Levy, *Ana Pauker*, pp. 221–5.

43 ASRI, Fond 'P', file 40009, vol. 21, p. 112.

44 Ionescu, *Communism in Rumania*, p. 152; and Deletant, *Communist Terror*, p. 178.

45 C. Popişteanu, 'Un epilog neaşteptat: Malenkov aprobă lichidarea lui Lucreţiu Pătrăşcanu', *Magazin Istoric*, no. 3 (March 1992), p. 39.

46 H. Nestorescu-Bălceşti, 'Structura Conducerii Superioare a Partidului Comunist Român', *Arhivele Totalitarianismului*, vol. 2, nos 1–2 (1994), p. 363.

47 The ten were Kofler, Herbert (Belu) Silber, Ion Mocsonyi-Stârcea, Alexandru Ştefănescu, Jac Berman, Emil Calmanovici, Victoria Sârbu, Harry Brauner, Lena Constante and Herant Torossian.

48 Quoted from Ionescu, *Communism in Rumania*, p. 156, n. 17.

49 *Cartea Albă a Securităţii*, vol. II, (1994), pp. 459–60.

50 See the deposition of Vasile Varga, a deputy judge at Luca's trial, dated 23 March 1968 for the party commission of enquiry set up to investigate the charges against Pătrăşcanu (copy in possession of the author).

51 Under the provisions of decree no. 3 of 1963, the sentence was modified to 25 years hard labour. Luca died of a heart attack on 23 July 1963. See 'Documentar Referitor la Procesul Privind pe Vasile Luca', Archive of the Executive Committee of the Central Committee of the RCP, no. 264/19, 18.02.1972, p. 2. I am grateful to Marius Oprea for retrieving this document.

52 Decree 421 of 24 September 1955 of the Grand National Assembly provided an amnesty and pardon for a number of offences. See *Buletinul Oficial*, no. 27, 24 September 1955.

Stalinist and anti-Stalinist repression in Yugoslavia, 1944–1953

Jerca Vodušek Starič

Terror and repression as part of the practice, method and technology of power implemented by different communist parties in the twentieth century derive from one source: the Leninist formula for revolution and the preservation of the so-called 'dictatorship of the proletariat'. The formula promulgated the rule of a party elite in the name and interest of the 'vanguard' proletariat, whose state of consciousness was as yet deficient. Leninism was the basis of Stalin's validation for absolute power, and, enriched by his interpretation, became the fundamental principle of the communist revolutionary agenda in the 1930s, documented beyond dispute in 1938 in the *Short Course on the History of the All-Union Communist Party (Bolsheviks)*, the infamous *Short Course*. The term 'terror'[1] in this context comprised violence and enslavement, both physical and psychological; mass killings; the inculcation of fear; labour camps and abuse of inmates (exposure to extreme climatic conditions; over-populated, unhygienic conditions; ideological and mental pressure; and last, but not least, physical terror – forced lack of sleep, beatings, executions), whose legal prerogatives were nil, down to a number of well elaborated means of political pressure, systematic lawlessness against opponents, ideological warfare, censorship, dispossession, deprivation, lack of basic freedoms and idolatry, among others.[2]

Leninism–Stalinism became the 'religion' and the ideological guideline for most of the communist parties of the twentieth century, including the Communist Party of Yugoslavia (CPY) from its creation in 1920 to its demise in 1990. Stalin perfected the legacy, as Lenin's 'best pupil', and expanded it with enforced industrialisation and collectivisation, the central planning system, the personality cult, the monolithic party structure and bureaucracy, and a discriminatory national policy. Both during and after Stalin's time, each communist leader became partly the follower and partly the author of his own personality cult, administering his own 'version' of the system, although the basic skeleton remained unaltered. Josip Broz Tito, who was prone to hedonistic living and luxury, invented a more consumer-oriented version, one ensuring a relatively higher standard of living in the 1950s, calling it self-management. Self-management by definition completely contradicted one of Lenin's basic principles – democratic centralism – which was the main axiom of the CPY and, by derivation, the constitution of Yugoslavia. All the abovementioned means of terror were at one stage or another put to use in communist Yugoslavia, and will be elaborated in some detail in this piece.

The rise of the Bolshevik CPY

The Communist Party of Yugoslavia formally came to power with the constitutional elections of November 1945. However, the story began long before that. The CPY covered a long road, establishing its strategies and tactics, refining its ideological profile and acquiring a strong position in the Comintern (and its clandestine successors after 1943) before gradually accessing power during the Second World War. The whole process was from the start based on violence and terror on one hand and strict party discipline on the other, both the unmistakable legacies of the Comintern. Yugoslav communists, at least the new generation that took over the party in the 1930s, were no exception. This is validated by any examination of the history of the CPY that reaches beyond the surface, inevitably challenging the myth created after the 1948 Tito–Stalin split and the many attempts to glorify the party's history or obscure its darker sides.[3] Therefore, it must be stressed at the beginning that the CPY and its affiliates – for instance, the national communist parties of Slovenia, Croatia and Serbia – throughout their existence adhered to the basic principles of communism: democratic centralism, the party as an *avant garde* of the proletariat and the secret police as the 'detachment of the revolution'.

The Communist Party of Yugoslavia was established in June 1920 at the Congress of Vukovar and adopted a programme declaring itself in favour of overt revolution. It changed its name from 'Socialist' to 'Communist' even before the Comintern imposed Lenin's 'Twenty One Points' laying down the conditions for membership in the International. The first wave of party violence followed soon after. Based on the Comintern assessment that revolutionary change was going to sweep over Europe and break up the 'Versailles system', the Yugoslav party embarked on several terrorist attacks, armed conflicts with the police and the army and violent strikes. As these intensified, the authorities banned communist activities for the first time in December 1920. After the attempt to kill the regent and the murder of the minister of interior, parliament banned the CPY in August 1921 and criminalised membership of it. In response, the party set up an illegal organisation and held meetings abroad, but did not relent in its policies. The communist youth set up proletarian action squads, the party organised workers' action committees and continued with the armed clashes, which resulted in the death of several young communist functionaries. Many went to prison and others fled, most to Moscow, where they received ideological education at different 'universities' and courses.

As a consequence, the party was torn apart by different policies. Left and right factions, abroad and at home, fragmented and stagnated in illegal organisations and prisons. Like several other member sections of the Comintern, the CPY came under threat of being dismantled by Moscow. In the mid-1930s, a new generation of communists emerged led by Tito, Edvard Kardelj, Milovan Djilas and others, all of whom adopted Stalinist methods. Thereby the CPY, with help from Moscow, initiated the process of Bolshevisation, unification and implementation of 'iron discipline'. Many 'old-timers', 'factionalists', 'Trotskyites' and 'opportunists' fell under NKVD investigation and were killed or sent to camps during Stalin's terror. At a meeting of the Comintern in January 1937, the general secretary of the CPY, Milan Gorkić, was removed from office and 'Walter' (Tito) was appointed organisational secretary with the task of consolidating the party. Gorkić and around 800 Yugoslav 'deviationists' became victims of the purges in 1937–38 and were executed by the NKVD. This meant the removal of almost all CPY cadres in the USSR, including several ex-secretary generals. Tito and his entourage never rehabilitated the victims of the purges or those they had expelled, not even after this was done in the Soviet Union in the 1950s.

At the outset of World War Two, the party had 3,500 members along with another 3,500 well organised and disciplined members of the Union of Communist Youth (SKOJ) out of a total population of around sixteen million. In 1939, the party declared itself neutral and the war 'imperialist'. However, many party members condemned the Soviet invasion of Poland and especially the attack on Finland. Some left the party, others were expelled. In the autumn of 1940, the CPY was already contemplating the war as an opening for revolution. Tito was ready and the party 'cleansed'. After a great deal of hard work, he said, the factions had been defeated, 'spies of the class enemy', even inside the leadership itself, had been unmasked and 'social-democratic influence' and 'sectarianism' were at last eradicated. The party had definitely become 'Bolshevik', soundly organised in harmony with true 'Leninist–Stalinist ways'.[4] The extent of this cleansing process in terms of victims and cadres expelled or eliminated is not known. Some Trotskyites, for example, never made it back from the French camps after the end of the Spanish civil war.

After the Axis occupation in 1941, the CPY organised and took over the leadership of the resistance movement, although in many parts of the country other political groups had already joined the movement. After the party declined to allow the resistance to become a proper coalition, many non-communists refused to cooperate. The party regarded those that stayed on as 'fellow travellers'. On the other hand, it labelled those who refused to join as 'white guardists' (Catholics), 'blue guardists' (those loyal to the Yugoslav Royal Government in exile), 'reactionaries' and 'fifth columnists'. The CPY soon decreed them 'traitors of the people' and thus subject to punishment, including execution. Needless to say, most of these were ideological categories deriving from the Soviet lexicon. In this way, 'counter-revolutionaries' became the primary enemy. In 1941, individual acts of terror were perpetrated, stipulated by a fierce campaign against political opponents and adjusted to circumstances in different parts of the country.[5]

The first revolutionary attempts, 1941–42

The first wave of terror and violence exhibited by the CPY towards other political groups came during the attempt at a revolutionary uprising in the 'October 1917' fashion, when the 'second phase of the revolution' was declared at the beginning of 1942. In the autumn of 1941, probably due to Stalin's speeches and the standstill on the eastern front, Tito and his Central Committee (CC) estimated that the Red Army would soon mount a counter-offensive, move west and lend them support. Therefore revolution was on the agenda. The call went out from the CC to the party that the time was right for the beginning of the intensified class struggle. All available means were to be implemented and fellow travellers were no longer needed.[6] Proletarian symbols were brought into the open and proletarian brigades founded. The CC urged the Slovene CC, for instance, to get ready for the next stage, to act directly against the 'fifth column' (the counter-revolutionary groups and political opposition) and correct the mistake of not killing enough of them.[7] The Slovene party leadership carried on along these lines throughout the summer of 1942, explaining that the Soviet–British Treaty signed in May 1942 was just a slight postponement of the world revolution. The outcome was the assassination of a number of prominent political figures, members of the clergy and wealthier peasants. This wave of terror initiated the civil war in Yugoslavia. The areas that were most affected were Montenegro, Herzegovina and Slovenia. In Serbia, the civil war began with the break between Colonel Draža Mihailović and Tito in November 1941, the latter's partisans soon leaving Serbia for Bosnia and Herzegovina to return in full force in 1944. In Macedonia, the enemy was the group of Vančo Mihailov and members of the Prizren League. Overall, the list included 'reactionary' politicians, freemasons and religious structures.

The exact number of victims attributed to the civil war is still uncertain. Slovenia is the only ex-Yugoslav republic where an approximately accurate death-toll will soon be known.[8] Here, the partisan movement executed most of the anti-communist forces they captured in September 1943. In a context of mass violence on all sides in Yugoslavia, some of the anti-communist political groups decided to seek cooperation with, or protection from, the German occupying forces and police, and hence the Slovene *Domobranci*, or 'home-guard', was founded. It is indicative that in 1944 there was almost an equal number of soldiers in both the party-led liberation forces and the homeguard in Slovenia, and the death-toll was approximately the same on both sides, around 2,500. As the war approached its end the number of victims grew.

The CPY relied on, and consulted regularly via telegram with, Dimitrov, the head of the Comintern, Stalin and Molotov. On the insistence of Stalin, who had just signed the Soviet–British Treaty, the CPY was compelled in 1942 to abandon the policy of open revolution and concentrate on a 'patriotic war'. This caused a dramatic change in strategy – the re-introduction of the 'popular front' policy, an emphasis on patriotic resistance and, later, the tactically successful policy of a gradual takeover of power. The French communists underwent a similar development in 1944 with analogous directives from Stalin. The dissolution of the Comintern in the spring of 1943 brought no change in the communication between the CPY and Dimitrov, Molotov and Stalin. Tito was known in NKVD intelligence circles as one of those communist leaders who consulted Stalin down to the smallest detail. Their correspondence was full of allusions to the 'common cause' and 'our line', reflecting the spirit of what Djilas called a 'communist-conspiring relationship'. Those on the outside had other words for it; in early 1944 the British reported it as a 'pathological admiration' of the Yugoslav communists for the Soviet Union, a religious communist zeal. Kardelj, a member of the Yugoslav Politburo, a close associate of Tito and leading party persona in Slovenia, often asserted that the USSR was 'our only true ally'. As the war approached its end, and especially after September 1944, this turned into open propaganda.

The takeover of power

The policy of intense political differentiation was one of the main leverages of the communist takeover of power in 1944–45, but also one that generated violence.[9] It was used all over the country where the communists prevailed, and even beyond. For example, Tito counselled the Albanian Communist Party in 1943 to 'put into effect a resolute political differentiation'. The CPY delegate to Albania was more frank: we shall do everything to ensure that the pro-British resistance leaders will either join the occupier or us; we shall not allow a third way.[10] The position was clearly ideological and for tactical reasons was rarely worded so openly in order not to alarm the western Allies and upset the flow of aid. But it was a frequent theme of party correspondence within the country and with Moscow. It also clearly demonstrates that the communists were set on stopping contacts with, and the influence of, the western Allies, especially the British. Such policies began in 1943 and escalated in 1944 as the fronts progressed.

As a consequence of these practices, fear expanded well beyond party circles in the last stages of the war. It crept into the consciousness of the population. At the same time, the party began the process of taking over complete control of the country. On the outside, for the benefit of the west and international political recognition, it demonstrated a willingness to compromise with the Royal Yugoslav Government in exile in London. Hence, Tito signed the Vis Agreement with Ivan Šubašić, the president of the Yugoslav Royal Government, in June 1944. The arrangement promised freedom of speech, the restoration of political parties, free and secret elections and the separation of powers: more or less the same substance as the Declaration on Liberated Europe signed a few months later by Stalin at Yalta. It was 'Strategy and Tactics' in the works.

However, on the ground in Yugoslavia the CPY was beginning to build up the system of a 'people's democracy', that is, the 'revolution from above'. The crucial years in this process were 1944–45. It was gradually introduced as the country was liberated and in the following years the system of a party and secret police state was honed to perfection. First on the agenda were the most important sites of power – the secret police, the judiciary and the army. The hold of the party over the liberation movement was ensured early on by two institutions it completely controlled, the secret police and the armed forces. The former was founded in Slovenia in August 1941 as the Security Intelligence Service (VOS), and the rest of the country followed in 1942. It was designated to fight the 'fifth column' and all other enemies of the partisan movement. Only reliable party members were permitted to sign up. It was this organisation that carried out the abovementioned assassinations of 'enemies' and 'traitors of the people' in the spring of 1942. With the help of the service, the party also started systematic surveillance and the assembling of files on all possible opposition, including members of the partisan movement itself.

In May 1944, Tito dismantled all existing services and personally founded the Yugoslav secret police – the Department for the Protection of the People (OZNA), whose primary task was to persecute all those who were hostile to the liberation movement. Later, it was specifically empowered to protect the revolution by dealing with 'political crimes'. OZNA was set up with the active participation of General-Lieutenant Nikolai V. Korneev, head of the Soviet military mission with the Yugoslav Supreme Command, who had joined Tito on liberated territory in February 1944. According to Yugoslav documentation, he belonged to the NKVD. In September 1944, the first dispatch of reliable party cadres was sent to Moscow for courses on intelligence work. They later became heads of departments in the secret police structure, a structure which bore great similarity to the Soviet Cheka. The Soviet mission in Slovenia simply lived in the OZNA headquarters. OZNA was directly responsible to the Minister of Defence, Tito, who appointed Alexander Ranković, a member of the Yugoslav Politburo, as its head. OZNA was assigned its own armed detachments, the Corps of People's Defence (KNOJ), and thus had a specific nature, being both a military and a political organisation closely tied to the CC and the party committees and secretaries in the field. Its task was to fight all 'anti-people's elements', meaning the leaders of different parties, the 'reaction', homeguardists, Chetniks and similar forces, the Gestapo, members of the German minority, suspects working for intelligence services, as well as members of the partisan forces and government (except the leadership of the CPY), and to persecute all hostile 'acts of a political nature'. Score settling against local associates of Nazi terror, who themselves were responsible for large-scale murders and atrocities, was also a key element here. As the war approached its end, OZNA was given the task of assembling data on all counter-revolutionary organisations, 'collaborationists' (the definition of the term was wide enough to include almost anybody) and 'enemies of the people', compiling lists and card-files on them. As the retreat of the German army progressed, the secret police carried out arrests and seized enemy archives. On this basis further arrests ensued.

The second element completely faithful to the CPY was the armed forces, or the National Liberation Army and Partisan Forces as they were officially called until their reorganisation into a centralised Yugoslav Army in March 1945. From 1941, these forces were led by commandants and commissars (without exception communists), and bound by a partisan oath. As these forces gained official recognition at the Tehran Conference, they introduced compulsory mobilisation and harsh mortal sanctions for those who evaded it or deserted. The party thus gained new means of imposing political influence, asserting political differentiation and ultimately of inflicting punishment.

The first revolutionary penal codes were introduced in 1944 along with the formation of military courts mandated to administer justice over the civil population, especially 'enemies of the people'. Judges were instructed to study Soviet law and the works of Andrei Vyshinskii, Stalin's prosecutor. The new legal system, as the party ruled, was to be based on the principles of Soviet legal theory and should incorporate the concept of 'ultra vires', the idea of social justice and the Soviet policy of punishment: confiscation of property and correctional labour in camps. In parallel, the institution of public prosecutor was set up on the Soviet model. Concentration camps were created for suspects sentenced to hard labour by order of the civil or military authorities. The camp rules were not new: the commandant had full authority over the inmates, and barbed wire, guards and watchtowers were in place. There were two types of camps – military and secret police. From 1946, the latter came under the jurisdiction of the ministry of interior. Finally, in February 1945 all pre-war legislation which was 'not in spirit with the achievements of the liberation movement' was abolished. Similar provisions were made for elections to the organs of the 'people's government', rulings on the confiscation and sequestering of property, and laws against saboteurs and war profiteering.

As the end of the war approached, the party perfected its pressure on other political parties. First, the partisan leadership ruled that parties as a whole could not join the Front, only individual members. This was a concept that originated in Slovenia in 1941; a few parties and groups jointly established the Liberation Front, but in 1943 all of them, except the CP, had to give up their party autonomy and were drawn into a monolithic organisation led by the party. Along with it 'old',[11] 'worn-out', 'rotten' and 'corrupt' party democracy was vilified and the alternative, the idea of complete political unity, was promoted. The National Liberation Front held its founding conferences all over Yugoslavia in 1944 and, with the exception of Slovenia, was renamed the People's Front at the end of the war. All who spoke against it were labelled 'enemies of the people' and those who did not join had little chance of employment and, subsequently, ration cards.

All other new political bodies, such as the workers' union, the anti-fascist women's front and the anti-fascist youth organisation, were set up on this model. With the liberation of Belgrade in October 1944, the party expanded its power over state institutions and ministries, installing reliable cadres and political commissars into the administration. The process of cleansing the administration had begun and went on for the next few years in blatant disregard of the principles of the Vis Agreement. The Yugoslav party, later the Communist League, from then on never abandoned the principle of unity of power; more so, in the two constitutions of 1963 and 1974 the Communist League became part of the state structure and its programme became that of the state and all mass political organisations.

The process of enforcing political unity in Yugoslavia varied in different parts of the country, corresponding to the interaction of the Anglo-American and Soviet alliance. In areas liberated first, like Serbia in the autumn of 1944, pre-war parties were allowed (the democrats, the radicals and others), whereas in Slovenia, liberated in May 1945, the notion of having no parties, just the Liberation Front, was strictly applied. At this stage Tito and his closest collaborators made two important visits to Stalin – one in September 1944, when the process of taking over the country began, and the other in April 1945, when the Soviet and Yugoslav governments signed the Treaty of Friendship, Mutual Aid and Cooperation. There is still no written evidence of these talks between Stalin and Tito, but considering the circumstances, it is most probable that key policy issues were discussed, such as the tactics of implementing a one-party system and procedures regarding the 'cleansing' of the country.

The cleansing operation

Terror and violence were the basis of the cleansing process that began as the country was liberated, culminating in the summer of 1945. A newly liberated territory initially came under military jurisdiction and then the cleansing started. The first organisation to step in was OZNA, the secret police. A few weeks later civil institutions took over, meaning the People's Front or the People's

Committees. At the local level, the party leadership and secret police were in control and any degree of political compromise or plurality was strictly a feature of the Provisional Government, headed by Tito and Šubašić, and the Provisional Parliament. OZNA carried out arrests on the basis of pre-prepared lists and quick interrogations. The arrested were then either 'liquidated' on the spot or sent to labour camps or secret police prisons for further investigation.[12] As a report on the district of Celje in Slovenia shows, in little more than two weeks in May 1945 1,004 people were arrested; 272 of these were sent to Celje (probably the local OZNA headquarters), 272 to the nearby concentration camps of Teharje and Hrastnik, and seventy were liquidated on the spot. From the Celje prison, seventy-five were 'liquidated', twenty sent to the camps and nine to OZNA headquarters in Ljubljana.[13]

At the end of May 1945, a large group of prisoners, comprised of various military groups and civilians, was handed over by the British authorities in Austria to the Yugoslav army. Fearing reprisals, they tried to make their way into territory held by the western Allies. Among them were some 12,000 Slovenes, a group of Montenegrin Chetniks, several hundred thousand soldiers of the Croat homeguard, mobilised by the Independent State of Croatia and led by the Ustashi, and many civilians fleeing Croatia. Other soldiers and civilians were captured on the run, while many stayed on and voluntarily surrendered to the authorities, convinced of their innocence and that nothing would befall them. All underwent the same process of OZNA 'selection' as described above.[14]

The mass of prisoners was 'liquidated' between the end of May and the end of July 1945. The victims, including women and children, were assembled in groups and tied two by two with telephone wire. Some were marched through cities and publicly humiliated and harassed. They were then taken by train and trucks into isolated woods, disused mine pits or trenches and shot in the back of the head or slaughtered; the pits were later mined and covered. In Slovenia, where the final operations of the Yugoslav army took place, there is evidence of 571 such locations; many are also identified in Croatia, but not much is known for the rest of Yugoslavia. The statistics of this 'cleansing' operation are not yet known, although OZNA kept records and carried out a census of the population in the summer of 1945. According to the demographer Vladimir Žerjavić, the wartime death-toll among the 'quisling' forces was 209,000, of whom 9,000 were Slovenes.[15] The Slovene project of compiling casualty lists of wartime and immediate post-war killings shows larger numbers, with 14,531 people killed (1 per cent of the population) in the cleansing operation up to January 1946. In Vojvodina and Srijem, by 1946, 9,668 people had been shot, among them 6,763 of German nationality.[16] We also know that a large number of armed and civilian Croats – approximately 100,000, according to army sources – were killed instantly when turned over to the partisan forces at the northern border in May 1945, while Žerjavić gives us a total figure of 50,000 of those killed in combat.

Documents indicate that in June 1945, almost 44,000 Croat soldiers were interned in camps.

The losses among the Croat population as a whole will probably turn out to be higher than estimated and the death-toll that can be attributed to the immediate post-war killings is likely to be, by percentage, among the highest in Europe. The cleansing operation in Yugoslavia continued in later years and by 1947, according to official data, KNOJ units had captured, killed or wounded 116,000 'Ustashi', 'Chetniks' and other 'members of bands' or 'enemy groups'.[17] Despite all the killing, Yugoslavia's camps were full – in July 1945 there were 115,440 prisoners, among them 81,376 German and 948 Austrian soldiers and officers, with the remainder mostly captured Croat forces and some Serb Chetniks. Those German nationals with Yugoslav citizenship who were not shot were assembled in camps (130,380, among them 58,821 women and 24,422 children) and expelled from the country at the beginning of 1946.[18]

The extent of the cleansing operation and the manner in which it was organised leave no doubt that the mass murder was carefully planned and executed by the Yugoslav army and OZNA. Recently discovered correspondence from 1946 between Tito's cabinet and Major Mitja Ribičič, the Slovene general secretary of OZNA, demonstrate that the order was given at the highest level – Tito, Ranković, and probably others from the CPY Politburo together with the central, federal and army OZNA leaderships. It is clear that they decided to keep the whole enterprise secret. It was not to be spoken of and unauthorised persons were not to be acquainted with the procedure.

Parallel to the mass killings was another process – trials before extraordinary courts. All regular courts were suspended from May to September 1945 and replaced with people's courts appointed by the newly elected local authorities, the people's councils. There were three kinds of extraordinary courts: military, with the authority of sentencing civilians; courts of national honour;[19] and, in December 1945, extraordinary senates for the persecution of sabotage, speculation and damage done to the reconstruction of the country. OZNA chose the defendants and prepared the indictments, working directly with their own cadres in the public prosecutor's office. The material it consigned to the court was sparse, and never contained all the interrogations. Court proceedings were quick; trials usually took a few hours. In the summer of 1945, at the military and courts of honour no witnesses for the accused were called, no appeal was permitted and the sentence was implemented immediately. Defendants were brought to court in groups (usually owners of industrial or other enterprises, and members of cultural or other organisations). The sentences were harsh, ranging from confiscation of property and disenfranchisement to hard labour and death penalties.

The outcome was that between 80 and 90 per cent of all industry was confiscated and handed over to state management. In many sectors, the nationalisation of private property passed in December 1946 merely formalised the existing situation. The private sector was slowly abolished in the trading business, which was nationalised in 1947, and in agriculture, with a land reform in 1945 which redistributed 1,566,000 hectares (mostly in Slovenia, Croatia and Vojvodina), setting a maximum limit of 10–35 hectares. Peasants were oppressed by different measures of the 'socialist transformation of the village' policy, by compulsory surrender of goods, low fixed prices for agricultural goods, and 'production' cooperatives. Later the state introduced harsher methods. In the meantime, the secret police continued to monopolise all persecution of political crime, even when civil courts were introduced. In the first year after the war the Slovene OZNA 'processed' approximately 5,000 citizens per month, meaning one in every twenty Slovenes.

All these procedures ran parallel to preparations for the elections, first local in the summer and then constitutional in November 1945. The provisional parliament and provisional government, appointed in March 1945, were dominated by the communists and gradually subverted all state institutions and civil organisations, dictated the electoral law, and by various means eliminated or disabled all existing political structures and bodies. After the war, the ministry of interior permitted only a few pre-war political parties to operate, mostly in Serbia. The CPY constantly increased pressure to integrate all parties into the People's Front. In Croatia, politicians from the Peasant Party and their representatives in the provisional government, Šubašić and Franjo Gaži, pleaded for permission to resurrect their party. It was one of the most popular parties in the country and had the distinct potential of becoming the strongest opposition party in Yugoslavia. The communists, therefore, did everything possible to degrade its leader, Dr Vlatko Maček, who fled the country in May 1945. Moreover, they adopted familiar tactics and created a parallel and loyal party – the Croat Republican Peasant Party – pronouncing it publicly as the legitimate heir of the pre-war Peasant Party. It immediately joined the People's Front. This tactic was replicated in several other cases (for instance, the Serb Peasant Party and the Slovene Christian Socialists). The leading pre-war political parties in Slovenia and Montenegro were still banned and completely disgraced publicly, while there were no attempts at all at party renewal in Bosnia and Herzegovina.[20]

The regime exerted direct secret police pressure on politicians, and what was left of the pre-war political elite were either in prison, doing hard labour, were disenfranchised or simply 'paid a little visit' and thus terrified. Pervasive reports instigated by agitprop, the party body for agitation, propaganda and media censorship, relentlessly advertised political unity and criticised the 'reaction', domestic and international. In the meantime, the CPY consolidated its own organisational structures based on the Soviet model – a cadre department, agitprop, commissions for the economy and political organisations, and a control commission, which appointed cadres to all segments of society, devoting special care to the secret police. A party secretary, who was not known publicly, was at the same time head of the local People's Front and people's council. In Slovenia, for example, 71 per cent of all communists obtained leading positions in the government, judiciary and enterprises, regardless of their qualifications.[21] The Soviet framework was not only applied, but the entire implementation was overseen by Soviet advisers.

The remainder of the pre-war political elite, now in opposition *en bloque*, had little possibility to influence the course of events. They made several attempts to involve the Allies by sending appeals on the internal political situation, the persecutions and the inadequacy of court procedures. On the eve of the constitutional elections of November 1945, the united opposition announced it would abstain due to political pressure and the nature of the electoral law. Nevertheless, the poll went ahead with only one electoral list, belonging to the People's Front, and attendance was proclaimed a duty. OZNA operatives were present to oversee the balloting and the turnout. The vote was cast with small balls that were lowered into big boxes, one for the Front's list and the other, 'black', for the absent opposition. The 'black' box was not lined and resounded loudly when the ball was cast. There were reports of transferring the balls from the 'black' box into the Front's and other anomalies. The elections passed with a large vote in favour of the People's Front led by Tito and events took their course. The constitutional assembly met, passed a new constitution and installed the system of people's democracy.

The consolidation of people's democracy

In spite of expectations, the CPY actually increased its political and police pressure after the elections. Immediately a new wave of the cleansing process started, and in local councils, the judiciary and the People's Front unreliable or hostile 'elements' were purged. Some previous sentences were overturned and large public court trials were organised at which there was always a high number of defendants with mixed provenance. Bishops were tried next to war criminals and pre-war politicians with saboteurs – all 'enemies of the people'. The remainder of the pre-war politicians, who had joined the People's Front in 1945, was now under constant OZNA surveillance. They were followed, surrounded with informants and their phones were tapped.

Meanwhile, the secret police was reorganised into departments and by hierarchy. An elaborate filing system was set up: category 2a was for 'anti-popular elements', 2b for their contacts, 3 for those under arrest, and so on. Dossiers were created on different topics, among them political parties, the churches and pre-war societies. Information was collected by a further wave of interrogations, the analysis of archives and an elaborate system of informants and agents. This system of informants established control over all sections of the population and was one of the most perverted instruments of the totalitarian state. It was perfected in the coming years and never ceased to exist; even today it is impossible to get testimony on such archival data.[22] In Slovenia alone, there were 4,198 such 'agents', while the number of people under control was 25,770. Besides such agent-informants, there existed a network of OZNA agent-officers working in governmental offices, enterprises, schools, local communities and other organisations that regularly reported on the political situation. In the spring of 1946, OZNA was renamed the Administration for State Security (UDBA) and transferred to the ministry of interior. The army kept its own counter-intelligence service and both became pillars of the new regime.[23]

There was another kind of terror that has not been discussed up to now: the terror of subjugating the population to a forcibly installed level of 'vulgarity' imposed in everyday life and omnipresent in the next decades. It was promoted by the leadership and had as leverage the socially inferior, the lumpen proletariat, who rose to positions of influence through the revolution and took pleasure in denigrating the pre-war cultural standards of the middle classes (the aristocracy was practically non-existent in Yugoslavia) and long existing rural and religious traditions. This vulgarity was imposed in behaviour, family relations, literature, architecture and the educational system, and was common to all totalitarian systems which aspired not only to control the mind, but also to transform human nature. At the same time, a new kind of purism was introduced, a negation of 'petit-bourgeois' manners, with propaganda and measures against make-up, fashion and table etiquette. Egalitarianism became a social value, often enforced. In the field of literature and arts, it was the time of socialist realism.

As the term 'people's democracy' by definition meant a transitional stage on the road to socialism in which the remnants of capitalism were to be eliminated, all other necessary measures were applied in Yugoslavia. Nationalisation of private property was only part of it; there was an abundance of measures that brought all sectors of the economy and civil life under state control. In this process a definite policy was discernible; it was coordinated with the Soviet Union, either by consultation with its ambassador or during the many visits of prominent Yugoslav party leaders to Moscow. The extent and nature of direct Soviet involvement in Yugoslavia were obfuscated, although mixed companies, sending cadres for adequate schooling to the USSR, and the involvement of Soviet experts and NKVD officers in the police, army and economy are all known facts. On the ideological front, by 1947 Yugoslavia was heavily engaged in the liquidation of social democracy, although it had no such party left to eliminate.

Throughout 1946–47 the CPY concentrated on the state and economic apparatus: the State Control Commission, State Planning Commission and preparations for the centrally based Five-Year Plan. New laws were passed on state ownership, local government and planning. The plan for 1947–51 was inaugurated in the spring of 1947 and predicted rapid industrialisation and electrification. Yugoslavia became an autarchic state. Its economy was directed towards the emergent Soviet bloc via signed treaties of friendship and mutual aid with all countries, starting with Poland in March 1946. Yugoslavia also followed the principle of the exchange of 'minorities' – Czechs, Ukrainians and Poles, who were Yugoslav citizens – with neighbouring countries. The exchanges started with the forcible 'repatriation' of Poles on the basis of an agreement in early 1946. Meanwhile reconstruction of the country was under way, introducing the cult of manual work, mass meetings, competition and compulsory measures. Youth and other shock brigades, based on high labour tempos and norms, emulated 'Stakhanovism' and became part of the fabric of everyday life. Civil servants 'volunteered' for manual tasks at weekends and even elections became competitions, not among candidates, but for the turnout. These were on the agenda for one or other local or state government, each bringing about a further purge. Whoever did not fit into this system was a 'saboteur', a 'reactionary' or an 'enemy of the people' and was variably punished. They might be ousted from a mass organisation or the party, disenfranchised, administratively punished, resettled or taken to the people's court. Every applicant for a job was screened by the secret police, especially those for leading positions. On the same principle, travel documents and passports were given out individually and after careful deliberation, in some cases by the highest party officials. Discrimination was part of the scheme – state social welfare was not given to the private sector, the previously condemned, clergy and peasants. The churches, both Catholic and Orthodox, were dispossessed by the land reform and their societies dismantled. Ecclesiastical ceremonies were obstructed in different ways and the clergy who didn't fall into the category of 'progressive' was carefully screened for behaviour during the war and were later often under daily supervision by UDBA agents. Many were imprisoned, sentenced and despatched to labour camps.[24]

The real power that hatched and enforced all these measures was the party and secret police, and not the civil authorities and mass organisations, as it would appear from newspaper headlines. All post-war standing orders for OZNA, UDBA and later the State Security Service, from 1947 to 1985, defined the enemy ('enemy of the people') in the following way: members of pre-war and wartime bourgeois political parties, the dispossessed bourgeoisie (and their offspring, as was added later in 1970), *kulaks*, advocates of bureaucratic, dogmatic and right-wing ideas and supporters of clericalism.[25] The secret police was required to report regularly to the requisite political organisations about such 'elements'.

In order to foment hatred for 'enemies of the people' and 'reactionary forces' and bring about the final defeat of the representatives of parliamentary democracy, big show trials were held in the early post-war period through to 1953. The first wave of show trials was in 1945–46, when large groups of defendants were tried for war crimes and collaboration with the enemy. In mid-1946 trials were mounted in Belgrade against the wartime minister of war and commander-in-chief of the Royal forces in Yugoslavia, General Mihailović. In Ljubljana the bishop, Dr Gregorij Rožman, was tried together with a renowned politician and member of the Allied Advisory Commission for Italy, Dr Miha Krek, (both in absentia) for war 'crimes'. In Zagreb the trial of Archbishop Dr Aloysius Stepinac took more than two weeks, implicating the church in wartime Ustashi policies and ending with a sixteen year prison sentence for Stepinac.[26]

In 1947, 'spy trials' began. They were organised almost simultaneously in Belgrade, Zagreb, Ljubljana and elsewhere. The accused were charged with subversive activities, espionage for the west, and often for their wartime activities, but the true guilt lay in their aspirations for the reinstatement of democratic rule. All charges were adorned with the necessary ideological terminology and suggestions of deeds against the 'people' and state. The highly publicised proceedings directly or indirectly implicated the personnel of western embassies and consulates, mainly those of the USA and Great Britain, who were accused of involvement in hostile activities against Yugoslavia and in some cases of organising contacts between Yugoslav 'terrorists' and foreign countries. One of the defendants in such a trial was the translator at the American embassy in Belgrade, M. Stefanović. He was arrested by the UDBA in April 1946, sent to court on 31 December 1946 and *inter alia* charged for alleged contacts with Mihailović. On 4 January 1947 he was sentenced to death. The UDBA interrogated other Yugoslav citizens employed by embassies, harassed them into becoming informers, and sometimes even detained diplomatic personnel.

It is hard to convey the momentum of these trials and even harder to present and evaluate the charges, owing to the notorious lack of regularity. Defendants were not allowed proper representation, were physically abused (beatings and night-time interrogations), and forced to write their own confessions. Court procedures were the usual public prosecutor's monologue, charged with political language and aggravated further by leading questions from the judges. The public assembled in court was carefully hand-picked and gave timely ovations. Some trials were transmitted outside on loudspeakers and collective farms, unions and other mass organisations wrote letters in support of the prosecution. It was all a well staged mass meeting.

The trials were intertwined with implications of incriminating connections left hanging in the air. This is best illustrated by the fate of Dr Dragoljub Jovanović, professor at the University of Belgrade and one of the left-wing leaders of the Serb Peasant Party in the inter-war period. He had joined the People's Front in 1945, became its vice-president and presented its programme to the first congress of the Front on 5–7 August 1945. He was also elected member of the provisional and later constitutional parliament and appointed to its presidium. In the aftermath of the November elections, his role became superfluous and he gradually came under suspicion. The first public attack came at the trial of Mihailović in June 1946, when he was indirectly accused of having links with the Chetniks. That autumn he was 'relieved' of all his political duties, and public accusations, or, rather, propaganda, against him intensified. This degenerated into physical attacks on the street. In May 1947, the UDBA arrested him and he was put on trial in October on charges that he had joined the Front in order to sabotage it and that he was a spy for the British intelligence service. He was found guilty and probably escaped the death sentence owing to diplomatic intervention, but was in prison for several years. The same fate befell a group of defendants in Zagreb headed by the leader of the Front's duplicate Croat Peasant Party and ex-minister, Dr Gaži, together with Dr Jančiković (who died in prison in 1951); and a similar cohort of left-wing liberals in Ljubljana, where the leading defendant, Dr Črtomir Nagode, was sentenced to death and executed, together with the dean of the Ljubljana Faculty of Law Dr Boris Furlan and Ljubo Sirc, both of whose death penalties were, after a few weeks, commuted to lengthy imprisonment.[27]

In 1948–49, in Slovenia alone a series of trials, culminating in several death sentences, were conducted against thirty-seven members of the communist party and high governmental officials accused of sabotage and working for the Gestapo during their imprisonment in the Dachau concentration camp during the war, the so-called 'Dachau trials'. The background of these trials is still not sufficiently clear. The arrests began in 1947 and some of the defendants belonged to the older generation, some had spent time at different party schools in Moscow before the war, while others were accused of adhering to social democratic ideals. In these cases procedures were slightly different. The suspects were first interrogated by a party commission, where they were supposed to admit to their 'objective and subjective' party guilt and confess. After that they were handed over to UDBA and their treatment became more severe. At the same time in Belgrade two members of the CPY Politburo, Andrija Hebrang and Sreten Žujović, were first relieved from office, then expelled from the party and arrested. Hebrang and some of the Ljubljana defendants 'committed suicide' in prison.

The true Stalinist phase

The split between Yugoslavia and the Cominform that erupted in the summer of 1948, not because of any rejection of Stalinism by Tito, but as a result of foreign policy differences between himself and Stalin,[28] had two main consequences. The first was Yugoslavia's well-known turn towards the west. What is rarely mentioned is the other side of the story. While inventing anew the basic principles of socialism, Yugoslavia also introduced even stricter Stalinist measures than before the split. Hence, it is surprising, and paradoxical, that 'anti-Stalinist' Yugoslavia was pursuing very similar policies as elsewhere in the Soviet bloc where full-blown Stalinism was being consolidated. For example, from 1949 to 1951 Yugoslavia embarked on a strict collectivisation policy, forcing peasants into collective land ownership and the establishment of 'peasant working collectives' which survived till the mid-1950s. Throughout this period there was a clandestine armed resistance in various parts of the country consisting of several small to medium-sized groups that had the support of the dissatisfied peasantry and clergymen. They were labelled 'bands', allegedly sponsored by the west, and were thus persecuted by the secret police, who regularly infiltrated informants into their ranks. By 1953 these groups had been destroyed.

The year 1949 started off with a more intense anti-religious policy and a renewed campaign of 'differentiation' among the clergy. It was part of the constant attempt to draw the Catholic church away from the Vatican and to conform to the concept of a national, or state, church. The regime tried to force the clergy to join the newly established state-sponsored association of priests, but the Vatican excommunicated many of those who did. Then a series of attacks, even physical assaults, and trials took place against priests and church officials. The peak of the process came in December 1952 when Yugoslavia broke diplomatic relations with the Vatican, expelled theologians from the universities and embarked on a harsh 'anti-clerical' campaign.

The split with the Cominform gave a glimmer of hope for the restoration of democracy, but the regime made sure that no opposition list would take part in the 1950 state and 1951 republic elections. It relied on the secret police to monitor all conversations, movements and meetings of the potential opposition, and to control their mail. All foreign post was routinely opened and transcripts documented. The Cominform purges, therefore, presented another opportunity for renewed differentiation and 'cleansing' within the party, this time justified by Tito's fear of Soviet (rather than western) invasion. The purges were officially directed against those who sided with Stalin and conducted 'organised hostile activities' or were connected with foreign intelligence services. But recent case studies show that the definition was interpreted in a broad sense. The party succeeded in converting some of its high-ranking Stalinist officials, while at the local level punishment was meted out for various offences and a variety of reasons. The process was facilitated by the introduction of administrative punishment, meaning a senate of three members of the ministry of interior passed judgement and sent people to labour camps without the formality of a trial. The official number of repressed communists was 16,312, but this figure is not final either.[29] Several new camps were set up for them, among them the most notorious two on the remote Adriatic islands of Grgur and Goli otok, where inmates worked in extreme heat, suffered constant physical torment from the UDBA and their fellow prisoners, and were under intense pressure to repent. Both camps functioned into the sixties and recent studies claim that 31,000–32,000 persons were imprisoned in Goli otok during this time, although some may have been 'ordinary' criminals as opposed to political prisoners.[30]

Nevertheless, the party spoke of democratisation and decentralisation and introduced a new concept of 'workers' self-management', a concept declared to be true to Marxism–Leninism, while condemning Soviet 'revisionism'. It also strove for public support with mass manifestations, letters of faithfulness and a series of well publicised congresses of the party itself (1948 and 1952) and all mass organisations. At the party congress of 1952, even the name was changed to the League of Communists of Yugoslavia, implying a new kind of policy which would not be dictatorial. But by early 1953, the orthodox party line had regained the upper hand.

The period of terror and physical repression was over by 1955 with the denunciation of Stalinist methods and increased reliance on western aid to build up the Yugoslav economy and military. Outright terror was now replaced by a refined secret police control and the shattering of any dissent with the help of secret agents and informers, many of whom were from the ranks of the potential opposition. Fear of physical reprisals had long been established in the consciousness of the people. Exemplary punishment sufficed, as the later cases of Djilas, Dr Dragotin Gustinčič, Mihailo Mihailov, Jože Pučnik and others, coupled with secret proceedings before army courts, showed. Everything was still directed towards one goal, socialism, which Yugoslavia achieved formally in 1963, and from then on the party line remained constant: self-management simply became another form of the 'dictatorship of the proletariat'.

Notes

1 Lenin had defined the key elements of a revolutionary party and its organisation, including the dictatorship of the proletariat. Texts by Stalin added practical definitions (the most important are *The Problems of Leninism* and *Strategy and Tactics*). For details on the concept of 'terror', see the Soviet party documents published in J. A. Getty and O. V. Naumov, *The Road to Terror: Stalin and the Self-Destruction of the Bolsheviks, 1932–1939* (New Haven and London, 1999).

2 For details, see L. Schapiro, *The Communist Party of the Soviet Union* (Cambridge, 1978).

3 Historiography even today is prey to the propaganda launched in 1949–53 and sustained by the Yugoslav leadership with its primary assertion that the Yugoslav communist movement was different and independent of Moscow from its beginning, more accurately from the 1930s on, since the years before Tito's rise to power were considered less relevant.

4 *Peta zemaljska konferencija KPJ: Kongresi, zemaljske konferencije, plenumi CK KPJ*, vol. I, part 10 (Belgrade, 1980), pp. 3–45.

5 During the war Yugoslavia was territorially divided among different occupiers (Nazi Germany, Fascist Italy and Hungary), while the Ustashi set up an independent state in Croatia. The Royal government was in London, divided by disputes on Serb–Croat lines and debilitated by endless discussion on the responsibility for the country's capitulation in April 1941.

6 J. B. Tito, *Zbrana dela* (Ljubljana, 1981), vol. 8, pp. 77, 218 and 235–6.

7 Tito, *Zbrana dela*, p. 113.

8 Slovenia is the only ex-Yugoslav republic with a project of compiling casualty lists of the wartime and immediate post-war killings carried out by the communists (and other armies). Its findings are being published on the website: Sistory.si. The Slovene population at the time was approximately 1,492,000. In the areas where civil war raged, there was a much larger death-toll than elsewhere (the average would be approximately between 2 and 4 per cent, while the losses in the broader Ljubljana region went up to 8.8 per cent) and, in the spring and summer of 1942, there was also a distinctive rise in the number of civilian victims. Most of the losses must be attributed to wartime operations and the occupiers' coercive measures, although a local study of the Notranjsko area (south west of the capital) shows that the largest death-toll can be attributed to the civil war. The latest comprehensive wartime figures are: victims of German forces – 33,853; of Italian forces – 6,472; and of partisan forces – 7,476. These numbers include both civilians and armed forces, but do not include the death-toll among those forcibly mobilised into the Italian and German armies.

9 The process was complex, analysed in detail by J. Vodušek Starič in *Prevzem oblasti, 1944–46* (Ljubljana, 1992), and *Kako su komunisti osvojili vlast* (Zagreb, 2006).

10 *Dokumenti centralnih organa KPJ, NOR i revolucija, 1941–1945*, vol. 18 (Belgrade, 1986), p. 335. See also Tito, *Zbrana dela*, vol. 23, pp. 3, 13 and 47.

11 As in the paradigm 'old Yugoslavia', which was being replaced by a 'new' people's state.

12 The term 'liquidation' was adopted at the time by the communist authorities and is still in use. It means killing without a court trial, often without so much as an interrogation. If there was an interrogation, it was short and basic: name, birth, residence, military unit or allegiance during the war.

13 J. Vodušek Starič, *Obračun: Slovenija v letu 1945* (Ljubljana, 1996), p. 97.

14 There was complete symmetry in the Soviet and Yugoslav repatriation policies, from the requests that all Soviet/Yugoslav nationals should be returned (willingly or not) to their countries, up to interrogations by NKVD/OZNA in camps, and sentencing without due court procedures.

15 V. Žerjavić, *Gubici stanovništva Jugoslavije* (Zagreb, 1989), p. 116.

16 OZNA procedures in Croatia are presented in N. Barić and Z. Radelić (eds), *Partizanska i komunistička represija i zločini u Hrvatskoj 1944–1946, Dokumenti* (Slavonski Brod, 2005), p. 324. We have no evidence of similar documentation published in other ex-Yugoslav republics.

17 *Završne operacije za oslobodjenje Jugoslavije* (Belgrade, 1986), p. 611. The estimated numbers of people killed vary from the lowest, 7,000 in Slovenia and 60,000 in

Croatia, to the highest, 30,000 for Slovenia, 200,000 for Croatia and 50,000 for Serbia. The exact number will never be known, but the lowest estimates have already been proven incorrect.

18 Barić and Radelić (eds), *Partizanska i komunistička represija*, p. 310.

19 According to OZNA reports, in Croatia 1,083 people were charged and 926 were sentenced by such courts, 699 to hard labour (Barić and Radelić (eds), *Partizanska i komunistička represija*, p. 262). But these numbers could be even higher, because in Slovenia alone in one of the seven regions 1,368 people were brought before this court, all were disenfranchised and some sentenced to hard labour. The court dealt with 30–40 cases per day.

20 Vodušek Starič, *Prevzem oblasti*, p. 170.

21 Vodušek Starič, *Prevzem oblasti*, pp. 211–13 and 293–7.

22 However, two volumes have recently been published in Bosnia listing all OZNA/UDBA agents in the republic.

23 Numbers give a relatively good picture: the Gestapo had 40,000 employees for 80 million citizens, the East German Stasi 102,000 for 17 million, while in the case of Slovenia there was one OZNA officer for 1,200 people, and that was in early 1946. If we add all the active agent-informants, then we get one OZNA agent per 282 Slovene citizens, which is close to the Stasi numbers (one per 167 citizens).

24 J. Pučnik (ed.), *Iz arhivov slovenske politične policije* (Ljubljana, 1996), pp. 141–7.

25 *Priročnik za delo milice na področju varstva ustavne ureditve – Strogo zaupno, uradna tajnost* (Ljubljana, 1985).

26 Most of the sentences mentioned have been annulled or the indictments withdrawn.

27 See Ljubo Sirc's memoirs, *Smisel in nesmisel* (London, 1968); *Med Hitlerjem in Titom* (Ljubljana, 1992); and *Dolgo življenje po smrtni obsodbi* (Ljubljana, 2010). The circumstances and place of death and burial of Dr Nagode are still unknown.

28 See L. Gibianskii, 'The Soviet-Yugoslav Split', in K. McDermott and M. Stibbe (eds), *Revolution and Resistance in Eastern Europe: Challenges to Communist Rule* (Oxford, 2006), pp. 17–36.

29 *Istorija Saveza komunista Jugoslavije* (Belgrade, 1985), p. 371. Twelve were participants in the Bolshevik Revolution, thirty-six in the Spanish republican armies, 2,300 were army officers and twenty-three were ministers, among others.

30 K. Bartošek, 'Central and Southeastern Europe', in S. Courtois et al. (eds), *The Black Book of Communism: Crimes, Terror, Repression* (Cambridge: MA, 1999), pp. 394–456 (here p. 425).

Stalinist terror in Bulgaria, 1944–1956

Jordan Baev

The declassification of formerly 'top secret' communist archives after the fall of the Berlin Wall in the autumn of 1989 has afforded many new opportunities for thorough and comprehensive research of the post-war Stalinisation process in Eastern Europe. In Bulgaria's case, this gradual declassification occurred over a relatively long two decade period, starting with the release of communist political archives in the early 1990s and finishing with the security and military records in the last few years.[1] Greater accessibility to this huge documentation for the entire era 1944–89 was a necessary precondition for creating a more precise and objective view of contemporary history since, in my opinion, personal testimonies and evidence should be used primarily as secondary 'critical oral history' sources. Nevertheless, even authentic archival documents must be evaluated very carefully bearing in mind the practical mechanisms by which official memoranda were created. In a political system of monistic personal rule, official information was frequently transmitted to the 'top' either in distorted form or 'accommodated' with the leaders' actual or perceived views. It was an open secret during the Cold War era that communist statistics were 'opportunistic fixes' or 'adjustments' of the real facts.

Another serious obstacle, which has impeded a detailed examination of Stalinist terror, is the relatively restricted access to relevant ex-Soviet archives. It is true that several documentary volumes have appeared in Moscow in the last decade or so, but they have tended to suffer from a selective editorial approach.[2] Meanwhile, on the basis of these selected sources some Russian historians have recently argued that the purges in the ruling communist parties during the Stalinist period were provoked by the east European leaders themselves, thus assigning only a secondary role to the Soviet masters.[3] However, a serious review of the political trials of László Rajk, Traicho Kostov, Rudolf Slánský and other east European functionaries (with the exceptions of the Lucrețiu Pătrășcanu case in Romania and the Koçi Xoxe affair in Albania) clearly demonstrates that the scenarios were written and directed by Moscow.

Bulgarian specificities

Central to the Stalinisation process in Eastern Europe is the question of national specificities versus generic commonalities among states. Bulgarian 'peculiarities' and similarities with other countries of the Soviet bloc have been discussed in various documentary and research publications in the last two decades,[4] and a few standard works have also appeared in English.[5] At least three or four interdisciplinary projects on Bulgarian communist, or socialist, rule (depending on one's conceptual framework) have been launched in recent years and all these parallel endeavours have stimulated a more thorough, consistent and balanced interpretation of post-war Bulgarian history and elucidated the precise mechanisms by which Stalinism was transposed to the country.

After the national liberation of Bulgaria and during the third Bulgarian kingdom (1879–1946) a relatively liberal constitutional law existed, but the political system in the country could hardly be defined as an entirely western-minded democratic model. In the severe socioeconomic circumstances of the post-First World War years, political violence was endemic and soon after a successful military coup in 1934 political parties were disbanded. Communist propaganda in the post-1945 period grossly exaggerated the 'armed anti-fascist resistance' led by the illegal communist party during the Second World War. Retrospectively, the number of 'anti-fascist victims and sacrifices' was over-estimated ten to fifteen times in order to justify the 'mass people's struggle' and the 'national uprising' of 9 September 1944. To be sure, in comparison with other Nazi allies like Hungary and Romania, there was a relatively active guerrilla movement in Bulgaria. But its actual role as a significant factor in the overthrow of the regime was exaggerated for many years. All these claims served as an important psychological reason and excuse for the total elimination of traditional conservative and liberal political forces immediately after the communist seizure of power.

Besides the lack of a genuine democratic political culture, there was a second 'foreign' factor: in contrast to other east European states, the Bulgarians traditionally had a positive attitude towards the Russians, even in their Bolshevik guise. Bulgaria was the only Nazi ally that did not send its troops to the eastern front and continued to maintain official diplomatic relations with the USSR during the war years. Bulgaria was also the first former Nazi satellite in Eastern Europe from which Soviet occupation troops were withdrawn (in December 1947), and they were not stationed there for the next forty years. The insistent aims of the American and British representatives on the Allied Control Commission for Bulgaria between October 1944 and September 1947 were based on the assumption and expectation that the early withdrawal of Red Army forces would contribute to a weakening of Soviet influence and promote the eventual political liberalisation of the country. This did not happen. Even the brutal interference of Stalin's so-called 'advisers' in the internal affairs of a formally independent state did not significantly change traditional pro-Russian feelings, and that situation was unique among Soviet bloc satellites during the Cold War (with the exception of Czechoslovakia until the Warsaw Pact invasion of August 1968).[6]

A specific circumstance, which existed for the first few months after the establishment of a 'Fatherland Front' government on 9 September 1944, was the peculiar composition of political power in the country. At the apex was a four-party coalition, in which the communists held only four of the sixteen ministerial portfolios plus one representative on the three-member regency council. Everywhere, however, real power belonged to the 'Fatherland Front' committees dominated by the communists. In the first couple of months the representatives of the non-communist parties officially did not protest against the mass purges, and even signed all regulations that formally legitimated the repression of 'fascists'. Those regulations would be used against themselves just two years later.

'Revolutionary terror'

The available data in the reports and correspondence of the Central Committee of the Bulgarian Communist Party and the state security directorate show without doubt that in the first two months after 9 September 1944 (especially between 11 September and 10 October) at least 3,000 to 5,000 people were killed intentionally and without any legal basis. These were active loyalists and employees of the old regime, mainly police and gendarme officers and functionaries, secret agents of state security, mayors, local activists of paramilitary nationalist civil formations and pro-Nazi organisations, as well as several activists of the opposing factions of the Internal Macedonian Revolutionary Organisation (IMRO). Among the victims of 'revolutionary terror' were also many totally innocent merchants, landlords and intellectuals, even accidentally arrested outsiders. The collective national memory still keeps alive unwritten stories of pay-offs of older personal and neighbourhood scores, masked under the slogan of 'political retribution'. A few authors have insisted that many more than 3,000 were killed in those days – from 30,000 to 200,000 persons – but this figure is reflective of an emotional counter-weight to the former 'anti-fascist' mythology and is without any solid documentary base.[7]

The driving force behind the initial round of non-judicial mass purges and killings of 'fascist elements' in September and October 1944 were the so-called People's Militia (*Narodna Militsia*) forces, created as early as 10 September by a special decree of the council of ministers. This totally new armed organisation was staffed almost exclusively by former guerrillas (partisans), recently released political prisoners, members of underground armed groups and other functionaries of the illegal communist movement against the former regime. One of the first leaders of the People's Militia with the rank of lieutenant colonel was the future leader of Bulgaria, Todor Zhivkov. On 3 October 1944 the regency council approved in the name of the young King Simeon II a special law of the 'people's court' directed against all former government members during the Second World War, but very soon thereafter, on 7 October, the chief of the People's Militia issued an order to stop all 'arbitrary' arrests and house searches. Most probably one of the reasons for this directive was the arrival on the same day of a British military mission to Bulgaria, composed of 110 personnel.

Political developments in Bulgaria in the first weeks after the Red Army invasion were dictated also by the behaviour of the Third Ukrainian Front occupation troops. It is worthy of mention that before the end of the war Soviet representatives not only downplayed the eventual process of 'Sovietisation', but also insisted on a policy of 'correction' and restriction of 'leftist errors', 'preserving' in this way the fighting potential of the Bulgarian army. This paradoxical tendency[8] could be explained by the fact that the main Soviet goal was to expel German troops from the Balkans, as well as by Stalin's long-standing intention to use Bulgaria's strategic location as a gateway to the Bosporus and the Black Sea straits in order to realise the old Russian dream of an outlet on to the Mediterranean. There were also important disputes with the western allies, such as the German settlement and the issue of Poland's future borders.

At the same time, the Soviet military administration became exceptionally jealous of the activities of the western representatives in Bulgaria and did everything to eliminate their influence in the region. In a secret cable to Marshal Fedor Tolbukhin, commander-in-chief of the Third Ukrainian Front, Stalin ordered:

> The group of English officers who came to visit [Colonel-General Sergei] Biriuzov should know:
>
> 1. Nobody is going to conduct negotiations with them, for there are no instructions from above;
> 2. All the groups that have arrived should be asked to go back immediately, for they are on the front line and they will not be allowed to go anywhere;
> 3. In future, if any foreign representatives arrive, they should be detained and not allowed to go anywhere without permission from the Supreme Command. No negotiations of any kind should be carried out with them.[9]

The Anglo-Soviet 'percentage agreement' on spheres of influence, suggested by Churchill and accepted by Stalin on 9–11 October 1944, played a fateful role in the post-war political development of the Balkan countries. In a secret message of 8 March 1945, prime minister Churchill confessed to US president Franklin Roosevelt:

> In order to have the freedom to save Greece, Eden and I agreed in October that the
> Russians should have the say in Romania and Bulgaria, while we are going to have
> control in Greece. Stalin kept strictly to this agreement during the 30-day battles
> against *ELAS* [Greek communist armed forces] in Athens even though it was very
> uncomfortable for him and his entourage. Now Stalin leads an opposite course of
> action in the two Balkan Black Sea countries. Despite everything, I'll be careful
> not to show that I know this, so that Stalin wouldn't say: I didn't interfere in your
> business in Greece, why don't you give me the same freedom in Romania?[10]

Highly characteristic for this period was the statement of the Soviet foreign
minister, Viacheslav Molotov, in a conversation with Bulgarian communist
leader, Georgi Dimitrov, immediately after the Potsdam conference: 'Basically,
these agreements are to our advantage. In effect, this sphere of influence has
been recognized as ours.'[11]

After the signing of the armistice agreement with the countries of the anti-
Nazi coalition on 28 October 1944, the new rulers of Bulgaria used to their
utmost Articles 6 and 7 and their provisions for 'the apprehension and trial of
persons accused of war crimes' and for the immediate dissolution of 'all pro-
Hitler or other fascist political, military, paramilitary and other organisations
on Bulgarian territory'.[12] Later, on 26 January 1945, a special law for the
protection of the people's authority was adopted. Article 1 postulated that
anyone who organised or led an organisation 'that had as its aim the overthrow,
subversion or weakening of the authority of the Fatherland Front would be
punished with life imprisonment under a severe regime or with death'.

Three days after the 9 September coup, thirty-four generals, ninety-one
colonels and forty-seven officers were dismissed from the armed forces
following an order by General Damian Velchev, the Bulgarian war minister. In
the next two months, using the provisions of the 'people's court' law, the
People's Militia arrested 746 officers, and investigated 687 more, no matter that
some of them were actively fighting Nazi troops in Yugoslavia and Hungary. In
November 1944, twenty-five professors were dismissed from Sofia University
and another twenty-nine intellectuals were expelled from the Union of
Bulgarian Writers, according to a new decree on the 'purgation' of 'fascist
elements' from academic and cultural institutions.

In the period December 1944 to April 1945 the so-called 'people's court' held
135 trials involving a total of 11,122 people accused of pro-fascist behaviour
and crimes. These trials were held under the legal framework of the 'Decree-Law
to try at the people's court all those guilty of Bulgaria's entry into the World War
against the allied nations, as well as of all the evil miseries linked with that war'.
Over 9,000 verdicts were pronounced, with a staggering 2,730 people sentenced
to death and 1,305 to life imprisonment. Among those sentenced to death were
three ex-members of the regency council to the minor King, twenty-two
ministers from various cabinets of the period January 1941 to September 1944,

sixty-seven former members of parliament and forty-seven generals and colonels from the armed forces.[13]

Soviet 'advisers'

The first Soviet representatives to appear in Sofia, on 10–11 September 1944, were not regular army regiments, but military intelligence and counter-intelligence (SMERSH) units led by General Alexei Vul, Colonel Boris Zaitsev and Colonel Sergei Zotov.[14] They displayed a keen interest in the files of the Bulgarian state security and police dealing with German, British and Turkish intelligence activities in the country.

One of the first NKGB and Military Intelligence (GRU) operations in Bulgaria in late September and early October 1944 was to activate former agents in local political circles. According to information addressed to the communist leader Vŭlko Chervenkov in 1950, in the initial weeks after Soviet troops entered Bulgaria in September 1944 Lieutenant-Colonel Iakov Savchenko, a former Soviet military intelligence officer in Sofia in 1941–42, reappeared in the country. The main task that he assigned to his former agents was to monitor the behaviour of non-communist political leaders and gather information about the activities of British and American representatives on the Allied Control Commission in Bulgaria. After his return to Moscow, Savchenko was replaced by another military intelligence officer resident during the war years, Colonel Leonid Sereda. Highly valued information came in 1945–46 from an agent (alias 'Brodsky'), who infiltrated the entourage of the Agrarian Party opposition leader Nikola Petkov. He sent various reports on confidential talks between Petkov and the American political and military plenipotentiaries in Sofia, Maynard Barnes and Major-General John Crane. Part of this information was delivered by General Pavel Fitin, the NKGB foreign intelligence directorate chief, to Bulgarian communist leader Dimitrov, the former secretary general of the Comintern and chief of the international relations department of the Soviet Communist Party in 1944–45.

The first NKGB 'instructors' were sent to Sofia in November 1945 under the cover of homecoming Bulgarian emigrants. Colonel Lev Studnikov was the main intelligence and security 'adviser' to Anton Yugov, the Bulgarian minister of the interior; Colonel Petr Golubenko was responsible for the reorganisation of the Bulgarian counter-intelligence service, and Colonel Ivan Zelenskii (Zalakis) for that of the Bulgarian militia. As happened almost everywhere in the newly established Soviet 'sphere of influence', former NKVD agents among the east European communist emigration to the Soviet Union during the inter-war years soon infiltrated the re-established security service apparatus. In 1947 a new group of Ministry of State Security (MGB) 'advisers', led by Colonel Mitia Trifonov, was sent to Sofia to 'help' in the communist purges of opposition leaders.

The next chief MGB 'adviser' in Bulgaria, General Stepan Filatov, even began to ignore the Bulgarian party's Politburo decisions and personally participated in the interrogation and torture of political prisoners. However, when Filatov started to invent new 'conspiracies' against certain Bulgarian Politburo and Central Committee members, he was recalled to Moscow in mid-1951 following a strong official protest to Stalin by the Bulgarian prime minister, Chervenkov. Filatov was soon sentenced together with his boss General Viktor Abakumov. During Stalin's lifetime, Soviet 'advisers' exercised direct control over the security services and had free access to special agents' information, a privilege not enjoyed even by most Bulgarian communist leaders and the minister of internal affairs.

Post-war political repression

Newly revealed documentation from the Bulgarian archives provides more information on one of the most controversial questions of Cold War history – whether Stalin's pre-election speech of 9 February 1946 or Churchill's 'Iron Curtain' address at Fulton, Missouri, on 5 March of the same year were the first official ideological indications of the beginning of the Cold War. These documents show that precisely in the middle of March 1946, that is after the Fulton speech, Soviet policy towards Bulgaria changed considerably (as well as towards Greece), gradually becoming harsher. In the discussions over the formation of a new Bulgarian government on 13 March 1946, no one proposed any changes to the appointment of non-communist ministers to some influential positions. The very same evening, however, an abrupt ultimatum from Soviet foreign minister Molotov arrived: 'You have to appoint a new minister of foreign affairs in place of [Petko] Stainov, because we do not trust him . . . The Stainov people abroad are a threat to stable relations with the USSR. This shouldn't last any longer.' On 18 March, a second telegram arrived from Molotov, criticising the leaders of the Bulgarian Communist Party: 'We are astonished by your modesty and lack of initiative in this assignment. The Yugoslav communists are much better and more active than you are.' The next day in a secret telegram from Dimitrov to Stalin and Molotov, the Bulgarian leader explained that the prime minister, Kimon Georgiev, had insisted that Stainov be given 'another lower position.' On 20 March Molotov replied: 'In order not to make the formation of the new government more difficult we believe that Stainov could be left temporarily in a less responsible position. Later on, however, you have to remove him from the government, for he does not deserve any trust.'[15]

The start of the Cold War in Bulgaria was also clearly indicated by the fact that the key post of minister of foreign affairs was resolved in favour of Soviet interests, communist predominance in the new Fatherland Front government became more pronounced and attacks on the anti-communist opposition were stepped up. Furthermore, in the next few months the Soviet leaders pushed for the organisation of a thorough purge among the Bulgarian officer corps. The best example of these actions was the fate of the war minister, General Velchev. After a visit to Moscow in June 1945 and talks with Stalin, Velchev seemingly gained a stable position supported by Dimitrov, who in November 1945 at a meeting with a group of generals declared that the communist party stood firmly behind Velchev.[16] However, from March 1946 Moscow urgently insisted on an immediate purge of the war ministry. At a secret tripartite meeting in Moscow on 6–7 June between Stalin, Tito and Dimitrov, the Soviet boss once again praised the Yugoslavs and criticised the Bulgarians for their 'insufficiently decisive measures', advising them to initiate a radical purge of the Bulgarian officer corps from top to bottom and to take the armed forces firmly in their hands. This was, perhaps, Stalin's first ever direct critique of a communist leader in Eastern Europe and it was to have major ramifications.

On 19 June 1946 the Soviet representatives on the Allied Control Commission for Bulgaria, Marshal Tolbukhin and Colonel-General Biriuzov, received a directive from Moscow instructing them to undertake measures to 'restrict the powers of war minister General Velchev and remove reactionary officers and generals from the Bulgarian armed forces'.[17] One month after Stalin's intervention, Velchev was dismissed from his post and in July to August mass dismissals of former royal officers started at the ministry. As a result, 1,909 officers were purged, many of them arrested on fabricated charges of 'militarily conspiring' against the regime. The investigations were 'assisted' by several Soviet state security instructors who had arrived in Sofia seven months earlier. Two years later, at a Cominform meeting in Bucharest, Bulgarian deputy prime minister Kostov provided a retrospective justification for the actions against Velchev:

> We are not going to hide from this friendly audience that our Soviet comrades, and especially comrades Stalin and Molotov, turned out to be better informed about our affairs than we were . . . In the middle of 1946, when we had the illusion that we could control our former war minister and the reactionary officers, comrades Stalin and Molotov called our attention to the unfavourable situation in the army.[18]

According to some accounts, from the end of the Second World War to September 1953 more than 106 political trials were held. Initially, the repressions were directed against the higher ranks of the army and the most vocal representatives of the 'old' political parties. Several 'army conspiracies' were exposed publicly in 1946–47, as a result of which nearly half of all 'Tsarist officers' were fired. The leader of the Bulgarian Agrarian Union, Dr Georgi M. Dimitrov, was sentenced to life imprisonment *in absentia*.[19] The chair of the opposition Social Democratic Party, Krastiu Pastukhov, received a five-year sentence, but in August 1949 he was found strangled in prison.

The announcement of the Truman Doctrine on 12 March 1947, which provided for military and economic support for Turkey and Greece and condemned the pro-communist regimes in Eastern Europe, caused anxiety within the ruling circle of the Soviet Union and its Balkan allies. The British representative in Sofia, John St Bennett, noted that: 'The speech of President Truman from March 12th caused great confusion and disturbance in the Government.'[20] The French minister, Jacques-Emil Paris, sent a similar report to the Quai d'Orsay.[21] The American envoy, John Horner, in a talk with his British colleague in June 1947, commented on the position of the Bulgarian government:

> The Truman policy in Greece and Turkey has raised wide-spread hope in Bulgaria that American (and British) interests would spread later on to Bulgaria and would lead to the replacement of the present government by a truly democratic one. The present government is disturbed by this reaction and is afraid of a possible war between the USSR and the Anglo-Saxon Powers. If a war like this occurs Bulgaria would be in the front line, facing neighbours ready to attack it, equipped with American aid . . . This makes the Communist government more anxious to defend itself and to show that it is able to protect Bulgaria's sovereign rights.[22]

The new international situation in the wake of the Cold War predetermined the elimination of political opposition in Bulgaria in the next few months. The leader of the parliamentary opposition and of the Agrarian Union, Petkov, was stripped of parliamentary immunity, arrested on 7 June 1947 on false allegations of treason and, after a show trial, was sentenced to death and executed on 23 September of the same year. Shortly before, Stalin and Dimitrov had discussed Petkov's execution in a confidential meeting and on 17 September the Bulgarian prime minister sent a coded cable to Kostov from Moscow:

> After the Anglo-Americans interfered and demanded the rescinding of the death sentence, the issue has acquired new dimensions in light of our domestic and foreign politics and calls for change of our initial plans. All that has a direct influence on Bulgaria's sovereignty and also encourages the activities of the reaction in our country. If we do not carry out the sentence, it would be considered . . . a surrender to outside interference and would undoubtedly encourage renewed intervention . . . Any wavering on this issue, to judge from the standpoint of the current situation in our country and abroad, might only cause damage. You should act firmly, with long-term state interests in mind. This is also the opinion of our [Soviet] friends.[23]

A special law banned the opposition Agrarian Union, dissolved its parliamentary group and many party activists were arrested. This repressive law affected more than 150,000 members and loyalists of the Agrarian Party. In November 1948 several former members of parliament and activists of the opposition Social Democratic Party were also charged, their leader, Kosta Lulchev, receiving a fifteen-year prison sentence.

After the defeat of the official political opposition in the second half of the 1940s, the most serious danger for the communist regime turned out to be the emergence of various armed groups in the regions of Sliven, Pazardzhik and the Rhodopi mountains in 1950–51. Some of these 'forest people' (*goriani*) squads numbered 50–70 combatants, among them several well-equipped fighters who had been trained in special centres in Turkey and Greece before illegally crossing the border or being transported to Bulgaria by aeroplane. As the efforts to destroy these groups through blockades, ambushes or secret posts proved fruitless, their liquidation was achieved mainly by infiltrating state security agents into their ranks and by carrying out counter-intelligence operations. According to Bulgarian state security reports, about 440 members of illegal armed squads were killed during the period 1949–56 and over 800 of their supporters in mountain villages were arrested.[24]

Bulgarian Gulags

The first concentration camp after the establishment of the Fatherland Front government was set up as early as the end of October 1944 in the village of Zeleni Dol in south-western Bulgaria. It was established in accordance with the provisions of the armistice agreement and on the instructions of the Allied Control Commission and it initially held citizens of Nazi Germany and its satellite countries – Austrian, Hungarian and other citizens, as well as Bulgarians who had married and thus formed families with such citizens. There were nearly 250 people detained there at the end of 1944 and early 1945.[25]

On 20 December 1944 the government adopted two laws: the decree for labour correction centres for criminals and the decree for labour correction centres for politically dangerous people. The laws were ratified by the three members of the regency council in the name of the minor King Simeon II. The first camp began functioning in January 1945 in the region of the town of Sveti Vrach (now Sandanski) and in April of the same year it was transferred to the region around the city of Dupnitsa–Bobovdol. In October 1945 the same camp was moved to the Bogdanov Dol and Kutsian mines near the town of Pernik, thirty kilometres from the Bulgarian capital. The first people there were former policemen, officers of the royal army and Russian White Guard émigrés. According to official statistics, the number of 'politically dangerous people' interned in 1945 was 3,298. In 1948 the Bulgarian authorities agreed with the request of the Soviet government to transfer to the USSR over 300 Russian emigrants, who had voluntarily served in Nazi army and police units.

From mid-1946 onwards, many representatives of the opposition Agrarian and Social Democratic parties were despatched to the camps, as were some anarchists. In 1948 a law was adopted that transferred the authority over prisons and camps from the ministry of justice to the ministry of internal affairs, with direct guidance being in the hands of the state security directorate. By September 1949 over 4,500 people were incarcerated in the labour camps. Additionally, existing documentation shows that in 1951 over 6,600 political prisoners were held in Bulgarian prisons, 2,360 of whom were sentenced, seventy-nine to the death penalty. In 1952, 2,799 were charged with political offences, 1,857 being sentenced in the same year, with more than 100 death penalties. In 1953, the last year of the 'total' terror, there were 6,523 political prisoners with 917 sentenced the same year, sixty-two to death. A total of 1,019 were sentenced for foreign 'espionage' for that same period. Several years later, in 1959, 1,650 people were in Bulgarian prisons serving sentences for 'counter-revolutionary activities'. Moreover, summary reports of the state security services acknowledged that while in 1953 about 4,600 'traitors of the Fatherland' (that is, political emigrants) were living abroad, a decade later their number had grown to 5,933.

The largest labour camp in Bulgaria – on the Danube river island of Persin near the town of Belene – was closed in September 1953. At the time, there was a total of 1,913 inmates in the camp, 1,732 of whom were there for political reasons. Another element that should be added to the labour camp statistics is the forced labour mobilisation of the period 1946–49 under the terms of the law on labour mobilisation adopted in August 1946. Under these provisions in 1949 alone over 2,000 people, among them 433 women, were arrested and forced to work without any payment. Another form of mass political repression was the internment and relocation of people from Sofia and other big cities to distant and under-populated areas of the country. The first wave of such relocations came in the autumn of 1945 and it concerned 326 relatives of the already sentenced (and many executed) ex-ministers, regents, parliamentarians, high military officers and police ranks from the former regime. In the period September 1945 to August 1953 a total of 7,025 families with 24,624 members were relocated and interned in different parts of the country.

A state security report from March 1951 provides another fearsome statistic, quite typical for the essence of a totalitarian state. At that time 207,396 persons were placed under 'strict surveillance' by the secret services, among them 79,473 former adherents of the banned opposition Agrarian Union, 34,551 social democrats, 14,150 ex-members of the 'Legion' mass organisation, 7,880 members of the former official youth organisation 'Ratnik', 3,870 members of the 'Zveno' party, 2,911 anarchists and 1,385 members of the Democratic Party.[26]

Internal enemies within the party

A year after the attacks on the political opposition, a new repressive wave followed, this time directed at the 'enemy with a membership card' inside the communist party. It was orchestrated by the Kremlin and 'supported' by MGB 'advisers' in Sofia and 'prosecutor squads' from Moscow. The most important show trial was that of Traicho Kostov, the former vice-prime minister in Dimitrov's cabinet and a secretary of the Bulgarian Communist Party. The first serious signals against Kostov were inspired by the Soviet embassy in Sofia in October 1948. He was accused of harbouring a 'nationalist attitude' towards Soviet representatives in Bulgaria for not providing them with full information about the real prices of Bulgarian foreign trade products. In early December, during a high level meeting in Moscow, Stalin directly accused Kostov of 'insincerity'. One month later at the constituent Comecon session in the Soviet capital, Stalin again hinted that a 'nationalistic' trend existed in the Bulgarian party, an insinuation which provoked further charges against Kostov from party leaders in Sofia. Consequently, in March 1949 Kostov was expelled from the Central Committee and several of his close collaborators were arrested. The Soviet chief security adviser, Colonel Trifonov, personally participated in the investigation, elaborated the chain of accusations against Kostov and concocted a new overall scenario, this time of espionage for Great Britain. On 13 April the Bulgarian interior minister discussed the 'Kostov case' with Stalin and Abakumov. Ten days later a secret operation codenamed 'Doctor' was launched to constantly shadow the movements of the former vice premier. Finally, on 20 June 1949 Kostov was arrested.

In the last days of June, Soviet security 'brigades' were despatched to Sofia and Budapest to 'assist' in the parallel investigations against Kostov and Rajk. The group in Bulgaria was led by Colonel Lev Shvartzman, known in Sofia as 'General Chernov'. The results were almost immediate: more high level Bulgarian party and state officials were detained in July and August. A secret visit to Sofia by the Soviet deputy minister of state security, General Ogoltsov, heralded a new direction for the 'Kostov case'. On 3 September Abakumov sent a report to Stalin which signalled that the 'British' connection was to be dropped in favour of a 'Titoist' orientation. Shvartzman delivered the new version to Sofia and, according to the testimonies of leading Bulgarian security officers in 1956, the final indictment was initially written and edited in Russian and then translated into Bulgarian. Following a sham trial, Kostov was sentenced to death and executed on 16 December 1949.[27]

An interesting facet of the trial, scarcely mentioned in contemporary historiography, is that it was accompanied by a top secret Soviet security mission. Between 18 October 1949 and 14 January 1950, a special regiment of 668 servicemen, armed with submachine guns and mortars, arrived clandestinely from Moscow via the Black Sea port of Odessa. These special forces, dressed in civilian clothes, took close guard of the main party and state buildings in Sofia, including the residence of the Soviet ambassador. Further security units from Kiev and Minsk were deployed in other large Bulgarian cities and disbursed along the borders with Yugoslavia, Greece and Turkey. The Soviet leaders left nothing to chance.

The fabricated trial of the former no. 2 Bulgarian communist leader ensnarled in turn the US diplomatic representative to Sofia, Donald Heath. In January 1950 ambassador Heath was ostentatiously declared 'persona non gratis' which logically resulted in the curtailment of diplomatic relations between the two countries. The wider global significance of this act was taken into consideration by the US State Department in a secret analysis in Washington dated 6 April 1950:

> The USSR is firmly resolved to limit as much as possible normal relations between the Soviet world and the United States. The severance of diplomatic relations with Bulgaria could be considered as a test meant to establish the extreme which the USSR is determined to reach in this respect.[28]

Nearly 100,000 communist party members were investigated and under surveillance in the period 1948–53, including some at the highest levels of the state administration, the party apparatus, army and the security services. During the mass purges of 1948–50 the whole staff leadership of state security was replaced, and in 1951 twenty-eight senior officers and 343 members of the secret services were fired. The total number of members dismissed from state security in the period 1949–56 was 5,108, but enrolment increased from 3,614 to 7,000. The informal apparatus of secret agents numbered 55,000 collaborators (informers, residents and safe-house keepers).[29]

Spiritual oppression

In parallel with the government's energetic atheistic propaganda campaigns, the security services instigated show trials and repressive actions against representatives of different religious denominations. The influence of the Catholic and Evangelist churches in Bulgaria was traditionally slight. That is why the communist regime's efforts were oriented initially to overpower the Orthodox church clergy, the Islamic imams and the Jewish rabbis. In 1948 growing pressure against the Holy Synod of the Orthodox church culminated in the arrests of several clergymen and bishops, while the head of the Bulgarian Orthodox church, Exarch Stefan, was forced to retire into 'voluntary exile' in a small monastery.

In March 1949 an open trial was held of fifteen representatives of the Evangelist church, five of whom were sentenced to life imprisonment for 'espionage in favour of British-American imperialism'.[30] A year later came purges against the 'agents of the Vatican'. Secret trials were held in the first half of 1952 against four Catholic priests, and in the autumn of the same year a show trial orchestrated by the communist regime followed the arrests of forty Catholic bishops, priests and ordinary lay church-goers. Four death sentences were pronounced and executed – against Bishop Evgeni Bossilkov, Father Josefat Shishkov, Dr Kamen Vichev and Father Pavel Dzhidrov. Many of the other accused received sentences of varying years of hard-regime imprisonment.[31]

Stalin's death did not significantly alter the political situation in the country, frequently described in the west as the most loyal Soviet satellite. From 1947 on there was no active and influential political opposition to the regime inside Bulgaria, while the political emigration abroad was rather fragmented and divided. A CIA national intelligence estimate of 4 April 1955 affirmed:

> Traditionally, through race, language, and culture the Bulgarians have been closely linked with the Russians . . . In view of the regime's effective security controls, close Soviet supervision, and the absorption of Bulgaria into the Soviet security sphere, there is little likelihood that organized resistance can develop under cold war conditions . . . The average Bulgarian is too engrossed in the daily struggle of living and too cowed by the police state to have time and energy left for resistance activities.[32]

Repercussions of the central European revolts, 1956

Similar to other east European countries, Khrushchev's 'secret speech' at the twentieth Soviet party congress in February 1956 caused tremors among Bulgaria's political elite. Illusions arose that there was a chance to liberalise the Stalinist regime. However, the changes introduced in Bulgaria at the beginning of April 1956 amounted to purely cosmetic measures undertaken with the Kremlin's direct participation and control. Under pressure from Khrushchev, Chervenkov, the Stalinist dictator, remained a member of the Politburo and of the Bulgarian government. According to most western diplomats and observers, Chervenkov continued to run party affairs from behind the scenes and Zhivkov's election to the position of party first secretary in 1954 represented merely a transitional compromise arrangement. Actually, it was to be a compromise that lasted thirty-five years until November 1989! The commission that came into being at the time to rehabilitate suppressed party members and liberate political prisoners also proposed highly imperfect measures which suffered, to a great degree, from internal contradictions. For example, in the case of the former deputy prime minister Kostov the commission found the accusations of 'spying' to be groundless, but it failed to retract the other charges against him of 'nationalism' and 'anti-Soviet sentiments'. Likewise, nobody in the former party leadership or in the security services was condemned for having tortured political prisoners. In this atmosphere, any overt manifestation of anti-communist opposition in Bulgaria in 1956 was out of the question regardless of certain social tensions which existed, mainly among intellectual and military party circles. These modest attempts to initiate an open public discussion were, however, cut short within a few months. The leading party organ embarked on a sharp propaganda campaign against 'petit-bourgeois laxity' among the intellectuals.

While armed clashes occurred in Hungary and Soviet forces launched 'Operation Whirlwind' at the beginning of November 1956, state security officers and the party apparatus in Bulgaria re-launched mass repression against anyone who had expressed discontent in the past or who had harboured views differing from the official Stalinist line. In a mere six days, from 4–9 November 1956, 564 persons were arrested, including 115 former opposition functionaries of the Agrarian Union and 251 other politicians who had been in power before the coup of 9 September 1944. The minister of internal affairs even proposed the formation in Bulgaria of armed 'workers' combat units', whose main task 'would be to nip counter-revolution and all manifestations of hostility in the bud, wherever they might arise'.[33]

The concentration camp near Belene was re-opened immediately after the Hungarian revolt and by the beginning of 1957 there were over 1,120 prisoners, among them the ex-prime minister Konstantin Muraviev and several former MPs and ministers of the Democratic Party. In June 1958 the number of interned people was 2,729, the greatest part of them being officially declared 'persons with criminal behaviour'. The Belene labour camp was finally closed after a report by Zhivkov on 27 August 1959 on the eve of the Soviet–American summit between Khrushchev and President Eisenhower in Geneva and soon after diplomatic relations between Bulgaria and the USA had been re-established. During its entire existence, 154 people died in captivity, 120 of them political prisoners. The practice of mass relocations of families of so-called 'enemies of the people' was also restored after October 1956. In April 1957, for instance, there were proposals for the resettlement of nearly 1,000 families of internal 'enemies'. In the next three years 1,651 families were relocated, with the total figures for the whole five year period (1956–61) numbering over 8,000 persons.[34]

The primary outcome of the Bulgarian leadership's reaction to the central European revolts of 1956 was a return to a fiercely repressive internal policy which lasted for over ten years. A CIA intelligence estimate from 4 February 1958 called Bulgaria the most 'Sovietised' country in the eastern bloc.[35] In contrast to the other Warsaw Pact states, during Zhivkov's thirty-five years of authoritarian personal rule there was no influential organised opposition movement in Bulgarian society.[36] The first serious 'heretics' and 'dissidents' to the regime appeared only in the last few years or even months of communist rule.

The establishment of the Stalinist regime in Bulgaria followed a pattern similar to that in other east European countries. It was marked by strict Soviet control and realised with energetic subordinate efforts by local communists. At the end of the 1940s, the mass purges of former ruling elites and the consequent elimination of the non-communist opposition under the slogans of 'anti-fascism' and 'proletarian dictatorship' entirely reproduced the Stalinist political model of a 'socialist state'. The further cleansing and eradication of all 'nationalist' trends inside the Bulgarian Communist Party disciplined its membership and instilled loyal obedience to Moscow in a situation in which accusations of 'anti-Sovietism' became more dangerous than those of 'national treason'. Although Stalinist terror in Bulgaria, as elsewhere, peaked in the period 1948–53, milder recurrences sporadically resurfaced, generally inspired by political crises in other east European states. It was quite typical for Bulgaria that from the beginning of the 1950s no organised political opposition existed inside the country, émigré groups were relatively weak and disunited, and for years the only resistance and challenge to the ruling elite came from within party circles. Logically and ironically, the strongest threat to Zhivkov's personal power was an unsuccessful military coup organised by pro-Stalinist party and military officials in April 1965. Thus, the long-term consequence of Stalinist terror was the preservation of a relatively monolithic political regime throughout the Cold War era.

Notes

1 According to the newly approved Law for State Security Dossiers, adopted by the Bulgarian parliament in December 2006, all police and security records kept at the ministry of internal affairs became available for the period 1944–90. However, a thorough examination of this huge documentation will take a long time judging from the fact that the files of the Investigation and Prison Departments alone (Archive of the Ministry of Internal Affairs (AMVR), Sofia, Record Groups 6, 12 and 63) comprise about one million pages.

2 T. Volokitina et al. (eds), *Sovetskii faktor v Vostochnoi Evrope, tom 1, 1944–1948* (Moscow, 1999); *tom 2, 1949–1953* (Moscow, 2002).

3 T. Volokitina et al., *Moskva i Vostochnaia Evropa. Stanovlenie politicheskikh rezhimov sovetskogo tipa 1949–53: Ocherki istorii* (Moscow, 2008).

4 For details on these publications, see K. Jordanova and J. Baev, *History of Bulgaria in the Cold War Era: A Bibliography, 1989–2004*, www.coldwar.hu (available from March 2009).

5 J. Bell, *The Bulgarian Communist Party from Blagoev to Zhivkov* (Stanford, 1985); R. Crampton, *A Concise History of Bulgaria* (New York, 2005); V. Dimitrov, *Stalin's Cold War: Soviet Foreign Policy, Democracy and Communism in Bulgaria, 1941–48* (Basingstoke, 2008).

6 In a very interesting report to the Foreign Office from May 1961, the British ambassador to Warsaw, Sir George Clutton, keenly perceived the national peculiarities of the Bulgarians comparing them to the Poles. See D. Dimitrov, *Sŭvetska Bŭlgariia* (London, 1994), p. 90.

7 An official report from December 1944 claimed that in September and October of that year approximately 5,000 people were declared 'missing'. In 1982 a state security officer composed, on the basis of existing documents, a list of 1,904 named 'fascists' killed in late 1944, and in 1991, following the downfall of the communist regime, a special governmental commission estimated that between 18,000 and 25,000 persons were killed in the first months after the September coup. For details, see D. Sharlanov, *Tiraniiata. Zhertvi i palachi* (Sofia, 1997), pp. 8–9.

8 This tendency is on record in a variety of western intelligence and diplomatic reports. See, for example, National Archives and Record Administration (NARA), Washington, RG 226, R/A, L 45284 and L 47437; Ministère des Affaires Étrangeres (MAÉ), Paris, Archives Diplomatiques, série Z, carton 65, dossier 1, vol. 8, no. 1006 and vol. 9, no. 670; The National Archive (TNA), Kew, Foreign Office (FO), Political, 371/43 591, pp. 32–3.

9 Central State Archive (TsDA), Sofia, CMF 18, no. 893/9, k. 43.

10 W. S. Churchill and F. D. Roosevelt, *The Complete Correspondence*, vol. 3 (Princeton, 1984), p. 489.

11 Cited from the English text: I. Banac (ed.), *The Diary of Georgi Dimitrov, 1933–1949* (New Haven, 2003), p. 377. For the Bulgarian original, see G. Dimitrov, *Dnevnik (9 mart 1933 – 6 februari 1949)*, ed. by D. Sirkov et al. (Sofia, 1997), p. 492.

12 The armistice agreement, special legislation and statistics in this section are cited from the documentary reader, *Narodna demokratsiia ili diktatura? Khristomatiia po istoriia na Bŭlgariia, 1944–48* (Sofia, 1992). In the period September 1944 to November 1945, the Bulgarian parliament did not function and, contrary to constitutional procedures, all new laws were promulgated as decrees by the regency council.

13 P. Semerdzhiev, *Narodniiat sŭd v Bŭlgariia 1944–45* (Sofia, 1997).

14 In these years the Soviet intelligence and security system comprised four main organisations: NKVD (renamed MVD in March 1946) – the Ministry of Internal Affairs; NKGB (renamed MGB in March 1946 and KGB in 1954) – the Ministry of State Security; GRU – military intelligence; and SMERSH (included in the MGB in March 1946 as its Third Directorate) – military counter-intelligence. Literally, SMERSH is an acronym of 'Death to Spies'.

15 TsDA, fond 146 B, newly declassified record no. 5032, t. 2, papka 10, ll. 5–12.

16 TsDA, f. 265 B, op. 1, a.e. 35, ll. 1–2.

17 Library of Congress, Washington D.C., Manuscript Division, General Dmitrii Volkogonov Papers, reel 6.

18 TsDA, f. 214 B, op. 1, a.e. 497, l. 6.

19 Following an abortive attempt to arrest him, Dr Dimitrov hid at the US political representative's residence and emigrated from Bulgaria in August 1945.

20 TNA, FO 371/66 905, p. 78.

21 MAÉ, Archives Diplomatiques, série Z, carton 68, dossier 1, vol. 27, p. 148.

22 TNA, FO 371/66 907, pp. 81–2.

23 Banac (ed.), *The Diary of Georgi Dimitrov*, pp. 427–8.

24 *Gorianite: Arkhivite govoriat. Dokumentalna poreditsa, 1944–49*, vol. 1, no. 16 (Sofia, 2001).

25 All data on concentration camps in this section are taken from P. Stoianova and E. Iliev, *Politicheski opasni litsa. Vŭdvoriavaniia, trudova mobilizatsiia, izselvaniia sled 1944 g.* (Sofia, 1991).

26 AMVR, f. 13, op. 1, a.e. 1822, l. 22.

27 M. Isusov, *Poslednata godina na Traicho Kostov* (Sofia, 1990).

28 *Foreign Relations of the United States. Diplomatic Papers, 1950*, vol. IV (Washington DC, 1980), p. 290.

29 J. Baev and K. Grozev, 'Bulgaria', in K. Persak and Ł. Kamiński (eds), *A Handbook of the Communist Security Apparatus in East Central Europe, 1944–1989* (Warsaw, 2005), p. 41.

30 One of the surviving victims testified in his memoirs that together with Bulgarian security officers the arrested clergymen had been interrogated by two Soviet 'advisers'. See M. Mateev, *Na slovoto ti se opovavakh: prezhiviana tragichna istoriia na edin osŭden v protsesa sreshtu evangeliskite pastori 1948–49* (Sofia, 1993), p. 60.

31 Zh. Tsvetkov, *Razpiatieto* (Sofia, 1994).

32 NARA, Record Group 263, entry 29, box 10 – CIA NIE 10–55, 'Anti-Communist Resistance Potential in the Sino-Soviet Bloc', 12 May 1955.

33 AMVR, f. 66, op. 1, a.e. 49, l. 11.

34 All figures in this paragraph are taken from Stoianova and Iliev, *Politicheski opasni litsa*.

35 NARA, Record Group 263, entry 29, box 10 – CIA NIE 12–58, 'Outlook for Stability in the Eastern European Satellites', 4 February 1958.

36 Open Society Archive (OSA), Budapest, fond 300, sub-fond 8, J. L. Kerr, 'Dissidence in Bulgaria', *RAD Background Report*, no. 156, 10 July 1978.

Purge and counter-purge in Stalinist Albania, 1944–1956

Robert C. Austin

The story of the consolidation of power by the Albanian Communist Party (ACP) is relatively well known. Despite better access to archives inside Albania since the 1990s, the picture that emerged with the works of Elez Biberaj, Anton Logoreci, Nicholas Pano, Peter Prifti, Stavro Skendi and Louis Zanga is still predominantly accurate.[1] Wherever communists took power, the process was decidedly violent and predatory with few real heroes. At the outset, the Albanian regime was no more or less deadly than others in the emergent Soviet bloc, especially in the aftermath of the Soviet–Yugoslav split, which – as other contributions in this volume show – led to wide-scale purges. In this piece, I attempt a synthetic treatment of the early years of what became, arguably, the harshest form of Stalinism in communist Europe long after Stalinism had been subject to reassessment elsewhere.

Albania has long been victim of a series of negative attributes – it was the most isolated, most Stalinist, most bizarre and, worst of all, generally known as the poorest country in Europe. It is true that the form of communism that Albania adopted in the weeks and months that followed the victory of the Albanian communists in 1944 set the tone for four decades of brutal rule with huge human and other costs. While Albania entered communism worse off in virtually every statistical measure, the regime's methods served to make the gap even wider when the country's belated transition from communism started in 1991. The legacy of early Stalinism, both in the economic and political realm, along with subsequent refusals to reform even in the wake of Stalin's death in 1953, ensured that Albania faced the most daunting of challenges when the impetus for change finally came.

The period between 1944 and 1956 is essential in understanding the nature of the regime and the shifts in Albania's external policy that followed. It is as important to recognise that Albania, as a small, weak, poor and often 'irrelevant' state, found itself primarily reacting to events outside its borders, a phenomenon which had significant implications for its domestic affairs. It is indeed a paradox that a country liberated by local communists rather than the Soviet Red Army in 1944–45 would find itself most tied to external pressures. The initial period also reveals a surprising amount of factional activity inside the ACP and an equally impressive range of intra-party debate. This centred on the unusual shifts in Albania's foreign alliances from Yugoslavia, to the USSR, to China and finally to an ultimately catastrophic form of self-reliance in 1976. External pressures and personality wars over control of the party–state apparatus created a series of purges, executions, exile and prison sentences that dominated Albanian society into the early 1980s. It also fed in to the most important and regrettable legacy of Albanian communism: the fostering of a siege mentality based on perceived external and internal 'enemies' that led to profound isolation. What allowed Albania to pursue policies that were at odds with the mainstream, even within the bloc, was the fact that the country was essentially peripheral.

Hence, the period 1944–56 is extremely important as it set the tone for Albania for the next forty-five years. Stalinism, which was characterised by massive and often bloody purges of the party, remained the cornerstone for maintaining party discipline long after the thaw of 1956 took hold in other Soviet-aligned states. Regardless of the erosion of Stalin's legacy and the softening of the edges, Albania's communists still revered the Soviet dictator as their source of modernity and political control. In fact, it was the use of purges, along with an obvious political acumen, that gave party leader Enver Hoxha the political longevity that was unrivalled among other communist leaders – only Yugoslavia's Josip Broz Tito and Bulgaria's Todor Zhivkov came close to Hoxha's forty-one years of rule (1944–85). As important, it would be an exaggeration to say that the ACP had achieved a high level of doctrinal purity by the end of the war. It was events between 1944 and 1956, but primarily between 1944 and 1948, that established Albania as a hard-line Stalinist state. In November 1944, as the communists celebrated their victory in the capital, Tirana, a number of significant and divisive questions remained on the table: what would be the nature of the relationship with the west, Yugoslavia and the USSR?; and was Stalinism an acceptable model to bring about Albania's transformation from semi-feudalism to a modern industrial society?

When the Berlin Wall came down in 1989, Albania held on to the epithet 'The last Stalinist outpost in Europe'. When scholars and analysts examine Albania, they often note that the country was the most Stalinist both in its economic and political agendas long after Stalinism had more or less disappeared elsewhere. Much of this is true. Albania, under the long-term dictatorship of Hoxha, maintained a strict adherence to Stalinism that was grounded in the early experiences of liberation and the post-war consolidation of power, and which became a key mechanism for Hoxha to preserve his often vulnerable position both inside and outside Albania.

Historical background

The legacy of Albania's wartime liberation struggle was instrumental in shaping the nature of Albanian Stalinism in the war's aftermath. When the Italians invaded on 7 April 1939, King Zog and his family fled Albania. This did significant damage to Zog's reputation as he had originally claimed he would stay on to lead the resistance. It also created a dangerous political vacuum in Albania. This is not to say that Zog left fertile ground for the growth of communism; only that his departure, along with large segments of the inter-war ruling elite, laid the foundations for a power struggle between a then nascent communist movement and conservative nationalists. Both groups had been sidelined by Zog's authoritarian state. The Axis occupation, first Italian and then German after September 1943, witnessed the emergence of two key factions seeking the removal of the occupiers and the creation of a new Albania – the communists and the *Balli Kombëtar* (BK), or National Front. Although communism had not been a major factor in inter-war Albania, it had made important gains prior to the Italian occupation, albeit lacking organisational unity.

The Yugoslav communists emerged as a central force in the creation and subsidisation of the Albanian communist movement, abetted by the Soviet Union, which, until 1948, allowed Yugoslavia to take the lead in Albanian affairs. Two members of the Communist Party of Yugoslavia (CPY), Miladin Popović and Dušan Mugoša, played important roles in the formation of the Albanian movement. Often the CPY's influence has been exaggerated owing to a dependence on Yugoslav sources, but while Tito's emissaries did not 'create' Albanian communism or the ACP their assistance during the war was nevertheless vital. Although various communist groups existed on the margins of society in the inter-war period, it was only in 1941 that three factions managed to unite to form a single party. Its first leader was Hoxha, born in 1908 in the southern town of Gjirokastër. Having studied in France in the 1930s and served in the Albanian counsel in Brussels, Hoxha had a certain cosmopolitanism and his experiences abroad exposed him to the main currents of Marxism in western Europe. As an ardent nationalist, deeply affected by Albania's historical experiences, and an able orator, he was the most logical choice as leader of the new party. Other influential figures included Mehmet Shehu, who was born in southern Albania in 1913 and who had fought in the Spanish civil war. During the Second World War, Shehu earned a reputation for extreme brutality orchestrating the wartime execution of Albania's northern tribal chiefs. David Smiley, a captain in the British army who served in Albania during the war, noted that Shehu 'seldom smiled except at other people's misfortunes.'[2] Koçi Xoxe, long heralded as the true proletarian in the party as he was a tinsmith, was, at least until 1948, second to Hoxha in terms of influence. However, both Shehu and Xoxe lacked Hoxha's undeniable popularity.

The communists, who in September 1942 formed the National Liberation Movement (NLM), which became the National Liberation Front in May 1944, were at first a broad coalition of nationalists and communists. Seeking to avoid being characterised as a communist front, the NLM based its programme more on nationalist appeals and a commitment to liberal democracy. It drew considerable support from the country's youth and the mass of poverty stricken peasants who had seen only marginal improvements in their quality of life under Zog. The *Balli Kombëtar* was founded in 1942 and in the early years of the liberation struggle the two groups managed to cooperate. Its leader, Midhat Frashëri, based the organisation's programme on calls for the creation of an ethnic Albania (that is, one that would include Kosovo) and a modern state along western democratic lines.

Kosovo, and its fate in the war's aftermath, played a key role in the subsequent battles inside the Albanian communist movement. The Axis incorporation of the region in 1941 had done much to rekindle interest in the Kosovo question, yet at the same time served to undermine resistance efforts. Regardless, the issue of an ethnic Albania figured prominently in the programmes of both parties. Cooperation between nationalists and communists, however, always remained tenuous at best. The NLM became concerned with the BK's growing strength and sought to undermine its influence, first through cooptation and then through fratricidal conflict. The main attempt at coordination took place at a meeting in the town of Mukja in August 1943. The resultant Mukja Accord continues to attract attention and with greater access to party archives, many questions about this subject can be answered. Representatives of both the BK and the NLM met and hammered out a plan for joint cooperation in the liberation struggle, forming the Committee for the Salvation of Albania.

Most important was the recognition that both groups would strive for the creation of an ethnic Albania. Hoxha, however, completely rejected the accord. In the first place, given the Serb attachment to Kosovo, the agreement on the region aroused deep concerns among Yugoslav communists, who no doubt put considerable pressure on Hoxha. This and other internal issues ensured that during the war the Albanian communists found themselves already working against domestic opponents. In 1943, Anastas Lulo and Sadik Premte were purged on charges of Trotskyism – Lulo was executed and Premte fled abroad. In the aftermath of the Mukja Accord, Mustafa Gjinishi, who had supported the agreement, was executed.[3] I emphasise the accord as it was critical in establishing the nature of the relationship between Albania and Yugoslavia and thus had a profound effect on the ACP.

Aside from Yugoslav pressure, it is doubtful that Hoxha, noted for his vanity, envisioned full cooperation with the BK on an equal footing. Also, since the Kosovars were both Gegs from the north and anti-communists, Hoxha did not attach much significance to the area as a wartime issue, but viewed its solution in the framework of the eventual victory of both Albanian and Yugoslav communism. Indeed, the struggle against northern opposition, embodied by the local Gegs and the Catholic church, was a key component of the purges and violence that accompanied the communist takeover in 1944. Hoxha thus took the Kosovo question off the table. Documents confirm that he considered Kosovo essentially a Yugoslav problem. The repudiation of the Mukja Accord ensured that the liberation struggle also became a civil war. After the collapse of Mukja, Abaz Kupi, a leading patriot, formed the Legality organisation, which was the only body in wartime Albania that called for the return of King Zog. Indicative of Zog's weak position in his homeland, coupled with the fact that so many of his supporters had been forced to flee, Legality remained forever on the fringe of the struggle for Albania's liberation and never received any substantive support from the Allied Powers. Zog's inability to achieve recognition in exile, and the disorganisation of the BK, were therefore important factors in the communist victory. Also, from the autumn of 1943 the new German occupying forces allowed Albania a measure of self-government, which bought off some members of the BK.

As elsewhere in the Balkans, the communists emerged as the most effective fighting force against the fascists and were thus accorded considerable aid from both Britain and the United States. However, the key factor in ensuring the success of the Albanian communists was the incompetence and disorganisation of their opponents. Moreover, since Zog had left the peasantry largely untouched, communist calls for social justice and land reform found a highly receptive audience. The outcome was a communist-dominated provisional government installed in Tirana on 29 November 1944. Without Soviet assistance, the Albanian communists had assured victory in their homeland even before the end of the war. This fact was to be of considerable importance to the new regime whose historical experiences became prominent in the shaping of policy in the years to come. Hoxha and his clique could not hide their elation, and possibly surprise, at their astounding success. Their enemies, both real and perceived, were to suffer as the party set about establishing itself as the single source of authority.

Consolidation 1944–49

Hoxha's government used all available means to consolidate itself and exhibited extraordinary impatience in implementing radical political and economic changes. A key component, as elsewhere in what was to become the communist bloc, was violence and repression. Reprisals were designed to eliminate rivals and intimidate ordinary people. A large number of opponents, especially in alternative movements like the National Front and Legality, were rapidly liquidated. Those who did not manage to flee the country were brought before a 'people's court'. Of special interest for Hoxha's communists was the Catholic clergy in the north, because, as in the days of King Zog's regime, they were 'the only well-organized force in Albania.'[4] At a meeting of the Central Committee in October 1945, Hoxha made clear his fear of the church and his reference to 'eliminating' its impact was equally obvious in its intent:

> It is not easy to work with the Catholic clergy. The clergy is influential in Shkodër and the surrounding region, and this influence cannot be eliminated merely by administrative measures. The Catholic clergy is a well-organized body with strong traditions and close links with external reaction and the Vatican.[5]

Hoxha went on to mention that the church had to be fought on the party's ground. Therefore, the Catholic church, which rejected Marxist ideology and opposed the formation of a communist state, was brutally suppressed by the authorities. This was deemed necessary also because the church possessed great human potential in that its members were educated, western-orientated and had marked influence in the north.

As a result, by 1946 all foreign priests were forced to leave Albania and church property was confiscated. In 1948 alone, eighteen Catholic clerics were executed and by 1952 all twenty-four high clerics had vanished, thirty-five priests were jailed for long terms, ten had disappeared and eleven were recruited into the army. In 1951, the independence of the Catholic church was made null by decree with the establishment of a national church totally dependent on the state. By 1953, 153 Catholic churches were taken over by the state and were destroyed or transformed into youth community centres.[6] The Islamic and Orthodox faiths did not fare much better. At the outset, religious instruction and attendance were discouraged and places of worship were gradually closed. Hoxha's obsession with religion as an obstacle to national unity and party control culminated in the Cultural Revolution of 1966–69, at which time Albania declared itself the world's first atheist state after the country's three religions – Islam, Orthodoxy and Catholicism – were essentially shut down and effectively eliminated. While relations between religious communities and the communist state had been strained everywhere in the Soviet bloc, only in Albania was some kind of compromise impossible.[7]

The attack on religious institutions coincided with an equally vicious crackdown on the numerically tiny intelligentsia. In an effort to make everyone toe the single 'party line', together with the fact that neither Hoxha nor Xoxe trusted intellectuals, a substantial cleansing took place between 1946 and the early 1950s. Parallel to the attack on the Catholic church, the hardest hit were the intellectuals in and around Shkodër in northwestern Albania. In a speech in October 1946, Hoxha declared that Albania's schools and culture 'must be cleansed of all reactionary ideologies.'[8] What this meant in practice was that the entire re-tooled intelligentsia had to serve the party alone, with special attention to the glorification of the partisans' success during the war. Those who chose to ignore the new rules faced prison or even execution. Some of the country's most influential figures, including writers, jurists and scholars, were incarcerated; others were executed. Prifti has calculated that ten intellectuals were killed and more than three dozen ended up in prison.[9]

Another critical task was to deal with the simple fact that the Albanian communist movement was primarily, though not entirely, a collection of Tosks from the south of the country. As Pano has pointed out, a large minority of Gegs, or northern Albanians, had little sympathy for the communists.[10] The hostility between Tosks and Gegs was made worse in that the communists, who were deeply linked with Tito's partisans, had little stomach for the notion of unification with Albanian-dominated Kosovo. For the communists, and the archives make this clear, Kosovo was essentially a Yugoslav problem.[11] Hoxha had no time for the additional headaches that would have accompanied assuming control there. As important, unlike other ethnic groups in Yugoslavia, the Albanians in Kosovo refused to cooperate with Tito's Popular Front.[12] For Tito, along with Xoxe, the Kosovo question would be solved by Albania's integration into Yugoslavia.

Some authors, notably Isa Blumi, have argued that the establishment of Hoxha's state and the terror that accompanied it must be viewed in the context of Geg–Tosk relations.[13] This is certainly part of the picture and does help to explain the degree of violence that accompanied the communist seizure of power, especially in northern Albania. In addition to the need to consolidate its position in areas where its support was weak, the party also had to develop a unified position on two crucial issues – policy towards Tito's Yugoslavia, which had played such a prominent role in Albania, and the attitude towards the west and the Soviet Union. Even before the communist takeover, some factions, notably one led by Nako Spiru, were calling for closer ties with the USSR. Others hoped that somehow Albania could balance itself between east and west. Hoxha's position in all this is unclear – like many communist leaders he was able to shift alliances depending on what the situation on the ground dictated. Forever the opportunist, Hoxha preferred to see which way the wind was blowing. These critical questions were only resolved with the Tito–Stalin split in 1948 and Albania's subsequent adherence to an orthodox Stalinist economic and political model.

As noted, the Albanian communists inherited an essentially feudal country dominated by a small group of large landowners. The first step was to eliminate these landed gentry whose power Zog had largely left untouched in exchange for them remaining out of politics. As such, the radical agrarian reform of 1945 had a huge impact as it completely destroyed the pre-war landowning class. Landowners with other sources of income lost all their land without compensation, and those who depended on agriculture saw their holdings reduced to

100 acres. Religious institutions also saw their land holdings reduced, while all forests and pasture lands were nationalised. This was a real windfall to the peasantry as some 70,000 landless or poor peasants received twelve hectares of land each. According to Logoreci, in less than a year the communists succeeded in eliminating the power of the landowner class, who had more or less run Albania since the Ottoman advance in the fifteenth century.[14] By one single decree, the communists effectively ended private agricultural property.

The communists also moved extremely quickly to establish control over what was a divided country with an incomplete national awakening. Although some historians, notably Bernd Fischer, have credited Zog with at least laying the foundations for a national consciousness, it was the communists who devoted themselves to eradicating what they perceived as obstacles to their vision of national unity and their absolute domination of all aspects of Albanian society.[15] Zog had left Albania more or less as he found it as his principal preoccupation was remaining in power. There were few schools, no universities, illiteracy was as high as 90 per cent and there was only limited infrastructure. The communist movement was the sole political force that emerged, albeit clandestinely, under Zog's authoritarianism. In power, they immediately seized control of the economy and worked to eliminate all aspects of non-communist foreign influence. One thing is clear, the Albanian communists' commitment to Stalinism, in both economic and political spheres, was unparalleled in the communist world. Their subsequent developmental strategy was firmly based on Stalin's *Economic Problems of Socialism in the USSR* (1952), and the adoption of Stalinism by the party leadership was entirely voluntary and not the 'result simply of subservience to the Soviet government.'[16] Stalinism, for Hoxha, was the only sure method for Albania's modernisation and communist control hit hard at what was essentially a traditional and patriarchal society serving to shatter the main tenets of pre-war life.

In the political realm, the communists immediately established special tribunals to try alleged war criminals, which in the end included not just those who collaborated with the Axis occupation, but anyone who seemingly opposed the policies of the new communist government. These trials were under the direct control of Xoxe, the minister of the interior and for all intents and purposes the party's number two man. Xoxe staged a series of show trials in January 1945 that resulted in hundreds of convictions and by the spring 'the communists succeeded in eliminating or discrediting a substantial portion of the pre-war political elite.'[17] The courts, under strict party control, meted out harsh sentences for any deviations. Special people's courts and military tribunals operated between December 1944 and January 1945 and were charged with rooting out war criminals and 'enemies of the people'. Skendi has calculated that 'hundreds of non-communists went to the gallows' and some sixty former ministers, deputies and high government officials were charged, of whom seventeen were executed.[18] Not a single person involved had any legal experience whatsoever and spectators were encouraged to weigh in on the proceedings.[19] Hoxha noted in one of his many volumes of memoirs that the crowds, both in and out of the court, declared: 'Long Live the people's justice! Death to the war criminals.'[20] The trials served three main purposes: to show to a largely uneducated population the extremely high price of dissent; to sow fear of foreign 'enemies' among society; and to eliminate party factions.

Throughout the communist period, figures for those jailed or internally exiled range from lows of 12,000–15,000 to highs of 50,000–60,000. Between 1945 and 1956, some 80,000 political arrests were made from a total population of less than two million. By 1961, reports estimated that fourteen labour camps existed near mines, industrial sites and other projects so as to take advantage of forced work brigades.[21] With the very pronouncement of the regime, the party established a system of special labour camps for those convicted. Party membership always remained out of reach for most people with no more than 3–4 per cent of the population claiming membership. Of that group, only 1,200 people really mattered. Events between 1944 and 1948 not only consolidated the party, but created a tiny and often related elite centred on Hoxha and a few other key families who grew increasingly isolated from ordinary Albanian society. The Albanian party retained its elite and nepotistic characteristics for the entire period of its rule.

The party relied on a vast network of Interior Ministry departments. Created on 20 March 1943 as a secret political police, the Directorate of State Security (*Drejtorija e Sigurimit te Shtetit*), popularly known as the Sigurimi, was one of the most shadowy secret police organisations in Eastern Europe. The Sigurimi was part of the Ministry of Internal Affairs, which also exercised authority over the judiciary and law implementation and enforcement. The political police eventually employed some 10,000 full-time agents with military rank, 2,500 of whom were assigned to the people's army, and reportedly a quarter of the adult population as part-time informers. Officers were generally career volunteers, recommended by loyal party members and subjected to careful political and psychological screening before finally being allowed to join the service. As elsewhere in communist Europe, they had an elite status and enjoyed many privileges designed to maintain their reliability and dedication to the party.

The Sigurimi boasted national headquarters and branches in each of Albania's twenty-six districts, and was organised into sections covering political control, censorship, public records, prison camps, internal security troops, physical security, counter-espionage and foreign intelligence. The political control section verified the ideological correctness of party members and ordinary citizens, monitored private phone conversations and correspondence, and purged the party, government, military and secret services of individuals closely associated with Yugoslavia, the Soviet Union and China after Albania broke off relations with each of these countries in turn, in 1948, 1961 and 1976 respectively.

Communist party purges

With much of the opposition to the communists eliminated by early 1945, the debate inside the party shifted to internal questions. What happened between 1944 and 1949 to many communists was as violent as the punishments meted out to nationalists, landowners, intelligentsia, Geg oppositionists and the Catholic church. The principal intra-party dispute was between moderates and hard-liners. The result was the first major purge of party ranks. Between 1945 and 1946, some 10 per cent of party members were expelled.[22] Although not entirely apparent at the time, the key issue centred on what was to be become an extremely violent clash between Hoxha and Xoxe. In essence, the fight between the two set off a prolonged battle that culminated in jail terms, executions and one suicide. The first battle involved relations with the west. Sejfulla Maleshova, poet of the partisan struggle, party ideologist and one-time minister of culture, had urged a softer line calling for good relations with both east and west. This ran counter to the pro-Yugoslav faction headed by Xoxe, who led the attack on Maleshova. At the sixth plenum of the Central Committee in February 1946, Xoxe accused him of upholding right-wing views on internal and foreign affairs and of advocating a 'completely opportunistic and liberal policy with regard to the relation which [Albania] should have with the Anglo-American imperialist countries.'[23] Pano suggests that Hoxha's initial sympathies were with the moderates, but that he saw the writing on the wall and joined the pro-Yugoslav group at least as a temporary move.[24]

In the wake of the sixth plenum Xoxe's faction initiated a dramatic purge of the party. Maleshova was expelled from the Politburo and the Central Committee and the debate over the orientation of Albania's foreign policy came to an end. The demise of Maleshova coincided with the aforementioned war on the intelligentsia which took place with Hoxha's full support. The series of arrests was a clear warning to people who cherished the hope of an independent Albania. At that point, Albania, with Xoxe's open support and Hoxha sitting on the fence, was moving towards integration with the Yugoslav federation.

The country's new constitution adopted in 1946 reflected the internal party situation and followed a decidedly Stalinist line. The cabinet placed huge power in Hoxha's hands when he was only thirty-five years old – prime minister, foreign minister, defence minister, commander of the armed forces and secretary general of the Albanian Communist Party. Xoxe remained interior minister and party organisational secretary. Hoxha held on to multiple positions until 1953 when he gave into some aspects of Khrushchev's de-Stalinisation by adopting a collective leadership. In 1946, Hoxha was the most powerful man in

Albania.[25] The moderates, essentially those who questioned both the over-whelming influence of the Yugoslavs and the growing hostility to the west, had been completely routed and Hoxha had joined Xoxe in denouncing the actions of Maleshova and others.

With the pro-Yugoslav faction in the ascendancy, relations between the two countries improved further with the signing of a Treaty of Friendship, Cooperation and Mutual Aid in July 1946. However, cracks in an otherwise perfect alliance began to appear with some in Albania decrying their loss of independence. For the Yugoslavs, economic aid was designed to ensure their political domination over Albania, but for many in the ACP economic and financial aid was expected to make the country economically independent. Party unity also suffered considerably over the question of how far Albania should go in its relations with Yugoslavia. For many communists, it seemed absurd to fight a war of liberation only to end up as part of the Yugoslav Federation.

After the fall of the Maleshova group, the axe eventually fell on Spiru, who had been sent to Belgrade to try to negotiate both better economic terms and more Yugoslav financial assistance. Spiru's visit to Belgrade only served to worsen relations with Yugoslavia and brought things to a head inside the Albanian party with Tito declaring that Spiru was the major obstacle to good Albanian–Yugoslav relations. Spiru and others opposed to Belgrade's growing and undeniable control over the Albanian state argued that the country was destined for permanent under-development. They were bitter about Albania's role in the envisioned economic cooperation agenda. Spiru rejected Yugoslav designs, which included an offer of a secret pact protecting Yugoslav interests in Albania in the event of a change of government in Tirana. With the support of his allies, in February 1947 Xoxe counter-attacked by orchestrating the expulsion of nine members of the people's assembly. They were charged with plotting against the state. The group included Maleshova, Kosta Boshnjaku, the director of the national bank, and others. Thereafter Xoxe turned his sights on Spiru, who, in late November 1947, allegedly committed suicide, likely avoiding either execution or a prison sentence. One source, at least, claims that Spiru was in fact murdered by Xoxe's secret police.[26] Whatever happened, Spiru's death removed the principal opponent of Yugoslav influence inside the Albanian party.

The story at this point is well known and little has emerged to alter the main facts previously established. By late 1947, Yugoslavia had decisive influence in Albania and Xoxe had already indicated that a merger of the Albanian and Yugoslav armies was inevitable – a first step towards eventual unification. Some 1,000 Yugoslav specialists were working in the country and the Yugoslav Communist Party even had a representative inside the ACP's Central Committee.[27] Equally telling was the fact that Albania was not invited to the founding meeting of the Cominform in September 1947 and nor was it later admitted to the organisation largely because the Yugoslavs were deemed capable of representing Albanian interests. This in itself is testimony to the peripheral role Albania maintained in the bloc.

At that time, Hoxha's position in the party was extremely weak, but the growing rift between Stalin and Tito was about to transform party dynamics. The eighth plenum of the ACP in February 1948, however, confirmed Xoxe's pro-Yugoslav position and Hoxha was forced to admit to past errors: he performed ritual self-criticism, saved himself and retained his position as party leader. The plenum brought with it multiple expulsions, including Spiru's widow, Liri Beleshova, and Shehu, Albania's best known military leader. The meeting even went so far as to approve the merger of the Yugoslav and Albanian armies and economies. Between early March and June 1948, Xoxe worked hard to eliminate all his opponents, especially Hoxha. However, the acrimonious break between Moscow and Belgrade on 28 June changed everything as Albania was the first in the bloc to denounce Tito. It was the only chance to alter Tirana's growing subservience to Belgrade and likewise Hoxha's only chance to save his life. The nature of the Tito–Stalin split is beyond the scope of this chapter. Suffice to say, it was primarily the Albanian question that caused the rift as Stalin was deeply disturbed by Tito's expansionist foreign policy.[28] In the aftermath of the split, a jubilant Hoxha repudiated all agreements with the Yugoslavs and sent the vast array of specialists and advisers packing. Life for Xoxe became increasingly precarious.

Unlike Xoxe, Hoxha worked slowly and meticulously to crush his opponents. His strategy, which amounted to piecemeal removal of Xoxe's key positions of influence, allowed him the time to consolidate his own position both within the party and with his new bosses in Moscow. Hoxha concluded economic agreements with Moscow to mitigate the loss of Yugoslav support. By September 1948 figures like Beleshova and Shehu were back, the latter taking over the crucial position of interior minister. Xoxe, who had quickly recanted, performed self-criticism and adopted an anti-Yugoslav stance, found himself and his key lieutenants demoted. This was only a temporary reprieve. Hoxha waited until the eleventh plenum in November 1948, which, at Moscow's insistence, officially changed the name of the Albanian Communist Party to the Albanian Party of Labour (APL), in order to expel Xoxe and his main allies. Xoxe's 'mistakes' were that he had always put his Yugoslav patrons first and Albania second and that he had driven Spiru to suicide. In the wake of the plenum, the late Spiru was rehabilitated. The first congress of the APL, also held in November, promoted a group of Hoxha supporters at all levels and Albania, at least until 1956, entered the fold as a satellite of the USSR.

Following his trip to Moscow in March 1949 to sign new trade agreements and to receive permission from the Soviets for his move on Xoxe and instructions on just how to proceed, Hoxha staged a secret trial of Xoxe and his allies between 11 May and 10 June. Accused of treason, Xoxe was shot on 11 June 1949. His supporters, principally the former head of the party control commission Pandi Christo, earned lengthy prison sentences. The state prosecutor, Bedri Spahiu, based his case on the group's alleged Trotskyism and Titoism. Xoxe confessed that he had organised his own faction within the party and had willingly collaborated with the government in Belgrade knowing full well that they planned to make Albania the seventh republic of Yugoslavia. Radio Tirana told listeners on 10 June that Xoxe was convicted as the 'chief bandit of the Trotskyite group of enemies of the people.'[29] The day after, it was announced that Xoxe had been executed, although Khrushchev claimed in his memoirs that Shehu had personally strangled Xoxe.[30]

George Hodos, in his important work on the period, has argued that the Xoxe trial was a copy of the 'classical Stalinist purges of the 1930s, transferred to a Balkan country', but was also 'the starting shot for the beginning of a new phase of show trials, the exception that proved the rule.' The big difference between the Xoxe trial and those elsewhere in the Soviet bloc was that Xoxe really was guilty of Titoism. Soviet agents took over from the Yugoslavs as advisers to the Sigurimi and engaged in the systematic torture of Xoxe and his followers for five months. His trial had repercussions far beyond Albania as it set in motion a series of other trials throughout the region on falsified charges of 'Titoism'. To invoke Hodos again, the trial sent a clear message to other satellite states about the dangers of breaking with Moscow, serving to brand opponents of the new line as criminals or agents of imperialism.[31]

Any attempt to rehabilitate Xoxe, even with Khrushchev's encouragement in the more relaxed climate of 1956, was rejected by Hoxha. Xoxe went down in history as a traitor who sought to create the conditions for a Great Serb empire in the Balkans. Hoxha insisted that under Xoxe the Interior Ministry had been conducting all kinds of surveillance activity against senior party members and that a dossier had been prepared on Hoxha himself. As far as the Yugoslavs were concerned, the attack on Xoxe was an attack on the workers' dimension of the APL. Writing on 14 June, Milovan Djilas, at that time a close associate of Tito, noted that 'every communist, every honest fighter for truth and justice, ought to examine his conscience over the innocent sacrifice of Koçi Xoxe.'[32]

The breakdown in relations with neighbouring Yugoslavia also intensified Albania's, and Hoxha's, adherence to the Stalinist line. As was often the case, it was external events that influenced developments inside the Albanian party. Hoxha became a lifetime Stalinist in 1949 in the wake of the rift with Yugoslavia. This is not surprising given the legacy of the preceding four years. However, in the aftermath of the split much work remained to be done in order to establish party unity. In the period 1948 to 1952, party membership actually dropped due to massive purges.[33]

The finishing touches, 1950–56

The execution of Xoxe, which was certainly one of the darkest episodes in Albanian communism, led not to calm and peace inside the party, but to a wave of dismissals and arrests which had parallels throughout the communist bloc. In an effort to eliminate the last vestiges of pro-Titoist, pro-Yugoslav and pro-Xoxe elements, a vicious purge took place starting in 1950. At the upper levels of the party, five out of twenty-one Central Committee members were expelled. At the grassroots level, some 12,000 people – an astonishing 25 per cent of the party – were excluded.[34] A verification process, which took place between April 1950 and September 1951, reviewed all party memberships. Nearly 4,000 people were expelled for 'hostile activities' and another 220 were let go for being 'unworthy'.[35] The aftermath of Xoxe's execution was definitely the high point of the purge campaign. At a party conference in 1950, Hoxha expelled Abedin Shehu, the minister of industry, and Niazi Islami, deputy communications minister, for 'anti-party' and 'anti-Soviet' activities. These expulsions were followed by a series of trials throughout the country designed to ferret out real and perceived 'Titoist' elements.

Attempts by the western powers, notably Britain and the United States, to topple Hoxha's regime only made matters worse as they reinforced Hoxha's mantra that Albania was encircled and under siege by internal and external threats and machinations. The actions of the so-called Committee of Free Albanians between 1950 and 1953 could not have come at a better time for Hoxha, who had consistently sought to create a siege mentality among the population. With support from both the UK and USA, several incursions into Albanian territory were undertaken, but the operations were betrayed by the British double-agent Kim Philby, who informed the Soviets, and through them the Albanians, of virtually every detail of the plan.[36] As a result, each incursion was met by Albanian forces. Hoxha had already announced in April 1950 that invasions were under way and that several arrests had been made.

Even today, aspects of what was called 'Operation Valuable' are unclear. It was either a paramilitary operation designed to overthrow Hoxha outright or to ascertain if enough opposition existed in Albania to permit his overthrow. Whatever the truth, we do know that a number of invasions did take place and that the whole business was a total disaster with only one person winning: Hoxha. As Sarah-Jane Corke has noted: 'Operation Valuable should never have been undertaken. It was reckless and foolhardy.' Of the sixty or so men who parachuted into Albania between 1949 and 1953, 'less than a handful survived to tell their story. Those who did survive had to contend with arrest and torture of their families.'[37] A bomb explosion at the Soviet legation in 1951 was also met with more internal house cleaning as events like these gave legitimacy to the regime and created the conditions for the elimination of dissent. It led to the demotion of Tuk Jakova, party organisational secretary, and Manol Konomi, minister of justice, among others.

By early 1953, Hoxha and Shehu were triumphant. However, the respite was only temporary as once again external developments called into question Hoxha's leadership. Just how Albania, as the most devout of Stalinist countries, would react to the winds of change in the USSR that accompanied Stalin's death in March 1953 was always unclear. Stalin's death came just as the two men had more or less succeeded in consolidating their hold on both the party and the nation. Not surprisingly given the potential for a coup or a serious challenge to their authority, neither Hoxha nor Shehu travelled to Moscow for Stalin's funeral. Nevertheless, this was odd given their devotion to the late dictator. Any reassessment of the Stalinist line had direct and dangerous consequences for Hoxha and his lieutenant. With the rapprochement between Khrushchev and Tito in 1955, there was a real fear that their days were numbered.

At the outset, Albania did make certain moves consistent with what was happening in Moscow. In 1953 a form of collective leadership was adopted with Hoxha relinquishing his posts as foreign and defence minister. In 1954, a further step was taken on this road when Hoxha gave up the prime ministership in favour of Shehu. These were small and in some ways cosmetic changes. The Albanian leadership, however, drew the line at a Soviet-encouraged rapprochement with Belgrade or any fundamental reassessment of the Stalinist economic and political model. This forced the party to begin looking for alternatives to an increasingly reformist USSR. While there is no space here to re-tell the story of Albania's bizarre shift from Soviet to Chinese satellite, it is enough to say that, as in 1948, external developments in the communist world acted to save Hoxha and Albanian Stalinism.

The dramatic events of 1956, especially Khrushchev's de-Stalinisation speech at the twentieth congress of the Soviet party in February and the Hungarian Revolution in the autumn, allowed Hoxha to stay in power and move even further away from the USSR and Yugoslavia. In the course of 1956, Soviet diplomacy was encouraging Hoxha to mend fences with the Yugoslavs and calling for some fairly significant changes in Albania's decidedly Stalinist developmental path with a greater emphasis on agriculture and less on heavy industry. Voices were heard within the party, too, advocating a softer internal and external line and it appears that the Hoxha–Shehu alliance was facing a serious challenge in the wake of change in the USSR and improved Soviet–Yugoslav relations. The first calls for reform came from the prosecutor in the Xoxe case, Spahiu, and Jakova, the vice-premier. Hoxha accused the latter of working with the Catholic clergy and both men were removed from their posts for 'revisionist' activity and sentenced to jail. Spahiu died at the hands of the police and Jakova faced internal exile until 1991. A key beneficiary of their demise was Ramiz Alia, who was later to assume the number two position in the party hierarchy following the alleged suicide in 1981 of Shehu, who had been 'exposed' as a foreign agent in the pay of multiple countries.

Khrushchev's 'secret speech' was a direct attack on the very basis of Hoxha's rule. According to Pano, Jakova, Spahiu, General Panajot Plaku, General Dalli Ndreu and his wife, Liri Gega, had garnered Yugoslav support and approval from the Soviets to gain control of the party in April 1956.[38] Documents indicate that there were serious demands from within for change and the rehabilitation of prominent members, even Xoxe. However, despite increasing pressure from the Soviets, Hoxha refused to rehabilitate Xoxe.[39] For Hoxha, and any objective observer for that matter, Xoxe had worked exclusively for Albania's union with Yugoslavia. If Hoxha is to be believed, the Jakova–Spahiu group attempted to take over the party with both Yugoslav and Soviet backing. Gega and Ndreu were consequently executed in November 1956. While pledging his support for the decisions of the twentieth congress of the CPSU and acceding to some modest changes to the party leadership, Hoxha had eliminated yet another challenge to his tutelage. What is more, in contrast to other countries in the Soviet bloc, the victims of the Albanian 'Titoist' purges never found themselves back in the fold.

Conclusion

What, then, if anything, was distinctive about the purges and counter-purges in Stalinist Albania? A crucial feature to bear in mind is that unlike Yugoslavia, where the party had unparalleled unity of command, the ACP found itself divided when it took power in 1944. It was rife with dissension – in fact, it was only by the early 1950s that party unity had been achieved through a variety of methods. Even then, it was a brief honeymoon as the death of Stalin in March 1953 and Khrushchev's subsequent de-Stalinisation speech again called into question Hoxha's leadership. The regime's internal and external insecurity drove events. It was certainly both factors that forced Hoxha to accept such a high degree of Yugoslav interference in Albania's domestic affairs from the foundation of the party in 1941 to the break in 1948. Throughout the communist bloc there were common features in the shift to a completely Soviet-style leadership, which in Albania was in place with the execution of Xoxe in June 1949. The adherence to violence and massive purges was not unique, but it was in some ways more easily done in Albania than elsewhere. The country's miserable inter-war political and economic legacy set it apart from other states – the legacy of Zog's personal authoritarianism meant that democratic impulses were severely under-developed, social democracy was virtually non-existent, only limited centres of resistance to the communists emerged during the war and those that did lacked unity or the support of Yugoslavia.

By the end of 1956, Hoxha had been able to remove all his opponents. This is not to say that purges, which had been the cornerstone of maintaining party control, were now a thing of the past. Indeed, routine and vicious cleansing of party ranks remained, although executions were replaced by prison sentences or internal exile. The aforementioned Cultural Revolution brought with it some significant changes to party structures. In 1967, Hoxha announced a programme to eliminate religious practices and 'bourgeois attitudes' among other threats to party discipline. Thousands of agitators took to the field to convince the people of the error of their ways. For the communists, the near total elimination of religion was considered one of their greatest achievements. In the 1970s, a purge of the cultural elite took place and, as we have seen, in 1981, bringing back memories of 1949, Shehu allegedly killed himself after being exposed as a foreign agent. Shehu, like Xoxe and so many others, disappeared from the official history of Albanian communism.

A statistical look at the party by 1960 provides a gloomy picture:

> Of the 14 Central Committee members elected at the foundation of the party in 1941, Hoxha was the only one still alive; . . . 14 of the 31 Central Committee members elected in 1944 had been liquidated and only 9 remained in office; and . . . of the original 109 members of the National Assembly, 17 had been shot, 15 imprisoned, 2 had committed suicide and only 29 were still politically active.[40]

What went on at the top was not radically different at the grassroots level. Hoxha and Shehu managed to maintain their primacy through constant and violent purging. The impact of this was felt throughout the country. Despite its small size, Albania, especially in the north, is rugged and inaccessible. Nevertheless, writing in 1971, Julian Birch noted that 'as far as it was possible to ascertain, party control and influence extends to the most obscure and backward villages, where portraits of Hoxha, and even Mao, as well as the routine Marxist slogans, are to be seen in abundance.'[41] Birch also observed the near total absence of outside knowledge among Albanians, with the regime systematically depriving them of any contact with foreign countries, travel, television and radio being virtually banned. Tight controls inside the country coincided with extraordinary security on the frontiers.

Emerging from the Second World War as an essentially feudal society with illiteracy estimated at over 80 per cent, Albanian communists used Stalinism as both an economic and political tool to enforce their vision of modernisation. More than any other communist elite, the Albanian leaders always applied solutions that were fiercely radical and ultimately by the book, combined with an absurdist siege mentality that convinced many Albanians that the world really was against them. The legacy of the inter-war period, which included poverty, illiteracy, superstition, tribalism and epidemics, meant that the Albanian leadership invariably took extremely strong measures. That said, Albanian

Stalinism was not merely a state-building tool; it was used by the communists to impose their vision of nation-building as evidenced most tellingly by the Cultural Revolution in the late 1960s. The end result when communism finally collapsed was a cowed and timid population cut off from the outside world, the near total absence of serious dissident movements and a completely destroyed economy. This ensured that Albania's transition to democracy after 1991 was fraught with setbacks and by far the most arduous in the region.

Notes

1   E. Biberaj, *Albania: A Socialist Maverick* (Boulder, 1990); A. Logoreci, *The Albanians: Europe's Forgotten Survivors* (Boulder, 1977); N. Pano, *The People's Republic of Albania* (Baltimore, 1968); P. Prifti, *Socialist Albania since 1944* (Cambridge: MA, 1978); S. Skendi (ed.), *Albania* (New York, 1956). Louis Zanga was an analyst with Radio Free Europe/Radio Liberty in Munich. His work in the RFE/RL Daily Reports and Research Reports is unrivalled.

2   D. Smiley, *Albania Assignment* (London, 1984), p. 56.

3   Enver Hoxha maintained that Gjinishi was a British agent who was killed in an ambush in 1944. See E. Hoxha, *The Anglo-American Threat to Albania* (Tirana, 1982), p. 224.

4   S. Skendi, 'Albania Within the Slav Orbit: Advent to Power of the Communist Party', *Political Science Quarterly*, vol. 63, no. 2 (1948), p. 265.

5   Cited in O. Pearson, *Albania as Democracy and Dictatorship* (London, 2006), p. 474.

6   I. Blumi, 'Hoxha's Class War: The Cultural Revolution and State Formation', *East European Quarterly*, vol. 33, no. 3 (1999), p. 307.

7   Logoreci, *The Albanians*, p. 155.

8   Prifti, *Socialist Albania*, p. 172.

9   Prifti, *Socialist Albania*, p. 171. Prifti provides a detailed list of names of those imprisoned or executed.

10 Pano, *The People's Republic of Albania*, p. 62.

11 For a discussion of the archives and the Kosovo issue, see R. Austin, 'Greater Albania: The Albanian State and the Question of Kosovo, 1912–2001', in J. Lampe and M. Mazower (eds), *Ideologies and National Identities: The Case of Twentieth Century Southeastern Europe* (Budapest, 2003), pp. 235–53.

12 J. Perović, 'The Tito-Stalin Split: A Reassessment in Light of New Evidence', *Journal of Cold War Studies*, vol. 9, no. 2 (2007), p. 43.

13 I. Blumi, 'The Politics of Culture and Power: The Roots of Hoxha's Postwar State', *East European Quarterly*, vol. 31, no. 3 (1997), p. 381.

14 Logoreci, *The Albanians*, p. 155.

15 See Bernd Fischer's seminal study, *King Zog and the Struggle for Stability in Albania* (Boulder, 1984).

16 A. Schytzer, *Stalinist Economic Strategy in Practice* (Oxford, 1982), pp. 5–6.

17 Pano, *The People's Republic of Albania*, p. 59.

18 Skendi, *Albania*, p. 104.

19   Logoreci, *The Albanians*, p. 85.
20   E. Hoxha, *Laying the Foundations of a New Albania* (Tirana, 1984), p. 529.
21   See D. Hall, *Albania and the Albanians* (London, 1994), p. 57.
22   Pano, *The People's Republic*, p. 66.
23   Cited in Pearson, *Albania as Democracy and Dictatorship*, p. 16.
24   Pano, *The People's Republic*, p. 67.
25   Pano, *The People's Republic*, p. 68.
26   See G. H. Hodos, *Show Trials: Stalinist Purges in Eastern Europe, 1948–1954* (New York, 1987), p. 8.
27   Perović, 'The Tito-Stalin Split', p. 45.
28   Perović, 'The Tito-Stalin Split', p. 34. See also L. Gibianskii, 'The Soviet-Yugoslav Split', in K. McDermott and M. Stibbe (eds), *Revolution and Resistance in Eastern Europe: Challenges to Communist Rule* (Oxford, 2006), pp. 17–36.
29   Cited in Pearson, *Albania as Democracy and Dictatorship*, p. 343.
30   S. Talbott (ed.), *Khrushchev Remembers* (Boston, 1971), p. 527.
31   Hodos, *Show Trials*, pp. 5 and 10–12.
32   Cited in Pearson, *Albania as Democracy and Dictatorship*, p. 347.
33   Prifti reported that party membership stood at 45,382 in 1948, but only 44,418 in 1952. Prifti, *Socialist Albania*, p. 30.
34   J. Birch, 'The Albanian Political Experience', *Government and Opposition*, vol. 6, no. 3 (1971), p. 374.
35   Pano, *The People's Republic*, p. 94.
36   For Philby's extremely interesting version of events, see his *My Silent War* (London, 1968).
37   Sarah-Jane Corke, *US Covert Operations and Cold War Strategy: Truman, Secret Warfare and the CIA, 1945–1953* (London, 2008), pp. 82 and 99.
38   Pano, *The People's Republic of Albania*, p. 118.
39   For details, see J. Halliday (ed.), *The Artful Albanian. The Memoirs of Enver Hoxha* (London, 1986), pp. 212–13.
40   Birch, 'The Albanian Political Experience', p. 376.
41   Birch, 'The Albanian Political Experience', p. 363.

List of major works cited

General works (including works on Stalinist terror in the Soviet Union)

Apor, B., Apor, P. and Rees, E. A. (eds), *The Sovietization of Eastern Europe: New Perspectives on the Postwar Period* (Washington DC, 2008)

Berend, I. T., *Central and Eastern Europe, 1944–1993: Detour from the Periphery to the Periphery* (Cambridge, 1996)

Conquest, R., *The Harvest of Sorrow: Soviet Collectivisation and the Terror-Famine* (London, 2002)

Corke, S.-J., *US Covert Operations and Cold War Strategy: Truman, Secret Warfare and the CIA, 1945–1953* (London, 2008)

Courtois, S. et al., (eds), *The Black Book of Communism: Crimes, Terror, Repression* (Cambridge: MA, 1999)

Davies, R. W. and Wheatcroft, S. G., *The Years of Hunger: Soviet Agriculture, 1931–1933* (Basingstoke, 2004)

Deák, I., Gross, J. T. and Judt, T. (eds), *The Politics of Retribution in Europe: World War II and Its Aftermath* (Princeton, 2000)

Figes, O., *The Whisperers: Private Life in Stalin's Russia* (London, 2007)

Gerlach, C. and Werth, N., 'State Violence – Violent Societies', in M. Geyer and S. Fitzpatrick (eds), *Beyond Totalitarianism: Stalinism and Nazism Compared* (New York, 2009), pp. 133–79

Getty, J. A. and Naumov, O. V., *The Road to Terror: Stalin and the Self-Destruction of the Bolsheviks, 1932–1939* (New Haven and London, 1999)

Glenny, M., *The Balkans, 1804–1999: Nationalism, War and the Great Powers* (London, 1999)

Goldman, W. Z., *Terror and Democracy in the Age of Stalin: The Social Dynamics of Repression* (Cambridge, 2007)

Gregory, P. R., *Terror by Quota: State Security from Lenin to Stalin (An Archival Study)* (New Haven, 2009)

Hagenloh, P., *Stalin's Police: Public Order and Mass Repression in the USSR, 1926–1941* (Baltimore, 2009)

Halfin, I., *Terror in my Soul: Communist Autobiographies on Trial* (Cambridge: MA, 2003)

Harris, J., 'Encircled by Enemies: Stalin's Perception of the Capitalist World, 1918–1941', *Journal of Strategic Studies*, vol. 30, no. 3 (2007), pp. 513–45

Hellbeck, J., *Revolution on my Mind: Writing a Diary under Stalin* (Cambridge: MA, 2006)

Hodos, G. H., *Show Trials: Stalinist Purges in Eastern Europe, 1948–1954* (New York, 1987)

—— *Schauprozesse: Stalinistische Säuberungen in Osteuropa 1948–1954* (Berlin, 2001)

Ilič, M. (ed.), *Stalin's Terror Revisited* (Basingstoke, 2006)

Judt, T., *Postwar: A History of Europe since 1945* (London, 2005)

Kuromiya, H., *The Voices of the Dead: Stalin's Great Terror in the 1930s* (New Haven, 2007)

LaPorte, N., Morgan, K. and Worley, M. (eds), *Bolshevism, Stalinism and the Comintern: Perspectives on Stalinization, 1917–53* (Basingstoke, 2008)

Leites, N. and Bernaut, E., *Ritual of Liquidation* (Glencoe: Illinois, 1954)

Martin, T., *The Affirmative Action Empire: Nations and Nationalism in the Soviet Union, 1923–1939* (Ithaca, 2001)

McLoughlin, B. and McDermott, K. (eds), *Stalin's Terror: High Politics and Mass Repression in the Soviet Union* (Basingstoke, 2003)

Medvedev, R., *Let History Judge: The Origins and Consequences of Stalinism*, revised edn (Oxford, 1989)

Mironenko, A. V. et al. (eds), *Istoriia stalinskogo Gulaga*. vol. 1: *Massovye represii v SSSR* (Moscow, 2004)

Overy, R., *Russia's War* (London, 1997)

Persak, K. and Kamiński, Ł. (eds), *A Handbook of the Communist Security Apparatus in East-Central Europe, 1944–1989* (Warsaw, 2005)

Schapiro, L., *The Communist Party of the Soviet Union* (Cambridge, 1978)

Schöpflin, G., *Politics in Eastern Europe, 1945–1992* (Oxford, 1993)

Shearer, D. R., *Policing Stalin's Socialism: Repression and Social Order in the Soviet Union, 1924–1953* (New Haven, 2009)

Studer, B. and Haumann, H. (eds), *Stalinistische Subjekte/Stalinist Subjects/Sujets staliniens: Individuum und System in der Sowjetunion und der Komintern, 1929–1953* (Zurich, 2006)

Suny, R. G., and Martin, T. (eds), *A State of Nations: Empire and Nation-Making in the Age of Lenin and Stalin* (New York, 2001)

Vinen, R., *A History in Fragments: Europe in the Twentieth Century* (London, 2000)

Volokitina, T. et al. (eds), *Sovetskii faktor v Vostochnoi Evrope, tom 1, 1944–1948* (Moscow, 1999); *tom 2, 1949–1953* (Moscow, 2002)

—— *Moskva i Vostochnaia Evropa. Stanovlenie politicheskikh rezhimov sovetskogo tipa 1949–53: Ocherki istorii* (Moscow, 2008)

Weber, H. and Mählert, U. (eds), *Terror: Stalinistische Parteisäuberungen 1936–1953* (Paderborn, 1998)

Zubkova, E., *Russia after the War: Hopes, Illusions and Disappointments, 1945–1957* (New York, 1998)

Memoirs, personal testimonies, eye-witness accounts

Böszörményi, G. (ed.), *Recsk, 1950–1953 – egy titkos kényszermunkatábor története* (Budapest, 2005)

Bouška, T. and Pinerová, K., *Czechoslovak Political Prisoners: Life Stories of 5 Male and 5 Female Victims of Stalinism* (Prague, 2009)

Danziger, C.-J. (i.e. Joachim Schwarz), *Die Partei hat immer Recht: Autobiographischer Roman* (Stuttgart, 1976)

Faludy, G., *My Happy Days in Hell* (New York, 1962)

Gabori, G., *When Evils Were Most Free* (Ottawa, 1981)

Györgyey, F. A., *True Tales of a Fictitious Spy: A Hungarian Gulag Grotesquerie* (King: North Carolina, 2005)

Kalniete, S., *With Dance Shoes in Siberian Snows* (Riga, 2006)

Kersnovskaia, E., *Skol'ko stoit chelovek*, edited by V. Pasat (Moscow, 2006)

Kirss, T. (ed.), *Estonian Life Stories* (Budapest, 2009)

Kuczynski, J., *Dialog mit meinem Urenkel: Neunzehn Briefe und ein Tagebuch*, 2nd edn (East Berlin and Weimar, 1984)

—— *Ein linientreuer Dissident: Memoiren 1945–1989* (Berlin, 1992)

—— *Ein treuer Rebell: Memoiren 1994–1997* (Berlin, 1998)

Leonhard, W., *Die Revolution entläßt ihre Kinder* (Cologne, 1955)

Loebl, E., *Sentenced and Tried: The Stalinist Purges in Czechoslovakia* (London, 1969)

—— *Stalinism in Prague: The Loebl Story* (New York, 1969)

London, A., *On Trial* (London, 1970)

Lukša, J., *Forest Brothers: The Account of an anti-Soviet Lithuanian Freedom Fighter, 1944–1948* (Budapest, 2009)

Margolius, I., *Reflections of Prague: Journeys through the 20th Century* (Chichester, 2006)

Margolius Kovaly, H., *Prague Farewell* (London, 1988)

Mateev, M., *Na slovoto ti se opovavakh: prezhiviana tragichna istoriia na edin osŭden v protsesa sreshtu evangeliskite pastori 1948–49* (Sofia, 1993)

Sára, S. (ed.), *Nehézsorsúak – magyarok szovjet rabszolgaságban* (Veszprém, 2006)

Scholmer, J., *Die Toten kehren zurück: Bericht eines Arztes aus Workuta* (Cologne, 1954)

Sirc, L., *Smisel in nesmisel* (London, 1968)

—— *Med Hitlerjem in Titom* (Ljubljana, 1992).

Slánská, J., *Report on My Husband* (London, 1969)

Šlingová, M. *Truth Will Prevail* (London, 1968)

Chapter 2. The Baltic states

Anušauskas, A. (ed.), *Anti-Soviet Resistance in the Baltic States* (Vilnius, 2006)

Balkelis, T., 'Ethnicity, Identity and Imaginings of Home in the Memoirs of Lithuanian Child Deportees, 1941–1952', in P. Gatrell and N. Baron (eds), *Warlands: Population Resettlement and State Reconstruction in the Soviet-East European Borderlands, 1945–1950* (Basingstoke, 2009)

Budryté, D., *Taming Nationalism? Political Community Building in the Post-Soviet Baltic States* (Aldershot, 2005)

Estonian State Commission on the Examination of the Policies of Repression, *The White Book: Losses Inflicted on the Estonian Nation by Occupation Regimes, 1940–1991* (Tallinn, 2005)

Feldmanis, A. E., *Masļenku traǧēdija – Latvijas traǧēdija* (Riga, 2000)

The Hidden and Forbidden History of Latvia under Soviet and Nazi Occupations 1940–1991: Selected Research of the Commission of the Historians of Latvia (Riga, 2005)

Jēkabsons, Ē. and Bambals, A., 'Latvijas armijas iznīcināšana un represījas pret tās karavīriem', in Latvijas vēsturnieku komisijas raksti 3. sējums, *Totalitārie režīmi un to represījas Latvijā 1940–1956. gadā* (Riga, 2001)

Kiaupa, Z., *The History of Lithuania* (Vilnius, 2004)

Laar, M., *War in the Woods: Estonia's Struggle for Survival, 1944–1956* (Washington, D.C., 1992)

Lasmanis, U., *Arveds Bergs: Politiskās apceres, ceturtā grāmata 1934–1941: Neizsūtītā trimdinieka piezīmes Pēdējais vārds* (Riga, 2000)

Mertelsmann, O. (ed.), *The Sovietization of the Baltic States, 1940–1956* (Tartu, 2003)

Onken, E. C., 'The Politics of Finding Historical Truth: Reviewing Baltic History Commissions and their Work', *Journal of Baltic Studies*, vol. 38, no. 1 (2007), pp. 109–16

Rahi, A., 'On the Current State of Research Into Soviet and Nazi Repressions in Estonia', in *Latvijas okupācijas muzējs gadagrāmata 2002: Varas patvaļa* (Riga, 2003)

Reklaitis, G., *Cold War Lithuania: National Armed Resistance and Soviet Counter-insurgency*, The Carl Beck Papers in Russian and East European Studies, no. 1806 (Pittsburgh, 2007)

Ronis, I. (ed.), *Kārlis Ulmanis Trimdā un Cietumā: Dokumenti un materiāli* (Riga, 1994)

Saleniece, I. (ed.), *1949. Gada 25. Martā izvesto balsis* (Daugavpils, 2008)

Smith, D., Pabriks, A., Purs, A. and Lane, T., *The Baltic States: Estonia, Latvia and Lithuania* (New York, 2002)

Strods, H., *Latvijas nacionālo partizānu karš*, 3 vols. (Riga, 1996-2003)

Strods, H. and Kott, M., 'The File on Operation "Priboi": A Reassessment of the Mass Deportations of 1949', *Journal of Baltic Studies*, vol. 33, no. 1 (2002), pp. 1–31

Swain, G., *Between Stalin and Hitler: Class War and Race War on the Dvina, 1940–1946* (New York, 2004)

Tininis, V. (ed.), *Komunistinio režimo nusikaltimai Lietuvoje 1944–1953 m.: Istoriné studija ir faksimilinis documents rinkiny II Tomas* (Vilnius, 2003)

Vīksne, R. and Kangers, K. (eds), *No NKVD līdz KGB: Politiskās Prāvas Latvijā 1940–1986: Noziegumos pret Padomju valsti apsudzēto Latvijas iedzīvotāju rādītājs* (Riga, 1999)

Chapter 3. Moldavia

Caşu, I., *'Politica naţională' în Moldova Sovietică, 1944–1989* (Chişinău, 2000)

Gribincea, M., *Basarabia în primii ani de ocupaţie sovietică, 1944–1950* (Cluj, 1995)

Moraru, A., *Istoria românilor. Basarabia şi Transnistria* (Chişinău, 1995)

Negru, E., 'Republica Autonomă Sovietică Socialistă, 1924–1940', in D. Dragnev (ed.), *O istorie a regiunii transnistrene din cele mai vechi timpuri până în zilele noastre* (Chişinău, 2007), pp. 268–72

Pasat, V., *Trudnye stranitsy istorii Moldavii, 1940–1950* (Moscow, 1994)

—— Surovaia pravda istorii. Deportatsii s territorii Moldavskoi SSR, 40–50 gody (Chişinău, 1998)

Postică, E., Rezistenţa antisovietică în Basarabia, 1944–1950 (Chişinău, 1997)

Scurtu, I., (ed.), Istoria Basarabiei, de la începuturi până la 1998 (Bucharest, 1998)

Şevcenco, R., Viaţa politică în RSS Moldovenească, 1944–1961 (Chişinău, 2007)

Şişcanu, E., Basarabia sub regimul bolşevic, 1940–1952 (Bucharest, 1998)

Stăvilă, V., De la Basarabia românească la Basarabia sovietică, 1939–1945 (Chişinău, 2000)

Ţaranov, V. et al. (eds), Kolektivizatsiia krest'ianskikh khoziaistv v pravoberezhnykh raionnakh Moldavskoi SSR. Dokumenty i materialy (Chişinău, 1969)

Ţăranu, A. et al. (eds), Golod v Moldove (1946–1947). Sbornik dokumentov (Chişinău, 1993)

Turea, L. and Turea, V., Cartea foametei (Chişinău, 1991)

Chapter 4. East Germany

Bruce, G., Resistance with the People: Repression and Resistance in Eastern Germany, 1945–1955 (Lanham: Maryland, 2003)

Epstein, C., The Last Revolutionaries: German Communists and their Century (Cambridge: MA and London, 2003)

Gieseke, J., 'German Democratic Republic', in K. Persak and Ł. Kamiński (eds), A Handbook of the Communist Security Apparatus in East Central Europe, 1944–1989 (Warsaw, 2005), pp. 163–219

Gniffke, E., Jahre mit Ulbricht (Cologne, 1966)

Grieder, P., The East German Leadership, 1946–73: Conflict and Crisis (Manchester, 1999)

Hurwitz, H., Die Stalinisierung der SED: Zum Verlust von Freiräumen und sozialde-mokratischer Identität in den Vorständen 1946–1949 (Opladen, 1997)

Kleßmann, C., 'Verflechtung und Abgrenzung: Aspekte der geteilten und zusammengehörigen deutschen Nachkriegsgeschichte', Aus Politik und Zeitgeschichte, B29–30, 16 July 1993, pp. 30–41

Klonovsky, M. and Flocken, J. von, Stalins Lager in Deutschland 1945–1950: Dokumentation, Zeugenberichte (Munich, 1993)

Leonhard, W., 'Im Fadenkreuz der SED: Meine Flucht von der Parteihochschule "Karl Marx" im März 1949 und die Aktivitäten der Zentralen Parteikontrollkommission', Vierteljahrshefte für Zeitgeschichte, vol. 46, no. 2 (1998), pp. 283–310

Major, P., The Death of the KPD: Communism and Anti-Communism in West Germany, 1945–1956 (Oxford, 1997)

Malycha, A., Die SED: Geschichte ihrer Stalinisierung, 1946–1953 (Paderborn, 2000)

Naimark, N. M., The Russians in Germany: A History of the Soviet Zone of Occupation, 1945–1949 (Cambridge: MA and London, 1995)

Neubert, E., 'Politische Verbrechen in der DDR', in S. Courtois et al. (eds), Das Schwarzbuch des Kommunismus: Unterdrückung, Verbrechen und Terror (Munich and Zurich, 1998), pp. 829–84

O'Doherty, P., 'The GDR in the Context of Stalinist Show Trials and Anti-Semitism in Eastern Europe, 1948–54', German History, vol. 10, no. 3 (1992), pp. 302–17

Otto, W., 'Erinnerung an einen gescheiterten Schauprozess in der DDR', *Jahrbuch für Historische Kommunismusforschung*, vol. 14 (2008), pp. 114–30

Pritchard, G., *The Making of the GDR, 1945–53: From Anti-Fascism to Stalinism* (Manchester, 2000)

Spilker, D., *The East German Leadership and the Division of Germany: Patriotism and Propaganda, 1945–53* (Oxford, 2006)

Stibbe, M., 'The SED, German Communism and 17 June 1953: New Trends and New Research', in K. McDermott and M. Stibbe (eds), *Revolution and Resistance in Eastern Europe: Challenges to Communist Rule* (Oxford, 2006), pp. 37–55

Stößel, F. T., *Positionen und Strömungen in der KPD/SED 1945–1954* (Cologne, 1984)

Weber, H., 'Schauprozeß-Vorbereitungen in der DDR', in H. Weber and U. Mählert (eds), *Terror: Stalinistische Parteisäuberungen 1936–1953* (Paderborn, 1998), pp. 459–85

Werkentin, F., *Politische Strafjustiz in der Ära Ulbricht: Vom bekennenden Terror zur verdeckten Repression*, 2nd edn (Berlin, 1997)

Wolkow, W. K., 'Die deutsche Frage aus Stalins Sicht (1947–1952)', *Zeitschrift für Geschichtswissenschaft*, vol. 48, no. 1 (2000), pp. 20–49

Chapter 5. Poland

Cienciala, A. M., Lebedeva, N. S. and Materski, W. (eds), *Katyn: A Crime Without Punishment* (New Haven, 2008)

Ciesielski, S., Materski, W. and Paczkowski, A., *Represje sowieckie wobec obywateli polskich* (Warsaw, 2002)

Dudek, A. and Paczkowski, A., 'Poland', in K. Persak and Ł. Kamiński (eds), *A Handbook of the Communist Security Apparatus in East Central Europe, 1944–1989* (Warsaw, 2005), pp. 221–83

Gross, J. T., *Revolution from Abroad: The Soviet Conquest of Poland's Western Ukraine and Western Belorussia* (Princeton: NJ, 2002)

Jarosz, D., *Polityka władz komunistycznych w Polsce w latach 1944–1956 a chłopi* (Warsaw, 1998)

—— *Polacy a stalinizm 1948–1956* (Warsaw, 2000)

Kamiński, Ł., *Strajki robotnicze w Polsce w latach 1945–1948* (Wrocław, 1999)

—— *Polacy wobec nowej rzeczywistości 1944–1948: Formy pozainstytucjonalnego żywiołowego oporu społecznego 1944–1948* (Toruń, 2000)

—— 'Schauprozesse in Polen 1945–1956', in U. Bräuel and S. Samerski (eds), *Ein Bischof vor Gericht: Der Prozeß gegen den Danziger Bischof Carl Maria Splett 1946* (Osnabrück, 2005), pp. 263–80

Kemp-Welch, A., *Poland under Communism: A Cold War History* (Cambridge, 2008)

Kersten, K., *Jałta w polskiej perspektywie* (London, 1989)

—— *Narodziny systemu władzy Polska 1943–1948* (Poznań, 1990)

—— 'The Terror, 1949–1954', in A. Kemp-Welch (ed.), *Stalinism in Poland: Selected Papers from the Fifth World Congress of Central and Eastern European Studies, Warsaw, 1995* (Basingstoke, 1999), pp. 78–94

Kopka, B., *Obozy pracy w Polsce 1944–1950: Przewodnik encyklopedyczny* (Warsaw, 2003)

Leinwand, A., *Przywódcy Polski Podziemnej przed sądem moskiewskim* (Warsaw, 1992)

Madej, K., Żaryn, J. and Żurek, J. (eds), *Księga świadectw: Skazani na karę śmierci w czasach stalinowskich i ich losy* (Warsaw, 2003)

Nalepa, E., *Oficerowie Armii Radzieckiej w Polsce 1943–1968* (Warsaw, 1995)

Osękowski, Cz., *Wybory do Sejmu z 19 stycznia 1947 roku w Polsce* (Poznań, 2000)

Paczkowski, A., *Referendum z 30 czerwca 1946 r. Przebieg i wyniki* (Warsaw, 1993)

—— *Pół wieku dziejów Polski* (Warsaw, 1996)

—— 'Poland: "The Enemy Nation"', in S. Courtois et al. (eds), *The Black Book of Communism: Crimes, Terror, Repression* (Cambridge: MA, 1999), pp. 363–93

Pietrzak, L., Poleszak, S., Wnuk, R. and Zajączkowski, M. (eds), *Rok pierwszy. Powstanie i działalność Aparatu Bezpieczeństwa Publicznego na Lubelszczyźnie (lipiec 1944 – czerwiec 1945)* (Warsaw, 2004)

Wnuk, R., Poleszak, S., Jaczyńska, A. and Śladecka, M. (eds), *Atlas polskiego podziemia niepodległościowego 1944–1956* (Warsaw and Lublin, 2007)

Wrona, J., *System partyjny w Polsce 1944–1950. Miejsce, funkcje, relacje partii politycznych w warunkach budowy i utrwalania systemu komunistycznego* (Lublin, 1997)

—— *Kampania wyborcza i wybory do Sejmu Ustawodawczego 19 stycznia 1947* (Warsaw, 1999)

Żaryn, J., *Dzieje Kościoła katolickiego w Polsce (1944–1989)* (Warsaw, 2003)

Chapter 6. Czechoslovakia

Blaive, M., *Promarněná příležitost: Československo a rok 1956* (Prague, 2001)

Evanson, R. K., 'Political Repression in Czechoslovakia, 1948–1984', *Canadian Slavonic Papers*, vol. 28, no. 1 (1986), pp. 1–21

Formánková, P. and Koura, P., *Žádáme trest smrti! Propagandistická kampaň provázející proces s Miladou Horákovou a spol.* (Prague, 2008)

Gebauer, F. et al., *Soudní perzekuce politické povahy v Československu 1948–1989. Statistický přehled* (Prague, 1993)

Hauner, M., 'Crime and Punishment in Communist Czechoslovakia: The Case of General Heliodor Píka and his Prosecutor Karel Vaš', *Totalitarian Movements and Political Religions*, vol. 9, no. 2–3 (2008), pp. 335–54

Jech, K. (ed.), *Vystěhování selských rodin v Akci K ('kulaci') 1951–1953: Seznamy a vybranné dokumenty* (Prague, 1992)

Kaplan, K., *Political Persecution in Czechoslovakia 1948–1972* (Cologne, 1983)

—— *Nekrvavá revoluce* (Prague, 1993)

—— *Stát a církev v Československu v letech 1948–1953* (Brno, 1993)

—— *K politickým procesům v Československu 1948–1954: Dokumentace komise ÚV KSČ pro rehabilitaci 1968* (Prague, 1994)

—— *Největší politický proces: M. Horáková a spol.* (Brno, 1995)

Kaplan, K. and Paleček, P., *Komunistický režim a politické procesy v Československu* (Prague, 2001)

Kaplan, K. and Váchová, J. (eds), *Akce B – vystěhování 'státně nespolehlivých osob' z Prahy, Bratislavy a dalších měst, 1952–1953* (Prague, 1992)

Lukes, I., 'The Birth of a Police State: The Czechoslovak Ministry of the Interior, 1945–48', *Intelligence and National Security*, vol. 11, no. 1 (1996), pp. 78–88

—— 'The Rudolf Slánský Affair: New Evidence', *Slavic Review*, vol. 58, no. 1 (1999), pp. 160–87

—— *Rudolf Slansky: His Trials and Trial*, Cold War International History Project, Working Paper No. 50 (Washington DC, 2006)

McDermott, K., 'A "Polyphony of Voices"? Czech Popular Opinion and the Slánský Affair', *Slavic Review*, vol. 67, no. 4 (2008), pp. 840–65

Pelikán, J. (ed.), *The Czechoslovak Political Trials, 1950–1954: The Suppressed Report of the Dubček Government's Commission of Inquiry, 1968* (London, 1971)

Pernes, J. and Foitzik, J. (eds), *Politické procesy v Československu po roce 1945 a 'případ Slánský'* (Brno, 2005)

Rupnik, J., 'The Roots of Czech Stalinism', in R. Samuel and G. Stedman Jones (eds), *Culture, Ideology and Politics: Essays for Eric Hobsbawm* (London, 1982), pp. 302–20

Skilling, H. G., *Czechoslovakia's Interrupted Revolution* (Princeton, 1976)

Chapter 7. Hungary

Balassa, Zs. W. et al. (eds), *Hortobágyi Kényszermunkatáborok 1950–1953* (Budapest, n.d.)

Balogh, M., *Mindszenty József 1892–1975* (Budapest, 2002)

Balogh, M. and Szabó, Cs., *A Grősz-per* (Budapest, 2002)

Baráth, M. (ed.), *Szovjet nagyköveti iratok Magyarországról 1953–1956 – Kiszeljov és Andropov jelentései* (Budapest, 2002)

Boreczky, B., 'Az Államvédelmi Hatóság szervezete, 1950–1953', in G. Gyarmati (ed.), *A Történeti Hivatal Évkönyve 1999* (Budapest, 1999), pp. 91–111

Borhi, L., *Hungary in the Cold War, 1945–1956: Between the United States and the Soviet Union* (Budapest and New York, 2004)

Farkas, V., *Nincs mentség – az ÁVH ezredese voltam* (Budapest, 1990)

Gyáni, G., 'A forradalom társadalomtörténeti paradoxonjai', in G. Gyáni and J. M. Rainer, *Ezerkilencszázötvenhat az újabb történeti irodalomban* (Budapest, 2007), pp. 87–104

Gyarmati, G. (ed.), *A Történeti Hivatal évkönyve 2000–2001* (Budapest, 2001)

Hódos, G., *Tettesek és áldozatok – Koncepciós perek Magyarországon és Közép-Kelet-Európában* (Budapest, 2005)

Kajári, E., 'Az egységesített BM államvédelmi tevékenysége, 1953–1956', in G. Gyarmati (ed.) *Államvédelem a Rákosi korszakban: tanulmányok és dokumentumok a politikai rendőrség második világháború utáni tevékenységéről* (Budapest, 2000), pp. 165–78

—— 'Bevezető a Belügyminisztérium Kollégiuma 1953–1956 közötti iratainak tanulmányozásához', in G. Gyarmati and K. S. Varga (eds), *A Belügyminisztérium Kollégiumának ülései 1953–1956*, vol. 1 (Budapest, 2001), pp. 24–7

Kiss, M., 'Péter Gábor Államvédelmi Hatósága', in I. Ötvös (ed.), *Variációk – Ünnepi tanulmányok M. Kiss Sándor tiszteletére* (Piliscsaba, 2004), pp. 135–41

Kiszely, G., *ÁVH – egy terrorszervezet története* (Budapest, 2000)

Lőrincz, J., 'A Sztálini büntetőpolitika és konzekvenciái a hazai büntető igazságszolgáltatásban', in *1956 szilánkjai* (Budapest, 2007)

Rákosi, M., *Visszaemlékezések 1940–1956*, vol. 2, I. Feitl et al. (eds) (Budapest, 1997)

Stark, T., *Magyar foglyok a Szovjetunióban* (Budapest, 2006)

Szakács, S. and Zinner, T., *A háború 'megváltozott természete' – Adatok, és adalékok, tények és össszefüggések, 1944–1948* (Budapest, 1997)

Varga, E. M. (ed.), *Magyar hadifoglyok a Szovjetunióban* (Moscow and Budapest, 2006)

Zinner, T., 'Az egyik gyújtózsinór a Rajk-Brankov ügyhöz (is)', in I. Okváth (ed.), *Katonai perek 1945–1958* (Budapest, 2001)

Chapter 8. Romania

Calafeteanu, I., 'Schimbări în aparatul diplomatic românesc după 6 martie 1945', *6 Martie 1945. Începuturile Comunizării României* (Bucharest, 1995)

Cartea Albă a Securității (Bucharest, 1995)

Ciuceanu, R., *Regimul penitenciar din România, 1940–1962* (Bucharest, 2001)

Deletant, D., 'Influența sovietică asupra Securității române 1944–1953' in *Memoria ca formă de justiție* (Bucharest, 1995), pp. 35–46

—— *Communist Terror in Romania. Gheorghiu-Dej and the Police State, 1948 to 1965* (London, 1999)

Fischer, M. E., *Nicolae Ceaușescu. A Study in Political Leadership* (Boulder, 1989)

Fischer-Galati, S., *The New Rumania. From People's Democracy to Socialist Republic* (Cambridge: MA, 1967)

Frunză, V., *Istoria Stalinismului în România* (Bucharest, 1990)

Ionescu, G., *Communism in Rumania, 1944–1962* (London, 1964)

Jela, D., *Cazul Nichita Dumitru. Încercare de reconstituire a unui proces comunist* (Bucharest, 1995)

King, R. R., *A History of the Romanian Communist Party* (Stanford, 1980)

Levy, D., 'Did Ana Pauker Prevent a "Rajk Trial" in Romania?', *East European Politics and Societies*, vol. 9, no. 1 (1995), pp. 143–78

—— *Ana Pauker. The Rise and Fall of a Jewish Communist* (Los Angeles, 2001)

Rusalii '51. Fragmente din deportarea în Bărăgan (Timișoara, 1994)

Tismăneanu, V., *Stalinism for All Seasons. A Political History of Romanian Communism* (Los Angeles, 2003)

Tismăneanu, V., Dobrincu, D. and Vasile, C. (eds), *Comisia Prezidențială pentru Analiza Dictaturii Comuniste din România. Raport Final* (Bucharest, 2007)

Chapter 9. Yugoslavia

Barić, N. and Radelić, Z. (eds), *Partizanska i komunistička represija i zločini u Hrvatskoj 1944–1946, Dokumenti* (Slavonski Brod, 2005)

Bartošek, K., 'Central and Southeastern Europe', in S. Courtois et al. (eds), *The Black Book of Communism: Crimes, Terror, Repression* (Cambridge: MA, 1999), pp. 394–456

Dokumenti centralnih organa KPJ, NOR i revolucija, 1941–1945, vol. 18 (Belgrade, 1986)

Gibianskii, L., 'The Soviet-Yugoslav Split', in K. McDermott and M. Stibbe (eds), *Revolution and Resistance in Eastern Europe: Challenges to Communist Rule* (Oxford, 2006), pp. 17–36

Istorija Saveza komunista Jugoslavije (Belgrade, 1985)

Peta zemaljska konferencija KPJ: Kongresi, zemaljske konferencije, plenumi CK KPJ, vol. I, part 10 (Belgrade, 1980)
Priročnik za delo milice na področju varstva ustavne ureditve – Strogo zaupno, uradna tajnost (Ljubljana, 1985)
Pučnik, J., (ed.), *Iz arhivov slovenske politične policije* (Ljubljana, 1996)
Tito, J. B., *Zbrana dela* (Ljubljana, 1981)
Vodušek Starič, J., *Prevzem oblasti, 1944–46* (Ljubljana, 1992)
—— *Obračun: Slovenija v letu 1945* (Ljubljana, 1996)
—— *Kako su komunisti osvojili vlast* (Zagreb, 2006)
Završne operacije za oslobodjenje Jugoslavije (Belgrade, 1986)
Žerjavić, V., *Gubici stanovništva Jugoslavije* (Zagreb, 1989)

Chapter 10. Bulgaria

Baev, J., *KGB v Balgaria: Satrudnichestvoto mezhdu savetskite i balgarskite tajni sluzhbi, 1944–1991* (Sofia, 2009)
Baev, J. and Grozev, K., 'Bulgaria', in K. Persak and Ł. Kamiński (eds), *A Handbook of the Communist Security Apparatus in East Central Europe, 1944–1989* (Warsaw, 2005), p. 37–83
Banac, I. (ed.), *The Diary of Georgi Dimitrov, 1933–1949* (New Haven, 2003)
Bell, J., *The Bulgarian Communist Party from Blagoev to Zhivkov* (Stanford, 1985)
Crampton, R., *A Concise History of Bulgaria* (New York, 2005)
Dimitrov, D., *Sŭvetska Bŭlgariia* (London, 1994)
Dimitrov, V., *Stalin's Cold War: Soviet Foreign Policy, Democracy and Communism in Bulgaria, 1941–48* (Basingstoke, 2008)
Isusov, M., *Poslednata godina na Traicho Kostov* (Sofia, 1990)
Jordanova, K. and Baev, J., *History of Bulgaria in the Cold War Era: A Bibliography, 1989–2004*, www.coldwar.hu (available from March 2009)
Ognyanov, L. Lalkov, M. (eds) *Narodna demokratsiia ili diktatura? Khristomatiia po istoriia na Bŭlgariia, 1944–48* (Sofia, 1992)
Semerdzhiev, P., *Narodniiat sŭd v Bŭlgariia 1944–45* (Sofia, 1997)
Sharlanov, D., *Tiraniiata. Zhertvi i palachi* (Sofia, 1997)
Stoianova, P. and Iliev, E., *Politicheski opasni litsa. Vŭdvoriavaniia, trudova mobilizatsiia, izselvaniia sled 1944 g.* (Sofia, 1991)
Tsvetkov, Zh., *Razpiatieto* (Sofia, 1994)

Chapter 11. Albania

Austin, R., 'Greater Albania: The Albanian State and the Question of Kosovo, 1912–2001', in J. Lampe and M. Mazower (eds), *Ideologies and National Identities: The Case of Twentieth Century Southeastern Europe* (Budapest, 2003), pp. 235–53
Biberaj, E., *Albania: A Socialist Maverick* (Boulder, 1990)
Birch, J., 'The Albanian Political Experience', *Government and Opposition*, vol. 6, no. 3 (1971), pp. 361–80.
Blumi, I., 'The Politics of Culture and Power: The Roots of Hoxha's Postwar State', *East European Quarterly*, vol. 31, no. 3 (1997), pp. 409–28

—— 'Hoxha's Class War: The Cultural Revolution and State Formation', *East European Quarterly*, vol. 33, no. 3 (1999), pp. 534–69

Fischer, B., *King Zog and the Struggle for Stability in Albania* (Boulder, 1984)

Hall, D., *Albania and the Albanians* (London, 1994)

Halliday, J. (ed.), *The Artful Albanian. The Memoirs of Enver Hoxha* (London, 1986)

Hoxha, E., *The Anglo-American Threat to Albania* (Tirana, 1982)

—— *Laying the Foundations of a New Albania* (Tirana, 1984)

Logoreci, A., *The Albanians: Europe's Forgotten Survivors* (Boulder, 1977)

Pano, N., *The People's Republic of Albania* (Baltimore, 1968)

Pearson, O., *Albania as Democracy and Dictatorship* (London, 2006)

Perović, J. 'The Tito-Stalin Split: A Reassessment in Light of New Evidence', *Journal of Cold War Studies*, vol. 9, no. 2 (2007), pp. 32–63

Prifti, P., *Socialist Albania since 1944* (Cambridge: MA, 1978)

Skendi, S. (ed.), *Albania* (New York, 1956)

Smiley, D., *Albania Assignment* (London, 1984)

Index

Note: 'n.' after a page reference indicates the number of a note on that page.

CPSIA information can be obtained
at www.ICGtesting.com
Printed in the USA
BVHW092116100119
537575BV00008B/68/P

9 780719 089022